Architecture and Collective Life

This book addresses the complex relationship between architecture and public life. It's a study of architecture and urbanism as cultural activity that both reflects and gives shape to our social relations, public institutions and political processes.

Written by an international range of contributors, the chapters address the intersection of public life and the built environment around the themes of authority and planning, the welfare state, place and identity and autonomy. The book covers a diverse range of material from Foucault's evolving thoughts on space to land-scraping leisure centres in inter-war Belgium. It unpacks concepts such as 'community' and 'collectivity' alongside themes of self-organisation and authorship.

Architecture and Collective Life reflects on urban and architectural practice and historical, political and social change. As such this book will be of great interest to students and academics in architecture and urbanism as well as practicing architects.

Penny Lewis is Programme Lead for the University of Dundee and Wuhan University Architectural Studies Programme, a job which involves teaching in China. From 1999 to 2007 she was editor of *Prospect*, the Scottish architecture magazine and a regular contributor to national papers and architectural journals. Her PhD on *The impact of ecological thought on architectural theory from 1968* remains an ongoing research interest alongside work on the city.

Lorens Holm is Reader in Architecture and Director of the Geddes Institute for Urban Research at the University of Dundee, where he runs the design research unit rooms+cities. His written work focuses on reconciling Lacanian thought on subjectivity with contemporary architectural/urban practice. Publications include *Brunelleschi Lacan Le Corbusier* (2010) and, with John Hendrix, *Architecture and the Unconscious* (2016). His papers have appeared in *Architecture and Culture*, *ARQ*, *Journal of Architecture*, *Perspecta*, *Critical Quarterly*, *Architecture Theory Review*, and *Assemblage*.

Sandra Costa Santos is an architect and academic with research in the fields of architectural theory and architectural design with a particular interest in housing and the home. She is a Senior Lecturer in Architecture, Architecture and Urban Planning, School of Social Sciences, University of Dundee.

Critiques: Critical Studies in Architectural Humanities
A project of the Architectural Humanities Research Association

Series Editor: Jonathan Hale (University of Nottingham)
Editorial Board:
Mark Dorrian (University of Edinburgh)
Murray Fraser (University College London)
Hilde Heynen (Catholic University of Leuven)
Andrew Leach (University of Sydney)
M. Christine Boyer (Princeton University)
Jane Rendell (University College London)
Adam Sharr (Newcastle University)
Igea Troiani (University of Plymouth)

This original series of edited books contains selected papers from the AHRA Annual International Conferences. Each year the event has its own thematic focus while sharing an interest in new and emerging critical research in the areas of architectural history, theory, culture, design and urbanism.

Volume 6: Architecture and Field/Work
Edited by: Suzanne Ewing, Jérémie Michael McGowan, Chris Speed and Victoria Clare Bernie

Volume 7: Scale
Edited by: Gerald Adler, Timothy Brittain-Catlin and Gordana Fontana-Giusti

Volume 8: Peripheries
Edited by: Ruth Morrow and Mohamed Gamal Abdelmonem

Volume 9: Architecture and the Paradox of Dissidence
Edited by: Ines Weizman

Volume 10: Transgression: Towards an Expanded Field of Architecture
Edited by: Louis Rice and David Littlefield

Volume 11: Industries of Architecture
Edited by: Katie Lloyd Thomas, Tilo Amhoff and Nick Beech

Volume 12: This Thing Called Theory
Edited by: Teresa Stoppani, George Themistokleous and Giorgio Ponzo

Volume 13: Architecture and Feminisms: Ecologies, Economies, Technologies
Edited by Hélène Frichot, Catharina Gabrielsson and Helen Runting

Volume 14: Architecture, Festival and the City
Edited by Jemma Browne, Christian Frost and Ray Lucas

Volume 15: Architecture and the Smart City
Edited by Sergio M. Figueiredo, Sukanya Krishnamurthy and Torsten Schroeder

Volume 16: Architecture and Collective Life
Edited by Penny Lewis, Lorens Holm and Sandra Costa Santos

AHRA provides an inclusive and comprehensive support network for humanities researchers in architecture across the UK and beyond. It promotes, supports, develops and disseminates high-quality research in all areas of architectural humanities.

www.ahra-architecture.org

Architecture and Collective Life

Edited by Penny Lewis, Lorens Holm and Sandra Costa Santos

LONDON AND NEW YORK

First published 2022
by Routledge
2 Park Square, Milton Park, Abingdon, Oxon OX14 4RN

and by Routledge
605 Third Avenue, New York, NY 10158

Routledge is an imprint of the Taylor & Francis Group, an informa business

© 2022 selection and editorial matter, Penny Lewis, Lorens Holm and Sandra Costa Santos; individual chapters, the contributors

The right of Penny Lewis, Lorens Holm and Sandra Costa Santos to be identified as the authors of the editorial material, and of the authors for their individual chapters, has been asserted in accordance with sections 77 and 78 of the Copyright, Designs and Patents Act 1988.

All rights reserved. No part of this book may be reprinted or reproduced or utilised in any form or by any electronic, mechanical, or other means, now known or hereafter invented, including photocopying and recording, or in any information storage or retrieval system, without permission in writing from the publishers.

Trademark notice: Product or corporate names may be trademarks or registered trademarks, and are used only for identification and explanation without intent to infringe.

Every effort has been made to contact copyright-holders. Please advise the publisher of any errors or omissions, and these will be corrected in subsequent editions.

British Library Cataloguing-in-Publication Data
A catalogue record for this book is available from the British Library

Library of Congress Cataloging-in-Publication Data
Names: Lewis, Penny (Penny R.), editor. | Holm, Lorens, editor. |
Costa Santos, Sandra, editor. | Architecture & Collective Life (Conference) (2019: University of Dundee)
Title: Architecture and collective life / edited by Penny Lewis,
Lorens Holm and Sandra Costa Santos.
Description: Abingdon, Oxon; New York: Routledge, 2021. |
Series: Critiques: critical studies in architectural humanities;
volume 16 | Includes bibliographical references and index.
Identifiers: LCCN 2021009429 (print) | LCCN 2021009430 (ebook) |
ISBN 9780367633912 (hardback) | ISBN 9780367633905 (paperback) |
ISBN 9781003118985 (ebook)
Subjects: LCSH: Architecture and society—Congresses.
Classification: LCC NA2543.S6 A62723 2022 (print) |
LCC NA2543.S6 (ebook) | DDC 720.1/03—dc23
LC record available at https://lccn.loc.gov/2021009429
LC ebook record available at https://lccn.loc.gov/2021009430

ISBN: 978-0-367-63391-2 (hbk)
ISBN: 978-0-367-63390-5 (pbk)
ISBN: 978-1-003-11898-5 (ebk)

DOI: 10.4324/9781003118985

Typeset in Univers
by codeMantra

On the eve of the outbreak of Covid19 the AHRA held a conference in Dundee exploring the relationship between architecture and collective life. The conference was advertised to a wide range of academic disciplines, to practicing architects and to other professionals and activist interested in the built environment.

Contents

List of figures x
List of contributors xv
Acknowledgements xx

Part I Contradictions in a common world **1**

1 Introduction 3
   Penny Lewis

2 A tale of two villages: Jane Jacobs, Marshall McLuhan and their visions of collective life 13
   Joan Ockman

3 Interview with Reinier de Graaf 31

4 Neofeudalism: The end of capitalism? 42
   Jodi Dean

5 Alternative models of tenure: Recovering the radical proposal of collective housing 55
   Martino Tattara

Part II New geography and the planners **69**

6 A proprietary polis: Silicon Valley architecture and collective life 71
   Claudia Dutson

7 Hyper-gentrification and the urbanisation of suburbia 82
   Ross Exo Adams, Tahl Kaminer, Maroš Krivý, Leonard Ma, Karin Matz, Timothy Moore, Helen Runting and Rutger Sjögrim

Contents

8 The dubious high street: Distinctiveness, gentrification and social value　　90
Aleks Catina

9 Zero-institution culture　　102
Louis D'Arcy-Reed

Part III　Authority　　113

10 Authorship and political will in Aldo Rossi's theory of architecture　　115
Will Orr

11 The heterotopias of Tafuri and Teyssot: Between language and discipline　　123
Joseph Bedford

12 Interruptions: A form of questionable fidelity　　145
Doreen Bernath

Part IV　The welfare state　　157

13 Constructed landscapes for collective recreation: Victor Bourgeois's open-air projects in Belgium　　159
Marie Pirard

14 Vienna's Höfe: How housing builds the collective　　170
Alessandro Porotto

15 Learning from Loutraki: Thermalism, hydrochemistry and the architectures of collective wellness　　182
Lydia Xynogala

16 BiG: Living and working together　　195
Meike Schalk, Sara Brolund de Carvalho and Helena Mattsson

Part V　Autonomy and organisation　　205

17 Design precepts for autonomy: A case study of Kelvin Hall, Glasgow　　207
Jane Clossick and Ben Colburn

18 Calcutta, India: Dover Lane – a cosmo-ecological collective life of Indian modernity　　218
Dorian Wiszniewski

19 The city of ragpickers: Shaping a faithful collective life during *les trente glorieuses*　　228
Janina Gosseye

Contents

20 Visions of Ecotopia — 238
Meredith Gaglio

Part VI Practice and life — **249**

21 Intraventions in flux: Towards a modal spatial practice that moves and cares — 251
Alberto Altés Arlandis and Oren Lieberman

22 Ethics of open types — 260
Davide Landi

23 The Age of Ecology in the UK — 274
Penny Lewis

24 *Opinions* – or, from dialogue to conversation — 284
Teresa Stoppani

25 Epilogue — 293
Penny Lewis and Vicky Richardson

The Wally Close — *305*
Robert Wightman
Tenement: The collective close — *309*
John Joseph Burns
Index — *317*

Figures

1.1	Chen Yang Jackson Heights, NYC 2021	4
2.1	Jane Jacobs near her home on Hudson Street in Greenwich Village, New York, 1961	14
2.2	Jane Jacobs, "The Missing Link in City Redevelopment," *Architectural Forum*, June 1956	15
2.3	Stills from *The City*, film shown at the New York World's Fair, 1939. Script by Lewis Mumford. The Garden City ideal as realised in the new town of Greenbelt outside Washington, D.C. "Never letting cities grow too big to manage…. The wife needn't feel cooped up on washing day. A little gossip or a friendly hand [of cards] is good for the complexion…."	17
2.4	Marshall McLuhan in Toronto, late 1960s	20
2.5	Protest against the Spadina Expressway extension by members of the Stop Spadina Save Our City Coordinating Committee (SSSOCCC), Toronto, 1970	24
2.6	Spread from Marshall McLuhan with Harley Parker, *Counterblast*, 1969	25
2.7	Stills from *The Burning Would*, 1970. Film by Marshall McLuhan with Jane Jacobs	27
3.1	Photo of Reinier de Graaf speaking at the AHRA conference in Dundee, November 2019	32
4.1	Photo of Jodi Dean speaking at the AHRA conference in Dundee, November 2019	43
5.1	Brussels: Dogma, *Do you see me when we pass? Housing Model for the Community Land Trust in Brussels*. Structural diagram	56
5.2	Brussels: Dogma, *Do you see me when we pass? Housing Model for the Community Land Trust in Brussels*. Four-room apartment	56
5.3	Brussels: Dogma, *Do you see me when we pass? Housing Model for the Community Land Trust in Brussels*. External view	59

Figures

5.4	Brussels: Dogma, *Do you see me when we pass?* View of the interior space of a unit	59
5.5	Brussels: Dogma, *Do you see me when we pass?* Interior view. Detail	62
5.6	Brussels: Dogma, *Do you see me when we pass?* Interior view. Detail	62
5.7	London: Dogma, *Do you hear me when you sleep?* Structural diagram	65
5.8	London: Dogma, *Do you hear me when you sleep? Proposal for a Cooperative House in London*. External view	66
5.9	London: Dogma, *Do you hear me when you sleep?* Rooms typologies	66
5.10	London: Dogma, *Do you hear me when you sleep?* External view	67
6.1	Apple, Facebook and Google corporate campuses pre-2009	72
6.2	Facebook Menlo Park Building 20 (MPK20) Gehry Partners, floorplan and desk locations redrawn by the author, 2019	73
6.3	New Facebook, Apple and Google campuses, 1st floor	75
6.4	Facebook's Menlo Park campus massing, illustration by the author, 2019	75
6.5	Location of the 'all hands' meetings at Facebook MPK20 and the Googleplex	77
6.6	All buildings owned or leased by Apple, Facebook and Google overlaying a satellite image of Silicon Valley	78
7.1	Anti-gentrification posters in Hackney Wick, London, 2018	83
7.2	A suburban street in London's Thamesmead area, 2018	86
8.1	The owners adorned this example of a traditionally decorated high street shop front on Blackstock Road, London, N4, in an idiosyncratic manner	91
8.2	The survey of the duration of occupancy of individual shops was published in the 'High Streets for All' report (GLA, 2017)	95
9.1	The Vessel, Hudson Yards, New York City, designed by David Chipperfield Architects	103
9.2	Another zero-institution? The V&A Design Museum, Dundee, Scotland, designed by Kengo Kuma & Associates	105
9.3	The New Art Gallery Walsall, designed by Caruso St John	108
10.1	The ABC Riverside Building at the Walt Disney Studios in Burbank, California. Rossi's final project was completed posthumously in 2001	116
11.1	Aula Magna, Tolentini Campus, IUAV, Venice	130
11.2	Front cover of *Il Dispositivo Foucault* (CLUVA, Veniezia, 1977)	131
11.3	Bicetre Prison by Louis Pierre Baltard (1816), from "Heterotopias and the History of Spaces" in *A+U* no. 121 (1980), 64–71	137
11.4	Jorge L. Borges's "Chinese Encyclopedia" cited by Foucault in the preface to *The Order of Things* and reproduced by George Teyssot in "Eterotopie E Storia Degli Spazi" *Il Dispositivo Foucault* (CLUVA, Veniezia, 1977)	138
11.5	George Teyssot's diagram of the grid of eight institutional spaces of sanitation in the town of Caen in "Eterotopie E Storia Degli Spazi" *Il Dispositivo Foucault* (CLUVA, Veniezia, 1977)	140

Figures

12.1	Veduta del Pantheon, by Gabriele Basilico, 2010	146
12.2–3	Kristin, after Miss Julie (2011), directed by Katie Mitchell and Leo Warner, adapted from August Strinberg's play from 1889, in collaboration with Schaubühne Berlin, produced and performed at Festival d'Avignon	148
12.4	Walking School (1971), project by Haus-Rucker-Co	152
12.5–6	Folly for a Flyover (2011), project by Assemble	153
13.1	The beach in Hofstade	161
13.2	Housing complex and recreational area in Frameries (the slag heaps are partly visible at top right)	162
13.3	The recreational forest in the South of Charleroi including pedestrian and cycling paths, an artificial swimming lake (bottom left), a stadium (centre) and an open-air theatre (right)	164
13.4	Axonometric view of the stadium for Charleroi	165
13.5	Master plan for the 'sanitation and planning' of Antoing	166
14.1	Bebel-Hof (1925–1927), layout plan and section	171
14.2	Schüttau-Hof (1924–1925), layout plan and section	174
14.3	Karl Seitz-Hof (1926–1933), layout plan	175
14.4	Fuchsenfeldhof (1922–1925), layout plan and section	176
14.5	Plan of Vienna (2019), showing the position of *Höfe*	178
14.6	*Höfe*, archival pictures of the collective courtyards (clockwise order): Bebel-Hof, Schüttau-Hof, Karl Seitz-Hof and Fuchsenfeldhof	179
14.7	*Höfe*, pictures of the current state of the collective courtyards (clockwise order): Bebel-Hof, Schüttau-Hof, Karl Seitz-Hof and Fuchsenfeldhof	179
15.1	Poster produced by the Greek Organisation for Toursim (EOT) heavily promoting Greece through Loutraki. The hydrotherapy building with its colonade at the foot of the mountain	183
15.2	Colonnade in the new municipal hydrotherapy centre	186
15.3	View showing the rapid construction that took place after the earthquake	187
15.4	The Karantanis bottling factory completed in 1963 with the mountain as backdrop	189
15.5	Cover of the *Loutraki Casino Review*, a weekly magazine covering the social life of the town in the golden 1930s era. The subtitle reads: Scientific, Critique, Social	190
16.1	Illustration by Inger Blomgren Larsson from the publication 'Vi bor för att leva' [We dwell for living]	196
16.2	A spread in the Boplats 80 [Living Place 80] exhibition catalogue showing BiG's model. Boplats 80 was meant as a follow-up of the famous 1930s Stockholm Exhibition	198
16.3	BiG's model, 'Ett litet kollektivhus' [A little collective house], at Boplats 80	198

16.4	Witness seminar with BiG, from left to right: Kerstin Kärnekull, Ingela Blomberg, Gunilla Lundahl, Inga-Lisa Sangregorio, Ann Norrby and Sonja Vidén at The Swedish Centre for Architecture and Design, April 2019	200
16.5	Some of the many publications written by BiG and individual members	202
17.1	Diagram of a typical depth structure, drawn by J. Clossick	210
17.2	Kelvin Hall Phase 1, architect's render	212
17.3	Analysis drawn by J. Clossick	213
17.4	Analysis drawn by J. Clossick	214
17.5	Analysis drawn by J. Clossick	215
17.6	Analysis drawn by J. Clossick	216
18.1	North East Corner of Prasad Mukherjee Road, Kalighat area intersection, a 'Bangal's' house	219
18.2	Ground Plan of Sukanya Mitra's House, a 'Ghoti's' house, 3 Peary Row, Maniktala, North Calcutta, built 1905. The Drawing Room is on the left side of the plan	220
18.3	Sukanya Mitra's House, Drawing Room, 3 Peary Row, Maniktala, North Calcutta, January 2017	223
18.4	Section, Plan and Elevation of Z's Precinct, Dover Lane, Ballygunge, Calcutta, January 2019	224
19.1	Infographic published in December 1954, showing the building activities of Emmaüs in and around Paris. 'Activités Emmaüs', *Faim & Soif* 6, n.p	231
19.2	Plans for the Emmaüs chapel at 'La Cerisaie' by Rainer Senn	233
19.3	Construction of the chapel at 'La Cerisaie', October 1955	234
19.4	The chapel at 'La Cerisaie', photographed in October 1955	235
20.1	'Ecotopia' Poster from *RAIN: Journal of Appropriate Technology* 2, no. 6 (April 1976)	239
20.2	'Ecotopia' Poster from *RAIN: Journal of Appropriate Technology* 2, no. 6 (April 1976)	239
21.1	Final state of a two-week improvisatory design and construction workshop with TU Delft students which led to the production of a public space including a public sauna, two adjacent volumes hosting a changing room, wood storage, chill-out and back stage rooms and a performance stage/public dance floor, in an area called Hiedanranta, in the outskirts of Tampere (Finland)	252
21.2	Initial steps in a 48-h improvisatory design and construction process leading to the construction of a small Finish sauna equipped with a stone fire place and activated through the combined efforts of its users who would need to flip it in order to make it receive the heat accumulated in the stones once the fire was put out after burning for hours	253

Figures

22.1	Photograph of the Rudolf in Helsinki by Davide Landi	261
22.2	Block layout by Davide Landi	263
22.3	Flat plan by Davide Landi	267
23.1	Image taken by author from Arcology – the City in the Image of Man – Published by MIT Press, New York (1970)	275
24.1	Giovanni Battista Piranesi, Parere, Plate IX (untitled), 410 × 645 mm. From *Osservazioni di Gio. Battista Piranesi sopra la lettre de M. Mariette…. E Parere su l'Architettura,…*, Paris: Firmin Didot, 1835–1839. (1st ed. Rome: Piranesi, 1765)	287
25.1	Jackson Heights Shop, Chen Yang 2021	294
25.2	Jackson Heights Subway, Chen Yang 2021	298

Back Matter

Photograph of models by Robert Wightman

A2.1	17–21 High Street	1722–1750s	311
A2.2	395 Gallowgate	1771	312
A2.3	Queen's Park Terrace	Alexander 'Greek' Thomson	1858	313
A2.4	Queen's Drive	W.M. Whyte	1884	314
A2.5	Afton Street	A.R. Crawford	1901	315
A2.6	Craigen Court	Ken McRae with McGurn/Logan/Duncan & Opfer	1989	316

Contributors

Jodi Dean is Professor of Political Science at Hobart and William Smith Colleges in Geneva, New York. She is the author of numerous books including *Democracy and Other Neoliberal Fantasies* (Duke 2009), *The Communist Horizon* (Verso 2012), *Crowds and Party* (Verso 2016) and forthcoming from Verso, *Comrade: An essay on political belonging*.

Claudia Dutson is a tutor and researcher at the Royal College of Art. Trained in architecture, and with a background in media, her research into the spatial tactics of Silicon Valley management cultures combines architectural analysis with critical theory and organisational studies. She is writing a book on the topic.

Reinier de Graaf is a Dutch architect and writer. He is a partner in the Office for Metropolitan Architecture (OMA), where he leads projects in Europe, Russia and the Middle East. His recent built work includes the Timmerhuis, a mixed-use project in Rotterdam widely recognized for its innovation in ways of working and living, sustainability and cost efficiency; and De Rotterdam, currently the largest building in the Netherlands. Reinier is the co-founder of OMA's think-tank AMO and Sir Arthur Marshall Visiting Professor of Urban Design at the Department of Architecture of the University of Cambridge. His book *Four Walls and a Roof: The Complex Nature of a Simple Profession* was named the best book of 2017 by the *Financial Times* and the *Guardian*.

Penny Lewis is Programme Lead for the University of Dundee and Wuhan University Architectural Studies Programme, a job which involves teaching in China. From 1999 to 2007, she was editor of *Prospect*, the Scottish architecture magazine and a regular contributor to national papers and architectural journals. Her PhD on *The impact of ecological thought on architectural theory from 1968* remains an ongoing research interest alongside work on the city.

Joan Ockman is an architectural historian, critic and educator. She is the Vincent Scully Visiting Professor of Architectural History at Yale School of Architecture and

Contributors

Distinguished Senior Lecturer at the University of Pennsylvania's Weitzman School of Design. She served as Director of the Buell Center for the Study of American Architecture at Columbia University from 1994 to 2008. She has also held teaching appointments at Cooper Union, Cornell, Harvard, and the Berlage Institute. Her book publications include *Architecture School: Three Centuries of Educating Architects in North America* (2012), *Out of Ground Zero* (2002), *The Pragmatist Imagination* (2000) and the award-winning anthology *Architecture Culture 1943–1968* (1993).

Martino Tattara is a founding partner in the architecture practice Dogma and Associate Professor at KU Leuven Faculty of Architecture. After graduating from the Università Iuav di Venezia, he obtained a postgraduate Master's degree at the Berlage Institute in Rotterdam and a PhD in Urbanism at the Università Iuav di Venezia with a dissertation centred on Lucio Costa's project for Brasilia. Dogma has recently exhibited at the Chicago Architectural Biennial in 2017, the Flemish Architectural Institute in Antwerp, the Seoul Architecture Biennale, the Sharjah Architecture Triennale in 2019 and the Biennale di Venezia 2021.

The Financialisation of European Global Cities Group at AHRA:

Ross Exo Adams, Assistant Professor and Co-Director of Architecture at Bard College and the author of Circulation and Urbanization (Sage, 2019). **Tahl Kaminer**, Reader in Architectural History and Theory and Director of Research, The Welsh School of Architecture, Cardiff University. **Maroš Krivý**, Associate Professor and Director of Urban Studies, Faculty of Architecture, Estonian Academy of Arts. **Leonard Ma** is a Canadian architect based in Helsinki, a member of New Academy, and currently teaches Urban Studies and Architecture at the Estonian Academy of Art. **Karin Matz**, an architect (B.Arch, Edinburgh College of Art and the University of Queensland; MSc Arch, KTH), a founding partner in the practice Secretary and a lecturer at the School of Architecture at KTH in Stockholm. **Timothy Moore**, Lecturer in the Department of Architecture at Monash University and director of Sibling Architecture based in Melbourne, Australia. **Helen Runting**, an urban planner (B.UPD, University of Melbourne), urban designer (PG Dip.UD, University of Melbourne; MSc UPD, KTH) and architectural theorist (PhD Arch, KTH); a founding partner in the practice Secretary, Chief Editor of the journal *PLAN* and co-editor of the publications LO-RES and Stockholmstidningen. **Rutger Sjögrim**, an architect (MSc Arch, KTH), a founding partner in the practice Secretary and a lecturer at the School of Architecture at KTH in Stockholm.

Joseph Bedford is Assistant Professor of History and Theory and coordinator of Thesis at Virginia Tech. His scholarship explores the intellectual history of architectural thought in the later third of the twentieth century through the encounter between philosophy, theory and architectural education. He holds a PhD in History, Theory and Criticism of Architecture from Princeton University and was the recipient of the 2008–2009 Rome Scholarship at the British School in Rome. He has taught at Princeton University, Pratt Institute and Columbia University and is the founding director of the Architecture Exchange, a platform for theoretical exchange between architecture and other fields, which houses an audio journal, books, workshops, oral history projects and curricula projects. He has published numerous book chapters and articles in journals such as *ARQ*, *AA Files*, *OASE*, *NYRA* and *Log*.

Doreen Bernath is an architect and a theorist across disciplines of design, technology, philosophy, visual art, media and cultures. Trained at Cambridge and the AA, she was awarded RIBA scholarship and selected as a finalist for the RIBA President's Award for Outstanding Thesis. She is currently a co-editor of *The Journal of Architecture* and a co-founder of the research collective ThisThingCalledTheory. She has published and lectured internationally, and teaches at the AA in PhD, MPhil Projective Cities, History and Theory and AAVS Uncommon Walks programs. She is also a senior lecturer at the Leeds School of Architecture, co-ordinator of postgraduate research and a leader of 'Cinematic Commons' MArch design and research studio.

Aleks Catina explores the potentiality of architectural resistance by researching the provincialisation of ironic ethos in the challenge to culturally dominant narratives of capital. He currently focuses on the strategies of detachment and difference employed in the advancement of decolonization agendas. He conducts his postgraduate research at Birkbeck, University of London, and teaches on a Senior Lecturer post at London Met. Aleks is the author of 'The Pillars of Uncertainty' (2021), a writing project of embodied irony, themed around the polyphonic rehearsal of ideas charting the borderlands of architectural purpose.

Louis D'Arcy-Reed is a social, political and cultural theorist specializing in the intersection of architectural and psychoanalytic inquiry. Utilizing facets of contemporary culture, media and filmic representations, D'Arcy-Reed presents interrogations on social and political control and the role of the built environment in the creation of cognitive and embodied urban fabrics.

Will Orr is a British-Canadian theorist and historian. In 2019, he completed a PhD at the AA, where he now teaches in the history and theory programme. His research focuses on the interplay between political and architectural theory from the 1960s to the present.

Marie Pirard is a part-time PhD student and teaching assistant at the University of Louvain. Her research focuses on the interplay between architecture, nature and leisure in the context of welfare and proto-welfare policies. Alongside her research and educational practice, she works at AgwA, a Brussels-based architecture office.

Alessandro Porotto, PhD is currently a postdoctoral fellow at Université catholique de Louvain, Belgium. He holds a PhD from École Polytechnique Fédérale de Lausanne, Switzerland (2018). His thesis investigated the Interwar housing projects in Vienna and Frankfurt through a comparative typo-morphological methodology. He is the author of the book *L'intelligence des formes: Le projet de logements collectifs à Vienne et Francfort* (MētisPresses, 2019).

Contributors

Lydia Xynogala is an architect and scholar. Through her design practice (ALOS) and theoretical research, she explores architecture's intersection with the natural environment. She is a doctoral fellow at the gta Institute for the History and Theory of Architecture, ETH Zurich.

Action Archive:

Alberto Altés Arlandis is currently an Associate Professor of Architecture at Bergen School of Architecture (Norway), where he continues to explore, work and think through love, care and 'the encounter' in design practice and pedagogy.

John Joseph Burns is an Architect at Holmes Miller in Glasgow. John has an interest in the historic architecture of his native city Glasgow and has exhibited his work exploring the city's Tenement history for the Glasgow City Heritage Trust and National Trust of Scotland. John also guest lectures for the University of Strathclyde on the architectural history of Scotland.

Sara Brolund de Carvalho is an artist, architect and educator. **Helena Mattsson** is professor in History and Theory of Architecture at KTH School of Architecture in Stockholm. **Meike Schalk** is an architect and associate professor in urban design and urban theory at KTH School of Architecture in Stockholm. Together, they founded the non-profit organisation **Action Archive** in 2013. The group approaches urban research through oral history and participatory historiography.

Jane Clossick is Senior Lecturer in Urban Design at the Sir John Cass School of Art, Architecture and Design and London Metropolitan University.

Ben Colburn is Professor of Political Philosophy and Head of Philosophy at the University of Glasgow.

Meredith Gaglio is an Assistant Professor of Architecture at Louisiana State University. She recently received a PhD in Architecture from Columbia University Graduate School of Architecture. Her work addresses the development and implementation of sustainable community planning and architectural strategies in the United States from the late 1960s through the early 1980s.

Janina Gosseye is an Associate Professor of Architecture at Delft University of Technology. Her research is situated at the nexus of 20th-century architectural and urban history on the one hand and social and political history on the other hand. Her most recent book is *Speaking of Buildings: Oral History in Architectural Research* (2019).

Davide Landi is a registered Architect and Researcher. He obtained his Master's Degree in Architectural-Engineering from the Università Politecnica Delle Marche and a second Master's Degree in Architecture from the Accademia Adrianea di Architettura e Archeologia. After his studies, Davide has worked as Architect and Researcher in a number of different countries including Japan, China, Italy and the United Kingdom. Now, he is a Lecturer in Architecture at the Department of Architecture and the Built Environment, UWE – Bristol. His writing on the notion of architectural types in contemporary culture and the ephemeral character of cities that the city's recent digital turn emphasised have been published on international peer-reviewed journals.

Oren Lieberman is the Head of the Portsmouth School of Architecture and Professor of Architecture at the University of Portsmouth (UK). He has developed a wide-ranging practice, as an architect, teacher, writer, publisher, and initiator and curator of events and exhibitions. His teaching and research focus on performative practices which entangle knowledge, methodologies and techniques from various disciplines, including architecture, performance, geography, anthropology, and sociology, and embody ethical and responsible engagements with ongoing worlding with other 'kin'.

Vicky Richardson is Head of Architecture and Drue Heinz Curator at the Royal Academy. She is a writer, curator and Visiting Lecturer at the RCA where she runs the Interior Urbanism Platform. Her recent exhibition, *What Where*, considers the relationship between Samuel Beckett and the design of a theatre in Barcelona, Sala Beckett. Vicky was previously Director of Architecture, Design and Fashion at the British Council. She is co-founder of the Lantao UK Fellowship for Chinese and British designers, and an Honorary Fellow of RIBA.

Teresa Stoppani is an architect, architectural theorist and critic. She teaches at the Architectural Association in London. She is an editor of the *Journal of Architecture* and sits on the steering group of the Architectural Humanities Research Association. She is the author of *Paradigm Islands: Manhattan and Venice* (2011) and *Unorthodox Ways to Think the City* (2019) and co-editor of *This Thing Called Theory* (2016).

Robert Wightman is a graduate of The Scott Sutherland School of Architecture & Built Environment in Aberdeen. His Master's project won the RIAS Andy MacMillan Drawing Award and commended in the RIAS Rowand Anderson Silver Medal. He was nominated for the RIBA Dissertation Medal for his writing on the work of Gillespie, Kidd & Coia. Currently, Robert works in a Dublin practice and teaches in the School of Architecture at the University of Limerick.

Dorian Wiszniewski Practitioner, Teacher, Theorist and Researcher, he teaches on the M Arch and directs the MSc Architectural and Urban Design and PhD Architecture By Design Programmes at the University of Edinburgh. His research interests include Ecosophy. Recent studies have focused on India, particularly the cities of Bombay, Calcutta and Ahmedabad.

Acknowledgements

Our sincere gratitude goes to Teresa Stoppani and Vicky Richardson for their help in the production of the book and to Trudy Varcianna at Routledge for her patience. It would be remiss not to mention somewhere all the wonderful student volunteers who made the conference possible.

Part I
Contradictions in a common world

Chapter 1

Introduction

Penny Lewis

You can think about architecture in many ways, but essentially, architectural inquiry falls into two camps. On the one hand, we write about buildings and places as designers and critics – making judgments about the qualities of a building in relation to the wider achievements of the discipline. These judgements are made based on an understanding of the legacy of the discipline across national boundaries and across time. We often observe and measure the quantities and qualities of a building or a city according to values that are historically specific and enduring. Vitruvius's *firmness, commodity and delight* remains a touchstone, to which we plug in contemporary concerns and judgements, for example, on sustainability and accessibility. At its core, this area of analysis is concerned with functional, formal, organisational, material and aesthetic questions, and the architect, the building or the city is the subject of inquiry.

In the second type of thinking, architects, urbanists, historians and critics are joined by geographers, urban theorists, social scientists, lawyers, philosophers, activists and policy makers. In this camp, architecture is both an expression of cultural impulses and something that shapes them. Architecture is understood as a product of its time and the conventions of the day. The vast majority of people in this second camp hold to the modernist idea that architecture expresses the 'spirit of the times.' However, they may also embrace the post-modern thesis that suggests that architecture is grounded on the longstanding values and associations accrued over time.

Hannah Arendt argues that individuals and communities are conditioned by the places in which they reside. "Men are conditioned beings because everything they come in contact with turns immediately into conditions of their existence," she writes

Figure 1.1 Chen Yang Jackson Heights, NYC 2021

in *The Human Condition*.[1] This study is based on the understanding that, to paraphrase Churchill, "we shape our buildings and afterwards they in return shape us."[2] Buildings and spaces are cultural products that provide an 'unconscious record' of the institutional and public values of their commissioners, and all buildings are in some way 'public' in that they are commissioned from within public systems that have very strong regulatory frameworks (e.g. today, safety and sustainability).

The content of this book straddles both camps, architecture as subject and object and as discipline and society. This distinction between creating conditions and being subject to conditions is central to the idea of architecture as a public or collective art. Architecture is both a public and simultaneously a private act, the product of communal needs or aspirations and the expression of private individual/institutional wealth. The authors, who participated in the AHRA conference in Dundee November 2019, are concerned with how we shape buildings and space and how these formations reflect and shape our lives. It's unusual to find both aspects of the discourse in one text, but between the two ways of thinking, there is a great deal of cross over; however, they are distinct and have a different purpose and output and it's worth making the distinction as well as enjoying the transgressions.

This tension between private interests and public needs is at the centre of city development, planning and architectural practice. This relationship impacts on every architect's and citizen's sense of what is possible. Colquhoun argues that the Modern Movement began life in the 19th century as a critique of poverty but adapted to become a tool for the reorganisation of the city to suit the interests of monopoly capitalism or state bureaucracy.[3] The idea that architecture will always be bent to the interests of the powerful is a compelling one; yet, the city is also the site of many different individual and shared interests, and it is sometimes a site of resistance. Life in the contemporary city demands a degree of public consensus and ownership in order to operate effectively. The relationship between the practice of architecture and the reproduction of political authority is nuanced and takes many different forms. Architecture is neither the medium nor the message, but it does align with the process by which the powerful assert their interests, and equally, it reflects the ways in which nations and communities arrive at a consensus on how to live together.

If today, architecture speaks to us – it speaks of the mediation of cultural values and the difficulties, we currently experience in arriving at a consensus. These complex and shifting processes of negotiation are evident in the planning process, and they have also been highlighted by the recent Covid-19 shutdown. We have witnessed the policing of the lockdowns, the construction of the Nightingale Hospitals and rise of urban road closures as acts of planning in the absence of a public consensus. Architecture murmurs something about the contradictions of our world but we are never quite in earshot. Architecture is 'read' and 'interpreted' in many ways regardless of the intentions of the architect or urban designer – contradictions abound. For Joan Ockman, there is the splendid and palpable contradiction between the interests of the residents of Greenwich Village in 1960 and the ambitions of post-war planners. For Alexander Michael Catina, the managerial language of placemaking sits in stark contrast to the reality of the High Street. Reiner de Graaf argues that happiness indicators mask the real meaning of the largely vacant real estate sculptures of Manhattan. Many of the essays in this book speak to the difficulty in establishing a sense of what is needed in the face of conflicting, shared and private interests. To talk about collectivity in these situations may seem naïve; in fact, one of the contributors to this book, William Orr, accuses the conference organisers of naivety. Despite his polemic, there is some weight to the idea that there is something essentially public about architecture and urban design and so one element of its practice is collective. Isi Metzstein, one of Scotland's most widely admired post-war architects, made a point of telling students that there was no such thing as a private building. Even a rich man's rural villa must have an approach and a public face and consequently a public responsibility.

Aldo Rossi said: "Architecture gives concrete form to society, it is intimately connected more than any other art or science…The contrast between the particular and the universal, between individual and collective, emerges from the city and from its construction, its architecture" (Aldo 1966 p21)[4].

Whether architecture provides a coherent expression of the needs and values of society at any given time depends on the authority of the people commissioning buildings and the level of consensus in society. Arendt argues that, from the middle of the 18th century, the flowering of music, poetry and, particularly, the novel, coincided with "a striking decline of all the more public arts, especially architecture" (Arendt 1998 p39). According to Arendt in the 19th century, architecture struggled to perform a public function because cultural life was focused on the private and intimate realm, an area in which there was little space for the practical arts. The public realm (where architecture had meaning) was increasingly seen as a place for the regulation of human behaviour and the promotion of conformity rather than a space for free association. This shift meant that there was very little opportunity to build with a clarity of intentions or as an expression of a public consensus. The production of *In What Style Should We build?* in 1828 by Heinrich Hubusch and Augustus Pugin's role in the so-called *Battle of the Styles* in the mid-19th century Britain seem to support Arendt' thesis[5].

One period that seems to run counter to Arendt's thesis is the one in which she lived as an American citizen in New York (1945–1975). We know it as the post-war period, but increasingly, authors such as Thomas Piketty have reclassified it as a golden age of social democracy. Whatever name you give to the three decades, it is evident that post-war reconstruction demanded a high level of state investment in housing, infrastructure and (in Britain and Europe) social welfare. On both sides of the Atlantic, economic expansion meant that there was a clear sense of public good often articulated through modernist built form. Reinier de Graaf refers to this period in which there was a positive environment for both commissioning and architectural production. For Piketty the three decades in which social inequality was tackled by the state sit in stark contrast to the Thatcherism and so-called neo-liberalism from 1980 to the present, in which the state appeared to retreat and social inequality grew.[6] Piketty's schema is mirrored in the fate of the architectural profession which found itself cast out of the public sector from the 1980s and became increasingly frustrated by the difficulty in producing high quality publicly funded buildings as the state's political priorities shifted. However, this narrative of a golden state-led post-war expansion brought to a brutal end by the miserable economic liberalism of Thatcher has many limitations. First, it's important to remember that the profession itself was articulating doubts about the capacity of the State to meaningfully meet public needs before Thatcherism[7]. Second, critics from the 1970s often described the so-called golden age as one in which technocrats in local authorities and City Hall used planning policy to take power out of the hands of the urban poor, the working class and radicals. The grass roots organisations of the 1970s, the squatters and the anti-redevelopment campaigners provide evidence to suggest a collusion between capital and state.

The 1951 Festival of Britain is often seen as marking the start of a new era, but it can also be seen as marking the high tide of cultural consensus in the UK. After 1951, a commitment to the modernist functional city with its national infrastructure, innovative building types and new open public realm began to erode pretty quickly. Although we interpret the buildings produced in the 1960s and 1970s as products of the post-war consensus, it's also the case that this consensus was dissipating rapidly and modernist architecture and planning was increasingly cast as an alienating and disruptive cultural force rather than a emancipatory one[8].

Some of those architects most closely associated with modernism, e.g. Le Corbusier and Team 10, were concerned to address symbolism and meaning alongside function, while the writings of Jane Jacobs, Robert Venturi and Colin Rowe articulated anxieties about the modern state and its planning in a more direct way. Joan Ockman's essay in this book describes the early ambiguities about state modernism in the work of Rudofsky and Van Eyck.

Colquhoun argues that the modern planning systems that emerged from the start of the 20th century undermined the possibility of giving form or meaning to the public realm and generated a more explicit split between private and public space[9]. Team 10's enthusiasm for clusters, repetitive units and 'association' bear witness to a general concern that something had been lost when 19th-century urban forms were replaced by less clearly defined modern ones. This anxiety about the organic and creative autonomy of the urban population was reflected in the work of French researchers at new research bodies such as CERFI, which featured in the AHRA conference session on Foucault led by Joseph Bedford.

Most of the essays in this book address this thorny question of 'the public' and its relationship with architecture and planning; they understand the public realm as something formed through and by public discourse. At the same time, many address the tension within the concept of the 'collective' in a market economy. At the end of the day, most buildings are paid for by private money or investment funds. They may be the outcome of a division of labour, a thriving local or international creative culture and a process of collaboration but they are rarely publicly owned. If members of the public have any impact or involvement in their conception and authorship, it is only as individual shareholders or private citizens, most public consultation lacks authenticity.

So, architecture sits at the centre of shared experience in a material world made up of the things that organise and give shape to our lives, but it is also largely alien to us – commissioned and designed by people who do not necessarily share our values or who are unable to clearly articulate their own. Louis D'Arcy-Reed's chapter on the construction of cultural icons in northern towns in the UK (Chapter 9) recognises that these building have often failed to contribute to a local sense of ownership or place while Claudia Dutson describes a different kind of indifference towards the new Big Tech developments in Silicon Valley (Chapter 6). Today, public commissioning is a complex process mediated by institutions and established patterns of behaviour. Led by fund managers and planning policy makers; it is largely technocratic rather than political and so it rarely touches the public imagination.

One of the questions we were not able to address in the conference itself was the meaning of the term collective life. What do we mean by 'collective'? Are we talking about trade unions or intentional communities, when we talk about 'life' do we mean the informal patterns and routines that we share in city, suburb or rural settlements as a result of basic co-operation or something vital or moral? Some of the answers to these questions can be found within the essays, there are a range of responses expressed. The history of the use of the term 'collective' in architectural and urban theory literature demands further research; the term commons is currently widely discussed but not collective. The term 'collective life' seems to originate in the 1840s; but it appears more frequently in the early part of the 20th century, in two contexts – to describe life in the USSR or China (collectivisation) and in sociological and psychological literature to describe shared civic values and neighbourhood associations. These shared or 'civic' values were seen by the social psychologist Gutave LeBon as an alternative to the political values of mob and socialism[10]. In this sense, the term is often used to express shared values that explicitly deny radical political connections. The idea of the 'collective' is at the centre of the work of the US sociologist and psychologist Mary Parker Follett in her work *The New State (1918)* written at the end of the First World War. Parker Follett (1868–1933) was a social and management theorist who played a important role advising Roosevelt on public democracy[11]. She pioneered the idea of community centres and participatory democracy. Her work seems to set the tone for US urban policy in the 1930s and for the opposition to US urban policy for much of the rest of the 20th century. She makes a case for a modern participatory state at the very moment that the activities of the state are expanding. For the urban elite, the expansion is designed to insulate the political class from the popular will; for others, including Follett, it is to give people a voice and some control over their environment.

Robert Goodman in his book *After the Planners* (1972)[12] charts the evolution of planning in the US from the early part of the 20th century and argues that, by the 1930s, planning was seen as the domestic equivalent of the White Man's Burden – an initiative to help the poor that were incapable of helping themselves. Jane Jacobs descriptions of her discussions with her planner friend in the 1950s suggest that this paternalistic attitude continued to pervade planning offices post-war. As early as 1972, Goodman was expressing concern at the way in which architects had adopted the role of the technocratic expert without any reference to building users. Goodman's experience as an expert helping low-income neighbourhood groups fight the consequences of urban renewal was recorded in the *New York Times* in 1972. "Goodman came to understand how conventional planning was often used as 'a mask of rationality, efficiency and science' to help maintain the status quo, and how participatory programs often helped maintain the mask by allowing the poor to administer their own state of dependency."[13]

Goodman questioned the idea that there was anything collective about the planning process or architectural design. He was a very different political animal from Parker Follett, and yet, they shared similar concerns about the nature of the emerging modern state and the manner in which it acted to take control away from ordinary people. Parker Follett argued for an Athenian style local democracy in which people would make collective decisions about the improvements and activities demanded in their own neighbourhood. As an adviser to Roosevelt, she provided a framework for the urban management that emerged from the 1930s and later she provided some inspiration for those that opposed this expert-led urbanism of the 1960s and 1970s. She makes a compelling argument for the collective mind and genuine process of self-government.

> To say that the social process is that merely of the spread of similarities is to ignore the real nature of the collective thought, the collective will. Individual ideas do not become social ideas when communicated. The difference between them is one of a kind. A collective thought is one evolved by a collective process. The essential feature of a common thought is not that it is held in common but that it has been produced in common.[14]

Parker Follett's ideas of a democratic state and communities organised on democratic principles are echoed in the work of Jane Jacobs post-war. In the early 1960s, the term collective is used more widely; for example, in *The Cosmological Eye* (1961),[15] Henry

Miller uses it as a counterpoint to the experience of modern man. While primitive man's life is entirely collective, writes Miller, modern man is largely individual and despite his aspiration for some shared experience, it alludes him. "As his sphere of influence widens his sense of isolation of loneliness increases."[16] Miller's critique of the alienating aspect of modern and urban life was expressed among architects and can be seen as a forerunner to the rise of post-modern architecture and its critique of modern planning.

In the USA, Robert Venturi was demanding complexity and contradiction in urban form and life, while in the UK Alison and Peter Smithson were exploring the joy of the ordinary and everyday patterns of urban life and writing about 'human association.' As such, it would be hard to deny the connection between the idea of the collective and the critique of modern planning.

For the AHRA conference organisers, the term seemed to touch on something even more fundamental – the fact that we are social animals and that urbanisation is spontaneously generated by urban life regardless of the specific form or the planning theory attempting to give shape to urban life. We were interested in renewing a discussion about how we made the world in which we live – a question that demands the meeting of architecture, planning and democracy. We imagined that it should be possible to speculate about the most appropriate arrangements for civic life at the same time as welcoming a democratic discourse rather than one excluding the other, as has often historically been the case. In retrospect, we didn't get very far in exploring the relationship between urban speculations, buildings and master plans and democratic life, but we began the discussion, and somehow Covid events overtook us.

Reinier De Graaf argues that language associated with collectivity – particularly, the word community is highly problematic – that community has its origins in pre-modern society and has quickly become associated with conservative and parochial social values. He argues that the ideas of community and placemaking have been used to guide urban policy to hide social inequality and disquiet. He describes how the rhetoric of community and happiness has been appropriated by the market to sell real estate or by bureaucrats to satisfy checklists. His analysis is engaging and rings true, but is he correct to argue that Jane Jacobs et al must bear responsibility for creating the language and vocabulary of the corporate placemakers? Ockman suggests that Jacobs' commitment to the free associations of the city could provide some inspiration for city dwellers and architects. Jacobs understood 'freedom as the reciprocal of community' rather than its polar opposite says Ockman – it's a very important observation for contemporary scholars.

The organisation of this book

The chapters in this book were selected from more than 200 papers and provocations that were delivered at the AHRA in Dundee in late November 2019. Papers were selected on merit from different panels, and they are organised loosely according to themes that draw upon the issues raised above:

Penny Lewis

The opening section of this book is made up of three essays and an interview from the conference's keynote speakers: Joan Ockman, Jodi Dean, Martino Tattara and Reinier de Graaf. Ockman takes a collaboration between Jane Jacobs and Marshall McLuhan (1911–1980) as the starting point for an analysis of a real and a virtual village in Chapter 2. Ockman makes a strong case for revisiting Jacob's work in the context of today's social relationships, highlighting the city as a site for 'new discoveries and unscripted encounters' as well as good neighbourhoods. Ockman's essay is followed by an interview with Reinier de Graaf, who delivered a polemic against city-marketing language on liveability, well-being criteria and urban league tables. For de Graaf, the popular placemaking discourse tells us little about the real nature of urban life and ignores economic relations and inequalities. Jodi Dean's chapter unpacks the changing nature of social relations, particularly in the USA, which she describes as neo-feudal. Dean paints a picture of a world in which we are subjects rather than citizens, and in which, the rule of law no longer operates particularly if you are poor and black and living on the periphery of the city. Drawing on the work of urban geographers, she paints a picture of the suburbs as the site of exploitation and urban resistance. Since the conference, the neo-feudalism thesis has become a focus of a much broader discussion about globalism, lockdowns, and social justice. We reflect on Dean's new geography, of rich urban core and impoverished hinterlands, in the conclusion. Martino Tattarra's essay and his practice's design work suggest some ways in which architects might subvert the existing arrangement of land values and development to provide good homes for urban workers.

Part 2 of the book looks at the idea of authority and collective life. Will Orr writes about, "an ideologically suspect notion of urban society and 'collectivity'." Orr's essay looks at Aldo Rossi's *The Architecture of the City* (1966) and asks why Rossi preferred to talk about 'the project' rather than 'planning.' He argues that 'the project' could accommodate the emerging 'anti-planning' sentiments among his contemporaries. For Orr, planning is equated with progress, and challenges to the plan (anti-planning) are aligned ideologically with neo-liberalism; Jane Jacobs and Aldo Rossi are included as part of this apparently reactionary trend. Orr encourages the reader to think about the question of authorship and the way the architect stands outside the collective output of the planning process and argues that Rossi's attempt to retain a sense of authorship is problematic. Joseph Bedford's essay looks at the evolution of Foucault's thinking, particularly in relation to phenomenology. In the late 1960s Michel Foucault became enmeshed in a series of research collaborative endeavours with architects, geographers, historians and sociologists, studying the history of housing, towns, health care facilities and the politics of space and themes of discipline and governmentality. Doreen Bernath's essay argues that interruptions are a necessary part of the collective and that gaps and mismatches are more significant than an imposed uniformity. The idea of being faithful to a common cause is replaced by the idea of infidelity – where there are parts but no whole or single voice. Bernath believes that the creator must make visible the organising or operative function of the work, turning the audience into collaborators rather than passive spectators.

Part 3 of the book covers the architecture and planning of the Welfare State, the process of post-war reconstruction and a variety of different relationships between designers and state planning. Marie Pirard looks at the work of Victor Bourgeois and the demand for healthy open-air facilities in the immediate aftermath of the war. Bourgeois was commissioned by the state to produce a number of public leisure facilities at a moment when health became a core concern of government and the body featured as both a mechanistic and mystical element in the imagination of modern architects. Bourgeois' landscapes and leisure buildings exploited the development of new earthworks plant – specifically diggers – and the new facilities tended to be earth buildings, embedded in the landscape and expressing an aspiration for social freedom. Alessandro Porrotto looks in detail at the design of some of Vienna's most famous social housing and Meike Schalk et al look at the emergence of new intentional communities in Sweden that emerged alongside the dismantling of some aspects of the welfare state and conventional forms of state procurement.

Part 4 looks at the changing shape of the urban landscape and the impact of these changes on the localised sense of place and community. Claudia Dutson's essay studies the new building types being developed in Silicon Valley. Her work is particularly timely given the current interest in the political and material power of the Big Tech corporations as wealth generators, employers and regulators of the speech and information in the digital world. Tahl Kaminer summarises the thinking explored in the AHRA panel on gentrification, one of the most significant effects of today's planning policy, and a trend that has sparked a broader debate about the changing character of the city. Louis D'Arcy-Reed explores state-sponsored cultural icons, while Aleks Catina looks at the death of the High Street.

Part 5 looks at autonomous forms of human activity and the idea of self-organisation. Janina Gosseye describes the work of one religious welfare organisation in France in the three decades from the end of the First World War, a period which she describes as the glorious 30 years. Gosseye argues that the planning of the built environment was one of the key areas in which the European welfare state's ambitions for redistribution were fulfilled. Meredith Gaglio looks at the early environmental campaigners involved in the publication of RAIN an alternative technology publication. Dorian Wiszniewski's study looks at three areas of housing in North and South Calcutta that now constitute heritage areas but have been overlooked by the authorities. He studies in detail how certain built forms and traditions have emerged from this introverted community within the densely populated city. Jane Clossick, architect, and Ben Colburn, philosopher, worked together to explore what we mean by the term 'autonomy' in relation to the built environment. They explore whether it is possible to design to enhance autonomy inspired by the idea of 'depth structure' a concept associated with Dalibor Vesely's communicative space.

Part 6 concludes the book beginning by looking at design work: Altes and Lieberman describe their own work and design process while Davide Landi analyses the design of spaces for communal living. Penny Lewis looks at the discussion on planning and ecology in the UK post-war with a particular focus on the work of the German émigré, EA Gutkind and the Independent Group. Teressa Stoppani explores how we generate theory *from* architecture. She suggests that theory is a collective or collaborative effort which involves the creation of a dialogue in which there is complexity and ambiguity. The concluding essay was written during the Covid lockdown. It aims to address the points raised by these essays in the context of the most extraordinary experience of what the *Economist* has called The Plague Year.[17]

Notes

1. Arendt, H, *The Human Condition* (1998) University of Chicago Press, London (First published 1958).
2. Churchill, W, Parliamentary debate in Hansard 28 October 1943 vol 393 cc 403-73. Churchill was speaking following the destruction of the Commons by bombing.
3. Colquhoun, A (1991) *Modernity and the Classical Tradition* MIT Press, Cambridge and London. Chapter on the concepts of urban space.
4. Rossi, A, *The Architecture of the City* (1982) Opposition Books, MIT Press, Cambridge and London.
5. Pugin, A.W *Contrasts* (2013) Cambridge University Press, Cambridge UK. First published in 1841
6. Piketty, T, *Capital in the 21st Century* (2014) Harvard University Press, Cambridge MA.
7. Brett, L (Viscount Esher) *A Broken Wave: the Rebuilding of England, 1940–1980* (1981), Allen Lane London.
8. Colquhoun (1991)
9. Colquhoun (1991)
10. Le Bon, G (1960) *The Crowd: A Study of the Popular Mind*, Viking Press (First published 1895)
11. Follett, M. P. (1998). *The New State. Group Organization the Solution of Popular Government*. United States: Pennsylvania State University Press.
12. Goodman, R, (1972) *After the Planners*, Pelican, London, p187.
13. Alperovitz, G (1972) 'Nothing Works' The New York Times 6 February
14. Follett, M. P. (1998). *The New State. Group Organization the Solution of Popular Government*. United States: Pennsylvania State University Press.
15. Miller, H (1961) *The Cosmological Eye*, New Directions Publishing, New York
16. Miller, H (1961) *The Cosmological Eye*, New Directions Publishing, New York p189
17. The Economist, December 2020.

Chapter 2

A tale of two villages

Jane Jacobs, Marshall McLuhan and their visions of collective life

Joan Ockman

"A big city is a place where you can buy a second-hand violin and keep a mistress." So Jane Jacobs once quipped. I thought I understood the second-hand violin and her point. But the mistress? Surprising coming from a woman. On one of her infrequent trips back to New York two years before her death to give an honorary lecture at City College, I had the chance to ask her about the statement. She laughed. "That was actually said by Oscar Stonorov."[1] Of course! It had to be a man. Stonorov was a Philadelphia architect and an early partner of Louis Kahn. But apart from the gendered innuendo, the meaning was clear enough. The value of a big city is directly proportional to its potential for unscripted encounters and new discoveries. It's a place where you can be part of something larger than yourself and where you can keep your secrets.

Freedom of the city

Urban freedom is one of the cardinal ideas that underwrites and animates Jacobs's most celebrated book, *The Death and Life of Great American Cities*, published in 1961.[2] In the open and vibrant city she wants, freedom is the reciprocal of community and bound up with it inextricably. A city worth the name fosters both. You can be alone together and together together. Jacobs wants collective experiences but not at the expense of singular ones; she wants both sociability and serendipity. To be sure, freedom can be *for* or *from*. Big American cities in the 1950s and 1960s were often, objectively speaking, crime-ridden, dangerous places. So it's not surprising to see a professional woman journalist

Joan Ockman

Figure 2.1 Jane Jacobs near her home on Hudson Street in Greenwich Village, New York, 1961
Photo: Ernest Sisto, *New York Times*

who was also a mother and a neighbour devote a large chunk of her book to questions of safety. Yet, Jacobs was unwilling to sacrifice one form of freedom to the other. Urban life should be as free as possible from unnecessary regulation, but also from physical and environmental threats. Both excessive control and excessive fear diminish the capacity of people to interact freely and productively with one another, stymying their sense of possibility. Freedom from control and fear is freedom for social relationships, and it is relationships – or, in a negative sense, the lack of them – that make a city what it is. Is it safe to take the subway home at one in the morning? Can you hold a demonstration in a park? What is it like, if you're black, to live in a building in a mostly white neighbourhood?

Jacobs invokes the phrase "freedom of the city" multiple times in *Death and Life*.[3] Her concept of urban freedom is not quite the same thing as Henri Lefebvre's "right to the city." It's more than a legally conferred entitlement. It's diffuse, experiential, experimental. It's the actualities of negotiating your everyday life with people beyond those in your immediate circle, people with different backgrounds, worldviews and claims. The city's spaces and places are the sites of this negotiation, and this process defines them, not the other way around. Freedom of the city has an aleatory character. As Sigfried Kracauer once wrote, "The value of cities is determined by the number of places given over to improvisation."[4]

Briefly put, urban freedom is the sense of potential that people living in a city share in common. Jacobs writes in *Death and Life*:

[What] we have to express in expressing our cities is not to be scorned. Their intricate order—a manifestation of the freedom of countless numbers of people to make and carry out countless plans—is in many ways a great wonder. We ought not to be reluctant to make this living collection of interdependent uses, this freedom, this life, more understandable for what it is.[5]

Essential to sustaining the city's intricate and intimate interplay between freedom and order for Jacobs are *diversity* and *density*. The latter two qualities in turn make possible her third d-word, *dynamism*. By 1956, when she made her debut as an urban thinker at a conference at Harvard's Graduate School of Design, she had already arrived at this constellation of ideas. The conference was intended to launch a new academic discipline, urban design, an intermediate scale of intervention between architecture and urban planning. The first was seen by Josep Lluís Sert, dean of the GSD and the conference organiser, as too object-oriented; the second as too abstract and quantitative. The event assembled many of the leading lights in the profession from around the United States. Along with Sert, the attendees included men like Lewis Mumford, Richard Neutra, Victor Gruen and Ed Bacon. The 'uncredentialed' young woman journalist from *Architectural Forum*, asked at the last minute to stand in for her boss, gave a lecture titled "The Missing Link in City Redevelopment." While most in the audience would not have disagreed with her indictment of urban renewal, the dominant policy of the day, especially as it was being ruthlessly carried out in her home city by Robert Moses, Jacobs ventured well out on a limb, calling attention to "… the hand-to-mouth

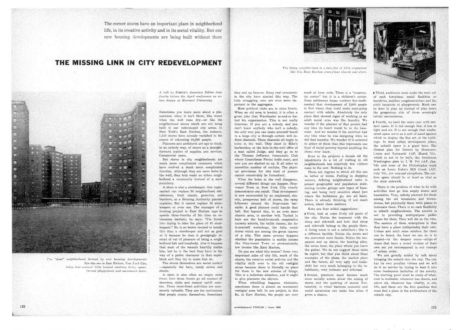

Figure 2.2 Jane Jacobs, "The Missing Link in City Redevelopment," *Architectural Forum*, June 1956

cooperative nursery schools, the ballet classes, the do-it-yourself workshops, the little exotic stores" that had so far escaped the notice of architects and planners. Such ostensible 'strips of chaos,' she asserted, have "a weird wisdom of their own not yet encompassed in our concept of urban order." "Notice the stores and the converted store fronts. Notice the taxpayers and up above, the bowling alley, the union local, the place where you learn the guitar," she advised. "All very ugly and makeshift but very much belonging to the inhabitants, intimate and informal."[6]

Counterintuitive as it may sound, Jacobs's ballet classes, bowling alleys and little exotic stores connect her to some of the most radical urban thinkers of the 20th century. Her love of the multifarious and granulated freedom of big cities was more than just a matter of picturesque charm. While the British Townscape movement would embrace her as a kindred spirit in the late 1950s, Jacobs's dense, diverse and dynamic city was closer in many respects to the urbanism of the Situationists at this date. Like Jacobs, the Situationists were not merely after an image, and like her, they recognised the value of the city's overlooked and marginal spaces, which were destinations for their 'drifts.'[7]

An even closer affinity exists between Jacobs's idea of collectivity and that of the architectural protagonists of Team 10, who published the first edition of their *Team 10 Primer* one year after *Death and Life*.[8] Even if they were insiders to the profession and she was decidedly an outsider, we can relate her famous "sidewalk ballet" to the "doorstep philosophy" put forward by Peter and Alison Smithson and, in a variation on the theme (influenced by Martin Buber), by Aldo van Eyck. For these rebels against modernist orthodoxy, the doorstep was the place of primary encounter 'between man and men,' the threshold where the individual and the collective met face to face.[9] For both Jacobs and Team 10, it was both a real and a metaphorical interface. What made the ebb and flow of life on the other side of one's doorstep so fascinating to observe was precisely its combination of familiarity and unfamiliarity. In the extended passage in *Death and Life* in which Jacobs waxes lyrical about the spontaneous choreography of identity and difference, she points to strangers as an ever-present element of urban life. Strangers are the 'natural proprietors of the street':

> Great cities are not like towns, only larger. They are not like suburbs, only denser. They differ from towns and suburbs in basic ways, and one of these is that cities are, by definition, full of strangers. To any one person, strangers are far more common in big cities than acquaintances. More common not just in places of public assembly, but more common at a man's own doorstep.[10]

This last statement calls to mind another contemporary theorist who, again despite his different context, was no less enamoured of the potential of new urban encounters. In a 1967 essay titled 'Semiology and Urbanism,' Roland Barthes writes of the *dimension amoureuse*, or 'erotic dimension,' of the city. Needless to say, eroticism for Barthes is more than a matter of the districts reserved for sexual transactions. "The city, essentially and semantically, is the site of our encounter with the other."[11] This may be the most compact summary of urban life ever written.

The concept of urban freedom is not, of course, exclusively modern. The saying *Stadtluft macht frei*, city air makes people free, goes back to the Middle Ages.[12] But imagine how liberating a city like New York must have been for the 20-year-old Jacobs, arriving in 1935 from small-town Scranton, Pennsylvania. A quarter century later, another woman trapped in a life too confining for her aspirations, Betty Friedan, would also recognise the city's emancipatory potential. Educated at an elite women's college during the Second World War and then finding herself consigned to a house in the suburbs with three children, Friedan was among the first to identify "the problem that has no name."[13] *The Feminine Mystique*, which appeared two years after *Death and Life*, exploded the myth of the 'happy housewife,' debunking the notion that a well-feathered nest stocked with plenty of consumer goods sufficed for a woman's well-being. In the 1960s, Friedan uprooted her family and moved to Manhattan and, with the founding of the National Organization of Women in 1966, helped launch the second wave of American feminism.

Notably, a man like Lewis Mumford, champion of small-scale regional cities against the overcrowded and unwholesome metropolis, had a different view of a woman's place. In *Death and Life*, Jacobs frontally attacks his Garden City ideal, the subtexts of which, she perceived, were docility under patriarchy, the stability of the traditional family unit, and the orderliness of everything-in-its-place. Jacobs would acknowledge later in her life that, among the various political battles she had fought during her career, feminism was never "an overt cause."[14] But Mumford, she stated, "seemed to think of women as a ladies' auxiliary of the human race."[15] He responded to her attack in *Death and Life* in his column in the *New Yorker* in a long review. Titled 'Mother Jacobs' Home Remedies,' it was full of barely disguised condescension for her amateurism and aesthetic philistinism.[16] Deriding her opinions as "a mingling of sense and sentimentality, of mature judgments and schoolgirl howlers," and the book as a celebration of "higgledy-piggledy unplanned casualness," grist for "dinner-table conversation," he criticised her prescriptions – shorter streets, wider sidewalks, mixed uses – for failing

Figure 2.3 Stills from *The City*, film shown at the New York World's Fair, 1939. Script by Lewis Mumford. The Garden City ideal as realised in the new town of Greenbelt outside Washington, D.C. "Never letting cities grow too big to manage…. The wife needn't feel cooped up on washing day. A little gossip or a friendly hand [of cards] is good for the complexion…."

to get at the deeper, structural problems faced by cities.[17] As he not incorrectly pointed out, her beloved Greenwich Village was hardly a typical model; had she turned her sights a 100 blocks north to, say, Harlem, she would undoubtedly have reached less naive conclusions. Later on, when he republished his book review in a collection of his essays, he toned down the sexism a bit, retitling it 'Home Remedies for Urban Cancer.' But he didn't alter his views.[18]

By the 1960s, Mumford was fully convinced that the American metropolis had not only exploded into a megalopolis but was well on its way to becoming a necropolis. He had been making a version of this argument since the start of his career, writing in 1925, "The hope of the city lies outside itself."[19] But, by 1961, when he published *The City in History* the same year that Jacobs's *Death and Life* appeared, reworking and updating his magnum opus *The Culture of Cities*, his tone was stridently moralistic and apocalyptic. Ironically, Mumford distrusted big government and centralised bureaucracy – the 'pentagon of power' – as much as Jacobs. Yet while he put his faith in a regional network of small urban centres, Jacobs sought solutions in the bottom-up, self-organising properties she saw as intrinsic to large cities. She regarded Mumford's position as fundamentally contradictory: "You can't decentralize centrally," she pointed out.[20] This axiom came from, of all people, Marshall McLuhan, with whom Jacobs would soon strike up a friendship – about which much more presently.

Mumford was by no means the only critic of *Death and Life*. The sociologist Herbert Gans attempted a more even-handed appraisal of the book, but his ultimate verdict was just as negative. In a review published in *Commentary* in 1962, 'City Planning and Urban Realities,' he faulted Jacobs's argument for the 'physical fallacy' that it shared, ironically, with the professional architects and planners she was criticising.[21] Her overemphasis on the design of streets and sidewalks led her to ignore less visible social, economic and cultural factors, from racism and poverty to the exigencies of the real estate market. He presciently predicted that her critique would be misappropriated by "those who profit from the status quo."[22] Previously, Gans and Jacobs had been on friendly terms; in *Death and Life*, she had cited his documentation, in an article published two years earlier, of the devastating effects of urban renewal on poor but stable neighbourhoods.[23] This article would become the basis of Gans's book *The Urban Villagers*, which appeared in 1962.[24] In his review of *Death and Life*, Gans further took Jacobs to task for generalising her own taste and values to a broad swath of post-war American citizens.[25]

Notwithstanding these expert opinions, though, the failures of urban renewal policy were palpable to most people by the early 1960s, not just in New York and Boston but also Chicago, St. Louis, Philadelphia and other cities that had eagerly availed themselves of Title I of the 1949 Federal Housing Act and its bulldozers. Jacobs's book thus struck a resonant chord, and the architectural profession had no choice but to respond. In 1972, the same year the first block of housing at the infamous Pruitt-Igoe complex in St. Louis was dynamited out of existence, Oscar Newman's *Defensible Space* appeared. Newman barely mentions Jacobs's name – only twice in passing, once to disavow her "unsupported hypotheses."[26] But the impact of her critique is implicit in his images of vandalised urban renewal projects built by modern architects and his efforts to propose 'defensible' solutions to the contradictions of security and surveillance in an open society.

The same photograph of the demolition of Pruitt-Igoe that appears on the back cover of Newman's book (taken from *Life* magazine) would be reproduced by Charles Jencks five years later in *The Language of Post-Modern Architecture*. For Jencks, the medium was the message. If late-modern architecture was the medium, the message was that its alienating forms had spawned dystopian cities. The messengers were, of course, modern architects and planners, and Jencks hailed Jacobs for having laid the blame squarely on their doorstep, so to speak.[27]

Jacobs would continue to have her defenders and detractors. Significantly, they would come from both ends of the political spectrum. This is not surprising; her politics resist easy categorisation. On the left, some accused her of a libertarian streak, while others applauded her activism, quoting her slogan "fix the buildings but leave the people" to refute charges that she had opened the floodgates to what would come to be known as gentrification.[28] Jacobs herself preferred to characterise her stance as that of "an old-fashioned pragmatist."[29] Her privileged method was empirical and observational, based on trial and error, what worked and what didn't. In the concluding chapter of *Death and Life*, titled "The Kind of Problem a City Is," she spells out her 'laboratory' method, taken from the biosciences:

> [A] growing number of people have begun, gradually, to think of cities as problems in organized complexity—organisms that are replete with intricately interconnected, and surely understandable, relationships. This book is one manifestation of that idea.[30]

Jacobs's early application of a theory of organised complexity to the analysis of urban behaviour, which she would elaborate in her subsequent books, remains among her most original contributions, and connects her thinking to contemporary urban discourse. In a speech in 1958, she describes New York's urban complexity as a 'crisscross network':

> The criss-cross of supporting relationships means, for instance, that a Russian tearoom and last year's minks and a place to rent English sports cars bloom well near Carnegie Hall.... It means that the Puerto Rican Orientation Club of East Harlem finds a place it can actually afford in a beat-up tenement basement—an unprepossessing place but a place of its own.... It means that tourists and the transients who stay in the city four or five years can continue enjoying the flighty bohemia of Greenwich Village, but only because the Village still has enough solid, rooted Italian families and sober-sided middle-class parents…[31]

Yet if, as here, her preference is always for forms of organic, bottom-up organisation, she was not too dogmatic to acknowledge that in a society of unequal life chances

Figure 2.4 Marshall McLuhan in Toronto, late 1960s
Courtesy of Information Services, University of Toronto

and wealth 'people do need help' from the government sometimes.[32] Apropos of old-fashioned pragmatism, her position recalls a distinction between commerce and commercialism once made by John Dewey. Replying to his anticapitalist critics, Dewey stated that while commercialism means "bondage to private interests," commerce signifies "intercourse, exchange, communication, distribution, sharing of what is otherwise secluded and private."[33] Jacobs would undoubtedly have endorsed this distinction. For her too, exchange and interchange, not profits, had the potential to engender positive change.

With or without propinquity?

In the early 1960s Jane Jacobs's blooming, buzzing, cheek-by-jowl vision of urban life found a receptive audience, as we have just said. Yet, at the same date, on the West Coast of the US, a different idea of complexity and collectivity was being articulated by an urban planner and sociologist at the University of California at Berkeley. In two essays of 1962–1963, "The Urban Place and the Nonplace Urban Realm" and "Order in Diversity: Community without Propinquity," Melvin Webber put forward the argument that urban theories based on the physical attributes of place failed to acknowledge the paradigm shift that had occurred since the Second World War. Attention needed to be turned from obsolete place-based theories to the 'nonplace realm' of communications. In the first of his two essays, he criticised architects and planners for clinging to a "small-scale, static, locational, and physical" frame of reference.[34] In the sequel, he reiterated that 'cityness' could no longer be understood in territorial terms. In a pluralistic and mobile society, urbanity was an increasingly complex 'communications system.' "Never before have men been able to maintain intimate and continuing contact with others across thousands of miles," he stated. He concluded by "flatly rejecting the contention that there is an overriding universal spatial or physical aesthetic of urban form."[35]

Webber's radical theory of urbanism (or post-urbanism) had a strong impact within academic planning circles. Yet, the ideas of a Canadian literary professor turned advertising consultant turned media guru were exponentially more explosive. Just as Jacobs's *Death and Life* was being published in New York, Marshall McLuhan was completing *The Gutenberg Galaxy: The Making of Typographic Man* in his home city of Toronto. Published in 1962, it would be followed two years later by the book that made him a household name, *Understanding Media: The Extensions of Man*. In *Gutenberg*, McLuhan telescoped thousands of years of civilisation in his genealogy of contemporary technology. Starting from archaic and tribal societies whose oral traditions privileged the ear and other non-visual senses over the eye, he leaped forward to 3500 BC, around when the invention of the phonetic alphabet ushered in a new visual culture of reading and writing. This culture would reach its climax in the 16th century with Gutenberg's invention of movable type and the mechanisation of print. But three centuries later, another revolutionary technology emerged. Radio and electronics challenged the regime of 'alphabetic man' and heralded the current epoch of television and the computer. McLuhan's linear reading of history was unabashedly techno-deterministic and teleological. But it was also, in his exhilarated telling, a circling back to the future: the advent of the electronic environment constituted a 'retribalization' of humanity, at once a retrogression to the acoustic and multisensory world of primitive times and an exponential expansion of the human sensorium, "global in extent."[36] This argument served as prequel to *Understanding Media*, in which he advanced the idea that the electronic universe was a prosthetic extension of human consciousness, capable of exploding society – or imploding it, as he had it – into universal interconnectivity.

A voracious reader, McLuhan conjured his media theory out of a heteroclite assemblage of sources, assimilated heretically. James Joyce was a primary inspiration; in his late novel *Finnegans Wake*, Joyce had pushed literary language to the limits of verbal expression. From the post-war science of cybernetics, McLuhan took the concept of feedback (or, as he preferred, 'feedforward'). Interest in architectural history led him to Sigfried Giedion, with whom he began a correspondence in the late 1940s, a moment when Giedion was turning his attention from the modern *Zeitgeist* of space-time back to the "beginnings of art."[37] McLuhan also absorbed Giedion's *Mechanization Takes Command* (1948), a history of 'anonymous' modern technology. Equally essential to McLuhan's technological telos was Lewis

Joan Ockman

Mumford's *Technics and Civilization* (1934), which was indebted in turn to the evolutionist perspective of the Scottish biologist and urban planner Patrick Geddes.[38] McLuhan picked up another of his key concepts, that of the 'extensions of man,' from the work of his friend Edward T. Hall, an anthropologist, who in *The Silent Language* (1959) had described a series of natural and man-made environments – from spiderwebs and cocoons to clothing, housing and weapons systems – as prosthetic devices.[39]

But, by far, the most famous idea that McLuhan put forward in *Understanding Media* was the 'global village.' The catchphrase immediately captured the popular imagination. Among McLuhan's sources was a statement made by Wyndham Lewis in a late book, *America and Cosmic Man* (1948). Written in Canada, where the Nova Scotia-born émigré author resettled temporarily during the Second World War and was befriended by McLuhan, Lewis's book hails the US as the prototype of a universal or 'cosmic' civilisation in which "the earth has become one big village, with telephones laid on from one end to the other, and air transport, both speedy and safe."[40] The global village would serve as a shorthand for McLuhan's vision of a human cosmos rendered intimately present and instantly available through electronic communications. The iconic passage in *Understanding Media* reads:

> After three thousand years of explosion, by means of fragmentary and mechanical technologies, the Western world is imploding. During the mechanical ages we had extended our bodies in space. Today, after more than a century of electric technology, we have extended our central nervous system itself in a global embrace, abolishing both space and time as far as our planet is concerned. Rapidly, we approach the final phase of the extensions of man—the technological simulation of consciousness, when the creative process of knowing will be collectively and corporately extended to the whole of human society, much as we have already extended our senses and nerves by the various media. Whether the extension of consciousness, so long sought by advertisers for specific products, will be 'a good thing' is a question that admits of a wide solution. As electrically contracted, the globe is no more than a village.[41]

Literary performance artist and provocateur, media evangelist and Pop culture celebrity, McLuhan would continue to promote his global village in written and spoken pronouncements until his death in 1980. In rhetoric ranging from arch and esoteric wordplay to vatic utterances, from self-contradiction to sheer bafflement, he insisted that his postulations were experimental 'probes' into the electronic future. He denied that he had any specific ideological affiliation. Indeed, his effusive but elusive writings make his politics even trickier to pin down than Jacobs's. Over the years, he would be variously branded a capitalist apologist, a counterculture humanist, a ludic Luddite and a right-wing Roman Catholic proto-post-modernist.[42] In an uncharacteristically direct interview published in *Playboy* magazine in 1969, he dilated on the political implications of the immaterial environment that he saw coming into being. Post-democratic and post-Tower of Babel, electronic interconnectivity would put an end to conventional electoral politics, he foresaw; instead of ballot boxes, there would be spontaneous manifestations of the popular will, which would express itself through daily plebiscites and other instant feedback mechanisms. Foreign languages would cease to be a barrier between people; the computer would instantaneously translate any code or language into any other, in time obviating the need for articulated languages altogether. Everyone would be bound together in "an integral cosmic unconsciousness" akin to "the collective unconscious envisioned by Bergson." A final, transcendent reunification would take place in "the mystical body of Christ … the ultimate extension of man."[43]

It is perhaps more the task of the psychologist than the historian to speculate on what lies behind McLuhan's half science-fiction, half theological eschatology. Yet, his yearning for an all-enveloping super-community in which atomisation is overcome through multisensory perception and unconstrained, unbounded communication may be understood as a response to the mechanistic divisions of late 20th-century urban existence. The big city, McLuhan states in *Playboy*, is a milieu of 'dissociated sensibilities' where 'uniformity and impersonality' reign. In the village, by contrast, 'eccentricity lingers,' making inevitable 'conflict and discord' but also 'love and harmony.' Retribalisation is the promise of sustaining differences while binding "the entire human family" into "a single universal membrane."[44] It is interesting to compare McLuhan's mystical poetics of reunification to Guy Debord's militant critique of the society of spectacle, with which it is contemporaneous. While it goes without saying that McLuhan and Debord occupy diametric ends of the ideological spectrum, both were driven by the ardent desire to overcome alienation and separation. Yet while McLuhan viewed the electronic environment as a medium of perfect transparency, the French theorist rejected all mediations, not least technological ones, as instruments of distortion and deception.[45]

It is also possible to connect McLuhan's metaphor of retribalisation – which he literalises in his 1967 book *The Medium Is the Massage* with a somewhat racist photograph of a group of naked African natives sitting in a circle animatedly exchanging stories – to the imagery of the primitive or vernacular village in the exhibition *Architecture without Architects*, curated by Bernard Rudofsky at the Museum of Modern Art in New York in 1964. *Architecture without Architects* reframed the kumbaya message of another exhibition, *The Family of Man*, staged at MoMA a decade earlier, in a more anti-colonialist and anti-Establishment spirit. Yet, in offering up non-Western patterns of settlement as antidote to the sterility of modernist urbanism, Rudofsky's photos of 'non-pedigreed architecture' provided a highly decontextualised and aestheticised argument.[46] In this respect, his approach differed from that of Aldo van Eyck, whose "doorstep philosophy" we mentioned earlier. Like Rudofsky, Van Eyck looked to the built environments of anthropological civilisations as a countermodel, although his immersive expeditions to the Dogon villages in Mali and the New Mexico Pueblo in the early 1960s differed from Rudofsky's more spectacularised approach. But taken all together, these and other atavisms of the day may be seen as the flip side of Jacobs's search for a 'missing link.'

Joan Ockman

Figure 2.5 Protest against the Spadina Expressway extension by members of the Stop Spadina Save Our City Coordinating Committee (SSSOCCC), Toronto, 1970
Photo: Fred Ross, Toronto Star. Courtesy: Getty Images

Between Greenwich Village and the global village

With the publication of *Death and Life* in 1961, Jacobs became a public figure and a celebrity, even receiving an invitation to speak at the White House. Her burgeoning reputation as a writer was soon matched by her practical successes in battling several notorious projects of Robert Moses. Having honed her skills as an activist in the late 1950s when she joined members of her Greenwich Village community in fighting a roadway that he was preparing to ram through the heart of Washington Square Park, she went on to out-manoeuvre a cabal of real estate interests and urban renewal proponents threatening her immediate neighbourhood on Hudson Street. She also joined with fellow New Yorkers in an unsuccessful last-ditch effort to save the original Pennsylvania Station from demolition and lent her energies to various other urban and political causes including protests against the Vietnam War. Finally, in an iconic David-versus-Goliath confrontation that would play out over two mayoral administrations, she took on Moses's project for the Lower Manhattan Expressway, a ten-lane traffic artery that was to slice across the southern edge of the neighbourhood subsequently to be known as SoHo and continue eastward. In 1963, her early actions against the expressway elicited a congratulatory letter from none other than Lewis Mumford, who, in a conciliatory gesture, expressed admiration for her efforts. Five years later, her ongoing activism resulted in an arrest for disorderly conduct, incitement to riot, and criminal mischief when she appeared at a public hearing on the expressway and ripped the tape out of the machine the stenographer was using to record the proceedings. This bad behaviour was rewarded a year later when a new mayor, John V. Lindsay, elected

A tale of two villages

in 1966, officially demapped LOMEX, citing the carbon monoxide fumes that would have wafted from it across Lower Manhattan. This momentous victory over the forces of urban renewal was duly recorded on 17 July 1969, on the front page of the *New York Times*, though eclipsed by a banner headline the same day announcing that three American astronauts were streaking across the sky to the moon in the spacecraft *Apollo 11*.

By this date, however, Jacobs herself had not only left New York City but the United States. Fearing that her two draft-age sons would end up in Vietnam (or else in jail), she and her husband pulled up stakes and moved to Toronto in the summer of 1968, relocating to an apartment on Spadina Road. Jacobs was hardly unpacked when she discovered that plans were afoot in Toronto for a major extension of the Spadina Expressway, slated to run from the northern suburbs into downtown Toronto and finish on the fringe of her new neighbourhood.

Meanwhile, the peripatetic McLuhan had also recently returned to Toronto from New York after spending a portion of the previous academic year guest-teaching at Fordham University in the Bronx (and also, after falling ill, undergoing serious brain surgery). In 1969, eager to make Jacobs's acquaintance, he invited her to join him for lunch at the University of Toronto Faculty Club. A lively friendship ensued. The two bonded over their shared opposition to the Spadina Expressway extension, and not long afterward McLuhan enlisted Jacobs's collaboration on a film that he wanted to make in support of a group of activists who were already protesting against it.[47]

Figure 2.6 Spread from Marshall McLuhan with Harley Parker, *Counterblast*, 1969

The local and global villages had rarely come closer together. By this point, the darker side of the global village was in full view. Two years earlier, Expo 67 in Montreal was themed 'Man and His World' and McLuhan's global village had served as something of an anthem, embodied in the geodesic dome designed by Buckminster Fuller (with McLuhan's blessing) for the US pavilion. Now, the techno-enthusiasm and optimistic humanism of Expo were tempered by geopolitical events. On the TV screen, anti-war protesters at the 1968 Democratic National Convention in Chicago, held two months after the assassination of aspiring presidential candidate Robert F. Kennedy, chanted, "The whole world is watching." McLuhan coauthored a book less cheery than his previous ones, *War and Peace in the Global Village*. This was followed by *Counterblast* in 1969, a reprise of Wyndham Lewis's short-lived Vorticist journal *Blast*, in which he assailed Toronto and other contemporary cities as antiquated and culturally vapid tourist destinations.[48] In his *Playboy* interview the same year, he elaborated on the obsolescence of physical cities:

> The cities, corporate extensions of our physical organs, are withering and being translated along with all other such extensions into information systems, as television and the jet—by compressing time and space—make all the world one village and destroy the old city-country dichotomy. New York, Chicago, Los Angeles—all will disappear like the dinosaur. The automobile, too, will soon be as obsolete as the cities it is currently strangling, replaced by new antigravitational technology.[49]

Jacobs too levelled an attack on the dinosaur city, although from a different perspective. In a newspaper article titled "A City Getting Hooked on the Expressway Drug," she expressed incredulity that Toronto – a city she considered "the most healthy and hopeful in North America" – was taking the first step to "Los Angelize" itself.[50] Was it possible that Toronto had learned nothing from recent experiences in the US?

But McLuhan was now also becoming increasingly concerned about things in his own backyard. Notwithstanding his affinity for the anti-gravity realm, he was up in arms about plans to erect four 'hideous high-rise slabs' close to his leafy neighbourhood of Wychwood Park, where he resided in a spacious Arts and Crafts-style house built at the turn of the 20th century. In 1970, turning his attention from the information highway to the one about to encroach on his city, he and Jacobs sat down for a free-wheeling conversation that was intended to generate the script for their Spadina Expressway film. The conversation jumped around in typically McLuhanesque fashion, and afterward, Jacobs was dubious that anything coherent could come of it.[51] She was pleasantly surprised when a local filmmaker brought in by McLuhan, David MacKay, succeeded in putting together an engaging 14-minute visual montage.[52] A medley of jammed and screeching highway traffic, car junkyards and other wreckage of automobile civilisation with a voice-over narration and a catchy theme song, the film was intercut with Toronto streetscapes and scenes of everyday life shot in locales the expressway would have obliterated. McLuhan titled it *The Burning Would*, a piece of wordplay taken from his touchstone *Finnegans Wake* (Joyce in turn riffing on *Macbeth*).

A tale of two villages

Figure 2.7 Stills from *The Burning Would*, 1970. Film by Marshall McLuhan with Jane Jacobs

Intended to be a wake-up call – it literally features a ringing telephone – the film helped rouse public opposition to the expressway, which got scrapped in 1971.

Epilogue: eyes on the street or eyes on the screen?

Five years apart in age, Jacobs and McLuhan were both free-thinkers, each with an iconoclastic and singular way of seeing things. Beyond this generality (which no doubt partly accounts for their mutual admiration), the two had more in common than first appears. Sharing a negative view of the late-modern city in the 1960s, they yearned for a freer and more sociable way of life, one based on dynamic and unscripted interactions. The etymological root that relates the words *community* and *communication* may be said to underlie their visions of, respectively, embodied and disembodied space.

A decade later, in the post-modernist climate of the 1970s and 1980s, Jacobs's ideas would become received wisdom, while the apostles of the nonplace realm would find fewer adherents. A representative of the generation of planners at Berkeley that followed Webber and his circle tried to have it both ways. In a 1981 essay titled "Place and Nonplace: The New Search for Roots," Donald Appleyard argued that while the reality of Webber's community without propinquity had in many respects come to fruition, it had also engendered its opposite, namely a "neighborhood movement ... in full swing." The fervour for historic preservation, the increased popularity of national parks and the resurgence of interest on the part of Americans in their family histories further attested to a collective 'search for roots.' Acknowledging Jacobs's key role in shifting public attitudes, he pointed to a new focus on humane urban environments where "life is the voluntary gathering of people in attractive and lively places."[53] Meanwhile, in 1977, the TV docudrama *Roots* became the most widely watched miniseries in the history of television. Adapted from a novel by Alex Haley about the multi-generational history of the family of a slave brought to the US from Africa, it drew 130,000,000

27

viewers to one or more of its eight episodes. In his widely read *No Sense of Place: The Impact of Electronic Media on Social Behavior* (1985), Joshua Meyrowitz identified a dialectic at work: as the new media were increasingly dissolving distinctions "between here and there, live and mediated, and personal and public," people were seeking more solid ground – even, paradoxically, on television itself.[54]

Nonetheless, within a few more years, McLuhan's dream of the globally interconnected electronic village would be resurrected. The rise of the internet and social media in the early 1990s saw those who had grown up in the 1960s counterculture – weaned on McLuhan and Fuller – leave behind the *Whole Earth Catalogue* in favour of new visions of digital democracy, virtual community, and cities in cyberspace.[55] McLuhan's euphoria momentarily seemed to have been justified. One more quarter century on, however, the consolidation of internet protocols in the hands of giant corporations and the trade-off of privacy for access are demonstrating that online culture is just as geared to cybercapitalism as to cybercommunity. McLuhan knew that centralised decentralisation was an oxymoron. But he remained remarkably naive about who would control and profit from the electronic revolution. No doubt Jacobs would have grasped this contradiction better.

In any case, it is clear today that the physical and virtual realms are no longer separable. Greenwich Village and the global village belong to a heterogeneous, interwoven system. The choice of corporeal space or cyberspace, of eyes on the street or eyes on the screen, is a false one. We live in association and dissociation, with propinquity and without. We form and perform our identities both on the doorstep and on the digital interface. We spend some of our time walking and some of it (a whole lot of it) watching. You can be taking a stroll in the park and the crazy person who just passed by you talking to herself turns out to have been speaking to someone on her cell phone. You can probably begin your search for a used violin better online than off. (I'm not sure about the mistress.)

In short, our lives are permeated with micro- and macro-cosmicity. We inhabit the world at hand and the world at large. To quote Marshall McLuhan quoting the other JJ – James Joyce – we are both "urban and orbal."[56]

Notes

1. This statement has always stuck with me although I have been unable to pin down where and when Jacobs uttered it. In a personal conversation following her delivery of the first Lewis Mumford Lecture (ironically enough – see note 13 below) at City College in New York on May 6, 2004, she confirmed that she had indeed said it and was quoting Stonorov.
2. Jane Jacobs, *The Death and Life of Great American Cities* (New York: Random House, 1961).
3. See *Death and Life*, 50, 86, 229, 379.
4. Sigfried Kracauer, "Stehbars im Süden," *Frankfurter Zeitung*, October 8, 1926; reprinted in Siegfried Kracauer, *Strassen in Berlin und anderswo* (Berlin: Arsenal, 1987), 51. My translation.
5. *Death and Life*, 391.
6. Jane Jacobs, "The Missing Link in City Redevelopment," *Architectural Forum*, June 1956, 133.
7. The Situationists' major platform at this date was "unitary urbanism," which they described as "not a doctrine of urbanism but a critique of urbanism," and it was based on their direct experience of the city: "UU is not ideally separated from the current terrain of cities. UU is developed out of the experience of this terrain and based on existing constructions." See "Unitary Urbanism at the End of the 1950s," *Internationale Situationniste* 3, December 1959, https://www.cddc.vt.edu/sionline/si/unitary.html.

8 Alison Smithson, ed., "Team 10 Primer 1953–1962," special issue of *Architectural Design*, December 1962; revised and published in book form as *Team 10 Primer* in 1968.
9 See A. and P. Smithson, "Draft Framework 4, 1956," concept document for CIAM X, in Max Risselada and Dirk van den Heuvel, eds., *Team 10: In Search of a Utopia of the Present, 1953–81* (Rotterdam: NAi, 2005), 49; and Aldo van Eyck, "Is Architecture Going to Reconcile Basic Values?" in Oscar Newman, ed., *New Frontiers in Architecture: CIAM '59 in Otterlo* (New York: Universe Books, 1961), 27.
10 *Death and Life*, 30.
11 Roland Barthes, "Semiology and Urbanism," originally published in Italian in *Op. cit.* 10 (September 1967); trans. in Roland Barthes, *The Semiotic Challenge* (New York: Hill and Wang, 1988), 199.
12 As Jacobs notes in *Death and Life*, 444. The saying originally referred to runaway serfs who acquired their freedom after residing in a city for one year.
13 Betty Friedan, *The Feminine Mystique* (New York: W. W. Norton, 1963), 13.
14 Letter from Jane Jacobs to Frank Mannheim, May 9, 2005; cited in Robert Kanigel, *Eyes on the Street: The Life of Jane Jacobs* (New York: Alfred A. Knopf, 2016), 394.
15 Jane Jacobs, "The End of the Plantation Age," Lewis Mumford Lecture, City College, 2004; in Samuel Zipp and Nathan Storring, eds., *Vital Little Plans: The Short Works of Jane Jacobs* (New York: Random House, 2016), 458.
16 Lewis Mumford, "The Sky Line: Mother Jacobs' Home Remedies," *New Yorker*, December 1, 1962, 148–179.
17 Ibid., 150, 158, 173.
18 Lewis Mumford, "Home Remedies for Urban Cancer," in *The Urban Prospect* (New York: Harcourt, Brace & World, 1968), 182–207.
19 Lewis Mumford, "Regions—To Live In," *The Survey: Graphic Number*, May 1, 1925, 151.
20 "Efficiency and the Commons," conversation between Jacobs and Janice Gross Stein, in *Vital Little Plans*, 377: "It seems that Marshall McLuhan was right when he observed that you can't decentralize centrally."
21 Herbert J. Gans, "City Planning and Urban Realities," *Commentary*, February 1962, 170–175.
22 Ibid., 175.
23 *Death and Life*, 271. See Herbert J. Gans, "The Human Implications of Current Redevelopment and Relocation Planning," *Journal of the American Institute of Planners*, vol. 25, no. 1 (1959), 15–26.
24 Herbert J. Gans, *The Urban Villagers: Group and Class in the Life of Italian-Americans* (Glencoe, IL: Free Press, 1962). The book was a first-hand account of the destruction of Boston's West End neighbourhood, a close-knit Italian-American working-class community condemned as a slum in 1953 and subjected to a brutal process of clearance, displacement and redevelopment.
25 Including those who preferred a more tranquil lifestyle in suburbia. Gans would investigate this subculture in his next book, *The Levittowners: Ways of Life and Politics in a New Suburban Community* (New York: Columbia University Press, 1967).
26 Oscar Newman, *Defensible Space: Crime Prevention through Urban Design* (New York: MacMillan, 1972), 25, 112. Among other vandalized modern housing projects documented by Newman was the Schuylkill Falls Housing Project in Philadelphia designed in 1953–1955 by Oscar Stonorov – he of the second-hand violin and mistress – which in the 1990s was destined to suffer the same fate as Pruitt-Igoe.
27 Charles Jencks, *The Language of Post-Modern Architecture* (London: Academy Editions, 1977). Jencks writes: "[Modern architecture] expired finally and completely in 1972, after having been flogged to death remorselessly for ten years by critics such as Jane Jacobs" (9–10).
28 *Death and Life*, 337.
29 Jacobs thus described herself in answer to a question from an audience member at the same Lewis Mumford Lecture referred to in notes 1 and 13 above. Asked whether she minded being misinterpreted by conservatives, she replied: "I was not an ideologist. I was really an old-fashioned pragmatist."
30 *Death and Life*, 438–439.
31 "A Living Network of Relationships," speech at the New School for Social Research in New York in 1958, in *Vital Little Plans*, 132.
32 Richard Carroll Keeley and Jane Jacobs, "An Interview with Jane Jacobs" (1985), in Fred Lawrence, ed., *Ethics in Making a Living: The Jane Jacobs Conference* (Atlanta, GA: Scholars Press, 1989), 18. Jacobs made this statement specifically in reference to the Thatcher administration and its treatment of poor people, insisting that public education, healthcare and other government services were essential provisions.
33 John Dewey, "Pragmatic America," *New Republic*, April 12, 1922, 186.
34 Melvin Webber, "The Urban Place and the Nonplace Urban Realm," in Melvin Webber, ed., *Explorations into Urban Structure* (Philadelphia: University of Pennsylvania Press, 1964), 80, 147.
35 Melvin M. Webber, "Order in Diversity: Community without Propinquity," in Lowdon Wingo, ed., *Cities and Space: The Future Use of Urban Land* (Baltimore, MD: Johns Hopkins Press, 1963), 42–43, 52.
36 Marshall McLuhan, *The Gutenberg Galaxy: The Making of Typographic Man* (Toronto: University of Toronto Press, 1962), 5.
37 Giedion's research would result in 1962 in the publication of *The Eternal Present: The Beginnings of Art. A Contribution on Constancy and Change*, based on his 1957 A. W. Mellon Lectures in the Fine Arts at the National Gallery of Art.

Joan Ockman

38. On McLuhan's indebtedness to Mumford, see James W. Carey, "McLuhan and Mumford: The Roots of Modern Media Analysis," *Journal of Communication*, Summer 1981, 162–178. Mumford, for his part, would distance himself from McLuhan and McLuhanism, becoming increasingly pessimistic about the direction in which modern technology was heading.
39. Edward T. Hall, *The Silent Language* (New York: Doubleday, 1959). In his next book, *The Hidden Dimension: An Anthropologist Examines Man's Use of Space in Public and in Private* (1965), Hall would develop a theory of physical spacing derived from an analysis of the flight patterns of migrating birds. Hall argued the applicability of his new social science of proximities, or proxemics, to problems of overcrowding in modern cities and housing.
40. Wyndham Lewis, *America and Cosmic Man* (Garden City, NY: Doubleday, 1949), 21.
41. Marshall McLuhan, *Understanding Media: The Extensions of Man* (New York: Signet/New American Library, 2nd ed., 1964), 19. Lewis Mumford, again (see note 38), appears to have been another important source of this idea, although his view of the global village's future was much less sanguine than McLuhan's. Cf. the following passage from his essay "Technics and the Future of Western Civilization," *Perspectives USA* 11 (Spring 1955), 80–81:

    As soon as we achieve the theoretic goal of annihilating distance entirely—as we now do for all practical purposes even without television when we telephone overseas—we come back again precisely to where we started: to the village world of face-to-face contact with over two billion villagers for neighbors, and at that point our human weaknesses, serious enough for a village society, become magnified…. Thanks to technics, men have become physically neighbors to people on the other side of the earth; but we have done little to make ourselves mental neighbors…. Certainly, the whole development of man himself, from small tribal units to cities and nations, from nations to leagues, unions, and empires, has been in the direction of unity and universality."

    I came across this previously unremarked statement by Mumford as the present volume was in publication and am grateful to the editors for allowing me to insert this reference to it.
42. See, among others, Grant Havers, "The Right-Wing Postmodernism of Marshall McLuhan," *Media, Culture & Society* 25, no. 4 (2003), 511–525.
43. "Playboy Interview: Marshall McLuhan. A Candid Conversation with the High Priest of Popcult and Metaphysician of Media," *Playboy Magazine*, March 1969; reprinted in Eric McLuhan and Frank Zingrone, eds., *Essential McLuhan* (New York: Basic Books, 1995), 262.
44. Ibid., 258–259.
45. See Guy Debord, *La société du spectacle* (Paris: Buchet/Chastel, 1967); English transl., *The Society of the Spectacle* (Detroit, MI: Black & Red, 1977): "If the spectacle, taken in the limited sense of 'mass media' which are its most glaring superficial manifestation, seems to invade society as mere equipment, this equipment is in no way neutral…" (paragraph 24).
46. See Bernard Rudofsky, *Architecture without Architects: A Short Introduction to Non-pedigreed Architecture* (New York: Museum of Modern Art, 1964). *The Family of Man* was curated by photographer Edward Steichen and designed by architect Paul Rudolph.
47. The local group spearheading the effort was the Stop Spadina Save Our City Coordinating Committee (SSSOCCC). Both Jacobs and McLuhan were members.
48. Marshall McLuhan with Quentin Fiore (designer), *War and Peace in the Global Village* (New York: Bantam Books, 1968); Marshall McLuhan with Harley Parker (designer), *Counterblast* (New York: Harcourt, Brace & World 1969).
49. McLuhan, "Playboy Interview," in *Essential McLuhan*, 262.
50. Jane Jacobs, "A City Getting Hooked on the Expressway Drug," *The Globe and Mail* (Toronto), November 1, 1969; reprinted in *Vital Little Plans*, 189.
51. See Jane Jacobs, "Making a Movie with McLuhan," *Antigonish Review* 74–75 (Summer–Autumn 1988), special issue on McLuhan, 127.
52. McKay had previously used a "multi-dynamic" image technique in a film for the Ontario Pavilion at Expo 67. The Spadina film was narrated by Colin Vaughan, an Australian-born architect, urban activist and McLuhan's neighbour. The credits ascribe the film's conception to McLuhan and identify Jacobs as consultant.
53. Donald Appleyard, "Place and Nonplace: The New Search for Roots," in J. I. de Neufville, ed., *The Land Use Policy Debate in the United States* (New York: Plenum Press, 1981), 51, 54.
54. Joshua Meyrowitz, *No Sense of Place: The Impact of Electronic Media on Social Behavior* (New York: Oxford University Press, 1985), 308. Meyrowitz's book was strongly influenced by McLuhan although not entirely uncritical of him.
55. See, for example, Howard Rheingold, *The Virtual Community: Homesteading on the Electronic Frontier* (Reading, MA: Addison-Wesley, 1993). For a historical perspective, see Fred Turner, *From Counterculture to Cyberculture: Stewart Brand, the Whole Earth Network, and the Rise of Digital Utopianism* (Chicago, IL: University of Chicago Press, 2006).
56. James Joyce, *Finnegans Wake* (New York: Viking Press, 1958), 601.

Chapter 3

Interview with Reinier de Graaf

After delivering a keynote at the AHRA 2019 conference, Reiner de Graaf talked to Penny Lewis about his work and the conference themes. His keynote was part of a larger critique he is developing of some of the more fashionable terms that have enveloped the world of architecture during past two decades. This critique will be published in his forthcoming book *Measures of Success* (Verso 2022). De Graaf is particularly scathing of idea of 'placemaking,' a term used by the media and policymakers to describe urban design and judge the quality of a place and life. The arrival of this term, he argues, has coincided with a shift in the commissioning of urban spaces and buildings, driven by the creation of profit rather than the public needs. In Dundee, he provoked a debate about the negative consequences of Jane Jacobs' work on urban theory.

PL: The theme of the conference was architecture and collective life; do you think it is possible to talk about anything 'collective' in connection with contemporary architectural practice?

RDG: Is it at all possible for architecture to express collective values? Look at our own work and our own portfolio over the last thirty years. Thirty years ago, most of our clients were public bodies. Today, 80%-odd of our clients are private entities who have a private agenda, an agenda which we are expected to respect and express. That puts the architect in a difficult position; often, his adherence to collective ideals is rhetoric at best. The architect becomes complicit in this game regardless of his intentions.

Contradictions in a common world

Figure 3.1 Photo of Reinier de Graaf speaking at the AHRA conference in Dundee, November 2019

We've gone from public clients to private clients, but, ironically, our contact with private users has only diminished as a result. Most of the private clients don't use the buildings they commission. They often build for speculative purposes. The architect used to build houses for an owner, and the owner interfered with what the architect did. There was a dialogue. If the client was not happy, he would tell the architect, and the architect would do things differently. This type of feedback is at the core of our profession, more than scientific research.

Then architects built for the welfare state, and people had a say through various community participation processes. Then property developers came. They hoped to attract inhabitants with their product, but they never met the inhabitants. The alienation from the people escalated.

The essence of architecture is that it's propositional. It elicits a reaction, and you use the reaction to adjust. If you ask people what they think, and their opinion is what generates the 'product,' then architects would no longer be needed.

PL: In Dundee you were very critical of Jane Jacobs. Why?

RDG: I struggle greatly with Jane Jacobs because sometimes people with their heart in the right place can do a phenomenal amount of damage and that is how I see her legacy. The idea of architecture as a propositional act applies clearly here. Jacobs' thesis is a critique, a critique that wouldn't have existed without [Robert] Moses. The critique is valid, but her panacea for the city has meanwhile proven to have its own drawbacks.

PL: You can read Jane Jacobs in many different ways. When I read her now I choose to read it as a sort of thesis against social and moral engineering. Joan Ockman identifies a commitment to liberal values of freedom,

Interview with Reinier de Graaf

autonomy and sociability. However, not many interpret Jacobs in this way. *Death and Life* tends to be seen as a design and behaviour management guide. As far as I'm concerned, it's a reflective, analytical piece, not policy guideline.

RDG: It's an open question, how much can you judge somebody based on what is being done in his or her name? To some extent you can't, but to some extent you have to. Somebody like Le Corbusier is judged based on the damage done by those who are trying to emulate him. Those who adhere to Jacobs, once they came into power, they set off an entirely different mechanism which was equally damaging, if not more, than the mechanism they had replaced.

PL: One of the strongest points in your presentation in Dundee was your critique of the idea of liveability. Can you explain why you are so suspicious of this idea?

RDG: I've produced a kind of genealogy of the term liveability, and ended up in Vancouver, where it was developed on the heels of all these kind of undemocratic decisions to have big freeway projects, to have neighbourhoods slammed to the ground in the name of modernisation.

In literature, it was Jane Austen who first used the term 'liveable' but in an ironic way, referring to a contemporary figure who wanted to show his money, who bought some countryside properties and essentially violated them in a very tasteless way, in the name of making them 'liveable.'

Then Lewis Mumford applied it to urbanism. He was very strongly influenced by Patrick Geddes, the biologist and sociologist, who saw the city as the prime manifestation of human biology. Since the mid-19th century, or even since the Industrial Revolution, the city is a contested territory between architects and planners on one side and sociologists and behavioural scientists on the other side. Where one side is posing as the creators, the other, who primarily sees the city as a living organism, is dealing with the fallout of those creations.

Patrick Geddes saw the city as a patient. You didn't create it, but as a doctor you surgically intervened when things went wrong, and if nothing was wrong, you didn't need to do anything. For Geddes and others, their prime technique was observation. For the planners, the prime techniques are composition and starting from scratch.

When you listen to Roger Scruton talking about Le Corbusier, you discover that that opposition has endured until this day. Many contemporary terms like 'placemaking' and 'liveability' are in a way the child of that same opposition.

PL: So there are observers and creators; how do you know which side of the opposition they come from?

RDG: Most of these terms are conveniently used by either side for the sake of their own argument. The same terms are used for very opposite ideological aims, that's the interesting thing.

PL: It's quite hard really to work out what that distinction is. Is the distinction between the capacity to project forward with a plan and to organise society

and the resistance that this generates? You're not saying one side's good and the other's bad…

RDG: Given the nature of my profession, I tend to be very suspicious of the behavioural scientists. I wrote somewhere that the problems with public space started as soon as we identified that there was something like public space. I think community is something very similar. Community is the spontaneous flipside of society, the *Gemeinschaft-Gesellschaft* tension.

A society, to some extent, is a construct, a political construct which can be assumed to operate in accordance with certain conventions, certain laws, while community is a bottom-up, spontaneous thing, out of which its logic spontaneously emerges. But to declare the community the new paradigm, to make the spontaneous a deliberate compositional element, that is to me a contradiction in terms.

PL: Are you saying is that there's a kind of social engineering implicit in placemaking?

RDG: Yes. For me these terms have a highly oppressive connotation. In certain places, where we are now facing a more oppressive situation through the re-emergence of autocrats and classical oppressive techniques. In other parts of the world, we are facing oppression through more subtle techniques, which manifest very often in the form of viciously good intentions and nauseating demonstrations of extreme virtue. There is no discussion, you are expected to agree and follow suit.

PL: The difficulty is that everything you've said about placemaking today could have been said by Jacobs in 1961 about redevelopment and Robert Moses. Isn't it the case that throughout the whole of the 20th century, there has been an overreach by the authorities?

RDG: Well, I don't know. Our profession is in a way a perpetual quest for freedom, and at the same time, it is a profession highly rooted in conventions and tradition. We progress by looking at those who went before us, repeating and modifying what they did. Occasionally, there is a technological breakthrough in the form of materials or construction technology, which allows us to make a leap forward and turn on its head whatever those before us were doing. Le Corbusier and Mies had a classical training, and one could say that their prototypes were the inversion of the classical principles, but still they remain indebted to the classical principles.

There is a problem with maintaining a certain amount of freedom presently. In the last 15 years, it has become more difficult to persuade those who seal our fate with 'non-linear' arguments. A lot of our work carries conviction because it relies on certain references, but once you have committees judging your work who are unfamiliar with the references, it's difficult.

Today, there are less and less architects in such committees. In 2019, we took part in the competition for the University of Milton Keynes where we had to present to a *gremium* [German for body or committee] of about 40 people, of which only one was an architect and he had purely an advisory role. Besides him, there was the director of the art museum who was susceptible to arguments. The rest insisted on 'measurable' things. "How does it benefit the community? In what way? How can you quantify this? What will be the amount of glare on a computer screen in a particular space? What is the capacity of the bicycle path?" I'm not denying the importance of those things, but they are all essentially things you make work, and I think all ten entries would have made those things work.

But you can look at this trend as a language problem. It seems to me that the current plethora of terms in our profession comes from an intentional drive to intoxicate the brain so that it can't think.

(Orwell talked about this in the novel 1984 – the note below). An architect is no longer an 'architect'; he is a 'built environment practitioner.' There isn't just 'placemaking'; there is 'healthy placemaking,' etc.

PL: Why do you think that happened?

RDG: I'm not sure what is going on. I think that there is a real will to democratise almost everything, which in itself is a good thing, but it allows an ever-larger body to speak about certain things, and for me, the weird effect is that things become undiscussable. There used to be something like an avant-garde, which was inextricably tied to an elite…

PL: Which avant-garde are you thinking about?

RDG: The avant-garde of the early 20th century, which is at the core of what we have been taught at the university in the late 20th century. That was a time characterised by an effort to industralise, democratise, mass produce, which was essentially engendered by an elite. I'm talking about Melnikov, Malevich, Kandinsky, the Bauhaus. But if the Bauhaus was the source of one of the most sophisticated types of architecture of the 20th century, its ultimate project was a kind of Houdini act, a disappearing act. The paradox is that once you achieve the largest possible numbers (mass production, the democratisation of architecture, of taste), the author is eliminated, and with it, the possibility to argue in any subjective manner.

Architects are a very particular species. Now, they are considered profound, the next moment laughable. The oration of any star architect relies on a certain suspension of disbelief; it relies on a benign audience to give them the benefit of the doubt because it only takes one raised eyebrow in the audience for that whole thing to fall apart. We do communicate through language, but there are certain aspects of creative professions that can never be fully framed in language, or at least not in the language of public policies.

PL: There has been an attack on the architectural and the political author, but I'm not sure that this an inevitable consequence of mass or democratic society.

RDG: No, but we see a very interesting development now where progressive constructs are deemed authoritarian. The European Union, an essentially wonderfully benign project, which probably presided over the greatest period of European peace, prosperity and happiness, is deemed an authoritarian construct. People like Prince Charles, somebody who is from such a privileged background, behave as if they are the advocate of the people. Donald Trump, a multi-billionaire, acts as the figurehead of blue-collar workers in America.

PL: Trump, Scruton and even Prince Charles are to some extent reacting against the bland, technocratic, managerial culture and language, the abandonment

of disciplinary conventions that you are criticising. I can understand why many people identify that.

RDG: I'm not a Prince Charles supporter, I'm not a Trump supporter, but I can clearly see why people identify with them. When I saw Trump's first speech in the Trump Tower in June 2015, coming down the escalator, I knew he was going to get elected. When he spoke, it was very clear, and the only thing the other side spoke about was how horrible he was. Same with Brexit. You could simply feel it coming. The writing is on the wall, and the whole world is in a state of denial about it, and I think the progressive side simply lacks a coherent answer, a populist answer if you want.

PL: It's hard to know what constitutes progressive nowadays, isn't it?

RDG: To get back to the term 'community,' as opposed to society, Margaret Thatcher once said: "Society? What is society? There are men, there are women and there are families, there's no such thing as society." I think a term like 'community' also feeds off wonderfully of a statement like that. When we talk about community, we focus on a smaller thing, and in a way, our mind is taken off the bigger thing.

Participation is another term used by the Right in order to cut back welfare so that people simply fend for themselves. They call it participation, but in fact it is a dressing-down of the welfare state.

Another thing is, again, placemaking. It strikes me that the cities that champion placemaking are the cities where there are enormous vacancy rates, where there is an enormous speculative ownership. For me all these terms are in fact a smokescreen for a number of utterly sinister trends.

PL: Perhaps place and belonging are important but I find that there's something unhelpful about someone like Jan Gehl and his approach to placemaking.

RDG: Yeah, I think Fred Kent and Jan Gehl are totally unhelpful people.

PL: Gehl and Krier before him were interested in neighbourhoods, but today it seems people fear being committed to things at a local level because it might be populist, right-wing.

RDG: When the Berlin Wall fell and the Soviet Union collapsed, the general presumption in the West was that it was only a matter of time before the entire world would be a liberal democracy. But that is proving increasingly wrong. The West, while economically dominant, is so massively outnumbered, and if there is such a thing as a global consensus, it's going to be a compromise way further removed from our home game than initially thought, which is why in the West you see an enormous pushback against globalisation.

PL: What do you think about customs and norms? You made the point that architecture is built on both convention and change. There's something about globalisation that is quite destructive in relation to norms and conventions. More recently norms have been seen as a problem or as oppressive, rather than being ways that people get along together.

RDG: I think norms are similar to globalisation. The more people have to agree on something, the more bottom-line that convention is and the more that convention is stripped of subjective idiosyncrasies. That might be what is happening to the

English language. It's shared by so many people in the world that it becomes unrecognisable for those who speak it well.

You can call that dumbing down, but all norms are a form of dumbing down, whether it's standardisation in the building industry or the removal of characters from the Chinese script. They are all attempts at simplification so that they can be understood by a larger number of people, a large number of people that can be mobilised to participate and propel things in a certain direction.

I find Ernst Neufert [the author of Architect's Data] highly fascinating. He was the big standardiser, once with the Bauhaus, then with the Nazis, only to become associated with the respectable West Germany. The curious thing is that he's only built two buildings, yet he's known by every architect. Once you surrender to his logic, it's almost scary to discover how little there is to be designed.

PL: **Let's talk about happiness. You're clearly very interested in what I would call the therapeutic agenda. Architects have spent the last twenty years appropriating the well-being agenda, arguing that well-designed schools give you better exam results, that hospitals with 'green' windows speed up healing, using behaviouralist arguments to suggest good design can make you happy.**

RDG: What irritates me about all the things you just mentioned is that many of the subjective wisdoms of today will be denied tomorrow. I think there is an embedded truth in architectural design which has a far longer history, which almost intuitively knows how to deal with light, how to deal with materials, how to deal with air, how to deal with a lot of these things.

It's very shocking to me how easily the architectural profession embraces every passing trend and meanwhile sacrifices its own body of knowledge. On the one hand, you have enormous hubris and snobbery amongst architects; on the other hand, there's an apparent lack of confidence in their own abilities. It's very strange to hear things like, 'green windows yield better exam results;' when a month later, another report comes out that proves the opposite. The market economy forces professionals to distinguish themselves competitively, which often leads them to prematurely embrace the latest trends in order to be the first – often more that than a genuine conviction in those principles themselves. It's this kind of condition of breathlessness that I find exasperating.

PL: **On the happiness agenda: you're putting forward a critique of the instrumentalism, and you're criticising the language. Are you also criticising the therapeutic aspects of this approach?**

RDG: What I'm trying to criticise is that all these terms, in my view, are an intentional distraction. I think the happiness agenda is promoted by certain political currents in order to reduce people's demands for material wealth. That 'material wealth doesn't make you happy' is often promoted by those who have all the material wealth. It's not that I deem happiness unimportant, but in this context, it is offensive. It is generally broadcast as an alternative ideology to people who are struggling economically – happiness as opium for the people.

We're currently working on a research project about the transformations in the healthcare system. With the baby boomer generation in retirement, the previous pyramid of a large working population supporting a small elderly population is inverted, and it's so striking how the ideology is almost immediately adapted. Healthcare has become a big business because so many people need healthcare. There is preventive healthcare to cut expenses of the medical system, and understandable as that is, it is an ideology which is a function of the state of things at a particular moment. The tendency to declare that ideology as absolute, like religion, is very dodgy. I remain very Foucauldian in this, in the sense that all absolute truths are the mere result of the power structures in place.

PL: Where do you stand in relation to the idea that there is an ideology based on a psychological outlook which sees us as vulnerable, or as the subjects needing psychological help?

RDG: Let's say you lose your job and you have no income. The consequences these days are a lot more severe than they were in the '70s and '80s. You lose your insurance. You lose your house. Your life changes beyond recognition. It is troubling when that happens to you, but the people giving psychological counselling suggest that it's your problem. That is probably the most repressive thing imaginable. Even in the most authoritarian regime you retain your psychological freedom to complain about it in private. Once the system enters the private domain – the psychological realm – it's the last stage of taking over the subject. By declaring it a psychological problem, it is implied that it's *your* problem and no longer society's problem.

PL: And the assumption is that you don't really have any real agency.

RDG: The aim is to prevent that you never get agency, because there's no room in your head once you're so sucked up by your own psychological problems.

PL: This aspect of ideology is all-pervasive, but it's rarely criticised. Even radical critics of today's society on the Left are prepared to see social problems in terms of our individual mental health.

RDG: That is the weird thing – the extent to which the Left allows itself to be fooled by a smokescreen. Of course, you cannot be against happiness, you cannot be against the community, you cannot be against participation. This is the ideological vocabulary of the Left, which is currently being deployed against the very principles of the Left: the emancipation of large groups from power structures, in an economic sense.

PL: There is a tradition of critical and progressive architecture which says it's always right to build, and that's the nature of the profession (e.g. Snozzi). Buildings produced in the current context may give concrete expression to a skewed set of values. Is it possible to build in a way that transgresses contemporary culture, or is it enough to just build?

RDG: With today's ethos, it's a compelling call to do nothing. Architecture suffers from the fact that it's an agent of whatever agenda those in power have. The repertoire of modern architecture was to build quickly, cheaply, simply and in a standardised way, so that as many homes could become available to as many people as possible. In the current context, building allows you to build cheaply not to make what you build available cheaply to more people but for profits to be maximised.

The same logic developed for one system serves a completely different purpose in another system. It is our duty to think about this. Architects will never control, nor create the economic system, but it is worth thinking about the role we are expected to play in any given economic system.

There is a perpetual loss of a bigger picture. Take the discussion about 'Black Lives Matter' for example. Very necessary, indeed. But it is crucial to recognise that it is part of a much larger problem. The fundamental problem in the US is the massive, ever-escalating economic inequality, which creates a platform for sexual abuse, for racial discrimination. Racism is a problem that comes from a power status quo, which is closely linked to an economic status quo. Despite supposed gains in civil rights, the US has escalated towards an ever-greater asymmetry ever since the 1950s, but nobody talks about that.

PL: The conference title was Collective Life, and there is an assumption that there can be a relationship between architecture and some kind of shared values. Is that flawed, given everything that you've said about the current conditions? Is that just wrong to think that there is a possibility of shared values?

RDG: No, but again I would contest that happiness, community, participation – in the way they're currently promoted – are shared values. Of course, shared values ought to be possible, because without them there is no basis for a society to exist, but what we're currently seeing is things that sound like shared values being hijacked by a particular strand of politics.

PL: Or all strands of politics actually, but each in a different way.

RDG: Politics by definition serves a partial interest. Politics are a form of subjectivity and are used by certain ideological camps. It's so interesting that the term 'participation' is used by both ends of the political spectrum to serve a completely different cause, at which point it almost forces a return to the ultimate meaning of the word.

There is a total mistrust of proposition. Anything that is propositional is in danger to be seen as a form of harassment in the current day and age, as an unwanted advance. There is always that moment of uncertainty when you propose something, without knowing whether what you propose is right. This is where designers are massively vulnerable.

For a designer, the essence of the creative moments is always the uncertainty. There is that moment in which you don't know whether you've gone totally crazy or stumbled across something profound. Without that moment, and without the legitimacy of that moment – the suspension of morals and preconceived ideas – the ultimate consequence is total creative stagnation.

PL: In terms of post-Covid, have you got any thoughts about what might change?

RDG: I don't know. I think this is going to go on for quite some time.

PL: I'm wondering what you think about the fate of the city under Covid?

RDG: Well, that's another interesting thing. The suburban house, the reliance on the car – the much-rejected suburban model – would actually be quite a good Covid model. The cellular office, dismissed as an unnecessary, sacrosanct testament to individuality, is all of a sudden very relevant again. It's a weird unravelling of the supposed progress we've made.

PL: So do you think we're going to see a return to the experience of the '70s, that people evacuate the city?

RDG: It's too early to tell, but you can see that happening. I was on holiday in the Netherlands this summer and didn't want to leave the countryside. I went on a bicycle trip from rural hotel to rural hotel, and it was phenomenally busy. All were fully booked. It was impossible to rent a house in the least densely populated part of the Netherlands.

PL: You guys were already looking at that anyway.

RDG: Well, Rem was – a man blessed with great foresight.

PL: In your book you are looking at the way in which the profession has been understood in relation to society; you describe a history in which architects have been part of the elite, forgotten, rediscovered, idolised, and treated as a cause for concern.

RDG: That's what I'm trying to argue: these stages that the profession has gone through have in fact been attempts to subject the profession to something extraneous and external. I think even the success and praise bestowed on the profession was in a way an attempt to get it under control. Success in itself is a very oppressing state, because once you have it, you need to have more of it, and it's also an imperative to repeat a success formula.

Note on Orwell's newspeak in 1984

In 1949, the Book of the Month club in the US had the rights to 1984 – but had indicated that they wanted to remove the appendix on Newspeak – Orwell refused to accept any changes to the text and the publisher backed down. According to his biographer, Michael Shelden, Orwell had learned about the impact of acts of censorship through his experience in the Spanish Civil War and his wartime work at the BBC. In the appendix *The principles of newspeak*, Orwell wrote that Newspeak would finally have superseded Oldspeak (or standard English) by about 2050. For Orwell, the control of language, its structure and vocabulary was a means to undermine the quality of independent thought.

> The purpose of Newspeak was not only to provide a medium of expression for the world view and mental habits proper to the devotee of IngSoc, but to make all other modes of thought impossible. It was intended that when Newspeak had been adopted once and for all and the Oldspeak had been forgotten, a heretical thought, that is a thought that diverging from the principles of Ingsoc – should be literally unthinkable, at least so far as thought is dependent on words. Its vocabulary was so constructed as to give exact and often very subtle expression to every meaning that a party member could properly wish to express, while excluding all other meanings and also

the possibility of arriving at them by indirect methods. This was done partly by the invention of new words and by stripping such words as remained of unorthodox meanings, and so far as possible of all secondary meanings whatever. To give a single example.

The word *free* still existed in Newspeak, but it could only be used in such statements as 'This dog is free from lice' or 'this field is free from weed. It could not be used in its old sense of 'politically free' or 'intellectually free', since political and intellectual freedom no longer existed event as concepts, and were therefore of necessity nameless… Newspeak was designed not to extend but to diminish the range of thought, and this purpose was indirectly assisted by cutting the choice of words down to a minimum.

(Page 241–242; 1955)

Orwell, G, *1984*, (1959) Penguin, London

Chapter 4

Neofeudalism

The end of capitalism?

Jodi Dean

Recall the line from Fredric Jameson, made famous by Slavoj Zizek and Mark Fisher, "it's easier to imagine the end of the world than an end to capitalism"; this no longer holds. A slew of active imaginings of an end to capitalism – or at least of radically different modes for the production and appropriation of the social surplus – populate popular culture: movie franchises like the *Hunger Games*, science fiction, dystopic fiction, *The Game of Thrones*, the array of survival-isms. The world continues after the zombie apocalypse, but it's not capitalist. Those few optimistic scenarios (like *Star Trek*) suggest some kind of post-scarcity. The dystopic versions rely on direct expropriation – violence, coercion and force. One might argue that "these non-capitalist economies are not part of a world anyone would want to live in." And that's my point: we can imagine an end to capitalism, but at least in the versions given to us by the dominant capitalist culture, it's hard to imagine wanting it. These non-capitalist futures seem worse than the present capitalism most of us in the global north think we have. They thus function ideologically to affirm capitalism as, if not inevitable, then at least better than the alternatives.

Not all post-capitalist dystopias are fiction. In recent years, conservative and libertarian economists have started to ask whether the future of the US is 'mass serfdom,' that is a property-less underclass only able to survive by servicing the needs of high earners (e.g. as personal assistants, trainers, child-minders, cooks and cleaners).[1] The most visible of these right-wing economists defend private property and suburban home ownership (i.e. construction and real estate), fossil fuels (cars, plastics and corporate agribusiness) and hold views of freedom and democracy associated

Figure 4.1 Photo of Jodi Dean speaking at the AHRA conference in Dundee, November 2019

with the American way of life (typically envisioned as white, straight, patriarchal and middle class). These conservative and libertarian economists oppose what they depict as the green elitism of sustainability, less-is-more, hipster downsizing, positioning these as outputs of Silicon Valley and Hollywood billionaire ideology of technology and high-speed rail. For them, neo-feudalism is a threat that calls for a defence of carbon capitalism.

My claim is that it's capitalism itself that is tending to neofeudalism. The capitalist dynamics that led to imperialism as the monopoly stage of capitalism (to use Lenin's formulation) that consolidate the "dominance of monopolies and finance capital" are today tending towards neofeudalism. Capitalism is producing its own gravediggers, but the gravediggers aren't proletarians; they are the tendencies transforming the system into something else.

Tendencies are not all-determining. There is a space for, a *need* for, political action. We are in the setting we describe, the picture we take. Capitalism is turning itself into a neofeudalism of new lords and new serfs, a micro-elite of platform billionaires and the massive service sector or sector of servants. Nevertheless, we can intervene and redirect it. In fact, we must. Communism – the internationalist, universalist and emancipatory egalitarian movement towards the abolition of private property and the division of labour – is the only political-economic arrangement that can provide a future for most of us.

By 'capitalism,' I mean a system where private property, waged labour and commodity production propel the self-valorisation of value. To maintain and legitimate itself, the capitalist system requires a particular state form, a bourgeois state of laws with claims to fairness and neutrality. Today's communicative capitalism is the system that is becoming neofeudal as its own processes intensify and turn in on themselves.[2] Not only has communicative capitalism transformed democratic participation into an endless loop of outrage replacing the meaning of communicative acts with their circulatory power, but its monopoly concentration, intensified inequality and subjection of the state to the market have transformed accumulation such that it now occurs as much through rent, debt and force as it does through commodity production. Globally, in the knowledge and technology industries, for example, rental income accruing from intellectual property rights exceeds income from the production of goods.[3] In the US, financial services contribute more to GDP than manufactured goods.[4] Increasingly, capital isn't reinvested in production; it's eaten up and redistributed as rents.[5] Thus, value is decreasingly self-valorising. Valorisation processes have spread far beyond the factory, into complex, speculative and unstable circuits increasingly dependent on surveillance, coercion and violence. In the complex networks of communicative capitalism, capitalism is turning itself into neofeudalism.

By 'communism,' I do not mean the end of politics in a reconciled and harmonious totality. As we learn from psychoanalysis, antagonism is irreducible; it goes 'all the way down.' Rather than heaven on earth, communism is the political form through which production for the sake of the capital accumulation of the few is replaced with production for the sake of meeting the needs of the many, a form for the collective self-emancipation of the proletarianised (Marx makes this point in his discussion of the Paris Commune in 'The Civil War in France').

Communicative capitalism is at a crossroads: communism or neofeudalism. Communism names that emancipatory egalitarian mode of association to which we should aspire and for which we have to organise and fight. Neofeudalism names the something worse to which capitalism is tending. It's what happens if we don't fight back.

Four features

Neofeudalism is characterised by four interlocking features: (1) the parcelisation of sovereignty; (2) hierarchy and expropriation with new lords and peasants; (3) desolate hinterlands and privileged municipalities and (4) insecurity and catastrophism. I'll address them each in turn.

Parcelisation of sovereignty

Marxist historians Perry Anderson and Ellen Meiksins Wood present the parcelisation of sovereignty as a key feature of feudalism. Two aspects of the parcelisation of sovereignty are important for understanding neofeudalism: fragmentation and extra-economic coercion. First, state functions are "vertically and horizontally fragmented."[6] Local arrangements occur in a variety of forms as different sorts of political and economic authorities claim right and jurisdiction. Arbitration and compromise take the place of the rule of law. The line between legal and illegal becomes weaker.[7]

Second, with the parcelisation of sovereignty political authority and economic power blend together. Feudal lords extracted a surplus from peasants through legal coercion, legal in part because the lords decided the law that applied to the peasants in their jurisdiction. Neofeudal lords like global financial institutions and digital technology platforms use debt to redistribute wealth from the world's poorest to the richest. In both the feudal and the neofeudal versions, economic actors exercise political power over a particular group of people on the basis of terms and conditions that the economic actors, the lords, set (e.g. what counts as permissible speech). At the same time, political power is exercised with and as economic power, not only taxes but fines, liens, asset seizures, licenses, patents, jurisdictions and borders. Under neofeudalism, the legal fictions of a bourgeois state determined by the forms of neutral law and free and equal individuals break down and the directly political character of society reasserts itself.

The fragmentation and extra-economic coercion characteristic of the parcelisation of sovereignty appear everywhere today. We might even say that they exert a structuring effect on political and economic action. Ten percent of global wealth is hoarded in off-shore accounts to avoid taxation, that is, to escape the reach of state law. Law doesn't apply to billionaires powerful enough to evade it. Correlatively, the largest tech companies have valuations greater than the economies of most of the world's countries. Cities and states relate to Apple, Amazon, Microsoft, Facebook and Google/Alphabet as if these corporations were themselves sovereign states – negotiating with, trying to attract and cooperating with them on their terms.

Another example: Foreign investors have the right to sue governments in international tribunals. Investors tend to sue when public interest regulations designed to protect water, communities and the environment threaten to reduce the value of their investments. A large number of such cases have been brought by Canadian mining exploration firms against Latin-American governments.

Sovereignty is parcelled, fragmented, on domestic fronts as well. Palestine is a clear example, as Israeli settlers under the protection of Israeli military forces illegally build up settlements on Palestinian land. An example from the US: cash-strapped municipalities use elaborate systems of fines to expropriate money from people directly, impacting poor people the hardest. In her recent book, *Punishment without Crime*, Alexandra Natapoff documents the dramatic scope of misdemeanour law in the already enormous US carceral system. Poor people, disproportionately, people of colour, are arrested on bogus charges and convinced to plead guilty to avoid the jail time that they could incur should they contest the charges. Not only does the guilty plea go on their record, but they open themselves up to fines that, if they can't afford to pay, will turn in to more fines and more charges. We got a brief look into this system of legal illegality and unjust administration of justice in the wake of the riots in Ferguson, Missouri that followed the murder of Michael Brown: "the city's municipal court and policing apparatus openly extracted millions of dollars from its low-income African American population."[8] Police were instructed "to make arrests and issue citations in order to raise revenue."[9] Like minions of feudal lords, they used force to expropriate value from the people.

Hierarchy and expropriation, new 'peasants' and 'lords'

Feudal relations are characterised by a fundamental inequality. Meiksins Wood emphasises that the distinct feature of feudalism in the West "is the exploitation of peasants by lords in the context of parcelized sovereignty."[10] Anderson reminds us of exploitative monopolies such as watermills that were controlled by the lord; peasants were obliged to have their grain ground at their lord's mill, a service for which they had to pay. So not only did peasants occupy and till land that they did not own but also they dwelled under conditions where the feudal lord was, as Marx says, "the manager and master of the process of production and of the entire process of social life."[11]

Already, in 2010, in his influential book, *You Are Not a Gadget*, tech guru Jaron Lanier observed the emergence of peasants and lords of the internet. This theme has increased in prominence as the tech giants have become richer and more extractive, their owners becoming billionaires on the basis of the cheap labour of their workers, the outsourcing of work to third party contractors, the free labour of their users, the tax breaks bestowed on them by cities desperate to attract jobs and the solidification of their monopolies. The tech giants are extractive. Like so many tributary demands, their tax breaks take money from communities. Their presence drives up rents and real estate prices, driving out affordable apartments, small businesses and low-income people.

Shoshana Zuboff's study of 'surveillance capitalism' brings out a further dimension of tech feudalism – military service. Like lords to kings, Facebook and Google cooperate with powerful states, sharing information that these states are legally barred from gathering themselves. Overall, the extractive dimension of networked technologies is now pervasive, intrusive and unavoidable. The tech giants have become masters of the entire process of social life. So while it's not quite right to say that the present is an era of peasants and lords, it is right to say that contemporary capitalist society is characterised by an intensification of inequality – more billionaires, greater distance between rich and poor and the solidification of a differentiated legal architecture that protects corporations and the rich while it immiserates and incarcerates the working and lower class.

'Platformisation' and land privatisation index tendencies towards the hierarchy and expropriation characteristic of neofeudalism. In *Platform Capitalism*, Nick Srnicek considers the effects of digital technology on capitalism. Even though technology companies employ a relatively small percentage of the workforce, their effects are tremendous, essentially remaking entire industries around the acquisition, mining and deployment of data. In fact, the smaller workforces are indicative of digital technology's neofeudalising tendency. Capital accumulation occurs less through commodity production and wage labour than through services, rents, licenses, fees, work done for free (often under the masquerade of participation) and data treated as a natural resource.

Srnicek defines platforms as "digital infrastructures that enable two or more groups to interact."[12] Positioning themselves as intermediaries, platforms constitute grounds for user activities, conditions of possibility for interactions to occur. Google makes it possible to find information in an impossibly dense and changing information environment. Amazon lets us easily locate, compare prices and purchase consumer goods from established as well as unknown vendors. Uber enables strangers to share rides. Airbnb does the same for houses and apartments. All are enabled by an immense generation and circulation of data. In other words, platforms don't just rely on data, they produce more of it. So, the more people use platforms, the more effective and powerful these platforms become, ultimately transforming the larger environment of which they are a part.

Two of the types of platform Srnicek considers are the cloud and the lean platform. The by now familiar cloud (which isn't a cloud but a bunch of energy-guzzling servers) features a broad array of on-demand computing services, typically storage, operating systems and applications. Companies don't have to purchase or host software of their own; they can subscribe to or rent it as needed. For example, Google sells access to its machine-learning processes like the "pattern recognition algorithms and audio transcriptions services."[13] Users of the processes pay Google for the service, and Google also collects the data generated through the use of the service. The cloud platform extracts rents and data, like land squared or reflexivised. Lean platforms are similarly reflexive, able to extract rent without property by relying on an outsourced workforce responsible for its own maintenance, training and means of work.[14] The primary examples are Uber and Airbnb, which reconfigure items of consumption as means of accumulation. One's car isn't for personal transport. It's for making money. One's apartment isn't a place to live; it's something to rent out. In each case, what was personal property becomes an instrument for the capital and data accumulation of the lords of platform: Uber and Airbnb. This tendency towards becoming-peasant, that is, to becoming one who owns means of production but whose labour increases the capital of the platform owner, is neofeudal.

Turning to land privatisation, over the past 40 years, over two million hectares of British public land (10% of Britain's overall land mass) have been sold to private buyers. According to Brett Christophers, this sell off has occurred at various levels from local to national, for various reasons and under various auspices in a "piecemeal and fragmented process."[15] Christophers points out that Marx saw the enclosure of the commons as a necessary condition for capitalist development insofar as this enclosure threw peasants off the land and forced them to sell their labour power in order to survive. Crucial to the new round of privatisation has been a different set of tendencies: "a rise in private-sector land-hoarding; Britain's growing transformation into a 'rentier' type economy—one increasingly dominated by rents paid by the many to the affluent, land-owning few; and widespread social dislocation."[16] The new privatisation is thus a move away from capitalism's profits and production and towards neofeudalism's rents and hoarding.

Cities and hinterlands

The third feature of neofeudalism is the spatiality associated with feudalism, one of the protected, often lively centres surrounded by agricultural and desolate hinterlands. We might also characterise this as a split between town and country, municipal and rural areas, urban communes and the surrounding countryside, or, more abstractly between an inside walled off from an outside, a division between what is secured and what is endangered, who is prosperous and who is desperate. Meiksins Wood says that medieval cities were essentially oligarchies, "with dominant classes enriched by commerce and financial services for kings, emperors and popes. Collectively, they dominated the surrounding countryside … extracting wealth from it in one way or another."[17] Outside the cities were the nomads and migrants who, facing unbearable conditions, sought new places to live and work yet all too often came up against the walls.

US hinterlands are sites of loss and dismantlement, places with fantasies of a flourishing capitalist past that, for a while, might have let some linger in the hope that their lives and their children's lives might actually get better. Remnants of an industrial capitalism that's left them behind for cheaper labour, the hinterlands are ripe for the new intensified exploitation of neofeudalism. No longer making things, people in the hinterlands persist through warehouses, call centres, Dollar Stores and fast food.

Politically, the desperation of the hinterlands manifests in the movements of those outside the cities, movements that are sometimes around environmental issues (fracking and pipeline struggles), sometimes around land (privatisation and expropriation) and sometimes around the reduction of services (hospital and school closings). In the US, the politics of guns positions the hinterlands against the urban. We might also note the way the division between hinterlands and municipality gets reinscribed within cities themselves. This manifests in both the abandonment of poor areas and their eradication in capitalist gentrification land grabs. A city gets richer, and more people become homeless – think San Francisco, Seattle and New York.

Finally, we could note the increased prominence of social reproduction theory as a response to 'hinterlandization,' that is, the loss of a general capacity to reproduce the basic conditions of liveable life. This appears in rising suicide rates, increase in anxiety and drug addiction, declining birth rates, lower rates of life expectancy and, in the US, the psychotic societal self-destruction of mass shootings. It appears in the collapsed infrastructures and undrinkable water. The hinterlands are written on people's bodies and on the land. With closures of hospitals and schools and the diminution of basic services, life becomes more desperate and uncertain.

Phil A. Neel's recent book, *Hinterland*, notes patterns between China, Egypt, Ukraine and the US. They are all places with desolate abandoned wastelands and cities on the brink of overload. Neel's account of the stratification and struggle across the international periphery echoes arguments made by International Relations scholars 30 years earlier. Already, in 1998, Philip Cerny was writing of the "growing alienation between global innovation, communication and resource nodes (global cities) on the one hand and disfavored, fragmented hinterlands on the other."[18] Cerny warned of the resulting exclusion and lumpenisation. As large geographical spaces are starved of infrastructure and support, he said, "many people will simply be 'out of the loop,' country bumpkins or even roaming deprived bands … forced once again to become predators or supplicants on the cities, as in the Middle Ages."[19]

Insecurity and apocalypticism

Finally, the fourth feature of feudalism important for thinking about neofeudal tendencies in the present is affective and subjective – insecurity, anxiety and apocalypse. These affective orientations link the first three categories together. There is good reason to feel insecure. The catastrophe of capitalist expropriation of the social surplus in the setting of a grossly unequal and warming planet is real.

A loose, mystical neofeudal ideology that knits together and amplifies apocalyptic insecurity seems to be taking form in the new embrace of the occult, techno-pagan and anti-modern.[20] Examples include Jordan Peterson's mystical Jungianism and Alexander Dugin's mythical geopolitics of Atlantis and Hyperborea. We might also note the rise of the so-called 'dark enlightenment' (Nick Land) and 'neo-reactionaries' such as PayPal's billionaire founder Peter Thiel who argues that freedom is incompatible with democracy.[21] In a lecture in 2012, Thiel explained the link between feudalism and tech start-ups: "No founder or CEO has absolute power. It's more like the archaic feudal structure. People vest the top person with all sorts of power and ability, and then blame them if and when things go wrong."[22] Along with other Silicon Valley capitalists, Thiel is concerned to protect his fortune from democratic impingement and so advocates strategies of exodus and isolation such as living on the sea and space colonisation, whatever it takes to save wealth from taxation. Extreme capitalism goes over into the radical de-centralisation of neofeudalism.

For those on the other side of the neofeudal divide, anxiety and insecurity are addressed less by ideology than they are by opioids, alcohol and food, anything to dull the pain of hopeless, mindless, endless drudgery. Emily Guendelsberger describes the stress caused by constant technological surveillance on the job – the risk of being fired for being a few seconds late, for not meeting the quotas, for using the bathroom too many times. Repetitive, low-control, high-stress work like that associated with work that is technologically monitored correlates directly with "depression and anxiety."[23] Uncertain schedules, lauded as flexible, unreliable pay because wage theft is ubiquitous, are stressful, deadening. They suggest that neofeudal apocalypticism, for some at least, may be individual, familial or local. It can be hard to get worked up about a climate catastrophe when you've lived catastrophe for a few generations.

I've shown how four elements of past European feudalism – parcelisation of sovereignty, hierarchy and expropriation, cities and hinterlands, and insecurity and apocalypticism – are relevant to present trajectories. Together, they let us see the present not as capitalist but as a neofeudalism born of capitalist processes as they intensify and turn back in on themselves. I am not making a historical claim about feudalism's fundamental structure or an empirical claim regarding all existing feudalisms. I'm drawing out tendencies that help us make sense of the present.

The political purchase of the neofeudal hypothesis

How, then, does the neofeudal hypothesis help us make sense of the present?

First, it lets us locate the primary conflict within capitalist processes. I reject the idea that the big confrontation today is between democracy and fascism. This makes little sense given the increasing power of oligarchs – financiers, media and real estate moguls, carbon and tech billionaires. Particularly striking is the way that a vicious new anti-communism has accompanied the political rise of the oligarchs in the US, Brazil, Hungary, Poland, the Czech Republic and the UK.

Viewing our present in terms of democracies threatened by rising fascism deflects attention from the fundamental role of globally networked communicative capitalism in exacerbating popular anger and discontent. Underlying the politicisation towards the right is economics: complex networks produce extremes of inequality, winner-take-all or winner-take-most distributions. The rightward shift responds to this intensification of inequality. When the left is weak, or blocked from political expression by mainstream media and capitalist political parties, popular anger gets expressed by others willing to attack the system. In the present, these others are the far right. Thinking in terms of neofeudalism thus forces us to confront the impact of extreme economic inequality on political society and institutions. It makes us reckon with the fact of billionaires hoarding trillions of dollars of assets and walling themselves into their own enclaves while millions become climate refugees and hundreds of millions encounter diminished life prospects, an intensifying struggle just to survive.

Second, the neofeudalism wager signals a change in labour relations. Today, the ideal of freely contracted labour that justifies and conceals coercive class relations is untenable. Not even the barest fantasy of freely given consent accounts for the social relations of wealth accumulation today. In the service-dominated economies of the global north, majorities work in service sectors. Some find that their phones, bikes, cars and homes have lost their character as personal property and been transformed into means of production or means for the extraction of rent. Tethered to platforms owned by others, consumer items and means of life are now means for their, the platform owners,' accumulation. Some of us enjoy the fantasy that our service is creative that we are members of a privileged class of knowledge workers. Yet, much of that work is increasingly done for free, maybe with a chance of pay. Knowledge workers, like day labourers, often have to compete for contracts – if they win, then they can work for a wage.

Most of us constitute a property-less underclass only able to survive by servicing the needs of high earners (e.g. as personal assistants, trainers, tutors, childminders, cooks and cleaners). A report from the Bureau of Labor Statistics says that, over the next ten years, the occupation that will add the most jobs is personal care aids, not health workers but aids who bathe and clean people.[24] The waged are further expropriated of their minimal incomes via unavoidable debts, fees, fines and rents. In the US, taxes on people are redistributed to corporations. For example, in 2018, 57 corporations, including Amazon, not only didn't pay taxes but received money back, tax rebates. The US government squeezes its citizens for money to pay out to corporations.

Third, thinking in terms of neofeudalisation enables us to identify a primary weakness of the contemporary left: those left ideas with the most currency are the ones that affirm rather than contest neofeudalism. Localism encourages parcelisation. Tech and platform approaches reinforce hierarchy and inequality. Municipalism affirms the urban–rural divide associated with hinterlandisation. Emphases on subsistence and survival proceed as if peasant economies were plausible not only for that half of the planet that lives in cities (including 82% of North Americans and 74% of Europeans) but also for the millions displaced by climate change, war and commercial land theft. Even worse, such emphases occlude the ever-worsening conditions for agriculture, as if droughts, floods and fires were not leading to crop loss around the world.

Those dwelling in the hinterlands face political, cultural, economic and climatic conditions that make it so that they can't survive through agricultural work. Approximately 50 countries are classified as low-income food deficit countries; most bear the initial brunt of the changing climate; most are in Africa. Universal Basic Income is a similarly untenable survivalist approach. It promises just enough to keep those in the hinterlands going – so long as they don't go to the cities where they can't afford to live. The fourth element, insecurity and apocalypse, takes shape in that left catastrophism preoccupied with extinction and the end of the world, as if the next 100 years or so just don't matter as well as in the renewed mysticisms around witchcraft and magic.

Taken together, these current left ideas suggest a future of small groups engaged in subsistence farming and the production of artisanal cheese, perhaps on the edges of cities where survivalist enclaves and drone-wielding tech workers alike experiment with urban gardens. Such groupings reproduce their lives in common; yet, the commons they reproduce is necessarily small, local and, in some sense, exclusive and elite, exclusive insofar as their numbers are necessarily limited, elite because the aspirations are culturally specific rather than widespread.

Popular left ideas mirror neofeudal tendencies as they converge via the abandonment of hinterlands, rural areas and small cities that have been left behind, and the cultivation of those elements of the urban that benefit the rich and educated (our robot future). Far from a vision anchored in the emancipation of the working class, the model can't see a working class. When work is imagined – and some on the left think that we should adopt a 'post-work imaginary' – it looks like either romantic risk-free farming or tech-work, 'immaterial labour.' By now, the exposes on the drudgery of call centre work, not to mention the trauma-inducing labour of monitoring sites like Facebook for disturbing, illicit content, have made the inadequacy of the idea of 'immaterial labour' undeniable. It should be similarly apparent that the post-work imaginary likewise erases industry, manufacturing, the production and maintenance of infrastructure, the wide array of labour necessary for social reproduction and the underlying state structure. Given that most cities are on coasts, this model lacks the institutional basis necessary for responding to the changing climate.

The neofeudal hypothesis thus lets us see both the appeal and the weakness of popular left ideas. They appeal because they resonate with dominant sense. They are weak because this dominant sense is an expression of tendencies to neofeudalism.

Jodi Dean

Communism?

As I mentioned at the outset, some outside the left have already formulated critiques of the present in terms of an emergent neofeudalism. The head of Russia's Federal Anti-Monopoly Service warns of increasing "economic feudalism … in which there is no private sector, no capitalistic relations, but vassals and lords."[25] His concern is with state involvement in the Russian economy, a concern echoed by Swedish market analyst Anders Aslund in an array of editorials on Russia's neofeudal capitalism.

Where these analyses of Russia see neofeudalisation as arising from the state, conservative and libertarian economists in the US see mass serfdom as the likely effect of green liberalism. According to Joel Kotkin, "the old economic regime emphasized growth and upward mobility. In contrast the new economic order focuses more on the notion of 'sustainability' – so reflective of the feudal worldview—over rapid economic expansion."[26] Presenting a division within the capitalist class as if it were a division between the many and the few (in other words, as a populist division), Kotkin places the oil and gas sector on the side of the people. High tech, finance and globalisation are the enemy, threatening "to create a new social order that in some ways more closely resembles feudal structures – with its often-unassailable barriers to mobility – than the chaotic emergence of industrial capitalism." In this libertarian imaginary, feudalism occupies the place of the enemy formerly held by communism. The threat of centralisation and the threat to private property are the ideological elements that remain the same.

These right-wing fears point to what the left needs to embrace, that is, to the communist alternative to neofeudalism. Returning to the four characteristics of neofeudalism, we can locate possibilities that, with political organisation and will, can be pushed in another direction.

Parcelisation can be reframed as the weakening of the nation state necessary for communist universalism. Rendered not as fragmentation but as the separation of elements that might be reconfigured into the new global state structures necessary for confronting the catastrophe, transnational organisations – from financial institutions, corporations and social media platforms to parties, issue alliances and political formations – suggest the plausibility of communising structures across and beyond nation states. It's not hard to imagine them repurposed as the institutions of global communism, devoted not to capital accumulation and protecting the hoards and privileges of the billionaires but to the emancipatory egalitarian flourishing of the many. Getting here requires political struggle – the capitalist class won't just roll over. But parcelisation reminds us that their power is more fragile than any of us often acknowledge. And it gives us a way to think about how an international communist state might take form out of a complex tangle of associations operating in ways that exceed the simple geometry of vertical and horizontal or the clichéd geography of local and global.

Lords and peasants, that is, hierarchy, inequality and expropriation provide a second opening. The communist path recognises this division as class conflict takes the side of the peasants and proletarianised. Such a trajectory already has momentum in the peasant organising carried about by Via Campesina, to use just one example.

Eliminating the lords, we abolish private property and seize the means of communication, production, transportation, etc., making production serve human need. It's not hard to dissolve trillions of dollars of fictitious capital – the capitalist system does this regularly. We'd just do it intentionally. And we'd need to deliberate on what sort of technologies we want and need and their real costs – for example, are we willing to do time in Coltan mines for the sake of cell phones? Do we want to abolish the collection of meta-data entirety or find ways to use it to better assess needs and uses? Liberated from the constraints of capital accumulation, we could finally grapple with fundamental choices regarding our collective life rather than having these choices determined for us and behind our backs.

With respect to cities and hinterlands, the end of an economy of capital accumulation makes possible the dissolution of the rural/urban divide and the division of labour that drives it. With a vision of communism mindful of the hinterlands, we open up new possibilities for organised struggle that build from current tendencies – we might think of the Maoist strategy of surrounding the cities. At any rate, the intensifying politics around migration and refugees, the class struggles unfolding in various forms on the outskirts of cities and the growing anger of the hinterland's dispossessed that we see vividly in France and in the electoral politics driving the rightward shift in the US, Hungary, Poland, Canada and elsewhere give us a setting of real struggle that is as yet undecided. There is nothing inevitable about the shift to the right. It's a matter of organising, of offering a politics that speaks to a wide array of human needs and concerns, that offers the possibility of flourishing.

Finally, instead of plagued by insecurity and apocalypticism, we can – and must – cultivate communist virtues of solidarity, courage, discipline and confidence, virtues that emerge out of and engender a sense of comradeship. Anything less dooms us to neofeudalism.

Conclusion

I've argued that capitalism is tending to neofeudalism. This does not mean that there are no longer capitalist relations of production and exploitation. It means that the other dimensions of capitalist production – expropriation, domination and force – have become stronger to such an extent that it no longer makes sense to posit free and equal actors meeting in the labour market even as a governing fiction. It means that rent and debt feature as or more heavily in accumulation than profit and that work increasingly exceeds the wage relation. It means that the state form associated with the bourgeoisie has been radically altered. Just as Lenin's account of imperialism as a stage of capitalism made clear that there were still capitalist relations, but in a new form, one where monopoly, finance and the territorial division of the world necessitated another analysis, so might neofeudalism lead us to a different appreciation of the forces communicative capitalism has itself produced. What happens when capitalism is global? It turns in on itself, generating, enclosing and mining features of human life through digital networks and mass personalised media. This reflexivisation produces new lords and serfs, vast fortunes and extreme inequality, and the parcellised sovereignties that secure this inequality while the many wander and languish in the hinterlands. Avoiding this – confronting this – requires organised political struggle for communism.

Notes

1. See, for example, Joel Kotlin, *The New Class Conflict* (Candor, NY: Telos Press, 2014).
2. For more on communicative capitalism, see my *Democracy and Other Neoliberal Fantasies* (Durham, NC: Duke University Press, 2009).
3. Richard Westa, *Periodizing Capitalism and Capitalist Extinction* (Basingstoke: Palgrave Macmillan, 2019), p. 221.
4. Ibid., 221.
5. Ibid., 224.
6. Ellen Meiksins Wood, *Citizens to Lords* (London, UK: Verso, 2008), p. 166.
7. Chris Wickam, "The 'Feudal Revolution' and the Origins of Italian City Communes," *Transactions of the Royal Historical Society* 24 (2014), pp. 29–55.
8. Alexandra Natapoff, *Punishment without Crime* (New York: Basic Books, 2018), p. 133.
9. Ibid., 134.
10. Meiksins Wood, *Citizens to Lords*, p. 168.
11. Perry Anderson, *Passages from Antiquity to Feudalism* (London: Verso, [1974] 2013), p. 183. Anderson is quoting Marx, *Capital*, Vol. 3.
12. Nick Srnicek, *Platform Capitalism* (Cambridge: Polity Press, 2017), p. 43.
13. Ibid., 62.
14. Ibid., 76.
15. Brett Christophers, *The New Enclosures* (London: Verso, 2018), p. 329.
16. Ibid., 4.
17. Meiksins Wood, *Citizens to Lords*, p. 172.
18. Philip G. Cerny, "Neomedievalism, Civil War and the New Security Dilemma: Globalisation as Durable Disorder," *Civil Wars* 1: 1 (February 1998), p. 45.
19. Ibid., 55.
20. I owe this point to papers given by Keti Chukhrov and Maria Chehonadskih at the 2019 meeting of the Radical Critical Theory Circle in Nisyros, Greece.
21. See Klint Finley, "Geeks for Monarchy: The Rise of the Neoreactionaries" (November 23, 2013), available online at: https://techcrunch.com/2013/11/22/geeks-for-monarchy/; and Peter Thiel, "The Education of a Liberation," *Cato Unbound* (April 13, 2009), available online at: https://www.cato-unbound.org/2009/04/13/peter-thiel/education-libertarian. I am indebted to Tomislav Medak for bringing Thiel's piece and position to my attention.
22. Keith A. Spencer, "Revenge of the Nerd-kings: Why Some in Silicon Valley are Advocating for Monarchy," *Salon* (April 13, 2019), available online at https://www.salon.com/2019/04/13/why-some-in-silicon-valley-are-advocating-for-monarchy.
23. Emily Guendelsberger, *On the Clock* (New York: Little Brown and Company, 2019), p. 125.
24. Derek Thompson, "Why Nerds and Nurses are Taking Over the U.S. Economy," *Atlantic* (October 26, 2017).
25. Available online at: https://www.themoscowtimes.com/2019/05/06/russian-watchdog-warns-states-role-in-economy-is-growing-a65497.
26. Kotkin, *The New Class Conflict*, p. 11.

Chapter 5

Alternative models of tenure

Recovering the radical proposal of collective housing

Martino Tattara

Housing crises seem to be an inherent feature of the capitalist city. Since the advent of industrialisation, many cities world-wide have been characterised by a scarcity in housing unfolding into poor living conditions for the urbanised masses and unaffordable rents. There was a crisis of supply in the 19th century; then after the First and Second World Wars, when bombing had made many homeless, there was a demand for housing reconstruction programmes. The housing crises of the last three decades have been understood as the outcome of the commodification and financialisation of the housing sector.[1] This current crisis involves the reduction of the average living space, the skyrocketing real-estate prices, the endless waiting lists to access public housing, gentrification, evictions and foreclosures, all the trademarks of today's city. Every major city in the world, from London to New York, from San Francisco to Shanghai, faces its own housing struggle.

As a remedy, cities have produced various solutions, often in the attempt to bypass the complexities of existing institutions by supporting civil society and community-led housing initiatives. Among these, we can think of the German *Baugruppen* or the Finnish *Ryhmärakentaminen*, models where individuals self-organise to finance the construction of their buildings. They have been highly successful in cutting out the costs of the middleman in the development process, in offering a degree of agency for residents in the arrangement of their domestic life and in equipping their buildings with some shared collective facilities. There is also the Small Sites Initiative,[2] launched in recent years by the Mayor of London, to promote a small scale and piecemeal approach to the urban housing problem by making available small parcels

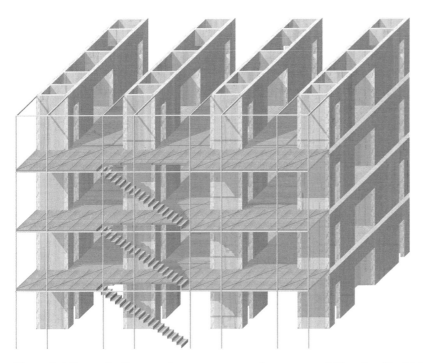

Figure 5.1 Brussels: Dogma, *Do you see me when we pass? Housing Model for the Community Land Trust in Brussels*. Structural diagram

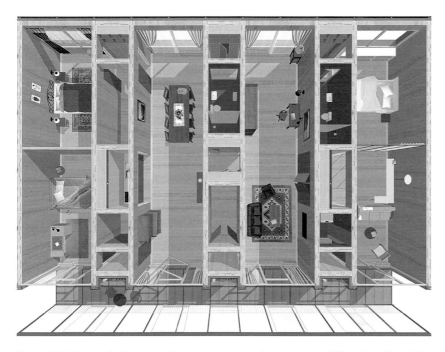

Figure 5.2 Brussels: Dogma, *Do you see me when we pass? Housing Model for the Community Land Trust in Brussels*. Four-room apartment

of public land and assisting in their development with housing cooperatives and other civic initiatives.

These projects, which have often developed into architecturally exciting designs, are the embodiment of what we generally refer to as 'collective housing,' namely residential projects characterised by a variable degree of collectivity among the inhabitants. These centralised and shared facilities, which were once associated with domestic labour such as cooking and washing,[3] are today mainly concerned with the sphere of leisure. And yet, to assess the efficacy of these proposals in relation to the present socio-economic challenges, one needs to admit that such initiatives are in most cases limited to those with access to credit and capital and with an appropriate amount of time and, given their intrinsically entrepreneurial character, are often lacking the mechanism to restrain the speculative ambitions of their inhabitants. While these initiatives are commendable in circumventing certain housing market mechanisms, nevertheless, they fail to address the original causes of the current crisis, to provide long-term solutions. They fail to address the issues of access to land and of home-ownership, real problems that need to be tackled in overcoming the origins of the present crisis.

It is through collective ownership – in the multiplicity of forms and models through which this idea can be exemplified – that the real collective nature of things emerges. In this essay, I want to address this relationship between the project of housing and alternative models of land ownership and housing tenure. In this relationship, there is real potential for the formulation of a new design agenda placing at its centre the problem of affordable housing. A few cases reveal how alternative tenure models can unfold into radical architectural propositions in terms of typologies, material definition and construction. I will conclude by presenting a couple of proposals developed at Dogma as collaborative projects between architects and two alternative housing initiatives in Brussels and London.

The problem of land property

As noted by Marx,[4] private property always involves the removing of something from the community. Home ownership is historically linked to the process of land privatisation that started in the 16th century in early modern England with the erasure of the ancient system of communal regulations and the forms of traditional tenure.[5] Land privatisation describes a process of dispossession – what has been defined as the legalised theft perpetrated by landlords with the support of the state through the invention of the institutions of property law, which allowed for customary communal rights to be suddenly swept away. This enabled new landlords to form large estates by uniting small pieces of land with the justification of (supposedly) improving agricultural efficiency.

The consequences of this process have been quite remarkable: land was suddenly transformed into a type of market commodity, like any other, making it possible for the first time to sell it in exchange for money, transforming it into the most important source of credit. To the point that, for landlords, owning land was not only a way to extract surplus from agricultural production but also to use it as collateral for a loan.

Marx defined this process as "primitive accumulation,"[6] which he saw as the precondition for the development of capital since the enclosure of common land-deprived peasants of their means of subsistence and turned them into landless proletarians to be exploited as wage workers. While this process initially and primarily concerned rural land, with the advent of the industrial city land privatisation became a fertile ground for landowners to speculate on land for housing. It was in this period that big metropolises such as Paris, New York and Berlin saw the emergence of dense housing typologies which were invented with the explicitly speculative goal of bypassing exorbitant land values and maximising profits from renting properties. These urban typologies, such as the Parisian *maison à loyer*, the Berliner *mietskaserne* and the New York tenement, still characterise today the residential landscape of each of those cities.

The divorce between the use and exchange value of land is today paramount everywhere, and land has become the financial asset par excellence, a situation which is worsening thanks to the chronic uncertainty of the financial economy that makes land the best form of collateral for debt. This has made for example land banking an important form of enclosure in many cities where vast plots of land remain empty as assets to back speculative investments. It is for this reason that alternative attempts to withdraw land from the market, and thus reclaim it for its use value, have become urgent.

To counter these conditions, various initiatives have attempted to reform land use towards a more cooperative and equitable model. One of the most radical initiatives was Ebenezer Howard's proposal for the 'Garden City' in which inhabitants would become direct stakeholders, thus preventing landlord control. It is significant to note that, while this model has been widely replicated in its urban spatial organisation, its land tenure logic has been unfortunately ignored or forgotten. Other past initiatives directly involved the state, especially when, after the Second World War, many European countries could secure public land for a massive injection of public housing. Yet, even in the heyday of the welfare state, the tacit political goal of many liberal-democratic states in Europe was to build a 'property owning democracy,' as it would be revealed later, in the 1980s, with the privatisation of social housing achieved through the 'right to buy' legislation, allowing housing tenants to purchase their homes at a heavily discounted rate.

The study of the history of landowning reveals the presence of alternative modes of land management, which are based on an understanding of land value as a collective resource. Many modern movements that support alternative forms of land acquisition claim the importance of this cultural heritage, drawing on the ancient traditions of native American, Indian and rural European communities and African tribes. A contemporary example is the Community Land Trust (CLT), first introduced into the US by Robert Swann in 1969 as an answer to the speculative development in farmland. In the 1980s, the CLT model also started to be implemented in urban areas, promoting the separation of the ownership of land from that of housing. While the first is to be retained by the CLT in perpetuity, therefore preventing land speculation, housing units could be purchased with long-term ground leases by interested owners. Nowadays, the CLT model is becoming increasingly widespread, expanding from the US and UK to European countries and representing one of the few viable

Alternative models of tenure

Figure 5.3 Brussels: Dogma, *Do you see me when we pass? Housing Model for the Community Land Trust in Brussels.* External view

Figure 5.4 Brussels: Dogma, *Do you see me when we pass?* View of the interior space of a unit

alternatives to the organisation of land without the interference of private developers. Yet, the observation of some recent housing projects realised for example in Brussels by the recently active CLT[7] reveals the development of quite conventional housing schemes in terms of spatial organisation, material definition and typologies, as if the political ambitions of its ownership model could not unfold into an innovative architectural agenda. This overview and the discussion of past and existing models of alternative forms of land tenure highlights the need for a transformation in the way in which access to land is conceived in contemporary society. It also brings to light the intricate relationship between aspects often considered completely disjointed in the discussion of housing, such as accessibility to land, housing ownership and architectural form.

Housing tenure, private ownership and alternative models

While home ownership has become the most widespread form of tenure in most European countries to the point that many households consider this as a sort of natural life-aspiration, it was only in the 1950s and 1960s under the pressure of emancipatory social struggles thriving both in Europe and the US and the need to protect private capital rights, that home ownership after it stagnated during the war picked up again and became central to the support for further capital expansion and the onset of housing financialisaton. Through the expansion of mortgages, homes started to be embedded in the global flaws of financial capital, the goal of which was the benefit of investors rather than homeowners. Through policies such as the Right to Buy in the UK (although approved in the 1980s as part of the Housing Act, it is since the Thatcher's election as party leader in 1975 that the Conservative Party began to move towards a wholesale advocacy of council house sales[8]), the promotion of tax incentives on mortgages, the involvement of the private sector in the provision of housing to low-income groups in the US, home ownership has become a cornerstone of neoliberal policies. With the state-supporting private ownership as the sole form of tenure, civil society initiatives have proven more effective in providing alternative models. Today, initiatives such as housing co-operatives offer a viable substitute to private home ownership by placing limitations on the speculative value of housing.

The inventor of the cooperative apartment house was Philip G. Hubert, an architect who identified in the cooperative model a possible solution to the dramatic housing shortage in New York at the end of the 19th century. At that time, residential property was mostly made up of townhouses and single-family houses. This situation prevented many people, including middle-class families, from owning a permanent home, thus forcing them to invest all their earnings in temporary living solutions. In this context, Hubert presented his idea of the Home Club[9]: affordable accommodation that combined the domestic arrangement of the European apartment with the transiency of the American hotel. Within the Home Clubs, housing units were kitchen-less and flexible. They accommodated different ways of living and were supported by centralised housekeeping and an abundance of collective facilities, such as lounges and meeting rooms. Besides introducing a new spatial model for collective living, the Home Clubs (eight prototypes were built in a few years in New York) were based on common ownership in a joint stock scheme. Organised as a corporation of shareholders, these were responsible for all aspects of the project, from management to maintenance. The most well-known example of this kind of arrangement is the Chelsea Hotel (1885) in New York, which included apartments of different sizes (all without kitchens), plus a large kitchen, central dining room and a lounge on the uppermost floor. The Chelsea Hotel not only became home to many artists and creators but also influenced, through its domestic arrangements, many thinkers, activists, feminists and utopian socialists of the time.[10]

In recent years, housing cooperatives have expanded in many countries and in some, such as Switzerland, where they have profited from legislative support and access to land, have become an important player on the housing market at the national level. Particularly relevant to the cooperative model are the limited equity housing co-operatives, which are owned and managed by a democratically governed, non-profit cooperative corporation, such as a tenants' union, but are different from other cooperative arrangements in that the price of the ownership shares is determined beforehand by the members of the associations themselves and is therefore not influenced by the fluctuations of the real estate market. Unlike traditional co-ops, there is a limit on the profit that members can make on the resale of their units. The below-market asking price, together with the restrictions on resale, keep the apartments insulated from increasing prices, thus making them an affordable option for generations of the city's low-income residents.

In any overview of counter strategies to home ownership, it is necessary to mention the mutual housing associations, which took their inspiration from the movements that emerged in Europe after the Second World War. For these associations, the property of buildings and land is permanently taken off the market and inhabitants rent the units from the associations by paying a membership fee and signing a lease that is calculated on the basis of their income. They are defined as expansionist organisations, since they aim to continuously subtract properties from the market to put them into collective ownership. An application of such a strategy is the German *Mietshäuser Syndikat* (Apartment House Syndicate),[11] which originated from the Freiburg squatter scene in the early 1980s in an attempt to permanently remove the buildings of a former industrial site from the real estate market. The *Syndikat*, which was officially funded in 1992 and that in 2017 counted 124 housing projects in Germany, aims at the appropriation and the reprogramming of existing capitalist forms of ownership. To prevent the selling-off of a property and ensure that every housing project is permanently withdrawn from the market, each syndicate project is divided into two main shares, owned by the users/inhabitants who form a cooperative of rent-paying stakeholders and by the *Syndikat* itself. In this way, the residents retain autonomy over the decision-making processes regarding development and the administration, while the right of veto of the syndicate prevents any attempts at privatisation and speculation.

Figure 5.5 Brussels: Dogma, *Do you see me when we pass?* Interior view. Detail

Figure 5.6 Brussels: Dogma, *Do you see me when we pass?* Interior view. Detail

WilMa 19, at Magdalenenstraße 19 in Berlin-Lichtenberg, is a good example of what the consequences of the application of the *Syndikat* logic are.[12] Part of the former administrative complex of the GDR Ministry of State Security, the building was put up for sale to the highest bidder after having been vacant for years. After bidding successfully and securing resources for the renovation, the future community of residents agreed on the principle of equal rent for all inhabitants, irrespective of the size of the apartment. Although small apartments would cost more proportionally in terms of construction, all inhabitants would pay the same rent, which was purposely kept below the threshold of five euros per square metre, to ensure that the building would be accessible to a socially diverse group of people, including those on low incomes and not contribute to the real-estate appreciation of the neighbourhood. This choice unfolded into a series of financial constraints during the renovation works, greatly limiting, for example, the possibility of making new openings within the prefabricated concrete panels of the existing structure (the infamous *Plattenbauweise*), of changing the layout of apartments or of insulating the house beyond what was strictly necessary to comply with the local regulations. Yet, to allow for the possibility of each household personalising its living unit, the principle of the *Terracottafliesenlösung* was invented, according to which each inhabitant could install a specific material at his or her own cost beyond the available terracotta tiles, provided that these extra elements became part of the property of the housing company, thus contributing to the appreciation of the building. To keep costs under control during renovation, each tenant had also to dedicate a certain number of hours to the construction so that specifically low-skilled activities such as removing old furniture, wallpaper and flooring could be performed without contractors.

Two proposals

During the past years at Dogma, we had the chance of working with some of the initiatives previously mentioned on housing collaborative projects in Brussels and in London. Our interest in these collaborations was motivated by the fact that they bring together issues of land ownership, housing tenure, construction and typology within a unitary design approach. Often, recent housing projects with alternative ownership models are generally based on standard construction techniques and rather conventional typological schemes. With our proposals, we were interested in reclaiming the experimental character of 'alternative' housing schemes from the past, which were often the site for typological innovation, technical advancement and social emancipation.

The first project concerns the development of a housing prototype in collaboration with the Community Land Trust Brussels (CLTB). CLTBs wanted to make housing as inclusive as possible. We provided a design strategy in which the architecture of the home expressed the cooperative form of land acquisition. Inhabitants live together and negotiate their own space; with a plan, based on the even subdivision of space, resulting in a sequence of equal bays framed by walls which contains all the fixed utilities of the living unit (bathroom, kitchen, etc.), while allowing for further partitions.

Following the bays structure, units can expand or shrink according to the needs. Following architect Avi Friedman, this concept of habitation was defined as 'evolutive housing,'[13] namely, the possibility for living units to accommodate as much as possible the transient nature of family living through years and decades. 'Evolutive housing' demands a different approach to building compared to traditional house forms. Within traditional housing, walls and partitions are rigid structures, and inhabitants are often confused on what the load-bearing walls and the simple partitions are. This spatial rigidity is further reinforced by the way building codes and ownership regimes force inhabitants to dwell within unchangeable boundaries. In the proposal, the idea of evolution of the living space is supported by a building system based on cross-laminated timber. Although more expensive as material than concrete, this has the advantage of allowing for a reduction in construction costs since parts can be assemble quickly and for inhabitants to participate in the construction process. A system of thick walls containing all the fix utilities such as bathroom and kitchen supports the possibility of arranging the rest of the units in different ways, using light partitions that can be easily mounted and dismantled by the inhabitants.

The second project concerns the development of a prototype for a cooperative housing organisation in London capable of meeting the ways of living and working of its young members.[14] The goal was to translate the cooperative ownership structure into a communal house that gives to its residents the opportunity to modulate sharing and privacy according to their needs and aspirations. Given the current economic situation, buying a house in London has become unaffordable to many, including middle-income workers, single people and families. In response to this situation, groups of individuals and families are coming together in small associations and cooperatives. While many of these associations are formed primarily with the goal of entering the housing market, others wish to take the opportunity of collective ownership to test a more communal way of living based on the implementation of a cooperative contract amongst inhabitants.

The project represents a prototype for a communal house for approximately 40 people, in which every inhabitant is equipped with a private room with shared kitchens, living rooms and terraces. These rooms can be grouped together in different ways, giving form to a multiplicity of households. The modular configuration allows for these households to evolve through time. This is possible due to the cooperative ownership system in which every member of the co-op owns a share of the whole building rather than a specific portion of it. The building includes spaces for work, providing the residents with office spaces, workshops and meeting rooms that can also be open to the local community. The use of timber for the structure and the main building components is motivated by the wish of the members to participate in the construction process and therefore favour the acquisition of those administrative and constructive skills that would reduce the need of external developers and contractors. The prototype is conceived as a repeatable structure that can be implemented in different sites, adapt to different urban conditions and thus resulting

Alternative models of tenure

in different configurations. Yet, the guiding principle remains the same throughout the various possible application, namely the idea of subdivision of the building based on individual rooms that can be brought together and give forms to different living spaces.

Conclusions

The solution to the problem of affordable housing is strictly interrelated to the problem of land accessibility and of housing tenure. Traditionally, these issues have been understood as detached from the field of design and as not having an impact on the development of the architecture of housing. The exploration of cases from the history of the discipline reveals rather the opposite, that a radically progressive and socially emancipatory domestic architecture is the result of the attempt to give a spatial and material definition to the immaterial dimensions of land ownership and housing tenure. The few examples of alternative housing ownership regimes that have been discussed are a clear embodiment of what the implications of living collectively are. If the nature of private property involves the removal of something from the community for personal exploitation, living collectively can be fundamentally achieved by going beyond the exclusive use of things.

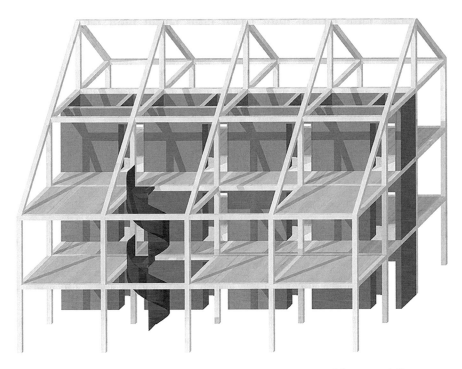

Figure 5.7 London: Dogma, *Do you hear me when you sleep?* **Structural diagram**

Martino Tattara

Figure 5.8 London: Dogma, *Do you hear me when you sleep? Proposal for a Cooperative House in London.* External view

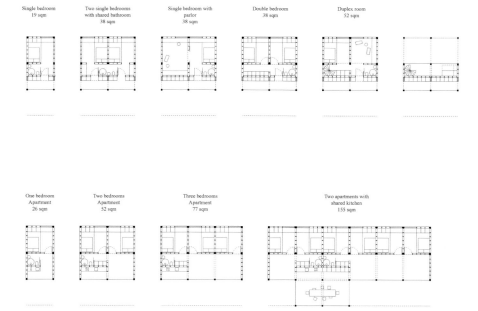

Figure 5.9 London: Dogma, *Do you hear me when you sleep?* Rooms typologies

Alternative models of tenure

Figure 5.10 London: Dogma, *Do you hear me when you sleep?* External view

Notes

1. David J. Madden and Peter Marcuse, *In Defense of Housing: The Politics of Crisis*, London: Verso, 2016.
2. See https://www.london.gov.uk/what-we-do/housing-and-land/land-and-development/small-sites/making-small-sites-available-small-builders
3. Dick Urban Vestbro and Liisa Horelli, "Design for Gender Equality: The History of Co-Housing Ideas and Realities", *Built Environment* 38, no. 3 (2012): 315–335.
4. Karl Marx, "Critique of Hegel's Philosophy of Right", *Marx & Engels Collected Works 3*, London: Lawrence & Wishart, 1975, 109.
5. Gary Fields, *Enclosure*, 1st ed., Berkeley: University of California Press, 2017, 23–44.
6. Karl Marx, *Capital: A Critique of Political Economy*, Vol. 1, New York: Penguin, 1976, 138.
7. On the experience of the Community Land Trust in Brussels, see Nele Aernouts and Michael Ryckewaert, "Beyond Housing: On the Role of Commoning in the Establishment of a Community Land Trust Project." *International Journal of Housing Policy* 18, no. 4 (2018): 503–521.
8. Daniel Stedman Jones, *Masters of the Universe: Hayek, Friedman, and the Birth of Neoliberal Politics*, Princeton: Princeton University Press, 2012, 305–311.
9. Elizabetsh C. Cromley, *Alone Together: A History of New York's Early Apartments*, Ithaca: Cornell University Press, 1990, 131–134.
10. Charles Matlack Price, "A pioneer in Apartment House Architecture: Memoir on Philip G. Hubert's Work", *Architectural Record* 36 (July 1974): 74–76.
11. Judith Vey, "Crisis Protests in Germany, Occupy Wall Street, and Mietshäuser Syndikat: Antinomies of Current Marxist- and Anarchist-inspired Movements and Their Convergence", *Capital & Class* 40, no. 1 (2016): 59–74; Lina Hurlin, "Mietshäuser Syndikat. Collective Ownership, the 'Housing Question' and Degrowth", in Anitra Nelson and François Schneider, *Housing for Degrowth: Principles, Models, Challenges and Opportunities*, London: Routledge, 2019, 233–243.
12. Juliane Seehawer, Die Häuser denen, die drin wohnen (Houses for Those Who Inhabit Them), Master's thesis, KU Leuven, 2019. (https://app.box.com/s/iansyqtm9rku64ltbaxdqnhmt0mw8pv6)
13. Avi Friedman, *The Grow Home*, Montréal: McGill-Queen's University Press, 2001.
14. The Sun Mutual Home Ownership Society Ltd (https://sun-coop.github.io).

Part II
New geography and the planners

Chapter 6

A proprietary polis

Silicon Valley architecture and collective life

Claudia Dutson

In 1981, as the silicon chip industry was being eclipsed by the 'miracle' economies of South Korea, Taiwan and Japan, Reyner Banham observed an architectural aesthetic for the technological age appearing in the Santa Clara Valley: "neat, silvery smooth and as slickly styled as an advanced computer: [...] super-smart buildings buried in luxuriant landscaping."[1,2] From computer research facilities, to laboratories and manufacturing plants, Silicon Style was "single-storey, rectangular, flat-roofed, sometimes very large – covering acres – but always very smart."[3]

At the height of the dotcom bubble, architecture critic Gwendolyn Wright described the 30-mile sprawl of the valley – stretching from Palo Alto in the north to Santa Theresa in the south – as a "seemingly endless pattern of flat, prosaic surfaces: Spanish-tile roofs, mirrored-glass walls, and cardboard classical colonnades attached to concrete panels, each building surrounded by a ubiquitous sea of lawn and parking lots."[4]

Silicon Valley remains a landscape of industrial lots and office-parks – cost-effective tilt-ups are the vernacular of the valley. Up until recently, only Apple had a purpose-built complex – Infinite Loop in Cupertino, a 1993 development by the Sobrato Organisation consisting of a ring of six buildings around a central green space. Facebook took over the former head offices of Sun Microsystems built in the mid-1990s: eight buildings strung along a private pedestrian 'main street,' the complex surrounded by parking. The Googleplex, a corporate campus built in 1994 for Silicon Graphics (SGI) by Studios Architecture (renovated by Clive Wilkinson Architects), is a mass broken into blocks and diagonally intersected by linked green squares.

DOI: 10.4324/9781003118985-8

Claudia Dutson

Between 2009 and 2011, Apple, Facebook and Google announced plans for new campuses in Silicon Valley. Instead of engaging experienced Valley architects like Gensler, HOK and NBBJ, they chose practices led by high-profile starchitects – Norman Foster, Frank Gehry, Bjarke Ingels, Thomas Heatherwick and Rem Koolhaas. As the first buildings neared completion, Silicon Valley became a topic of inquiry for architectural journalism, less for the architecture itself which has not drawn favourable criticism, and more for what it might say about the dominance and permanence of digital companies in public (and private) life. Speculation proliferated about the type of person that these buildings are for – the Silicon Valley tech worker.

To critically assess the campus and its role in the construction of the subjectivity of the tech-worker, while resisting the cultish tropes put forward Dave Eggers' novel The Circle, I have traced the historical development of the architecture of Silicon Valley as a co-evolution of the management philosophies of early tech spin-outs and start-ups. The campus, I propose, is not so much 'edifice complex' – on the contrary, I argue that this is not an architecture of representation, but an architecture of organisation. As such, the campus is the spatialisation of management and the production of identity and subjectivity through the physical manifestation of protocols and practices.

The campus designates a particular type of work environment apart from the down-town office or the business park. While it draws explicitly on the university typology, other formative influences include the research lab, the factory and the creative's studio.[5]

When a company commissions their own campus, the brief to the architects includes lessons learned in their original leased properties – operational spatial strategies which are repeated, refined and extended in the new campus designs. As each company acquires further land for the next iteration of campus (due to complete between 2021 and 2023) they continue to experiment with this emergent architectural typology. This typology has a number of key features that are not so much aesthetic as they are strategic and relational – particularly in how they construct the identities of

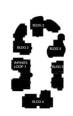  

INFINITE LOOP
Apple
Sobrato Organisation (1993)

Sun Microsystems
BAR Architects (1995)

1 HACKER WAY
Facebook
Gensler (2012)

Silicon Graphics Inc.
Studios Architecture (1997)

GOOGLEPLEX
Alphabet Google
Clive Wilkinson (2003)

Figure 6.1 Apple, Facebook and Google corporate campuses pre-2009, illustration by the author, 2019

their employees. Apple, Facebook and Google have their own cultures – with which their architecture in some way aligns – however, each design while formally different shares properties: the buildings are all low-rise (between one and four storeys) and the floorplates largely contiguous bringing together a very high number of employees on one floor (around 2,500 to 3,000).[6]

Apple is secretive and exclusory, calling engineers 'designers' and tech support workers 'geniuses.' Facebook prefers a stripped-back aesthetic, encouraging its employees to 'hack' the space. Google is open and participatory, employees identify as 'googlers,' 'gayglers,' 'dooglers,' 'jewglers,' 'brewglers' and so on. However, no singular identity is stable – something that the statistics on job mobility in Silicon Valley underscore:[7] a Googler can become a 'hacker' and then a 'genius' fairly readily. The formation of Silicon Valley was itself a result of job-hopping and disloyalty, beginning with William Shockley's departure from Bell Labs to form his own laboratory with his brightest staff in 1955. When eight of these left Shockley to form their own company, Fairchild Semiconductor, spin-out culture was established – many technology companies in the Valley trace their founding back to the Fairchildren.[8]

The Silicon Valley way of doing things originates in the management styles of high-tech companies in the mid-20th century, early start-ups who positioned themselves in contrast to corporate America by challenging top-down models of management. Hewlett Packard, who invented "management by wandering around,"[9] Varian Associates, who encouraged their employees to buy into the company through stock options,[10] and Intel, who pioneered non-hierarchical working, encouraged a focus on the individual, risk-taking and an entrepreneurial spirit.[11] Employees were highly motivated, felt autonomous and had a stake in the company's success.[12]

Silicon Valley companies recognise that work is a fundamental component of a person's life, their management philosophies enable the realisation of an employee's full potential. Apple, Facebook and Google have long known that the campus is the site where personal desires for meaningful work are enfolded within company missions, and the architecture facilitates the provision of well-being, the manufacture of shared objectives and the quest for self-actualisation.

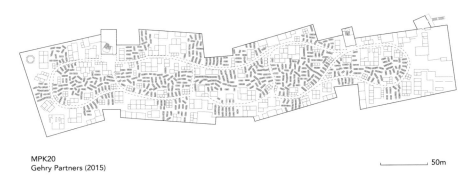

MPK20
Gehry Partners (2015)

50m

Figure 6.2 Facebook Menlo Park Building 20 (MPK20)
Gehry Partners, floorplan and desk locations redrawn by the author, 2019

Architectural critics have much to say (often mockingly) about Silicon Valley's vibrant interior finishes, free perks, jargon and unusual working practices: "an executive is practising tai chi by the cactus garden while another jiggles in a robotic massage chair nearby."[13] Accounts differ only subtly from the depiction in Eggers' novel of the campus as holiday club:

> I began to see these offices as cruise ships, happy heterotopias in which the sameness of work is made bearable by variety. You can choose your desk (sitting, standing, treadmill), your lunch (burrito, raw, sushi), your mode of transportation (walking, biking, shuttle, and if you must, car), your location (workstation, breakaway area, courtyard, all with Wi-Fi), but you need to be there and be available.[14]

But the aesthetic and cultural references synonymous with Silicon Valley architecture can overshadow the spatial tactics at work – which are not so much about trapping the employee or tricking them into working longer hours. The ongoing 'war for talent' is certainly at play; however, the assumption that perks and attention to well-being are a compensation for the tediousness of computer work is to miss the central premises of Silicon Valley culture. Employees are not shopping around to find the best remuneration for their skills; rather, they look for the company where they can do their best work.

This radically shifts amenities and working culture from operating as transactional to transformational. Instead of ameliorating monotony in work, perks are integrated with management practices premised on the belief that work itself is fulfilling and is even the route to self-actualisation. The amenities on offer remove barriers to being able to work for their employees, leaving them with more time and capacity to realise their full potential. The repetitive is made bearable by making company missions to 'change the world' tangible through the development of live projects with a global impact that connect seemingly inconsequential acts of updating code to effect.[15]

How buildings learn

The campus is the materialisation of lessons learned in research labs in the mid-20th century, a key prototype being the asbestos-clad Building 20 at MIT, a case study for Stewart Brand's 1994 book How Buildings Learn. An outcome of the layout of Building 20 is the serendipitous encounter – attributed to the dominance of lateral circulation in the low-rise building: "in a vertical layout with small floors, there is less research variety on each floor. Chance meetings in an elevator tend to terminate in the lobby, whereas chance meetings in a corridor tended to lead to technical discussions."[16] The horizontality of Silicon Valley campuses – while also a product of sprawl, planning restrictions on height and the genesis of the low-rise industrial type – is a specific aim in the design of Apple, Facebook and Google, who specify maximum square-footage of floorplates challenging the local Floor Area Ratio (FAR) limits.[17]

A proprietary polis

Facebook's MPK20 (Menlo Park Building 20) houses 2,700 desks in a non-hierarchical 430,000 square feet of continuous floor-space – a single room with no corner offices, no desks with-a-view and no executive washrooms. The architectural envelope is determined by interior logics, analogous to Kevin Roche and John Dinkeloo's sprawling fractal form to democratise Union Carbide's Connecticut headquarters through affording every office a view of the landscape.[18] Yet, unlike the Roche Dinkeloo project, ideas come from the companies themselves who have been incubating spatial experiments and gaming their working environments over years spent in industrial lots and business parks.

Apple Park brings together 12,000 people in one building over four loops terminating at a single cafeteria capable of seating 4,000 people at once – the culmination of Steve Jobs' theories about collaboration realised at Pixar in 1999. Google's original brief for the Bay View campus specified that no employee be more than a two-and-a-half-minute walk away from any other colleague. Proposals by Bjarke Ingels and Thomas Heatherwick for Charleston East and North Bayshore – terraced open workspaces underneath a vast canopied roof for around 3,000–5,000 workers – qualified for bonus FAR allocations. With their new campuses still under construction, Google has

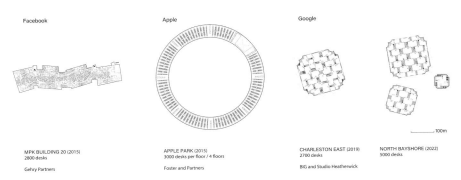

Figure 6.3 New Facebook, Apple and Google campuses, 1st floor, floorplans redrawn by the author, 2019

Figure 6.4 Facebook's Menlo Park campus massing, illustration by the author, 2019

constructed a small prototype in Sunnyvale to test the performance of open-plan working. At 1212 Bordeaux, a "giant mock-up that people can interact with,"[19] Google is – as well as assessing the impact of lighting, air quality and acoustics on the productivity – conducting experiments on the optimal density of employees on a single floor.

When Facebook announced plans to build a signature complex in 2011, architect Frank Gehry offered his services. Facebook initially said no – Gehry had to prove his worth to Zuckerberg whose first question to him was "Why would someone of your reputation want to do this?"[20] Gehry, usually appointed for his ability to deploy the Bilbao effect, was asked to tone down design flourishes.[21] Facebook said of the new Campus "It's better to think of it as a refinement of our current campus [rather] than a separate design altogether […] though it will no doubt have certain touches added by the Gehry team." One hundred thousand feet larger than MPK20 is the Gehry-designed MPK21 – another single floor office that further iterates on the concept, keeping elements of the interior architecture found in Facebook's earlier headquarters: the glass-walled conference rooms and bare walls waiting to be 'hacked' were features in the former Palo Alto office. Even the polished concrete floors with factory markings are not Gehry touches but part of the Gensler 2011 redesign of the Sun Microsystems complex.

Proprietary architecture

A series of buildings enclosing a green space is often a synecdoche of campus; however, the origin of the term campus is the Latin for field – its first documented use at Princeton in 1774 referred to the large field that separates the college from the town.[22] This proprietary separation of the tech-campus from the civic realm prefigures the considerable impact on the small cities they occupy: Apple owns or leases 67% of office space in Cupertino, while Google's initial campus expansion would have taken all the remaining zoned land in Mountain View. Campus conjures up an idyllic setting for work under the California sun; yet, it also brings gridlock, rising house prices and a shortage of space for small businesses outside the tech industry.

Although apparently premised on autonomy and self-sufficiency, the ecology of the campus is dependent upon the military–industrial–academic complex that transformed the Santa Clara Valley from apricot orchards into the world's foremost technology region – and the tech companies make the most of their strategic proximities with institutions and industries.[23] Plugged into the collegiate networks of the university, the research centre and defence contractors, the typology of campus consciously reproduces spatial programs from these environments within their architecture. While the canteen and green spaces are an obvious continuity of university life, the use of "war rooms"[24] and "all hands"[25] meetings is derived from factory logistics.

The all-hands meeting operates like a company 'town hall,' borrowed from civic forums the concept aims to transform the one-way communication of information down to workers from management into a two-way conversation. Employees can ask candid questions to the company – reinforcing their participation in and connection to the organisation's goals. But there is a second important layer to the 'all hands' gathering that further enlists the subjectivity of the tech worker as more than just stakeholder.

When Larry Page and Sergey Brin hold their weekly 'TGIF' (Thank God It's Friday) meeting at the Googleplex[26] and Mark Zuckerberg convenes all hands to the Full-Circle canteen, employees from the intern and software engineer, to the data scientist or art director, repeat a format that takes place on the factory floor of a major defence contractor in nearby Sunnyvale. Occupying the eastern edge of Moffett Airfield, where Google is building their Caribbean campus, is the Lockheed Martin Complex whose assembly lines once delivered the Trident and Polaris Inter Continental Ballistic Missile. Members at all levels of a production cell gather for their daily meeting, performing a protocol derived from the Toyota Production System (a combination of logistic, linguistic and socio-technical practices to assure quality through continuous incremental improvement).

In the factory, each and every employee, no matter their status, is required to come up with at least two actionable improvements to the process every month. At Facebook, anybody can submit a question directly to 'Mark' who will, it is reported, answer candidly about any aspect of the company's running. Zuckerberg also announces a fix-of-the-week – a "behind-the-scenes engineering fix or accomplishment that others may not be aware of that has made a difference."[27] The meeting format in both the factory and tech company is a process that enables – or rather demands – the active participation and engagement of all staff, reinforcing the idea that every small act or practical suggestion has the potential to contribute towards the company's success.

At Facebook, this is underpinned by the work of the Analogue Research Lab (ARL), an important mediator between the architecture and the occupiers of the space, the company culture and the employees and between the CEOs and the individual coding engineer. Begun as an employee initiative to take over an unused basement room at the Palo Alto campus for artistic projects, the ARL was set up to make tangible artworks and posters using old letter-press and printing equipment. During all hands meetings, runners will deliver notable quotes (usually from Zuckerberg or COO Sheryl Sandberg) to the lab – who will publish the 'mic-drop' moments directly as posters and paste them up around campus before the meeting is over.[28]

Where the meeting reinforces a sense of doing important work – small tasks are noticed and celebrated, anyone can contribute an idea – critique is welcome and even cultivated throughout the campus, contributing further to the unique collective

Figure 6.5 Location of the 'all hands' meetings at Facebook MPK20 and the Googleplex, plans redrawn by the author, 2019

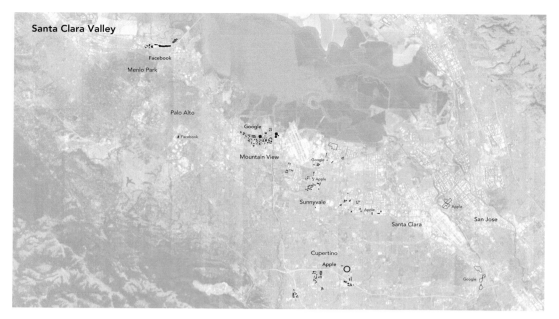

Figure 6.6 All buildings owned or leased by Apple, Facebook and Google overlaying a satellite image of Silicon Valley, illustration by the author, 2019

citizenry of the employees. As well as being a communications team for Facebook, ARL is an art studio and workshop where employees can try their hand at screen-printing their own posters to 'hack' the walls of the campus. Along with company slogans such as "MOVE FAST AND BREAK THINGS," "WHAT WOULD YOU DO IF YOU WEREN'T AFRAID" and "LEAN IN," a group or individual can use the printing press to reproduce political slogans supporting the cause of their choice. Fred Turner illustrates the incorporation of wider political issues into the company culture, documenting the posters at his visit to Facebook:

> "TAKE CARE OF MUSLIM BLACK WOMEN+FEMMES QUEER LATINX NATIVE IMMIGRANT P.O.C. TRANS DISABLED INCARCERATED L.G.B.T.Q.+ FRIENDS FAMILY & COMMUNITY." Another [poster] features the motto of Act Up, "Silence=Death," underneath a large pink triangle. And here and there, prominent among the maybe seventy posters in all, you can see portraits [...] of Holocaust survivor and author Eli Wiesel, and even labour leader and co-founder of the United Farm Workers Dolores Huerta.[29]

Turner concludes that images of activists and Black Lives Matter marchers are "hollowed of the hard work of movement organizing."[30] At Facebook, the act of screen-printing might take longer than a digital like; nonetheless, it "render[s] political dissent into just another mode of self-expression."[31] No longer required to provide only labour, the employee is expected to bring their full selves to work,[32] demonstrating their advocacy at a company that maintains their political impartiality.

Louise Mozingo argues that the campus is "a nostalgic copy of the suburban architecture of 20th Century corporate giants (IBM, Bell, Union Carbide and General Motors) recalling a post-war era of de-urbanisation, white-flight and retreat from civic engagement in the United States."[33] While the campus has its roots in the mid-20th century, it is the West Coast upstarts that sought to challenge the corporations' approach to management that has had the most profound influence on the campus type. There is, as Mozingo observes, a distinct political and civic impact of the campus on Bay Area cities, as the companies that claim to 'make the world a better place' create a separate polis within their walls – a proprietary polis.

In 2020, the tech campus articulates a new relational aesthetics of Silicon Valley that organises more than expresses; the relations between the employees and the company, between the employees with one another and between those inside the campus, and those outside. The collective subjectivity of the elite, highly educated, mostly white and male employees – believing themselves to be politically astute, critically aware and engaged in highly important and impactful work – is mediated through the architecture of the campus. From the provision of amenities, the elicitation of productivity and sense of belonging, the cultivation of collaboration, to the sense of purpose and meaning the employees get from their work, and even existential critique and political discourse – the campus contains it all.

In the proprietary polis, a high level of global political awareness and involvement is explicitly cultivated, while each company maintains that they are merely a technology or platform. Apple, Facebook and Google celebrate their singular achievements of rising to corporate power, as if by accident, by hustling in garages and dorm-rooms – as the volume of land leased, bought and developed by them transforms the entire Valley. As each company's success is indebted to what Annalee Saxenian calls the 'Regional Advantage' of the Californian military–industrial–academic complex,[34] the campus itself is a disavowal of the localised context in which they are headquartered.

Post-Covid

The global pandemic has prompted immediate changes in work, raising questions about the viability of the vast complexes favoured by Silicon Valley: indeed, several press articles cite the 'death' of open-plan working. However, while Twitter announced that homeworking may become permanent, Facebook and Google have been cautious about declaring the end to the campus. Short term, the future is remote-working, but sustaining team cohesion and the sense of belonging that characterises the companies' successes is more challenging. At Facebook, half may continue working from home long term, and at Google, CEO Sundar Pichai maintains that the team cohesion underpinning effective homeworking is built on initial physical team-building and will diminish with time.

With so much invested in cultures of belonging and serendipitous connections, the fate of the proprietary polis is not yet sealed. Open-plan buildings can be readily adapted to lower density occupation, and the campus affords tightly controlled access. Tech companies have both the physical and tech infrastructure – as well as the will – to create a proprietary bio-polis.

Notes

1. Reyner Banham, "Silicon Style," *Architectural Review*, Vol. 169 (May 1981): 284.
2. Reyner Banham, "Arts in Society: Down in the Vale of Chips," *New Society*, Vol. 56, no. 971 (25 June 1981): 532.
3. Banham, "Down in the Vale of Chips."
4. Gwendolyn Wright, "The Virtual Architecture of Silicon Valley," *Journal of Architectural Education*, Vol. 54, no. 2 (November 2000): 89.
5. Facebook's MPK20 is also influenced by Gehry's own architecture studio.
6. Facebook MPK20 holds 2,700 in one room, Apple Park 2 has 12,000 in a four-storey building, and Google's Charleston East is expected to house 5,000 employees over two floors.
7. Bruce Fallick, Charles A. Fleischmann, and James B. Rebitzer, "Job Hopping in Silicon Valley: Some Evidence Concerning the Micro-Foundations of a High Technology Cluster," *The Review of Economics and Statistics*, Vol. 88, no. 3 (August 2006): 472–481, 472, 474.
8. Turner, *From Counterculture to Cyberculture: Stewart Brand, the Whole Earth Network, and the Rise of Digital Utopianism* (Chicago, IL: University of Chicago Press, 2008), 150.
9. Hewlett Packard, *The HP Way: Hewlett-Packard Company Report* (1977), http://www.hp.com/hpinfo/abouthp/histnfacts/publications/measure/pdf/1977_07.pdf.
10. Wright, "The Virtual Architecture of Silicon Valley," 89.
11. Gideon Kunda, *Engineering Culture: Control and Commitment in a High-Tech Corporation* (Philadelphia: Temple University Press, 2009), 90, 71, 77.
12. Kunda, *Engineering Culture*, 8–9, 67, and Hewlett Packard, *The HP Way*, 8–9.
13. Oliver Wainwright, "Inside Facebook and Friends: A Rare Tour around Tech's Mind-boggling HQs," *The Guardian* (22 May 2016), https://www.theguardian.com/artanddesign/2016/may/22/nap-pods-and-rooftop-parks-how-silicon-valley-is-reinventing-the-office.
14. Alexandra Lange, *The Dot-Com City: Silicon Valley Urbanism* (Moscow: Strelka Press, 2012), 15.
15. During the Arab Spring, Google launched an automated voicemail-to-twitter application in collaboration with Twitter that allowed protestors to circumvent the social media blackout implemented by President Mubarak. Egyptian protestors could communicate with the world through social media by calling a phone number and leaving a voice message, which would be automatically tweeted with a hashtag of the country. Gabe LaMonica and Taryn Fixel, "Starting a Revolution with Technology," *CNN*, 17 June 2011, http://edition.cnn.com/2011/TECH/innovation/06/17/mesh.technology.revolution.
16. Brand, How Buildings Learn, 27.
17. Allison Arieff, Benjamin Grant, Sarah Jo Szambelan, Jennifer Warburg, "Rethinking the Corporate Campus: The Next Bay Area Workplace," SPUR Report (April 2017): 30.
18. Reinhold Martin, *Utopia's Ghost: Architecture and Postmodernism, Again* (Minneapolis: University of Minnesota Press, 2010), 132–136.
19. Lydia Lee, "Google at 1212 Bordeaux by Parabola," Architecture Record, 4 June, 2018, https://www.architecturalrecord.com/articles/13435-google-at-1212-bordeaux-by-parabola.
20. Paul Goldberger, *Building Art: The Life and Work of Frank Gehry* (New York: Alfred A Knopf, 2015), 410.
21. Ryan Tate, "Facebook Vs. Frank Gehry," *Wired Magazine*, 29 March 2013, https://www.wired.com/2013/03/facebook-vs-frank-gehry/.
22. "Campus," *OED Online* (Oxford University Press, March 2017), accessed 24 April 2017, http://www.oed.com/view/Entry/ 26840? Reinhold Martin and Karambadi Baxi propose that "a landscape with multiple tenants is a 'park,' while a similar complex with a single tenant is a 'campus.'" Reinhold Martin, Karambadi Baxi, *Multi-National City: Architectural Itineraries* (Barcelona: Actar, 2007), 31.
23. Annalee Saxenian, *Regional Advantage: Culture and Competition in Silicon Valley and Route* (Cambridge, MA: Harvard University Press, 1996), 128.
24. The War Room is drawn directly from Toyota, an "Obeya" is a space for meetings, where all the information needed is pasted around the edges of the room, as in a military operations room.
25. The "all hands" meeting has a long history in Silicon Valley and was one of the key management principles of Intel. Tom Wolfe, "The Tinkerings of Robert Noyce: How the Sun Rose on Silicon Valley," *Esquire Magazine* (December 1983), 360.
26. Google recently announced, after tensions between employees and management, to radically alter the format of the meetings to minimise leaks and controversial questions – they will be held once a month instead of weekly.
27. Kurt Wagner, "Mark Zuckerberg Shares Facebook's Secrets with all His Employees, and almost None of it Leaks," *Recode.net*, 5 January 2017, accessed 25 June 2018, https://www.recode.net/2017/1/5/13987714/mark-zuckerberg-facebook-qa-weekly.
28. Katherine Schwab, "Want a glimpse of Facebook's soul in 2019? Look at its internal propaganda lab," *FastCompany.com* (20 Feb 2019), https://www.fastcompany.com/90308216/want-a-glimpse-of-facebooks-soul-in-2019-look-at-its-internal-propaganda-lab.
29. Fred Turner, "The arts at Facebook: An Aesthetic Infrastructure for Surveillance Capitalism," *Poetics* (March 2018), 53.

30 Turner, "The arts at Facebook," 56.
31 Turner, 56.
32 An inspirational quote attributed to Sheryl Sandberg is Bring Your Whole Self to Work. "I don't believe we have a professional self Monday through Friday and a real self the rest of the time. It is all professional and it is all personal" Sandberg quoted in Sarah Frier, "How Sheryl Sandberg's Sharing Manifesto Drives Facebook," *Bloomberg.com* (27 April 2017), https://www.bloomberg.com/news/features/2017-04-27/how-sheryl-sandberg-s-sharing-manifesto-drives-facebook.
33 *OED Online* (Oxford University Press, March 2017), http://www.oed.com/view/Entry/26840?
34 Annalee Saxenian, *Regional Advantage: Culture and Competition in Silicon Valley and Route* (Cambridge, MA: Harvard University Press, 1996), 128.

Chapter 7

Hyper-gentrification and the urbanisation of suburbia

Ross Exo Adams, Tahl Kaminer, Maroš Krivý, Leonard Ma, Karin Matz, Timothy Moore, Helen Runting and Rutger Sjögrim

Suburban belts and outer-city areas in global cities such as Vancouver, London and New York are undergoing little noticed structural, social and formal changes. Demographics, local cultures, lifestyles, morphologies and densities are transforming in reaction to the exodus of both poor and middle class from the inner-city areas. The exodus is brought about by extreme forms of gentrification, referred to as 'super-gentrification,' 'hyper-gentrification' or 'third,' 'fourth' or 'fifth'-wave gentrification. Of these forms of gentrification, we argue, hyper-gentrification, as discussed in this chapter, is specifically the result of a process in which housing has become 'financialised.' All three issues – the transformation of the outer-city, the hyper-gentrification of the inner-city and the financialisation of housing – are current processes and rarely brought together under the same explanatory umbrella. Our research group aims to address this lack by interrogating the changes taking place in European global cities.

Our AHRA panel included six initial forays into this territory, three of which discussed hyper-gentrification and financialisation, while the others took a closer look at outer-city areas of Amsterdam, Berlin, London and Stockholm. In this chapter, we outline some of our preliminary hypotheses and initial findings. In particular, we are interested in showing not only how abstract economic forces shape our cities but also the specific manners in which these manifest themselves in different cities – namely, the argument that while the forces operating on European global cities may be similar, as a result of path dependencies their outcomes are distinctive and particular.

Hyper-gentrification

The diverse and often contradictory uses of 'hyper' and 'super' gentrification share an understanding that the process in question is one in which already gentrified inner-city neighbourhoods are undergoing a new phase of gentrification. This process involves sky-rocketing real-estate values that are beyond the reach of the vast majority of locals, including many well-off middle-class residents (Figure 7.1). Hyper-gentrification is more than simply a new phase in the process, as it undermines the tenets of some of the leading gentrification theories, as will be explained below.

Discussions of super-gentrification so far emphasised a change in the figure of the gentrifier – no longer 'the artist' or 'the yuppie,'[1] the gentrifier is now a senior manager in the financial sector, can purchase expensive housing in gentrified neighbourhoods without need for a mortgage and employs a professional team in modifying and upgrading the home.[2] This figure has been expanded to cover all 'super rich' individuals investing in properties abroad, whether employed in the financial sector or not.[3]

We find this discussion to be of limited value and will instead develop our argument from more recent contributions that focus on the flows of capital across borders instead of on the figure of the gentrifier.[4] Such a focus not only bypasses the all too common and problematic individuation of responsibility typical of anti-gentrification campaigns and of contemporary society more generally (e.g. the discussion of climate crisis and individual responsibility) but also offers, we believe, a more rigorous understanding of the key processes taking place. In order to differentiate this process from

Figure 7.1 Anti-gentrification posters in Hackney Wick, London, 2018
Photograph courtesy of Anna Bateson.

the one focused on the gentrifier (which we refer to here as 'super-gentrification'), we use the term 'hyper-gentrification.'

The two most influential gentrification theories, the 'consumerist' explanation by David Ley and the 'productivist' rent-gap theory of Neil Smith, as well as the theories that have been derived and developed from these, all presume a moment of equilibrium or saturation, a moment in which gentrification peaks.[5] For Ley, this would be achieved once the new social group of white collar employees has fully replaced working class, migrants and poor in inner-city areas; for Smith, this would happen once the 'rent gap' vanishes – that is, once the real-estate values rise to the level in which the potential land rent of a plot is fully reflected in the real-estate value. Hyper-gentrification undermines these theories, as a local rent gap becomes a minor concern in these global processes and Ley's white-collar employees and their cultural preferences become irrelevant. A neighbourhood can be hyper-gentrified whether homes are populated by the super-rich owners, renting students or left empty. The process becomes dependent on international flows of capital, surpluses and crises elsewhere and hence partially or completely detached from local earnings.

The financialisation of housing

What then are the 'flows of capital' driving hyper-gentrification? While we tend to think of gentrification processes in terms of displacement by increasingly wealthy classes of elites, the ease with which capital enters the city now extends beyond direct investment into real estate. Through increasingly sophisticated instruments of finance, investments into global cities can now become an increasingly abstract matter. While the entry of financial capital already began in the 1970s, these early investments were primarily focused on the supply of mortgage finance. Mortgages, once securitised into assets that are sold on stock markets, promised safe and stable return for investors as there was an underlying physical asset that could be foreclosed on in the event of default. Mortgage finance became the bedrock on which the current financialised economy is built, serving as the underlying asset for a range of financial securities and derivative products that have driven economic growth for the past half-decade.[6]

In the wake of the 2008 financial crisis, driven in no small part by the growing distance between mortgage-backed securities and their underlying assets, real estate became a target for investment not just by individual landlords, but by international private equity firms. With a dearth of profitable investment opportunities in equities and bonds in the aftermath of the crisis, firms such as Vanguard and Blackrock expanded their portfolios of 'alternative assets,' raising capital by issuing new shares and using their access to credit to purchase foreclosed assets of mortgage default at substantial discounts. Aided by the booming property management sector, these financial entities operate in effect as secondary landlords, subjecting local rental housing stock to the demands of global financial markets. In effect, anyone can be a landlord by owning shares in portfolios of alternative assets. The expansion into securitised rental housing investment has become the standard for institutional investors as well. Since 2015, PFA, Denmark's largest commercial pension and the fifth largest in Europe, has more than tripled its holdings in alternative assets. Earlier this year, it purchased a real estate portfolio worth over 1 billion euros in Berlin.[7] This process, dubbed by Raquel Rolnik as the 'new wave of financialisation,' has proven extremely lucrative.[8] With limited social housing provision – destroyed in neoliberal reforms and prior gentrification cycles – renting from these financial entities is often the only option in the residential market.

As wages stagnate, real-estate prices are driven to unimaginable heights, bearing little relation to the realities of their use. Investment-driven real-estate growth in global cities is an increasingly abstract matter. Buyers now no longer need to even visit the physical location of their assets, but rather, as in any abstract investment, scrutinise them based on a range of parameters such as their proximity to city centres, to major transport and internationally defined landmarks or the availability of high-end luxury amenities. The growing popularity of investment in global cities as a place to deposit capital, a phenomenon Andy Yan describes as the 'hedge city,' is predicated on the perceived stability and openness of internationally recognised cities such as London, New York or Vancouver.[9] The 2008 financial crisis also exposed two types of investment: investment seeking safety and lower risk, focused on the gentrified inner-cities of global cities and more speculative investments seeking opportunities for higher returns in conditions of risk elsewhere. The latter, in effect, can be described as investment in areas in which a large rent gap – a global rent gap – has been created. Often enough, the same investors are involved in both as a means of mitigating risk.[10]

The urbanisation of suburbia

A key outcome of the hyper-gentrification of inner-cities has been the exodus of out-priced middle-class residents. In earlier gentrification cycles, it was the poor, the unemployed and migrants who were dislocated, primarily from areas that used to house the unskilled labourers of industrial society in proximity to their places of work. One of the destinations of this exodus has been the outer-city, the suburban belt of the global city (Figure 7.2).

The relocation from city centre to outer-city is a familiar phenomenon; yet, the current process is distinctive from earlier phases. The large-scale suburbanisation of the 1950s had a strong Fordist anchoring: factories relocating from city centre to periphery in order to realise state-of-the-arts assembly lines in one-floor, large 'warehouse' buildings; unionised, skilled labourers demonstrating their ascent into middle class by moving to suburbia to live in detached homes; the dour conditions of neglected inner-city slums, primarily housing unskilled – and increasingly unemployed – labourers and poor.[11]

Of course, even as 'the return to the city' (of capital, of middle class) gathered pace in the 1980s and 1990s, many young city-centre renters chose to relocate to the periphery where larger homes with gardens could be purchased for less,[12] particularly when they decided to 'settle' – marry, have children. But in both these cases, the choices made by middle-class individuals tapped into and reflected society's own

Figure 7.2 A suburban street in London's Thamesmead area, 2018
Photograph courtesy of Anna Bateson.

perception of warranted forms of living: suburbia as the symbol of 'middle classness' in the 1950s; suburbia as 'the right place' for family life in the 1980s. Now, it is the inner city that is valorised by the post-Fordist, post-industrial society; yet, the economically 'productive' middle class, like the 'unproductive' poor, are being priced out from it.

It is little wonder that housing has become in many cities and countries a major political issue in recent times. Whereas the earlier cycles of gentrification were seen as a minor, local issue, 'gentrification' and housing are now major news items. The dislocated poor and middle class, unlike their progenitors, have not embraced suburban lifestyle – a lifestyle no longer valorised by society – but instead have invested in urbanising the outer city. Artists and artist studios, chic cafes, cycling paths and enhanced 'street' life are all emerging in parts of the global city that were until recently dormitory areas associated with cars, detached homes, back gardens and barbeques. Some cities, such as London,[13] have specifically identified the suburban belt as a focus of future housing and densification. The process underway will erode over time the differences between the current inner and outer city: in typologies, morphologies, culture, politics and lifestyle. Hence, we call this process the 'urbanisation of suburbia.' Currently, it is restricted to those cities suffering from hyper-gentrification, that is, global cities; yet, in certain conditions, it could spread elsewhere.

Amsterdam, Berlin, London, Stockholm

In Amsterdam, a 'pioneer' of cultural-led gentrification and a city in which planners and city council still hold significant sway, large-scale urban renewal projects in the van Eesteren-planned western garden suburbs and in Amsterdam Noord have involved reduction in social housing availability, new build and a deliberate deployment of artist-run-spaces, artist studios and cultural events as a means of improving the reputation of the areas. In effect, the city council has applied to outer-city neighbourhoods the same regeneration strategies used in the inner city in the 1990s and 2000s. Densities in these areas are rising, and lifestyles previously limited to city centre and inner city are now integrated into the suburban condition, as evidenced by new 'urban beaches,' laidback cafes, a 'cool' student hotel and artist spaces – all previously absent in such areas but now ubiquitous.

In Berlin, for decades a city with limited available jobs and low salaries, its recent job and population growth can be attributed to the international image of the city, brought about by its vibrant cultural sector – sustained through the housing availability and low rents in the inner city. Yet, the low property prices and international image have also encouraged international investment in housing since the 2008 crisis, highlighting a rent gap within and beyond Germany. The combination of the 'safe' German economy and real-estate 'opportunities' in Berlin was catnip to investors. Some of the largest owners of residential properties in the city are private companies with ties to finance capital. The largest among these is Deutsche Wohnen, a subsidiary of Deutsche Bank, which owned in 2011 around 115,500 homes.[14] In total, large companies (companies with more than 1000 homes) own a majority of rental homes in the city. Strong corporate interests, a powerful interventionist city council and a radical anti-gentrification movement have created a uniquely volatile situation.

In inner-city London, the combination of high property prices and the effects of austerity on local council budgets have led to the systematic demolition of post-war council housing, affecting the 'secure' tenures of council tenants and owner-occupiers alike. As a result of the housing crisis, the poor and the middle class have been relocating further afield, with the outer-city boroughs as a key destination. Many of these leafy, suburban neighbourhoods are currently undergoing dramatic change, with high-density residential towers invading the territory of low-rise and low density.

In Stockholm's suburbs, which follow a ring-like pattern that see early modernist structures give way to prefabricated post-war housing and eventually villa areas, densification strategies include the insertion of non-suburban typologies into the outer city. Apartment buildings, towers and perimeter-block structures challenge the scale of 'infill.' As such, these insertions of alterity into the uniformity of suburbia must be disguised, reducing their presence and visual impact by means of 'camouflage.' Multi-family housing behaves as suburban villas, towers are hidden behind balconies and built form is granularised, stepped, fragmented and decorated: densification is deemed necessary, but the political backlash must be averted, and any link to modernism – with its attendant social project of housing for all – severed. All these examples indicate the different trajectories underway in Europe's global cities; all point to similar issues and pressures and identify changes underway in the outer cities; yet, their manifestation is nevertheless particular and distinct due to disparate conditions.

Gentrification and 'collective life'

A point of departure for us is the understanding of the city as a political community, as a means and form of social and spatial organisation. In this sense, the dynamics of the global city have seen its spatial and social forms increasingly shaped not by the political community, but by abstract, international pressures and forces driven by global imbalances. Finance capital, in conditions of minimal regulation, easily 'flows' from one market to another, invested, reinvested or de-invested in manners in which traditional commodities or labour cannot. The reconfiguration of housing as a financial commodity necessarily effects the collective life of the city – it diminishes housing as a key social resource; it de-valorises housing's use value; it infuses increased precariousness into the lives of individuals, communities and cities. It reduces local governments' capacity to shape the city. And, as we will show, it is also remaking the form and culture of cities, urbanising suburban areas and radically transforming the urban and suburban demographics, with increased diversity of ethnicity and class emerging in the outer city while the inner city is becoming, at least on the level of class and age, more homogeneous and uniform.

Notes

1. Neil Smith, 'Of Yuppies and Housing: Gentrification, Social Restructuring, and the Urban Dream', Environment and Planning D, *Society and Space*, Vol. 5 (1987), pp. 151–172; Rosalyn Deutsche; Cara Gendel Ryan, 'The Fine Art of Gentrification', *October*, Vol. 31 (Winter, 1984), pp. 91–111.
2. Loretta Lees, 'Super-Gentrification: The Case of Brooklyn Heights, New York City', *Urban Studies*, Vol. 40, No. 12 (November 2003), pp. 2487–2509; Tim Butler and Loretta Lees, 'Super-Gentrification in Barnsbury, London: Globalization and Gentrifying Global Elites at the Neighbourhood Level', *Transactions of the Institute of British Geographers*, New Series, Vol. 31, No. 4 (December 2006), pp. 467–487.
3. Loretta Lees, Hyun Bang Shin, Ernesto Lopez Morales, *Planetary Gentrification* (Cambridge: Polity 2016).
4. Manuel B. Aalbers, 'Revisiting "The Changing State of Gentrification" Introduction to the Forum: From Third to Fifth-Wave Gentrification', *Tijdschrift voor Economische en Sociale Geografie*, No. 1 (2019), pp. 1–11, DOI: 10.1111/tesg.12332, Vol. 110.
5. See, for example, David Ley, 'Alternative Explanations for Inner-City Gentrification: A Canadian Assessment', *Annals of the Association of American Geographers*, Vol. 76, No. 4 (December 1986), pp. 521–535; Eric Clark, 'The Order and Simplicity of Gentrification – a Political Challenge', in *The Gentrification Reader*, edited by Loretta Lees, Tom Slater and Elvin Wyly (London; New York: Routledge), pp. 24–29; Neil Smith, *The New Urban Frontier: Gentrification and the Revanchist City* (London; New York: Routledge, 1996); Loretta Lees, Tom Slater, Elvin Wyly, *Gentrification* (New York; London: Routledge, 2008).
6. See Adam Tooze, *Crashed: How a Decade of Financial Crisis Changed the World* (New York: Viking, 2018).
7. Richard Lowe, 'Danish Pension Fund PFA Buys More than €1bn of German Real Estate', *IPE Real Assets*, 13 August 2018, https://realassets.ipe.com/news/danish-pension-fund-pfa-buys-more-than-1bn-of-german-real-estate/realassets.ipe.com/news/danish-pension-fund-pfa-buys-more-than-1bn-of-german-real-estate/10026206.fullarticle (accessed 13 March 2020).
8. Raquel Rolnik, *Urban Warfare: Housing under the Empire of Finance* (London: Verso, 2019).
9. James Surowiecki, 'Real Estate Goes Global', *New Yorker*, May 26, 2014, https://www.newyorker.com/magazine/2014/05/26/real-estate-goes-global (accessed 13 March 2020).
10. For some relevant discussions, see Michael Byrne, '"Asset Price Urbanism" and Financialization After the Crisis: Ireland's National Asset Management Agency', *International Journal of Urban and Regional Research*, DOI:10.1111/1468-2427.12331, pp. 31–45; Christopher Niedt and Brett Christophers, 'Value at Risk in the Suburbs: Eminent Domain and the Geographical Politics of the US Foreclosure Crisis', *International Journal of Urban and Regional Research*, DOI:10.1111/1468-2427.12413 pp. 1094–110.
11. Peter Marcuse, 'Do Cities Have a Future?', in *The Imperiled Economy: Through the Safety Net*, edited by R. Chery (New York: Union of Radical Political Economists, 1988), pp. 189–200.

12 Considering the skyrocketing prices of inner-city and city centre homes today, it is easy to overlook the fact that prices in city centre were higher than elsewhere also before the later gentrification cycles, particularly in areas in proximity to transport and good schools.
13 GLA, 'London Plan 2016' (London: GLA, 2016), p. 13, https://www.london.gov.uk/what-we-do/planning/london-plan/current-london-plan/london-plan-2016-pdf (accessed 21 February 2020).
14 Savills, 'Ownership Structure of the Residential Market' (Savills Germany, 2019), https://pdf.euro.savills.co.uk/germany-research/eng-2019/spotlight-ownership-structure-of-the-german-residential-market.pdf (accessed 13 March 2020).

Chapter 8

The dubious high street

Distinctiveness, gentrification and social value

Aleks Catina

In the words of the former Mayor of London, Boris Johnson, "the high street is the heartbeat of London's business community. It epitomises the distinct culture and character of our city to visitors from across the world."[1] This statement introduces one of the two Greater London Authority (GLA) publications from 2014, which both present a summative and somewhat self-celebratory assessment of the strategies suggested to business and local authorities for the regeneration of London's high streets. They overlap, not very coherently, on what it means for high streets to reinvent themselves, so as to be 'welcoming, diverse, distinct and growing.' Distinctiveness is mostly related to an idea of regeneration as spectacle. The 'aesthetic language' of the renewed high street experience alludes to a contemporary version of what Barbara Jones has called the "powerful traditions encompassing shop keeping in England, governing display, packaging and publicity" (Figure 8.1) to frame the stage of 'social and cultural significance' of these contemporary public spaces.[2] Based on the above, recommendations are made to independent traders and local authorities, such as a list of designers they can employ. Further, casual reference is made to a desired contemporary appearance, detailing a rich material palette to be considered in the renewal and rebranding of shop fronts.

To combat the populist agenda of creating literal *Potemkin Villages*, whose colourful facades aim to disguise the real economic state of London's high streets, many architects stress the 'local' aspect of the regeneration as a platform for architectural practice that can be experimental and socially responsible.[3] To enable effective criticism of the idea of social architecture in this scenario, it is important to understand the concepts that underpin the language of guidance documentation and the brief and

Figure 8.1 The owners adorned this example of a traditionally decorated high street shop front on Blackstock Road, London, N4, in an idiosyncratic manner. Examples of these spontaneous practices, described by Barbara Jones in *The Unsophisticated Arts* (1951), are few and far between in London. This old shop is located in an area which has recently been identified for renewal and regeneration. In 2017, Islington Council published the *Finsbury Park Shops Visual Merchandising Workbook* (Office S&M). Professional designers and architects were hired to generate a visual shift, in keeping with recent guidance by the GLA. Can a centralised drive towards sophistication reproduce an authentic, sustainable high street?

Photograph taken by the author, 2020

how they have evolved. The gap between an understanding of distinctiveness in theory and in practice is symptomatic of the *wicked problem* of the high street.[4]

Distinct places

The most important question in relation to London's high streets is are they really 'dying' at all, in a social sense? Griffiths and others (2008, 1155–1188) have argued that that principles conducive to the social sustainability agenda need to be based on the re-discovery rather than the alteration of the urban realm.[5] The economic impact of planning policies in the 1980s, the emergence of the online economy and the financial, political and health uncertainties clearly impact on the rate of shop vacancies, changing consumer behaviour, etc. The current measures implemented on social spaces in an attempt to counter the spread of Covid-19 can be seen as the latest chapter in a narrative that is bound to redefine the future experience of the high street as well as impact on the prospect of its economic renewal.

On a historical timeline spanning back to the economic depressions of the late 20th century, it has been argued that the core social functions that high streets perform have resiliently adapted to changing circumstances. The most in-depth urban realm studies on the high street therefore resist an emphasis on an ideal model and derive their conclusions about future sustainability on a loose-fit model, which embraces the difference and peculiarity of places. The 'link-place' model is based on a positive appraisal of the mature mixed-use street's potential for continuous social and economic adaptability.[6] Simply put, the report proposes that wider infrastructural considerations around access and traffic flow paired with a bespoke treatment and re-evaluation of the physical environment can guide effective policies of renewal. The process of *rediscovering* (rather than re-inventing) hereby aims to foreground the importance of the resilient social-economic structures that opportunistically inhabit existing spaces as the basis for future improvements.[7] Validation for such assertions of resilience can also be found in sources predating the academic literature of the last decade, for instance, in the description of Dalston Lane at the height of the recession in the 1990s.[8] Surprisingly, many elements echoed in later scholarly studies regarding sustainability, and principles of resilience are described by mere observation of the urban realm, even in the state of 'blight.' The lesson from this kind of anecdotal evidence of urban survival and adaptation is that distinctiveness cannot be measured by the character of a physical environment alone, but must include the way in which social and economic ecologies evolve and express their presence within it. Upon close ethnographic and geographical study, these high street ecologies or networks reveal that the cornerstones of social sustainability and inclusion are barely understood by planning authorities who often aspire to an unattainable homogenisation based on image-focused design thinking.[9]

Politics of distinctiveness

"Banality has taken root like a relative from abroad invited to stay because their foreignness seemed interesting, before realising they were tiresome and refused to leave."[10] The New Economic Foundation (NEF) 2005 report on 'clone towns' introduced a definition of 'distinctiveness' that has influenced the vocabulary of subsequent policy documents. The central assumption is that the visual culture of local independent trade can play a role in renewing the 'dying high street' the identity of which has been eroded by generically designed outlets of multi-national chains lacking in cultural resonance of what the NEF's report has dubbed 'home towns.' In this context, distinctiveness denotes the added social value that independent trade offers to the social experience of the public realm. In opposition to the globalist agenda, the NEF perspective defines the social value of such imagery as an expression of belonging, enabling the formation of social bonds or self-organisation in guild-like grass-root structures.

An alternative, market-oriented perspective, embraced by successive Conservative UK governments, argues that high street decline is the product of out-of-town retail developments and could be reserved if local authorities enable local stakeholders to mimic the strategies of big businesses, structured around the expressed needs of a local customer base.[11] The former NEF approach emphasises the added interpersonal experience value of independent trade on mixed-use street. The latter Conservative approach stems from the maxim that 'local people know best' when it comes to goods and services provided, and that self-management by local interest groups will implement change according to their best knowledge and business sense.[12] These influential propositions, despite originating in opposing political sides, both weigh in on socio-economic renewal by informing concepts of distinctiveness, as seen in the introduction, vis-à-vis the broader idea of high street regeneration.

NEF has been criticised for projecting on a restorative nostalgia for the 'ideal' high street of the home town.[13] On the other hand, its suggested political identity of independents operating as a collective and across neighbouring planning authorities holds the possibility of different socio-economic relations within that appeals to architectural modes of thinking about the urban realm. The map of the *East London Trader's Guild* (ELTG), lovingly illustrated by Adam Dant, captures this idea in one evocative image. Supported by the NEF, the ELTG's vision of an interest group of traders expanding across local authority boundaries spurs a sense of grass-root self-organisation and collective consciousness.[14] The map can be read as a survey of issues around which independent traders organise locally (for instance, the cluster of the 'guardians of the arches' behind Haggerston Station). The cover reads: "A map of small businesses for those who seek quality, distinctiveness and character." Only at closer inspection, one will be prompted to read the ELTG map as a geographically distorted record of an emerging socio-economic pattern, which, over three editions, traces the migration of affluent shoppers from London's economic core to the suburbs.

Sophistication and reference

"The projects are significant in enhancing the distinctiveness of Blackhorse Lane and creating a diverse, mixed neighbourhood."[15] The future of the high street as a place of re-imagining socio-economic relations – based on the notion of distinctiveness promoted by the NEF concept of the quality of the home town – has become the dominant reference for design practice to pick up, even in suburban areas of London where distinctiveness can be applied to social cohesion based on the common experience of migration. The allusion to the dominant appearance of the historical British high street 'with a twist' offers design professionals a platform to market their services by reclaiming the unsophisticated arts of visual merchandise of the shop front for the 21st century. This development marks an expansion of the cultural field of production into the formerly spontaneous practice of decorating the exterior of the shop. With professional expertise, come sophistication and taste regarding the specific appearance of distinctiveness and character. In terms of visual strategy of place-making, distinctiveness can be used as prompt or as a culturally specific signifier. Rather than serving any means of political consciousness envisioned by the NEF, it can be employed to 'sell housing,' for example, by manufacturing an image of exclusivity.[16] As such, the cultural reference maintains its currency on the regeneration agenda.

Scott's statement illustrates how architects tend to conflate cosmetic improvement with social value. The notion of creating or re-creating communities through regeneration underpins the pseudo-scientific methodology of place-making.[17] This is the frame for the casual conceptualisation of distinctiveness in guidance documentation for high street regeneration. The mapping of the physical possibilities and opportunities of a site falls within the realm of architectural expertise. Scott's artistic attempt to include the mapping of existing socio-economic conditions does not lend itself to the same architectural design thinking that can lead to an improvement of the physical appearance of the urban realm. As Patrick Wright found in the ruins Dalston Lane in East London in the 1990s, the high street, pushed to the margin of extinction by market forces, tends to resiliently persist as social form of peculiar networks long after its visual appeal has faded. Wright observes that the unsophisticated form seems to endure precisely because it is not designed but is organically defined within the discarded urban fabric. In other words, the principles of resilience are structurally inherent to the social network that adapts to a particular physical setting over time. They are neither brought about nor scaffolded by the artificiality of design thinking that centres on image-making.

The common aphorism that each high street is different (London alone boasts 600), and the realisation that 'selling stuff' is but one aspect of its socio-economic viability has not yet informed the complexity and social dimension of the definition concept of distinctiveness.[18] As a result, the social high street regeneration can be linked to the potential of 'creeping gentrification,' whereby success is measured by economic affluence, signalled by sophisticated appearance. It is not that the concept of distinctiveness can unlock the wicked problem of the high street; the ongoing, galloping decline of high streets points towards a validation of assumptions that no place-specific design interventions will yield sustainable socio-economic effect.[19] However, if the aim of architectural practice is to engage with the social reality underlying the problem of the experience of the public realm, distinctiveness can be seen a critical starting point of a wider review of what we talk about when we talk about the social role high streets play outside London's Central Activity Zone.

The paradox of affluence

Policy-orientated publications by governing bodies tend to equate success with affluence. This can be illustrated on the persistent use of precedents of 'popular and distinctive' high streets that often present decontextualised snapshots rather than an evolving picture of social relations. The postcode E5 in Hackney, London, is an example of an area that has experienced radical social change over the last decade. The ongoing gentrification has had an impact; many long-term habitants from the area have moved on, selling up or being squeezed out by galloping rents. However, it is these places that are repeatedly drawn on to exemplify the 'high street for all' in successive publications by the Greater London Authority and others (Portas Report, 2011), which point to E5 as a lesson in social value, exemplary governance and business success.[20] While these observations are by no means incorrect, they each promote a 'before and after' perspective where the critical factor is essentially, radical gentrification (Figure 8.2). On the one hand, a representative historical snapshot of three adjacent shops indicates the transformation that has taken place in Lower Clapton: the car spares supplier, a run-down betting shop and the long-abandoned shop of 2008 have been turned into a vet practice, a co-working cafe and a hip barber shop. On the other hand, a journey through the neighbourhood today will swiftly reveal that the majority of tenancies around the high street have become unaffordable for the people who made up the local community a decade ago.[21] Dubbed 'the worse place to live in Britain' in a hotly debated Channel 4 documentary in 2006, the opportunity to snap up cheap property for development did not go unnoticed. By 2017, the borough is the most expensive place to live in the UK in relation to average income. With regard to the theme of distinctiveness of a place

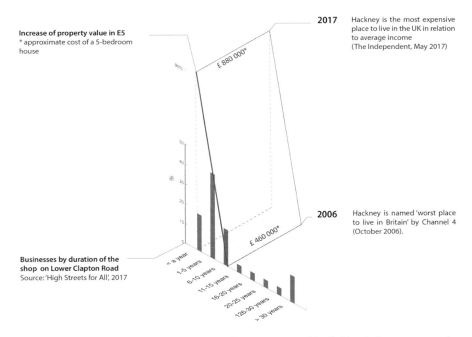

Figure 8.2 The survey of the duration of occupancy of individual shops was published in the 'High Streets for All' report (GLA, 2017). Four out of five shops have arrived on the street over the last decade, with half of the shops setting up since 2012. There is however a second side to this story. If one plots the increase in local house prices on the original graph, the cause for the apparent boom seems to be down to the impact of gentrification in Lower Clapton Road area that triggered the influx of new shops rather than a 'natural' growth. The relation between these sets of figures has not yet been analytically understood. It is however feasible to suggest that a population exchange has taken place, with the arrival of a more affluent client base, that coincided with the upturn in the high street's fortunes

that sustains a diverse community over time, gentrification in Lower Clapton presents a process of loss of a sense of the 'local,' compared to other places in London, where high streets perform the core functions attributed to their social value.

The paradox presented by distinctiveness with regard to social suitability in the literature shapes the problem designers face when engaging with the physical renewal of high street environments. It is, after all, the incentive of lessening the detrimental impact of gentrification by strategically assuming a mitigating role of communicators between policy makers and the community that attracts practices pursuing a social agenda to the high street projects. The ideas of 'local' and 'social' are thereby conflated under the heading of place and community, as entities that the designer can actually engage with through direct experience.[22] Closest to the architect's mode of thinking is the premise taken by urban design, which, in the case of the high street, can be understood as a discipline concerned with the 'art of place.' From the local authority client's view, the added value of architectural involvement in the process of regeneration, particularly in relation to distinctiveness, is a visual language of cultural reference, assumed to contribute to a distinct and welcoming mixed-use street environment that preforms economically. An exemplary set of case studies can serve to start questioning how implementing visual renewal through the conceived image relates to designing responsive to the social grain of a particular setting. The regeneration projects by Jan Kattein Architects (JKA) exemplify a take on distinctiveness that aims on the social values enabling experience economy on the high street, which underpins existing relationships.

Leyton High Road

JKA's pioneering scheme on Leyton High Road has been widely commented on in reference to 'other places,' such as the affluent Notting Hill, due to the flamboyant use of colour and shop signage. The parodic play on the cliché of the ideal high street closely observes the local authority's objectives to create a visitor-friendly visual environment as part of the boroughs public image (see Introduction). The visual shift introduced pays homage to the 'unsophisticated arts' of merchandising display of a by-gone time, while a carefully curated treatment of an extensive shop front homogenies the overall appearance, introducing a village-centre-like postcard image. Acutely aware of the superficiality of the original brief with regard to a social agenda, the architects stress that the physical intervention is but a by-product to the engagement process with the local trading community.[23]

Half of the time spent on the project was used to conduct personal conversations with shop owners and punters, reframing the aims of the project in dialogues on the high street as an open discussion around expectations in relation to socio-economic needs. Today, the relative success of the project can be measured against the criteria of distinctiveness not only by the fact that eight years on many of the traders that profited from the original scheme are still there, and a variety of new traders from diverse backgrounds have set up shop, but that those who opted out and remained 'unbranded' have not been displaced. The light-touch temporality of the changes made by JKA in 2011 become accentuated as the characteristic visual clutter of the typical suburban London high streets makes a return, indicating an organic relation between community and place. This said, the steady reversal of a superimposed aesthetic order that aimed to introduce qualities of particular taste and distinction can be understood as re-socialisation of the high street as a public realm, long after the gaze of Olympic tourists has ceased to pass judgments on the peculiarity of form and expression of the social life of the locals.

Francis Road

Francis Road is a detached stretch of mixed-use street embedded in a large residential zone. A socio-geographical study of this case would likely yield concerns with regard to the social sustainability of this detached local centre. Despite underpinned by a thorough process of meaningful and pioneering consultation work with the local community and delivering an attractive project to the client, Francis Road has seemingly caused an abrupt local shift of gentrification. An approach to 'making it look nice' perhaps over-emphasises the place aspect. Somewhat removed from the context of a wider urban infrastructure, the regeneration of Francis Road has created a intently localised boom in house prices that can be compared to Lower Clapton in Hackney, on a miniature scale. The concept of distinctiveness can be seen as a critical factor in evaluating the resulting social change over time. To what extent, the resulting population exchange is seen as unavoidable or even desirable in accordance to the client's brief is thereby of fundamental importance to understanding the role the architect assumes in the process of regeneration. Ironically, the principle of the duty of care that holds architectural practice accountable to the interest of client/budget holder can be seen to undermine a wider societal duty to challenge the brief in terms of its long-term social sustainability. The introduction of terms such as 'instagramable' into the vocabulary of commercially minded briefs reflect the cultural shift towards the emerging experience economy (see, #francisroad on Instagram). In this context, architects are pushed to define their strategic role as enablers of social processes on the high street in ever more complex, conflicting and uncertain terms. The challenge is for distinctiveness to be appreciated as a value statement relating to the social character of a place rather than its image value.

Blue House Yard

JKA's most experimental high street project to date, Blue House Yard (BHY) in Harringay, illustrates how the social agency of the architect is not solemnly defined by the consultation process but can powerfully and directly influence how the client's brief is structured and the project is procured.[24]

In the redevelopment of a redundant council property that includes an abandoned car park, JKA defied standard procedures by becoming their own contractor.

By that means, it was so possible to directly involve members of the local community in the construction of the project's simple wooden-frame structures. The resulting social hub, inhabited semi-permanently by micro-workshops of makers and artists, is handed back to the community as an envelope for a multitude of possible future programmes.

Attention was given that the initial 'visual shift' was followed up by highly visible, yet gradual change on the site. The strong social aspect of challenging the conceived space implemented by standard procedures of regeneration projects was founded on the participatory mode of space production.[25] The 'lived space' created in this process bears the hallmark of a disruptive spatial practice, akin to the precedent cases that lie outside the frame of reference of capitalist production.[26]

At BHY, the conventional process of conception and planning is challenged by allowing the architectural imagery to be perceived as 'made' rather than 'given.' The highly original response of spatial production defines social distinctiveness as a means of making the mixed-use street environment economically accessible to non-traditional means of business. The 'slow burn' approach to finding a new programme for the site, whereby the new identity of the BHY as place is allowed to evolve through the trial-and-error process of start-ups and micro-enterprises, removed the pressure of creating an instantly 'branded place,' without compromising its distinctive appeal as a public stage for emerging, inclusive social networks. Although agents of gentrification keenly await results framed by a conventional regeneration framework, BHY can instil optimism regarding emerging principles of a spatial practice that defies the simplistic logic of 'selling places' as secondary to social sustainability.

The particular, the peculiar and the dubious

As newly refurbished shop fronts all over London now conceal an increasing number of vacant shops, the place-making images of regeneration should be questioned. References to distinctiveness are often abstract, ahistorical, linked to teleological expectations of economic renewal and growth and packaged in a language that alludes to aesthetics. A concept of distinctiveness gains in social value, if it stems from participatory dialogue between the members of a "discursive community."[27] The immediate interest lies in defining common ground and constructing meaning collectively, which however retains the peculiarity of a specific community in the appropriation of an abstract concept, such as distinctiveness, to a specific social setting. This process can address a central insight gained from years of research into the wicked problem of the high street, namely that each high street is different. Distinctiveness can therefore not 'mean' the same everywhere. However, the seemingly *natural* occurrence of gentrification in areas such as Hackney and, on a smaller scale, Francis Road indicates that the formulation of a social value of regeneration tends to benefit those members of the collective whose cultural capital or economic interest are closest aligned with the dominant culture of a deregulated market economy.[28] As a profession epitomising the aspiration of this social class for sophistication, architects are tasked with creating inclusive processes that expand the social pool of the 'knowing audience' – those who are enabled to inform the meaning of images of renewal – to include members of community least imitated in the ways the regeneration of their urban environment can lead to personal financial gain. This responsibility does not merely reflect an immediate social concern of inclusion; in economic terms, the assimilation of vastly different places to the same economic principles can create a monoculture that is less resistant to crisis, jeopardising the core social value of high streets as inclusive and adaptable urban space.

Distinctiveness can be viewed as a contemporary version of architectural term 'character,' which has its own long architectural tradition. Whether cultural significance can be the result of dubious images, such as Cornish fisherman huts in suburban London, can ultimately be addressed by theoretical and philosophical inquiry. Speaking of irony, Richard Rotry's unimaginable scenario of a continuously self-conscious social culture has long become the norm through the societal impact of ubiquitous social media use.[29] It is by no means surprising that architecture, where it aims to be a social practice, must respond to the social currency of image-production of the age and its relation to the experience economy. However, it is in this context of investigating the future definitions of distinctiveness, as an undetermined factor of social complexity and discursive meaning-making in the public realm, can aid a wider critique of perceived wisdoms on social practice.[30]

Following Bourdieu, Paul Jones has suggested that architects would be misled into thinking that the symbolism of embodied cultural capital extends naturally beyond the field of cultural production of architecture. This ultimately leads to questioning the assumptions and projections of the dominant culture, which currently pursues a political campaign around distinctiveness and shaping the high street in its own image. In order to enable a pluralistic, more complex reading, I have tried to offer a nuance in thinking about distinctiveness by highlighting that particularity is different from peculiarity. On the one hand, the architect is a detached agent, acting upon the collective realm to enhance the particular physical appearance that distinguishes one high street from another. On the other hand, she cannot disregard the unique and peculiar form of the existing social network that will be affected by her work. If we are to take a step towards reclaiming distinctiveness for social practice, then architects will need to recognise the primacy of the peculiar rather than the particular.

Notes

1 Opening statement by London Mayor Boris Johnson, *Action for the High Street*, GLA (Summer 2014).
2 Barbara Jones, *The Unsophisticated Arts* (London: Architectural Press, 1951), 154.
3 Mark Goodwin, "The City as Commodity," in *Selling Places: City as Cultural Capital, Past and Present*, edited by Gerry Kearns and Chris Philo (Oxford; New York: Pergamon, 1993), 138:
> Regeneration is [..] based on restoring private sector confidence by encouraging investment through the preparation and marketing of land and infrastructure. Public subsidy is used as a prime element in this property value 'hype' (Klausner, 1987), but also crucial is the creation and subsequent marketing of a new image of the area.

4. Matthew Carmona, "London's Local High Streets: The Problems, Potential and Complexities of Mixed Street Corridors," in *Progress in Planning* August 2015. Reference to the high street as a wicked problem is made in the introduction to one of the most complete surveys of research concerning London's high street of recent years. It seems appropriate to remind us of Horst Rittel's original definition of wicked problems in the context of high street regeneration: "A class of social system problems which are ill-formulated, where the information is confusing, where there are many clients and decision makers with conflicting values, and where the ramifications in the whole system are thoroughly confusing."
5. Sam Griffiths, L. Vaughan, M. Haklay, and C. E. Jones, "The Sustainable Suburban High Street: A Review of Themes and Approaches," *Geography Compass* 2 (July 2008), 1155–1188.
6. Peter Jones, Marion Roberts, and Linda A. Morris, *Rediscovering Mixed-Use Streets: The Contribution of Local High Streets to Sustainable Communities* (The Policy Press, 2007).
7. Fiona Scott, "High Street Productivity," in *Suburban Urbanities*, edited by Laura Vaughan (UCL Press, 2015), 204–222.
8. Patrick Wright, "Around the World in Three Hundred Yards," in *A Journey Through Ruins: The Last Days of London* (University Press, 2009).
9. Suzanne Hall, "High Street Adaptations: Ethnicity, Independent Retail Practices, and Localism in London's Urban Margins," *Environment and Planning A: Economy and Space* 43, no. 11 (1 November 2011): 2571–2588. https://doi.org/10.1068/a4494.
10. New Economics Foundation, *Clone Town Britain, The Loss of Local Identity on the Nation's High Streets* (NEF, 2005), 5. For more on the NEF's concept on distinctiveness see *The 2010 Clone Town Report* (NEF, 2010).
11. Mary Portas, *The Portas Review: An Independent Review into the Future of Our High Streets* (uk gov 2011), 55.
12. Alex Lord, Michael Mair, John Sturzaker, and Paul Jones, "The Planners' Dream Goes Wrong? Questioning Citizen-Centred Planning," *Local Government Studies* 43, no. 3 (4 May 2017): 344–363. https://doi.org/10.1080/03003930.2017.1288618.
13. Sam Griffiths, et al, "The Sustainable Suburban High Street," 1155–1188.
14. "Adam Dant's Map of East End Trades," Spitalfields Life, Accessed 8 September 2020. https://spitalfieldslife.com/2018/11/30/adam-dants-map-of-east-end-trades/.
15. Fiona Scott, "High Street Productivity," 219.
16. All-Party Parliamentary Small Shops Group, *High Street Britain: 2015* (London: House of Commons, 2006), 60: "The reduction in local shopping facilities and associated environmental decline (vacant/boarded up premises; disjointed/sprawling retail area; and so on) could trigger population losses – whilst good quality local shopping facilities can 'sell' housing in an area, turning it into a desirable place to live and creating distinctiveness, the converse can occur if core facilities are missing."
17. Stephen Marshall, "Refocusing Urban Design as an Integrative Art of Place," *Proceedings of the ICE – Urban Design and Planning* 168 (1 February 2015): 8–18.
18. Suzanne Hall, *City, Street and Citizen: The Measure of the Ordinary* (Routledge, 2012).
19. Doreen Massey, "Geographies of Responsibility," *Geografiska Annaler*: Series B, Human Geography 86, no. 1 (March 2004): 5–18. https://doi.org/10.1111/j.0435-3684.2004.00150.x.
20. We Made That, L. S. E. Cities, *High Streets for All* (GLA, 2017).
21. Josie Co, "Hackney Homes Are Most Expensive in UK Relative to Average Wages," *The Independent*, 12 May, 2017, Accessed 8 September 2020. https://www.independent.co.uk/news/business/news/hackney-homes-most-expensive-uk-average-wages-north-london-a7731981.html.
22. Paul Jones and Kenton Card, "Constructing 'Social Architecture': The Politics of Representing Practice," *Architectural Theory Review* 16, no. 3 (1 December 2011): 228–244. https://doi.org/10.1080/13264826.2011.621543.
23. Jan Kattein, "Talking Shops: How to Keep the High Street Alive," *Riba Journal*, 2 June 2017, Accessed 9 July 2019. https://www.ribaj.com/intelligence/high-street-regeneration-jan-kattein-architects-london.
24. "Members' Tour: Blue House Yard, Jan Kattein," *Architecture Foundation*, Accessed 1 October 2019. https://www.architecturefoundation.org.uk/events/members-tour-blue-house-yard,-jan-kattein.
25. Henri Lefebvre, *The Production of Space* (Wiley-Blackwell, 1991).
26. An interesting architectural precedent to compare the Blue House Yard project to is Ranko Radović's *Gradić Pejton* in Belgrade, 1971. Of particular interest is the 'self-built' aspect in the creation of urban space. Despite its temporary character, it is still in use, almost half a century on.
27. Linda Hutcheon, *Irony's Edge: The Theory and Politics of Irony* (Routledge, 1994). The 'discursive community' includes all who contribute to a shared process of 'deciphering' a signalled intention in relation to a given social context in three states of constructing appropriated meaning (how irony happens): relational, inclusive and differential. Can these discursive attributes inform a less top-down discourse around the role of distinctiveness in the process of high street renewal?
28. Paul Jones, "Putting Architecture in Its Social Place: A Cultural Political Economy of Architecture," *Urban Studies* 46, no. 12 (2009): 2519–2536.
29. Richard Rorty, *Contingency, Irony, and Solidarity* (Cambridge University Press, 2007), 87: "I cannot imagine a culture which socialized its youth in such a way as to make them continually dubious about their own process of socialization."
30. Paul Jones, "Putting Architecture in Its Social Place," 2009.

References

All-Party Parliamentary Small Shops Group. 2015. *High Street Britain: 2015*. London: House of Commons, 2006.

Carmona, Matthew. "London's Local High Streets: The Problems, Potential and Complexities of Mixed Street Corridors." *Progress in Planning* (August 2015): 1–84. https://doi.org/10.1016/j.progress.2014.03.001.

Goodwin, Mark. "The City as Commodity." In *Selling Places: City as Cultural Capital, Past and Present*, edited by Kearns, Gerry and Chris Philo, 145–162. Oxford; New York: Pergamon, 1993.

Griffiths, S., L. Vaughan, M. Haklay, and C. E. Jones. "The Sustainable Suburban High Street: A Review of Themes and Approaches." *Geography Compass* 2 (July 2008): 1155–1188.

Hall, Suzanne M., "High Street Adaptations: Ethnicity, Independent Retail Practices, and Localism in London's Urban Margins." *Environment and Planning A: Economy and Space* 43, no. 11 (November 2011): 2571–2588. https://doi.org/10.1068/a4494

———. *City, Street and Citizen: The Measure of the Ordinary*. London: Routledge, 2013.

Hutcheon, Linda. *Irony's Edge: The Theory and Politics of Irony*. 1st edition. London; New York: Routledge, 1994.

Jones, Barbara. *The Unsophisticated Arts*. London: Architectural Press, 1951.

Jones, Paul. "Putting Architecture in Its Social Place: A Cultural Political Economy of Architecture." *Urban Studies* 46, no. 12 (2009): 2519–2536.

———. *The Sociology of Architecture: Constructing Identities*. Liverpool: Liverpool University Press, 2011

Jones, Paul, and Kenton Card. "Constructing 'Social Architecture': The Politics of Representing Practice." *Architectural Theory Review* 16, no. 3 (1 December 2011): 228–244. https://doi.org/10.1080/13264826.2011.621543.

Jones, Peter, Marion Roberts, and Linda Morris. *Rediscovering Mixed-Use Streets: The Contribution of Local High Streets to Sustainable Communities, Public Spaces Series*. Bristol: Published for the Joseph Rowntree Foundation by The Policy Press, 2007.

Kattein, Jan. "Talking Shops: How to Keep the High Street Alive." *Riba Journal*, 2 June 2017, Accessed 9 July 2019. https://www.ribaj.com/intelligence/high-street-regeneration-jan-kattein-architects-london.

Lefebvre, Henri. *The Production of Space*. Translated by Donald Nicholson–Smith. Malden, MA: Wiley-Blackwell, 1991.

Lord, Alex, Michael Mair, John Sturzaker, and Paul Jones. "The Planners' Dream Goes Wrong? Questioning Citizen-Centred Planning." *Local Government Studies* 43, no. 3 (4 May 2017): 344–363. https://doi.org/10.1080/03003930.2017.1288618.

Marshall, Stephen. "Refocusing Urban Design as an Integrative Art of Place." *Proceedings of the ICE - Urban Design and Planning* 168 (February 2015): 8–18.

Massey, Doreen. "Geographies of Responsibility." *Geografiska Annaler: Series B, Human Geography* 86, no. 1 (March 2004): 5–18. https://doi.org/10.1111/j.0435-3684.2004.00150.x.

New Economics Foundation. *Clone Town Britain, The Loss of Local Identity on the Nation's High Streets*. London: NEF, 2005.

———. *The 2010 Clone Town Report: Re-imaging the High Street, Escape from Clone Town Britain*. London: NEF, 2010.

Portas, Mary. *The Portas Review: An Independent Review into the Future of Our High Streets*. London: Department for Business, Innovation & Skills and Ministry of Housing, Communities & Local Government, 2011.

Rorty, Richard. *Contingency, Irony, and Solidarity*. 25. Cambridge Univ. Press, 2007.

Scott, Fiona. "High Street Productivity." In *Suburban Urbanities: Suburbs and the Life of the High Street*, edited by Laura Vaughan. UCL Press, 2015. https://doi.org/10.2307/j.ctt1g69z0m.17

We Made That, L. S. E. Cities. High Streets for All. Greater London Authority (report), 2017.

Wright, Patrick. *A Journey Through Ruins: The Last Days of London*. Paladin, 1992.

Chapter 9
Zero-institution culture

Louis D'Arcy-Reed

For many cities around the world, intervention-based redevelopment of place reveals layers of gentrification, elitist functions, sanitised spaces and or an increase in privatised areas of the city. While some critics proclaim that a new paradigm (such as Patrik Schumacher's fierce arguments for Parametricism; an extraction of neo-liberalist design and systems) is required for the profession of architecture to address society's biggest challenges – the environment, living arrangements, technology, to name a few – the desire to redevelop cities has attracted privately backed financial investments in order to future-proof themselves against decline, thereby enabling the big-business of hiring star architects to deliver master plans or showpiece architectural projects as an appropriate design tool in city redevelopment.

The problem, however, is in delivering such schemes, cities run the risk of constructing a series of 'zero-institutions,' disorientating its residents through an architectural parallax – an effect whereby the position or direction of an object appears to differ when viewed from different positions – creating narratives that eschews the conventional quality or condition of presenting a narrative of place at odds with a city's natural rhythm or evolution.

The structural anthropologist, Claude Lévi-Strauss (1908–2009), developed the idea of the 'zero-institution' as an empty signifier with no determinate meaning. Later, the philosopher Slavoj Žižek (b. 1949) identified iconic multi-functioning arts complexes at the heart of our cities as today's contemporary zero-institution. By way of extension, zero-institutions become an ideology to synthesise the city and its inhabitants, occupying both physical and cognitive space. Yet, these new zero-institutions, in the

Zero-institution culture

Figure 9.1 The Vessel, Hudson Yards, New York City, designed by David Chipperfield Architects
© Antony-22

guise of 'high-architectural intervention,' often reject existing identities or the semantic weight associated with an environments' history, enabling the regeneration of place and zero-institutions to exist in plain view of dynamic urban fabrics.

Using examples from contemporary architecture and synthesising theory from Lévi-Strauss and Žižek, this chapter argues that the blurring of semantic space and historicity of place are a strategic motif of the zero-institution which appeals to base psychoanalytical desires of spectators; new identities of place are formed where the idea of meaning is resigned to socio-political motives. Urban grains consisting of parallax 'gaps' with zero-institutions at their centres become fertile domains for architectural discourse to consider the manipulation of narrative structure and the resultant cognitive effects upon the culture of our cities.

Zero-institutions

The notion of the zero-institution is adapted from Claude Lévi-Strauss's anthropological study of Amazonian tribespeople in *Triste Tropique* (1955). Lévi-Strauss, famous for his structuralist approach to anthropology, posited that immutable deep structures exist in all cultures, and consequently, all cultural practices have homologous counterparts in other cultures – in other words, that all cultures are proportionate – and that every culture can be understood in terms of these opposites. "From the very start," he wrote, "the process of visual perception makes use of binary oppositions."[1] In *Do Dual Organizations Exist?* (1956), Lévi-Strauss called the 'zero-institution':

> a kind of institutional counterpart to mana [magical, religious and spiritual power inherent to tribal hierarchies], the empty signifier with no determinate meaning, since it signifies only the presence of meaning as such, in opposition to its absence: a specific institution which has no positive, determinate function – its only function (…) signalling the presence and actuality of social institution (…) in opposition to its absence, to pre-social chaos.[2]

Slavoj Žižek expands upon Lévi-Strauss's view of the "empty signifier with no determinate meaning,"[3] where the 'zero-institution' becomes central to the concept of architectural parallax, particularly, the contemporary arts centre:

> Big performance-arts complexes, arguably the paragon of today's architecture, try to impose themselves as a kind of architectural zero-institutions. Their very conflictual meanings (…) is the presence of meaning as such as opposed to non-meaning…[4]

Žižek's observations feed into his theory of the architectural parallax, which is, in its ordinary sense, the apparent difference in an object or the position of an object when it is viewed from different perspectives.[5] Yet, what differentiates Žižek's perspective is in its philosophical twist that the observed difference is not simply 'subjective.' It is, in effect, objective,[6] where "an 'epistemological' shift in the subject's point of view always reflects an 'ontological' shift in the object itself."[7] As a result, the object, in the shifting perspective of the parallax, is both itself and not itself; the parallax view renders the object uncanny.[8]

Whilst the parallax extends into the realms of architectural uncanny of Vidler (1992),[9] which, in itself, is an extension of the uncanny in psychoanalysis first discussed by Jentsch (1906) and Freud (1919), the uncanny is an effect that emerges at the latter end of zero-institutional building (discussed later). Žižek makes clear that

> the parallax gap is thus not a matter of our shifting perspective (…); things get interesting when we notice that the gap is inscribed into the 'real' building itself – as if the building, in its very material experience, bears the imprint of different and mutually exclusive perspectives.[10]

The zero-institution for Žižek, emblematic of its functionality to a myriad of concerns – contemporary art, theatre, performance, music and accompanying social spaces – is a fertile typology of architecture to other functions and forms. One can recognise such structures within cities across the globe, which are ever increasingly, central to city redevelopment or revitalisation plans. They also vary in scale; consider cultural

Figure 9.2 Another zero-institution? The V&A Design Museum, Dundee, Scotland, designed by Kengo Kuma & Associates
© Hufton+Crow

zero-institutions to re-invigorate post-industrial towns and cities in the United Kingdom over the 1990s and 2000s or New York City's recent Hudson Yards development scheme; whilst not centred on an arts complex, it houses a divergent typology of 'zero-institutional' architecture.

Narrating zero-institutionalist interventions

Today's cities are rife with messages upon the psyche. As a result, the historic transgression of place and, therefore, the historic and evolving narrative of place, raises the question of whether architecture can function independently of homogenising cultural identifications.[11] Western architecture exists in a capitalist dichotomy in which leading philosopher and Frankfurt school member Theodor Adorno claimed that functionalism in architecture – by which he meant not its practicality, but its sensuous meaning – cannot exist in an irrational society.[12] The irrationality of the built environment is therefore dictated by neoliberalist directives to construct the city's new narratives. Whilst this nudges upon the socio-political organisms within architecture, the contribution to narratives of place remains intrinsic to an identity.

Austin suggests "a successful narrative environment will prompt embodied perception, physical action and intellectual change or transformation."[13] Therefore, the city transmits a reliance on the intellectual account to yourself of who you are, and the place you are in, and your bodily schema; it is expected that stimulation is required to create desire to enter and engage with a narrative space. A "dialectical tension between the expert and amateur"[14] exists upon encountering urban fabrics that links to the existence of an incommensurability between community and audience in Žižek's Parallax, a concept we could describe as radical passivity.[15] Radical passivity builds on

Walter Benjamin's encounter with architecture by either 'rapt attention' or a 'noticing in incidental fashion.'[16]

If one considers the impact of zero-institutional architecture rupturing narratives through the creation of a Žižekian parallax, and the resultant uncanny implications on conscious and interpretation of the built environment, the question emerges of how is this so? Do not zero-institutions become immutable objects?

Phenomenological to psychoanalytical

Architectural projects often contain numerous phenomenological tools, but for the zero-institution, strategic psychoanalytic methods implicate subjects to become aware of, but also affected by the new intervention. For example, the zero-institution synthesises the physical space of the city, the plastic and real assemblage of the architecture and the metaphysical spectacular across both objective and subjective dimensions, demoting "phenomenology (…) to a base concept, which constructs space from subjective experience."[17] The zero-institution eschews tradition, becoming a powerful mediator of the objective and subjective within the city experience and shares the phenomenological capacity to morph urban environments from conscious markers of being, to powerful modulators of inclusion and exclusion.

However, the zero-institution has developed a capacity to reduce itself to base psychoanalytic desires, in evoking the uncanny quality in which they "…bear the imprint of different and mutually exclusive perspectives."[18] For Anthony Vidler, "the uncanny is not a property of the space (…); it is in its aesthetic dimension, a representation of a mental state of projection that precisely elides the boundaries of the real and unreal in order to provoke a disturbing ambiguity, a slippage between waking and dreaming."[19] Therefore, an integral qualitative tension always exists within the uncanny, where architectural responses can both marginalise and exacerbate internal anxieties.

The uncanny then begins to form dismembered states of environments, where fragmentation occurs between cultures, spatial relationships, cognitive functions and architectures. In Vidler's assessment of the uncanny, the role of architecture sought to deviate from any reconciliation but fostered a detachment from the body and modularity. As zero-institutions develop newer forms of abstraction to deal with the trauma of the past, and one's own guilt associated with nostalgia, technological and engineering advancements disassociate architecture further from its users. For example, Vidler discusses parametricism here, citing the work of Coop Himmelb(l)au, "…for the generation of a whole range of psychological responses that depend on our faculty of projecting onto objects states of mind and body."[20]

By extension, the uncanny presents a typology – or perhaps architectural methodology – inherent of zero-institutions to continually reproduce feelings of anxiety in buildings that articulate both a new territorialisation of environment but also detachment from its user's perspective. Perspective is at once visual but also embodied. Recall Žižek's zero-institution containing "…Their very conflictual meanings (…) is the presence of meaning as such as opposed to non-meaning…."[21] Where this observation relies on the postmodernist approach in architecture of a multitude of systems, the zero-institution behaves similarly, where their contemporaneity is characterised by antinomies and asynchronies: the simultaneous and incompatible social inequalities, differences that persist.[22] The inscribed non-meaning of the zero-institution allows a hierarchical order to materialise, underlying the institutional goals of a state.

One could begin to view this psychoanalytically where notions of unconscious projection or the transference of feelings are projected to alleviate conflicts or social disparity. Expanding upon this, the architect Alejandro Zaera-Polo of FOA notes a social antagonism which embodies both the building and the image it presents; "Institutions cannot simply rely on performances themselves to provide a sufficient attraction; the building must create an 'experience' and a 'sense of place' for its demanding audience."[23] The zero-institution's psychical 'power' and ability to territorialise an environment manages to obfuscate the reality redevelopment causes. It becomes a function of the built environment that necessitates "…observation, diagnosis, and treatment, and it is diagnosis that stands today as one of the more urgent and important interdisciplinary methodological hurdles between architecture and psychoanalysis."[24]

Exposing zero-institutional psychodynamic effects

Perhaps, the true first example was embodied by Rogers and Piano's Centre Georges Pompidou, Paris, which hallmarked the cultural complex across multi-disciplinary platforms and the power to actively play a role in the regeneration of the urban fabric. Conceived soon after the student rebellion of the late 1960s, the Pompidou Centre in Paris became a privileged place where culture was offered to the masses as a proof of democratisation[25] and, in turn, delivered an uncanny blurring of boundaries for Parisians. President Pompidou's desire to create a cultural legacy, in an obverse of his conservative politics, administering the world's first openly democratic 'Pop' building:

> … to define a different relationship with culture. No longer elitist, culture was now meant to get off its pedestal and enter the flux of life. Instead of being secluded in a temple or mausoleum, it had to be spread in a new kind of public forum, in a bazaar…[26]

It was in the "Completely out-of-context (in historical Paris), but also by the application of the pop principle of 'happening'(…)," notes Marinelli,[27] "…a 'strange object' capable of (…) arousing a sense of stupefaction (…) it was nevertheless supposed to break the traditional barriers existing between culture and people." The first zero-institution ascended into the urban and architectural realm, through a blurring of democratic messages, a de-compartmentalisation of elitist culture, re-branding the historicity of the Marais and an uncanny inverse between a flexible monumentality and removal of substantial urban fabrics.

Over the course of the Millennium, the New Labour government (1997–2010) of Great Britain implemented fierce regenerative programs across the country,

Figure 9.3 The New Art Gallery Walsall, designed by Caruso St John
© Louis D'Arcy-Reed

elevating cultural institutions and as a by-product, zero-institutions, to "…necessary, fixtures of a well-furnished state."[28] In 2001, the completion of Caruso St John's New Art Gallery Walsall was seen as a positive force for the town, revitalising a future desire to attract investment and tourism. Unfortunately, the institution fell victim to the 2008 financial crisis, raising concerns of the council. Nevertheless, the gallery is still open, but isolated by the idiosyncratic nature of Walsall's fabric, a reality of political inaction. Walsall proves the physical and psychological dichotomy in zero-institution architecture – it is a method of exposing different layers, which all converge upon the object as component of narrative: the new zero-institutionalist structure to provide meaning while also conveying absolutely no new meaning for place. In a successful narrative of place, the story continues and progresses; yet, for Walsall, this has halted. Instead, the zero-institution exists in a state of passive reading – "A reading acquired more through disinterest (désinteressement) than interest, [that] has a radical potential to change the reading"[29] – of place and stagnation.

In New York City as part of the 2004 Bloomberg-Pataki Hudson Yards synthesis, created the Special Hudson Yards District, changing about 301 acres from manufacturing and commercial to mostly commercial/offices and residential.[30] Costing $25 billion, the urban restructuring project drew fierce criticism for its questionable funding through the combination of the EB-5 visa exchange private donation scheme and gerrymandering. Officials managed to re-categorise lower Manhattan and Central Park as economically distressed areas funnelling funds from low-income communities in Harlem. At the centre of the redevelopment sits Thomas Heatherwick's Vessel (completed 2019 – Figure 9.1).

Vessel has attracted staunch criticism for its use, and ableism as a structure – an Escher-esque open object made up of staircases and viewing platforms raising 46 metres, wrapped in glass and copper-coloured steels – made further news for managed access and third-party ownership of photographs of the object. It is today's purest example, and the pinnacle of the architectural zero-institution, and moves beyond an art-object or sculpture.

"Forming the heart of this new district," Heatherwick[31] writes on his studio's website, "Vessel represents the intention for Hudson Yards to create a meaningful public legacy for New York;" yet, at the same time, one can argue that there is no determinate purpose or legacy relating to the Hudson Yards development; unless a legacy is dictated by the money in one's pocket. Perhaps, subconsciously, Vessel represents fiscal dalliance bound in aesthetic spectacle or its parallax quality bordering on the uncanny. Comprehensively, Vessel exemplifies the empty signifier with no determinate meaning, since it signifies only the presence of meaning as such in opposition to its absence: a specific institution which has no positive, determinate function – its only function is the purely negative one of signalling the presence and actuality of social institution as such, in opposition to its absence, to pre-social chaos.[32]

In 1980, the social urbanist William H. Whyte described 'triangulation' as the mutual act of looking at something that fostered strangers to interact with each other – perhaps, the modern equivalent for architects and developers is the zero-institution; both inspire awe and appeal to desire, but ultimately become nothing more than a momentary object reduced to the exorbitant uncanny. Shifting the conscious interpretation of place by blurring the ownership of spaces, and the 'meaning' attached to such interventions, only seeks to exteriorise the unequal narratives of place within urban fabrics. By consistently prescribing zero-institutions at the heart of urban fabrics does nothing more than imply the spectre of power hierarchies for place. The meaning of place is obfuscated by non-meaning; what we had is now managed by others, thereby having no meaning upon our psyche.

Notes

1. Claude Lévi-Strauss, "Structuralism and Ecology." *Information* (International Social Science Council) (February 1973).
2. Slavoj Žižek, *The Parallax View* (Cambridge, MA: MIT Press, 2009).
3. Claude Lévi-Strauss, "'Do Dual Organizations Exist?' Structural…" In *Edmund Leach: An Anthropological Life* (Cambridge: Cambridge University Press, 2001).
4. Slavoj Žižek, *Living in the End Times* (London: Verso Books, 2011), 257.
5. Matthew Beaumont, "The Politics of the Visor," *City*, 22, no. 1 (2018): 65.
6. Ibid., 66.
7. Žižek, *Living in the End Times*, 244.
8. Beaumont, "The Politics of the Visor," 66.
9. Anthony Vidler, *The Architectural Uncanny: Essays* (Cambridge, MA: MIT Press., 1999).
10. Slavoj Žižek, "The Architectural Parallax," in *The Political Unconscious of Architecture*, ed. Nadir Lahiji (Farnham: Ashgate Publishing Ltd., 2011), 253.
11. Gülsüm Baydar, "The Cultural Burden of Architecture," *Journal of Architectural Education*, 57, no. 4 (2004): 19–27.

12 Theodor Adorno, cited in Peggy Deamer, "(Un)Free Work: Architecture, Labour and Self-Determination," *Architectural Design*, 88 (2018): 16–23, 19.
13 Tricia Austin, "Scales of Narrativity," in *Museum Making*, eds. S. MacLeod, L. Hourston Hanks and J. Hale (London: Routledge, 2012), 109.
14 Dorian Wiszniewski, "City as Museum, Museum as City," in *Museum Making*, eds. Suzanne Macloed, Laura Hourston Hanks, and Jonathan Hale (London: Routledge, 2012), 126.
15 Ibid.
16 Walter Benjamin, cited in Ibid.
17 Lorens Holm, *Brunelleschi, Lacan, Le Corbusier* (London: Routledge, 2010), 9.
18 Žižek, "The Architectural Parallax," 253.
19 Vidler, *The Architectural Uncanny: Essays*, 11.
20 Ibid., 75.
21 Žižek, *Living in the End Times*, 257.
22 Terry Smith, "What is Contemporary Art?" in *Radical Museology*, ed. Claire Bishop (London: Koenig Books, 2014), 19.
23 Alejandro Zaera Polo, "The Politics of the Envelope: A Political Critique on Materialism," C-Lab (Graduate School of Architecture: Columbia University, 2008).
24 Martin, "Psychoanalytic Diagnosis in Architecture and Urban Design," 6.
25 Francesco Proto, "The Pompidou Centre: Or the Hidden Kernel of Dematerialisation," *The Journal of Architecture*, 573.
26 Renzo Piano, cited in Renzo Piano, P. Buchanan (Turin: Allemandi & Co., 1993), 49.
27 G. Marinelli, *Il Centro Beaubourg a Parigi: 'Macchina' e Segno Architettonico* (Bari: Dedalo, 1978), 201.
28 Carol Duncan, "Art Museums and the ritual of Citizenship," in *Interpreting Objects and Collections*, ed. Susan Pearce (London: Routledge, 1994), 279.
29 Wiszniewski, "City as Museum, Museum as City," 128.
30 David Halle and Elisabeth Tiso, *New York's New Edge: Contemporary Art, the High Line, and Urban Megaprojects on the Far West Side* (Chicago, IL: The University of Chicago Press, 2015), 270.
31 "Heatherwick Studio | Design & Architecture | Vessel," 2019, http://www.heatherwick.com/project/vessel/.
32 Žizek, *The Parallax View*, 7.

References

Austin, Tricia. 2012. "Scales of Narrativity." In Suzanne MacLeod, Laura Hourston Hanks, and Jonathan Hale (Eds.) *Museum Making*. London: Routledge, 107–118.
Baydar, Gülsüm. 2004. "The Cultural Burden of Architecture." *Journal of Architectural Education*, 57:4, 19–27.
Beaumont, Matthew. 2018. "The Politics of the Visor." *City*, 22:1, 63–77, DOI:10.1080/13604813.2018.1423815
Buchanan, P. 1993. *Renzo Piano*. Turin: Allemandi & Co.
Deamer, Peggy. 2018. "(Un)Free Work: Architecture, Labour and Self-Determination." *Architectural Design*, 88, 16–23. DOI:10.1002/ad.2296
Duncan, Carol. 1994. "Art Museums and the Ritual of Citizenship." In: Susan Pearce (Ed.) *Interpreting Objects and Collections*. London: Routledge, 279–287.
Foster, Hal. 2013. *The Art-Architecture Complex*. London: Verso Books.
Halle, David, and Elisabeth Tiso. 2016. *New York's New Edge: Contemporary art, the High Line, and Urban Megaprojects on the Far West Side*. Chicago, IL: The University of Chicago Press.
Holm, Lorens. 2010. *Brunelleschi, Lacan, Le Corbusier*. 1st ed. London: Routledge.
Levi-Strauss, Claude. 1956. "'Do Dual Organizations Exist?' Structural…" In S.J. Tambiah (Ed.) *Edmund Leach: An Anthropological Life* (2001). Cambridge: Cambridge University Press.
Levi-Strauss, Claude. February 1973. "Structuralism and Ecology." *Information (International Social Science Council)*, 12:1: 7–23. DOI:10.1177/053901847301200101.
Marinelli, G. 1978. *Il Centro Beaubourg a Parigi: 'Macchina' e Segno Architettonico*. Bari: Dedalo. [Google Scholar]
Martin, Timothy. 2016. "Psychoanalytic Diagnosis in Architecture and Urban Design." In: John Hendrix and Lorens Holm (Eds.) *Architecture and the Unconscious*. London: Ashgate Press.
Proto, Francesco. 2005. "The Pompidou Centre: Or the Hidden Kernel of Dematerialisation." *The Journal of Architecture*, 10:5, 573–589. DOI:10.1080/13602360500463156
Rendell, Jane. 2017. *The Architecture of Psychoanalysis*. London: IB Taurus and Co.
Sklair, Liz. 2008. "Iconic Architecture and Capitalist Globalization." In Peter Herrle and Erik Wegerhoff (Eds.) *Architecture and Identity*. Berlin: LIT.
Small, Zachary. 2019. "The Financing Of Hudson Yards Is Worse Than Its Architecture." Hyperallergic. https://hyperallergic.com/494907/the-financing-of-hudson-yards-is-worse-than-its-architecture/ [Accessed 29 July 2019].

Smith, Terry. 2014. "What is Contemporary Art?" In: Claire Bishop (Ed.) *Radical Museology*. London: Koenig Books.

Vidler, Anthony. 1999. *The Architectural Uncanny: Essays*. Cambridge, MA: MIT Press.

Wiszniewski, Dorian. 2012. "City as Museum, Museum as City." In: Suzanne Macloed, Laura Hourston Hanks, and Jonathan Hale (Eds.) *Museum Making*. London: Routledge, 119–131.

Zaera Polo, Alejandro. 2008. "The Politics of the Envelope: A Political Critique on Materialism." C-Lab. Graduate School of Architecture: Columbia University, Vol. 17, 76–105; Available online at http://c-lab.columbia.edu

Žižek, Slavoj. 2005. *Interrogating the Real*. New York: Bloomsbury.

Žižek, Slavoj. 2006. *How to read Lacan*. London: Granta Publications.

Žižek, Slavoj, 2009. *The Parallax View*. Cambridge, MA: MIT Press.

Žižek, Slavoj. 2011. "The Architectural Parallax." In: Nadir Lahiji (Ed.) *The Political Unconscious of Architecture*. Farnham: Ashgate Publishing Ltd., 253–296.

Žižek, Slavoj. 2011. *Living in the End Times*. London: Verso Books.

Part III
Authority

Chapter 10

Authorship and political will in Aldo Rossi's theory of architecture

Will Orr

Aldo Rossi's *The Architecture of the City* (1966; trans. 1982) presented a paradigmatic reflection on the situation confronting the architectural discipline following the widely acknowledged collapse of the Modern Movement. Together with the lesser known essay, "Architecture for Museums" (1966; trans. 2013), it set out a strategy to re-imbue the architect's work with the political and social weight sought, but ultimately lost, by the Modern Movement. Despite its particularities, Rossi's attempt established some of the key assumptions still underpinning contemporary debates regarding the political significance and agency of architectural practice. Rossi developed the principles of architectural autonomism, and his work contributed to the foundation of the post-modern discipline. Where the modernists attempted to integrate and shape social and technical development within the more or less utopian perspective of planning, Rossi, prominent but not alone among his contemporaries, moved decisively away from planning and towards something else: what can be called the "autonomous project."[1]

Despite its reputation for criticality, the autonomous project's opposition to 'planning' places it within the neoliberal paradigm as the latter evolved over the past 50 years. We have been told by Rossi, Jane Jacobs and their followers, as much as by Friedrich Hayek, that planning is at best misguided and, at worst, evil. There are clear reasons why a nominally professional discipline, such as architecture, might adopt an anti-planning stance when hostility to planning (political-economic as much as urban and architectural) defines the economic and political ideology of its institutional milieu. Linked to this historical confluence, we can read in the move away from the modernist programme an attempt to re-centre the discipline around one of its traditional

Figure 10.1 The ABC Riverside Building at the Walt Disney Studios in Burbank, California. Rossi's final project was completed posthumously in 2001

The image is available under the Creative Commons CC0 1.0 Universal Public Domain Dedication https://commons.wikimedia.org/wiki/File:Disney_studios_burbank_abc_building_riverside.jpg.

mandates: authorship. In this light, Rossi's work can be read as an attempt to stabilise the professional position of the architect through a theory of architectural authorship.

In what follows, I will outline how this institutional goal mediated Rossi's other political and disciplinary propositions, leading to a number of contradictions. Seen from a contemporary perspective, these contradictions fall into greater relief. Overall, proletarianisation and increasing class stratification within the office have called architecture's professional character into question, and with it, the notion of authorship. Both within the discipline and without, the accelerating breakdown of the neoliberal consensus has opened the way for renewed contestation over architecture's political and economic role in society. I hope to contribute to this struggle by tracing an influential line of its genealogy within architecture theory.

A theory of architecture as a search for authorship

In *The Architecture of the City*, Rossi combined aesthetic propositions and metaphysical axioms on the permanence and necessity of architecture, with concrete historical analyses of urban and economic development. The result is a highly original synthesis in the form of a 'theory of architecture.' But in what sense is it a 'theory' and in what sense does it address 'architecture'? The nature of Rossi's thinking at the time can be better understood by way of the essay, "Architecture for Museums," originally given as a lecture to Giuseppe Samonà's course at the IUAV in 1966 (2013, 5). The essay has a programmatic character and contains some of Rossi's clearest statements of intent:

> At the risk of appearing naïve, I propose to trace a truthful and appropriate theory of design, in other words forming a theory of design as an integral part of a theory of architecture. To talk about a theory of design I have to say first what I think architecture is. I shall give some definitions of the term "architecture"; I shall then go on to say by which criteria architectural design should be inspired, and what are its relations with architectural history.
>
> (2013, 25)

For Rossi, the question of 'architecture' and the question of 'design' were separate but intimately linked. The practical goal, 'to trace a truthful and appropriate theory of design,' required a kind of ontological foundation in the concept and history of its apparent object, 'architecture.' The idiosyncratic theoretical search that fills the pages of *The Architecture of the City* focuses almost entirely on the latter. Why did Rossi feel the need to take this highly abstract detour in order to arrive at a productive theory of design?

Both for western post-war architecture in general, and Italian architecture specifically, there are historical reasons for this. By the mid-1960s, Rossi's interests, emerging from debates within Italian urbanism of the late 1950s,[2] moved away from urban planning (and what might be called a 'quantitative' approach to the city) towards a qualitative interest in 'architecture.' This reflected the changing political conditions of planning practice of the time. The *centro-sinistra* (centre-left) government of the Christian Democrats and Italian Socialist Party had just sabotaged their own planning reform bill, dashing the hopes of many progressive architects and planners. Notable among them was a young Manfredo Tafuri, who in a 1992 interview claimed that this failure, and the inadequate response by major architects, forced him to abandon design practice entirely (Tafuri, Passarini 2000, 31). Taking the opposite approach to Tafuri's, Rossi sought to enter deeper into design through its theorisation. In "Architecture for Museums," he presented this trajectory as historically necessary:

> It is in certain periods, like ours, that one senses the need of building up a theory which is then taken up as the basis of the creative process, as the basis for what one is doing. I know that for many there is no need for a theory: a part of the Modern Movement has stated that theory had been overcome by method and that modern architecture has to be found in method.
>
> (2013, 26)

This distinction between Modernist 'method' and what he sought under the name 'theory' places Rossi in the larger international and historical context of the collapse of the Modern Movement. Modernist 'method' was problematic, not merely for its technical limitations, but because it called into question the architect's raison d'être by transforming creative authorship into technical execution (Tafuri, 1998, 21). Thus, behind the concept, 'architecture,' lays the subject, the architect, whose objectification under political and technical oversight was underway. The major stake of Rossi's theory of design was therefore the survival of the discipline itself, legible in the way he constantly tied practical concerns back to fundamental ones: "It seems to me that to formulate a building in the most concrete way possible, especially at the design stage, is to give a new impulse to architecture itself" (1982, 118).

Contradictions

In *The Architecture of the City*, the majority of Rossi's political discussion occurred in the final chapter; however, from the early pages, Rossi associated 'architecture' with social community:

> I use the term architecture in a positive and pragmatic sense, as a creation inseparable from civilized life and society in which it is manifested. By nature it is collective. As the first men built houses to provide more favourable surroundings for their life, fashioned an artificial climate for themselves, so they built with aesthetic intention. Architecture came into being along with the first traces of the city; it is deeply rooted in the formation of civilization and is a permanent, universal, and necessary artifact.
>
> (1982, 21)

Having posited this trans-historical essence as the foundational value from which to develop his theory, Rossi had difficulty reconciling it on two fronts: first, that such nigh-metaphysical functions can be practiced by a concrete disciplinary figure (the architect), and second, that 'civilisation' (in the abstract) can be represented by real societies.

The former became explicit in the contradiction between Rossi's thesis that architectural qualities are produced gradually through 'collective' use and the underlying goal of appropriating this production within design.[3] We might ask of what use his theory could be to designers, if Rossi had discovered that architectural quality was *not* invented through design, but developed over the real life of the urban artifact? In Pier Vittorio Aureli's reading, this problem represents Rossi's attempt to bring together 'typology' and 'event' into a 'difficult whole.'[4] The tension between extended collective use and the conscious authorship of the individual also suggests a return to the Renaissance dynamics of linguistic norm and creative transgression, which Tafuri would later identify with *sprezzatura*.[5] It is important to note here that the Modern Movement had its own version of the tension between the 'collective' masses and the disciplinary individual. However, for modernism, it had a material rather than a linguistic register. For example, Le Corbusier's *Vers une architecture* (1923) sought a privileged position for the architectural expert on the grounds that, as a planner, the architect could overcome urban society's class antagonisms.

Rossi's second contradiction concerns precisely the problem of class. He attempted to maintain a concrete awareness of the class character of society – "I maintain that the history of architecture and built urban artefacts is always the history of the architecture of the ruling classes" (1982, 23) – while claiming the pivotal and positive role of abstract 'collectivity.' Crucially, both contradictions involve the notional character of the 'collective' within Rossi's theory. That the history of architecture be tied to the history of a particular class implies the non-neutral character of the abstract 'collectivity' posited above. Were Rossi to connect the underlying class basis of architectural production to its concrete outcomes – in other words, using the concrete collectivity of class instead of an abstract 'collectivity' – his theory would gain a consistent grounding in political economy.[6] However, in departing from planning towards a qualitative theory of architecture, Rossi had broken the link between architectural objects and the political-economic context of their production. In fact, he argued that changes in the mode of production do not affect the city in any significantly qualitative way. Admitting its controversial character, he called this his "thesis of spatial continuity" (1982, 63).

Furthermore, Rossi used scalar concepts like the 'urban artifact' to bracket out the economic organisation of the city. Yet, he would not go so far as to ignore political economy altogether. One clear example of this negotiation concerns the role of the state and the distribution of property:

> Several theorists have asserted that state ownership of property—that is, the abolition of private property—constitutes the qualitative difference between the capitalist city and the socialist one. This position is undeniable, but does it relate to urban artifacts? I am inclined to believe that it does, since the use and availability of urban land are fundamental issues; however it still seems only a condition—a necessary condition, to be sure, but not a determining one.
>
> (1982, 141)

The distinction between a 'necessary' and a 'determining' condition marks the boundary between the unformed and the formed as well as between the city overall and the discrete 'urban artifact': "Ultimately, however, behind and beyond economic forces and conditions lies the problem of choices; and these choices, which are political in nature, can only be understood in light of the total structure of urban artifacts" (1982, 141). For Rossi, form is determined by 'choice' and is linked to a subjectivist understanding of politics. This was clearly stated in "Architecture for Museums": "The subjective element in architecture has the same tremendous importance it has in politics. Both architecture and politics can be and have to be understood as sciences, but their creative moment is based on decisional elements" (2013, 26). Two important questions follow: who or what is the subject making such choices and why is the economic organisation of the city – the 'plan' – not itself a political choice?

Choice and political will

It was Tafuri's argument in "Toward a Critique of Architectural Ideology" (1969; trans. 1998), that, for the Modern Movement, the ideal arena of 'choice' was the planning of society. However, '…once the Plan came within the scope of the general reorganization of production, architecture and urban planning would become its objects, not its subjects' (1998, 21). Choices having ceased to exist at the level of the plan, Rossi sought a change of terrain without relinquishing the political import of the architectural subject. While extra-architectural subjects like classes and states make planning choices, it falls to the architect to make formal choices.[7]

Here, the two contradictions discussed above interact: if the collective in its true form functions at the level of the political-economic – its 'choices' being beyond or outside of architecture – then what 'collective' remains bracketed under Rossi's terms? In what sense, is it 'political' and which of its 'choices' can be appropriated by architecture? Despite the contradictions, Rossi defiantly maintained this position in the final pages of *The Architecture of the City*:

> Urban architecture—which, as we have repeated many times, is a human creation—is willed as such; thus the Italian piazzas of the Renaissance cannot be explained in terms of their function or by chance. Although these piazzas are means in the formation of the city, such elements which originally start out as means tend to become ends; ultimately they are the city. Thus the city has as its end itself alone, and there is nothing else to explain beyond the fact of its own presence in its own artefacts. This mode of being implies a will to exist in a specific way and to continue in that way.
>
> (1982, 162)

That architecture be 'willed as such,' the object of a choice where 'means tend to become ends,' highlights precisely the ideological confluence at stake. For the architect, this would be the ideal point at which collective authorship coincides with individual authorship: a shared class ideology "registered in stone" (1982, 162). It would be the happy coincidence in which 'architecture' is as necessary for bourgeois ideology in general as it is for the professional architects in particular.

The project: will to architecture as will to ideology

Rossi's example demonstrates how architectural discourse, driven by institutional necessity to self-preservation and disciplinary renewal, has tended to produce an ideologically suspect notion of urban society. It did this for clear defensive reasons: after the collapse of the Modern Movement, only a spurious collectivity was capable of re-investing the architect with strong authorial power and social agency.

It would appear to follow that a theory of design, of the politically engaged sort Rossi sought under autonomist terms, would be neither conceptually plausible nor politically desirable. However, ideology does not operate by abstract logic. It is because of Rossi's position within a specifically professional ideology that he concludes *The Architecture of the City* with an example of Slavoj Žižek's famous "I know very well but…" (1989), framing the 'will to architecture' as a magical solution. This paradoxical quality is what makes Rossi's work exemplary rather than exceptional. Recalling Rem Koolhaas's apt phrase: "the greatest theoretician is the greatest obscurantist" (1994, 110), it reveals the extent to which 'theory' conforms to deeper forces and interests. In Rossi's case, the only reason the gambit succeeded was because it coincided with the abandonment of Keynesian economic planning measures in the latter decades of the century.

Despite its conceptual problems, and even against its nominal politics, his theory of architecture functioned and continues to function as a post-planning disciplinary paradigm. In the present moment, it exerts an especially powerful attraction. By simultaneously countering the technophilic determinism of much prevailing architecture culture, while lying within prevailing political-economic assumptions, it offers the appearance of radical critique with the safety of professional conservatism.

As we struggle today to transform the deteriorating and pathological structures of capitalist society, we must confront the ways in which our own thoroughly ambiguous disciplinary and institutional position mediates our thought and practice. We must fight to shape the political–economic character of state institutions, planning and production, for they are exposed to diverse ideological mediations. However, driven by professional-class interests, architecture theory has too often pursued a direct role in ideological mystification. We must free ourselves from this persistently dubious position.

Notes

1 For the larger significance of 'planning,' I draw upon Manfredo Tafuri's notion of the "ideology of the Plan." See Manfredo Tafuri, 'Toward a Critique of Architectural Ideology,' trans. Stephen Sartarelli, in *Architecture Theory since 1968*, ed. K. Michael Hays (Cambridge, MA: MIT Press, 1998), 6–35. While Tafuri extensively treated the crisis of planning, he ultimately never characterised its disciplinary successor. I use 'project' to define the ideological paradigm that replaced planning after the collapse of modernism and the crisis of the welfare state. For a detailed discussion, see William Hutchins Orr, *Counterrealisation: Architectural Ideology from Plan to Project* (PhD thesis, Architectural Association and The Open University, 2019), http://oro.open.ac.uk/61433/.
2 For a detailed discussion of this context, see Mary Louise Lobsinger, 'The New Urban Scale in Italy: On Aldo Rossi's L'architettura della città,' *Journal of Architectural Education* 59, no. 3 (February 2006), 28–38.
3 Rossi did partially recognise this problem: *The Architecture of the City*, 29. There is much more to be said on this than space allows. See Orr, 211–217.
4 While Aureli is at pain to present his reading of Rossi as an alternative to that which foregrounds the question of 'autonomy,' Aureli simply assumes autonomy by never linking 'type' or 'event' to anything outside disciplinary bounds. In contrast, I understand Rossi's contradictions as a manifestation of his autonomism. See Pier Vittorio Aureli, 'The Difficult Whole' *Log* 9 (Winter/Spring 2007), 39–61.
5 "The 'highly general' (*generalissima*) theory of *sprezzatura* is profoundly connected to the notion of a language in perpetual metamorphosis and to the transgressive impulses driving it; between the 'collective that speaks' and the individual subject, 'a dynamic relationship is recognized.'" Manfredo Tafuri, *Interpreting the Renaissance*, trans. Daniel Sherer (New Haven, CT: Yale University Press, 2006), 5.
6 In a 2010 text, Angelika Schnell argued that Rossi's introduction to the 15th Triennale di Milano (1973) associated 'collective creation' with production under socialism. However, as we will see, *The Architecture of the City* explicitly avoided this reading, as did Rossi himself over a career attempting to

reproduce the 'collective' within capitalist relations. See Angelika Schnell, 'The Socialist Perspective of the XV Triennale di Milano: Hans Schmidt's Influence on Aldo Rossi,' trans. Fiona Fincannon, *Candide* 2 (07/2010), 33–72.

7 The power to manipulate form is of course the easiest terrain on which to claim authorial agency, but because of its immediacy, it can also be construed as a kind of moral imperative:

> Foregrounding form might be at odds with most theories premised on the determining role of 'content' such as economy, technology, program and so on. Yet we believe that form needs to be recognized not only as something arbitrarily imposed, or as a symptom of something 'deeper' (superstructural), but more as an attempt of intervention, that has the possibility (and the responsibility) of altering the structure of things.

Aureli and Tattara, 'Architecture as Framework: The Project of the City and the Crisis of Neoliberalism,' 39.

Chapter 11

The heterotopias of Tafuri and Teyssot

Between language and discipline

Joseph Bedford

This chapter traces two interpretations of Michel Foucault's concept of heterotopia in architecture through the interconnected writings of Manfredo Tafuri and George Teyssot between 1968 and 1980. It does so as an exercise in the intellectual history of the field, demonstrating the ways that architecture operates as a discourse that draws upon ideas from other fields in order to be part of a larger dialogue and negotiate larger changes in society, politics, economics and history. The concept of heterotopia is perhaps one of the most polymorphous notions in architecture, if not in all of the humanities, and as such, it lends itself well to this exercise. It has had a complex life within various fields from literary criticism, anthropology, art, geography, urban history and many others and, within each of these, has been interpreted in different ways by different people at different times. Much of the semantic range of Foucault's concept has to do with his text "Of Other Spaces" which, as Peter Johnson puts it, was "briefly sketched and somewhat confusing."[1] It was not a text that he wished to promote or champion, given that he barred its official publication for much of his life. It was likely highly speculative and perhaps Foucault himself felt that it did not fit well within his larger body of work. The text that follows will explore the differences between an interpretation of the concept of heterotopia that privileged the idea of language and one that privileged the idea of discipline. It will map these differences against the larger historical and political context in order to reveal antagonisms within the field, particularly surrounding architecture's relationship to the history of the Left.

Joseph Bedford

Language

Manfredo Tafuri's interpretation of Foucault's concept of heterotopia was based primarily on his reading of Foucault's remarks on the concept in the preface to *The Order of Things*[2] and on Tafuri's interest in the general theme of language, critique and history. For Tafuri, the concept of heterotopia was related to Foucault's reflections on the condition of language within the present historical situation, and Tafuri's interest in it lay in his concern with the role of architectural language, in particular within the present historical situation of political struggles. For Tafuri, the present historical condition of language was that it was unmoored from any natural mediating relationship between subjects and their objects. Tafuri was interested in the relative autonomy of language for political reasons because within it, the realm of language could constitute a form of ideological critique, particularly through its construction of what he called "negative utopias."

Yet, Tafuri was also concerned about this present historical condition of language or the interpretation of it. He feared that if the disconnection between language and natural reality was celebrated too much or if it entirely lost its dialectical interplay with reality, then it would no longer have any political impact. This led Tafuri on several occasions to offer critical commentary of Foucault for indulging in the idea of such a total disconnection between language and reality. Foucault's concept of heterotopia thus partially informed Tafuri's theoretical position between 1960 and 1980, and his view that the contemporary architectural languages of the neo-avant-garde – such as those of James Stirling or Aldo Rossi – *might* serve as a form of critique. It was precisely in the tension he saw between the reduction to an architecture of pure language and play and the appeal to the functionalist ideal of the modern movement that Tafuri glimpsed in the work of Stirling and Rossi a manifestation of potent ideological critique with political implications. Yet, at the same time, Foucault's concept of heterotopia also partially helped Tafuri to crystallise his political opposition to post-structuralist discourses emanating from Paris, which he feared would undermine the real political struggles of class antagonism by rendering them merely discursive with no relationship to a real material basis.

Tafuri's engagement with Foucault's work began as early as 1968 in his essay "Architecture as Indifferent Object and the Crisis of Critical Attention," published as the second chapter of *Theories and Histories of Architecture*.[3] Here, Tafuri offered an architectural history that was framed explicitly as a parallel to the diagnostic history offered by Foucault in *The Order of Things*; one that narrated the construction and dissolution of *man* through the development of the human sciences. As Tafuri put it at the outset of the chapter: "The archaeology of the human sciences, tried by Foucault, can then be checked against the history of architecture."[4]

The architectural history that Tafuri offered ran from Alberti and Borromini, to Blondel, Perrault, Campbell and Burlington, to Winkelmann, Burke, Ledoux, Morris, Camus, Mezieres, Speeth and Lequeu. It narrated the shift of the centre of gravity of architectural meaning from meaning being located "auratically" (à la Benjamin) in the architectural object to meaning orbiting primarily around the emergent figure of *man* from the 16th to the 18th century. As Tafuri wrote, art and architecture now "reject[s] the communication of transcendental dogmas in order to speak to man of the history of humanity."[5] Yet, for Tafuri, no sooner had the figure of man been constructed as a reflective and critical being than had that same figure been annihilated. The critical attention that "man" gave to objects was subsequently displaced by a historical condition of distraction; a condition central to processes of modernisation that Tafuri understood as intertwined with capitalist development. No longer could works of architecture be understood as objects of "man's" critical attention, based, as Tafuri put it, on "images of high intellectual content." Instead, architecture had become "consumed" or "absorbed" into what he called "everyday" "absent-minded perception."[6]

After comparing Foucault's history with that of architecture, Tafuri concluded by reflecting upon a certain anguish which he detected in the contemporary work of architects like James Stirling, whom he described as being caught "half-way" within the dissolution of man and his objects. Such anguish was, for Tafuri, a result of being pulled between two poles: on the one hand, that of hope in the reconstitution of an architectural object that speaks publicly to a critically attentive audience and, on the other hand, the abandonment of hope and the completion of the historical destruction of architectural language as a negative critical gesture.

Three years later, in 1971, Tafuri elaborated again upon his theme of the historical destruction of language in his description of the "negative utopias" of Giovanni Battista Piranesi. In "G.B. Piranesi: Architecture as Negative Utopia," Tafuri highlighted the manner in which Piranesi in such projects as his *Carceri* series explicitly sought to construct impossible realms within language and representation able to critique present historical conditions.[7] Tafuri had not yet explicitly conflated his idea of a negative utopia with Foucault's idea of a heterotopia, as he would do in the coming years. Yet, the similarities between these concepts already pointed in this direction. A negative utopia, for Tafuri, meant something like an impossible space of representation that was able to challenge, negatively, the order of the world through its dissolution. As Tafuri put it, Piranesi's *Carceri* was an "unequivocable attack" upon language as "a mode of acting upon the world."[8] Piranesi's representations of prisons were literally impossible spaces not least because they were composed of perspectival fragments that could not be geometrically resolved as a coherent object. They were thus a negative utopia because they disturbed the order of architectural language, challenging it or critiquing it.

Three years on, Tafuri addressed Foucault's writing once again in his 1974 lecture at Princeton University, "L'Architecture dans le Boudoir: The language of criticism and the criticism of language," published in *Oppositions* 3 that year,[9] now conjoining his reading of the preface to *The Order of Things* with his reading of Foucault's 1970s inaugural lecture at the College De France, "L'ordre du discourse."[10] Tafuri began by referring to *The Order of Things* in the opening remarks of his essay to evoke the theme, already indebted to Nietzsche, of a historical condition in which language has become so emancipated from its reference as to become "silent."[11] Yet, reiterating his 1968 remarks from *Theories and History*, Tafuri saw such an emancipation as ultimately futile and impossible. Again, Tafuri took Stirling as exemplary for being torn between the "reduction of the architectural object to pure language" and his commitment to the "anti-linguistic" – that is, purely functional – tradition of the modern movement, exemplified by Hannes Meyer. As Tafuri put it, Stirling was caught between "the universe of signs and the domain of the real,"[12] and it was this dialectical tension between language and real material history that held out the possibility for critical expression within architecture.

Tafuri then turned to Foucault's "L'ordre du discourse" to support his argument that the universe of signs and the domain of the real must be held in tension and that such a tension was essential for a conception of history as progressing forward through symbolic moments of struggle. Tafuri commented, for example, on a section of "L'ordre du discourse" in which Foucault presented two distinct types of discourses, an everyday speech that passes away and a speech that constitutes the new and which remains:

> The discussions "which are spoken" throughout the days and exchanges which pass away with the very action which pronounced them; and the discussions which are at the origin of a certain number of new acts, of words which pick these up, transform or tell of them; in other words, discussions which remain indefinitely beyond their own formulation, and which *are said*, have been said, and remain still to be said.[13]

The key point here for Tafuri was that these "levels of linguistic organization," as he called them, were indeed distinct. As Tafuri observed when recapitulating this passage in his contribution to *Il Dispositivo Foucault*, "These are two types of discourse."[14] In 1974, Tafuri's use of Foucault's remarks about everyday speech versus historical speech acts was situated within a context in which he sought to criticise the work of contemporary architects like Robert Venturi for no longer desiring to communicate through their architecture. For Venturi, according to Tafuri, architecture was

> dissolved into an unstructured system of ephemeral signals. Instead of *communication*, there is a flux of information; instead of an architecture as language there is an attempt to reduce it to a mass-medium, without any ideological residue; instead of an anxious effort to restructure the urban system, there is a disenchanted acceptance of reality …[15]

For Tafuri, "architecture as language" had to maintain its relation to ideology, and precisely insofar as it worked to change the world around it or was at least in a dialectical engagement with the transformation of reality. What Tafuri called the reduction of architecture to pure language, to "the point of speaking about its own isolation," without *any* connection to the transformation of reality, exemplified a problematic collapse between these two levels. Venturi had collapsed functional architecture into a linguistic architecture in a manner that merely echoed, though in reverse, modern architecture's collapse of a linguistic architecture into a purely functional architecture.

"It is Foucault himself who recognizes the outcome of such an approach," Tafuri wrote, and as he went on, "the elimination of the displacement between those discussions 'which are spoken' and those 'which are said' cannot be realistically accomplished."[16] It was a recognition that was illustrated by Tafuri by citing a second passage by Foucault from "L'ordre du discourse," in which Foucault relayed the idea evoked by Borges of a criticism without any object to criticise:

> The radical repeal of this displacement can only be a game, utopia or anxiety. A game after Borges, of a commentary which will be nothing more than the reappearance, word for word (yet this time solemn and long-awaited) of the object of the comment itself: the game, once again, of a criticism which speaks endlessly about a work which does not exist.[17]

Two years on, in "Ceci n'est pas une ville" of 1976, Tafuri offered one of the earliest interpretations of Foucault's concept of heterotopia, though already, the concept was clearly refracted through his near-decade-long critical dialogue with Foucault.[18] Here, Tafuri sought to build directly upon Foucault's discussion of heterotopia in the preface to *The Order of Things* as a representational incongruity made possible by the disjunctive operations of montage. In place of Foucault's 1966 reference to Lautréamont's infamous operating table upon which an umbrella and a sewing machine could encounter one another "for an instant, perhaps forever,"[19] Tafuri turned to that other surrealist image which had interested Foucault, Magritte's pipe and the conflicted encounter on his canvas between image and word. In this view, while the canvas/table usually helped to constitute order, Lautréamont's and Magritte's montages were heterotopic because they "undermined" or disordered that order. As Tafuri put it:

> The "shock" montage carried out by the historical avant-gardes had, in fact, paved the way which Foucault himself has defined as heterotopy, secretly undermining language 'by devastating syntax in advance and not only the syntax that constructs sentences but also the less manifest syntax which "holds together" words and things (side by side and in front of each other)'.[20]

Tafuri, however, nonetheless made his emerging criticism of Foucault clear that a purely heterotopic disordering of the field would not *necessarily* be emancipatory. It might equally lead to a new kind of order that only reigned invisibly in the now scattered field of fragments. In Tafuri's words: "The point not seized by Foucault is this: that the 'secret' devastation of language is a subterfuge for safeguarding a principle of synthesis in which a new solidarity rules among the fragments of order disordered."[21]

The years between 1976 and 1980 were crucial years of debate in Venice, in which Tafuri was engaged in heated discussion with George Teyssot about the work of Foucault and the political implications of Foucault's views about language and power. During these years, Tafuri taught seminars on Piranesi and revised once more his interpretation of the "negative utopias" of Piranesi, now conflating them, problematically for Teyssot, with Foucault's concept of heterotopia.

As Teyssot argued, on reflecting back on the conflicts between them in Venice over the interpretation of Foucault's concept of heterotopia, Tafuri's idea of "negative utopia was of one artist, Piranesi, while Foucault's heterotopias were never the production of subjective wills. I had written on the concept of heterotopia, and we went through a real conflict because of what I was saying."[22] The distinction at the heart of the conflict between Tafuri and Teyssot was their respective interpretations of heterotopia as an idea about language, linked to the possibility that it might support a critique of ideology, and as an idea about space, linked to the disciplining of society.

Teyssot's reading of heterotopia operated at a more spatial register and drew upon Foucault's later writing on the concept of heterotopia in "Of Other Spaces," though his interpretation quickly collapsed Foucault's concept of heterotopia into Foucault's discourse on discipline. Teyssot was interested in the possibility of a method of architectural history that analysed architecture's role in the rationalisation of the modern world through its functions of disciplining of the social body, participating in the reorganisation of categories of knowledge.

Tafuri's reading of heterotopia, by contrast, continued to operate at the level of language and never moved far from Foucault's first remarks on the concept in the Preface to *The Order of Things* or Foucault's writing about language. In spite of the debates in Venice between 1976 and 1980, Tafuri continued to emphasise the radical possibilities of language articulated by Foucault in 1966, and not for lack of understanding of Foucault's later writing, but as a result of a principled opposition, which he shared with his colleagues in Venice, Massimo Cacciari and Franco Rella, towards the implications of Foucault's conception of power as something dispersed within the social body, and which language as a medium of communication has no symbolic relation to.

Perhaps, purposefully, Tafuri continued to conflate his reading of Piranesi's work as a "negative utopia" when he re-wrote his 1971 article for republication in *The Sphere and the Labyrinth* in 1980, transforming its title into "'The Wicked Architect': G. B. Piranesi, Heterotopia, and the Voyage." Tafuri also now inserted the passages he had drawn from the Preface to *The Order of Things*, which he had used in "Ceci n'est pas une ville," into his Piranesi article, cementing his interpretation of heterotopia as a key to the ongoing critical function of language, adding: "One could very well apply to this [Piranesi's] obsessive technique of assemblage Foucault's definition of heterotopia."[23]

Il Dispositivo Foucault

If Tafuri had remained concerned primarily with the Foucault of *The Order of Things*, *The Archaeology of Knowledge*, and "L'ordre du discourse," it was because, as we have said, he remained fascinated by Foucault's discussions about language and resistant to his shift in the 1970s towards a new analytic of power mapped out through his work on the histories of disciplinary institutions. In these years, Foucault was engaged in research into the history of prisons, housing and urban planning, which transformed society not simply through new systems of knowledge but through what he began to call, a *dispositif*, a "heterogeneous ensemble consisting of discourses, institutions, architectural forms, regulatory decisions, laws, administrative measures, scientific statements, philosophical, moral and philanthropic propositions."[24]

Foucault had, of course, written extensive histories of the emergence of medical practices and asylums in *The History of Madness* and *The Birth of the Clinic*, and in many ways, his studies of prisons in the early 1970s were extensions of these histories; yet, by the 1970s, the context around Foucault's work had shifted significantly, becoming ever more politicised and creating a unique circumstance out of which his research emerged and by which its results were received. An unusual situation in France emerged in the 1970s, following the events of May 1968, as culturally enlightened figures such as André Malraux were appointed to key government posts, and an extraordinary period of State sponsorship of architectural and urban research began to blossom which facilitated a number of experimental research organisations.[25]

The most famous of these was the Centre d'études, de recherches et de formation institutionnelles (CERFI) founded by Felix Guattari in 1965, a collective of radical social science researchers that saw themselves as being on the radical Left, but as having explicitly broken away from the communist party in terms of their theoretical orientation. Then, there was CORDA, the Comité pour la recherche et le développement en architecture, a research committee created in 1972 by the director of the ministry of cultural affairs, Jacques Duhamel. During the 1970s, CORDA ran nearly 200 research initiatives around four principal areas: the theory, epistemology and pedagogy of architecture; operational processes and architectural conception; the integration of architecture in its environment and systems of production for the social use of architecture.[26]

Foucault had begun working with CERFI in 1972 on a grant-funded project that would lead towards the publication of several projects: *L'espace Institutionnel de l'architecture entre 1750–1850* with Bruno Fortier, *Les équipments du pouvoir* with Gilles Deleuze and Felix Guattari and *Les équipements sanitaires*.[27] In September 1975, Foucault signed a contract with CORDA for a research project titled "L'histoire de l'apparition de la notion d'habitat dans la pensée et la pratique architectural au XVIII et XIX siècles" that lead to the publication of *Les machines a guerir (aux origines de l'hopital moderne)* with Fortier and the *Politics of space in Paris at the end of the Ancien Regime*, and later, *Politiques de l'habitat (1800–1850)*.[28]

In all this, Foucault was now situated within a much larger milieu of researchers in Paris that included architects, historians, sociologists, historians of science and geographers – figures such as Blandine Barrett-Kriegel, François Béguin and Anne Thalamy – who were collectively developing a new and influential methodological approach to architectural history that might hope to reveal a different understanding of architecture's relationship to power; one based *less* on understanding architecture as a form of language able to *communicate* – in Tafuri's term – and instead based *more* on understanding architecture's function in disciplining and normalising the social body through the coercion of more individuated and subjective everyday dimensions of experience.

Just as Tafuri was continuing to publish his various commentaries on Foucault's conception of language, the cumulative impact that these architectural research projects emanating from Paris and the political events that joined Italy to France at the end of the 1970s would lead to a debate within the Department of Critical Analysis and History at the Institute for Architectural History at IUAV in Venice between Manfredo Tafuri, Massimo Cacciari, George Teyssot and Franco Rella over the influence of Foucault's work – a debate that served as the site of contestation between Teyssot and Tafuri's interpretations of heterotopia.

The debate was held on one day, on 22 April 1977 in the aula Magna at the Tolentini campus in Venice (Figure 11.1), and the transcripts of the presentations were published that December in the book *Il Dispositivo Foucault* (Figure 11.2). The event was much anticipated, and its influence went well beyond Venice. As just one example, a party of Spanish architects including Beatriz Colomina drove from Barcelona to attend the seminar on Foucault and to report on it in *Carrer de la Ciutat*.[29]

That the seminar on Foucault was named after a concept which had only appeared in Foucault's research for the first time in 1975, and that the front cover of the publication featured a "panoptic" circular-form hospital plan, indicates the degree to which the *Il Dispositivo Foucault* event was ultimately preoccupied with the problematic of Foucault's conception of power as put forth in the pages of *Discipline and Punish*. Indeed, it was a preoccupation that had its roots in theoretical debates throughout the Left in France and Italy.

Left intellectuals in France and Italy had been increasingly turning to the role of culture and society as an ideological ground of class struggle and were adopting new

Figure 11.1 Aula Magna, Tolentini Campus, IUAV, Venice
© Università Iuav di Venezia, Laboratorio Fotografico, Umberto Ferro

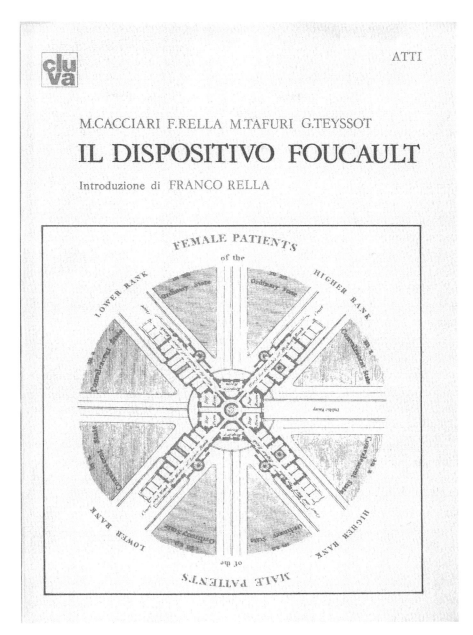

Figure 11.2 Front cover of *Il Dispositivo Foucault* (CLUVA, Veniezia, 1977)
Image Courtesy of Cluva Libreria Editrice

conceptual tools from linguistics, semiotics and psychoanalysis in order to develop a critique of power as it operated within culture and society rather than within the State or Parliament. Where the Italian Communist Party (PCI) held firm to Marxist orthodoxies regarding workers seizing control of the instruments of the State in order to advance the class struggle, a new radical Left had emerged that readily used the experimental writings of French intellectuals such as Foucault, Gilles Deleuze and Felix Guattari to help them advance extra-parliamentary strategies of political action based upon the contestation of the organisation of society: structures of the family, the relation between society and the individual, and the individual's desires and consciousness. Often, these new strategies involved rejecting the very existence of the State-form, its institutions and parliamentary protocols.

The years between 1975 and 1977 in Italy were also especially tense due to a rise in Left-wing terrorism. There were bombings in public spaces and on trains in major cities that killed several dozen people, and the radical Left terrorist group, Brigate Rosse, kidnapped the prime minister in 1978 and conducted a public trial through letters issued to the media over the course of a month before dumping his dead body midway between the headquarters of the PCI and the Christian Democratic headquarters in Rome – the two parties to the "historical compromise" which had angered radicals on the Left. To traditional members of the PCI, such terrorist groups were mixed-up with these new theoretical strategies. Francoise Dosse describes well the scenes in Bologna in 1976 in which over 8,000 people gathered in the city over many days filling the streets. With older members of the PCI effectively cowering inside the townhall, various groups gathered outside – some violent and brandishing weapons and some carrying Foucault's *L'Ordre du discours* and Guattari's *Anti-Oedipus* and talking about "desiring machines."[30] Such intellectual connections between Bologna and Paris were further indicated by the petition signed by Foucault, Deleuze, Guattari, Barthes, Sartres, Sollers and Kristeva in July 1977 against the perceived repression of the Italian autonomist movement in Italy.[31]

In such a political context, the seminar on Foucault in Venice in April 1977 was designed as a trial not only on the proper name of Foucault but on the new theoretical conception of Left-wing politics emanating from Paris and spreading throughout the world. Of the group gathered in the seminar to discuss Foucault's work, Massimo Cacciari was the most critical of Foucault, though Tafuri was not far behind. For Cacciari, Foucault was too concerned with reflecting upon forms of discourse and not concerned enough with the realities of existing practices of power politics in the institutions of the party, parliament and the State. Cacciari and Tafuri's position on politics could be said to have more in common with Mario Tronti and Claude Lefort's efforts to affirm the autonomy of the political, disentangling it from the social.[32] Yet, as Sandro Mazzadra has pointed out, the autonomy of the political became caught up in disappointments about the "historical compromise" between the Communists and Catholics.[33] A compromise which Franco "Bifo" Berardi described as "an alliance between the PCI and the Christian Democrats … aimed at avoiding social confrontation" and which only confirmed that the "parliament was against the movement."[34] In this sense, Cacciari and Tafuri opposed the mounting tide of pressure of the youth movement in Italy and its reduction of politics to the social. Cacciari's commitments to the autonomy of the politics of party, parliament and the state would indeed be made clearer still after the seminar, as he left his teaching post at the IUAV in order to become the mayor of Venice.

According to Tafuri, however, Cacciari went too far in his dismissal of Foucault and largely reduced the ideas in *Discipline and Punish* to Gilles Deleuze's interpretation of them in his review of *Discipline and Punish*. This review, along with Deleuze's review of *The Archaeology of Knowledge*, was published almost immediately in Italian in *Deleuze. Saggi, colloqui, interviste* in 1976.[35] Here, Deleuze imputed to Foucault his own critical diagnosis of the traditional communist party's conception of power and positioned Foucault's work as a theoretical critique of the idea that power is centralised in the State or parliamentary system and that it is something that the Left should no longer seek to possess using the traditional tactics of seizing control of the State apparatus.[36] As Deleuze put it, "As the postulate of localization, power would be power of the State and would itself be located in the machinery of State."[37] Instead, according to Deleuze, "Foucault shows that, on the contrary, the State itself appears as the overall effect or result of a series of interacting wheels or structures which are located at a completely different level."[38] That different level, Deleuze went on, was "characterized by immanence of field without transcendent unification, continuity of line without global centralization, and contiguity of parts without distinct totalization: it is a social space."[39]

Tafuri was right to point out the degree to which Cacciari's reading of Foucault was thus coloured by Deleuze's interpretation of his work. Indeed, in his own contribution to *Il Dispositivo Foucault*, Cacciari slips between a critique of Foucault and that of Deleuze, challenging what he describes as the "disarticulated" "anarchic dispersion of the Political, understood simply as disciplinary techniques."[40] Foucault, Deleuze and Guattari together, then, were taken by Cacciari as equally symptomatic of the problematic nature of the new strategies that were being pursued by the Left in Italy; strategies that turned away from politics and power as they had been traditionally pursued by the Left, towards a new approach by which the Left sought to modulate or transform individual subjectivities and navigate *within* the microphysics of power.

Tafuri's contribution to *Il Dispositivo Foucault* sided largely with the position of Cacciari in challenging Foucault's notion of power as "dispersed" and "disseminated," as destroying the institutional sites of power in which Tafuri understood political struggle to take place. Tafuri's paper began by questioning Foucault's genealogy as demonstrated in his *History of Madness* and *History of Sexuality*, insofar as genealogy opposed itself to history by rejecting a search for origins and seeking only to trace the ruptures between discourses. Yet, for Tafuri, the fragmentation of the many discourses that Foucault traced was never brought into connection with one another in any larger system within Foucault's work: "The various languages do not interpenetrate, the various places of power are impermeable to each other."[41]

Tafuri's text then returned to some of the same passages he had earlier drawn from Foucault's "L'ordre du discourse" and used in his "L'Architecture dans le boudoir," now reframing them to work against Foucault. Having previously observed Foucault's "recognition" of the Borgesian absurdity of a criticism that has no object to criticise, Tafuri returned to this point and, in doing so also accused Foucault's own more literary writings, such as his writings on Bataille, Roussel or his descriptions of Velazquez's *Las Meninas* as exemplifying that very absurdity. "Foucault seems to endlessly comment on a text that does not exist."[42] And, as such, as Tafuri put it, Foucault himself seems to attempt the annulment of the difference between different types of discourse, between those "levels of linguistic organization" as Tafuri had called them in 1974.[43]

Thus, despite his fascination for Foucault's ideas about language, Tafuri argued alongside Cacciari that Foucault's shift in the site of politics from institutions of power towards the terrain of language remained only at the level of the analysis of discursive breaks, which served for Foucault as a political practice in its entirety. As Tafuri put it, "there is no need to practice power."[44] Foucault's work, Tafuri went on, more damningly, could only ever be a "pre-text:" "the analysis of the text, for Foucault, is nothing more than a pretext, in the literal sense of the term."[45]

> Every text for Foucault is a pretext, in the sense that it is a real *pre-text*: it is a text *that comes before and after*, too soon and too late. What is it that Foucault absolutely cannot investigate, once he isolates practices of discourse from practices of domination, from practices that have a precise political content?[46]

The answer Tafuri gives to the question he posed towards the end of his text returned him to the long-traced conception of heterotopia as that impossible space in which things of a different order can be brought together. Yet, rather than that space being merely an impossibility, Tafuri asserted that that space was in truth a space of conflict and struggle – as if to suggest that this is precisely what Foucault could not investigate:

> In "Ceci n'est pas une pipe," what holds together the image of the pipe and the words that describe it? For Foucault, it is an impossible space; but we will call it that "space of conflict," which Foucault ignored. ... This "dissemination" of traces won't allow any "reconstruction," and especially it won't allow any "space of conflict" or "space of struggle."[47]

"Foucault seems to want to ignore the real conflict," Tafuri concluded, adding that "signifying practices and those of power do or don't exist in a space of real, managed, and political power." Against Foucault's genealogy, what Tafuri referred to as "historical space" was precisely not dispersed, it was instead a "space of conflict" that starts from texts as "elements of real power ... that is exercised over things and relations of production."[48]

In October, that same year, Tafuri went on to generalise his concerns not just about Foucault, but about the entire emanation of post-structuralist writing from Paris including those of Blanchot, Barthes, Deleuze and Derrida. Writing in "The historical 'project'" in *Casabella*, he argued in a manner echoing his position put forward during the *Il Dispositivo Foucault* seminar, that

> The danger that menaces the genealogies of Foucault—the genealogies of madness, of the clinic, of punishment, of sexuality—... lies in the

reconstruction of the microscopically analysed fragments as new units autonomous and significant in themselves. What allows me to pass from a history written in the plural to a questioning of that very plurality?[49]

That is, the danger was that that fragmentation could only devolve downwards and could not grasp historical space as a space of larger struggles and conflicts. Tafuri went on to embellish further on that "danger":

> By willingly taking on the plural aspects of objects themselves written in the plural … these critical languages prevent themselves from crossing the threshold that divides language from language, one system of power from other systems of power. They can break up works and texts, construct fascinating genealogies, hypnotically illuminate historical knots glossed over by facile readings. But they must necessarily negate the existence of the *historical space*.[50]

Discipline

According to David Stewart, commenting on the English translation of Teyssot's contribution to *Il Dispositivo Foucault*, Teyssot's contribution to the Venice seminar should be viewed as an "attempt to salvage something of the notion of heterotopia"[51] not as a poetics, which he implies it became with Tafuri, but as a history of the spatial disciplining that enabled modern society to come into being. For Teyssot, heterotopia was a key concept within a larger framework of Foucauldian thought about the relationship between knowledge and power and urban modernisation. It thus addressed in his view precisely what Tafuri feared, the reduction of the Political to social discourses; yet, in doing so, it opened up the possibility of new methodological approaches to architectural history, which Teyssot wanted to advance further.

George Teyssot was closely associated with the milieu directly surrounding Foucault in Paris in the mid-1970s. He had completed his doctorate at the IUAV in 1971, and after a year of study at Princeton University (1971–1972), he returned to Europe where he commuted between Venice and Paris between 1973 and 1978, teaching and researching. In Paris, Teyssot continued to collaborate with the Institut d'Etudes et de Recherches Architecturales (IERAU) at the Ecole d'Architecture de Paris-Belleville,[52] and in the context of his trips to Paris, he became part of an informal seminar that Foucault held in 1975 under the domed canopies of the old *Bibliothèque Nationale*. Foucault had just published *Discipline and Punish* in February 1975, and Teyssot recalls that sometime between 1974 and 1975, he visited Louis-Hippolyte Lebas's La Petite Roquette with Foucault, a prison built in 1830 for minors, children and women.[53]

At that time, Teyssot was exploring the archives of the Conseil des Bâtiments Civils at the Archives Nationales, conducting research that investigated the larger relation between governance, territory and security; themes explored by Foucault in his Collège de France lectures in the same years.[54] During this time, Teyssot collaborated on publications with Bruno Fortier, an architect central to the research milieu around Foucault.[55] One can thus observe in Teyssot's contribution to the *Il Dispositivo Foucault* seminar a desire to demonstrate or perform something of the methods of research being developed in Paris, perhaps more so than a concern to defend the new radical Left politics of the time that Teyssot and Cacciari saw in Foucault's work.

Teyssot put forward his position in the debates in Venice thus not only through his text "Eterotopie e storia degli spazi" (Heterotopias and the history of spaces) which he wrote for the seminar,[56] but also more so through his organisation of a major international conference titled "Architettura, programma e istituzioni" in October 1977, organised by Teyssot and Paolo Morachiello and published under the title *Le Macchine Imperfette* in 1980. The conference clearly had a polemical function in Venice to bring research work underway in Paris into contact with the Venice school. That the participants – including Jacques Guillerme, Jean-Claude Perrot, Christian Deviller, Robin Evans and Manfredo Tafuri – were brought together under the sign of Foucault's inspiration is made clear by Teyssot's efforts to invite Foucault himself to speak at the conference – an invitation he declined.[57]

Given this context, Foucault's concept of heterotopia was now once more problematically conflated with something else, less with the concept of "negative utopia" and, instead, with the concept of discipline. In "Heterotopias and the history of spaces," for example, Teyssot used the concept of heterotopia to describe 19th-century prisons or hospitals in which the regularisation of space, separations, discontinuity and ordering were brought about by a new instrumental form of architecture built by reformers and engineers. Of Louis-Pierre Baltard's Bicetre Prison (1816) (Figure 11.3), for example, included by Teyssot in the *A+U* republication of the text, he wrote that "There is a regular and heterotopic separation between the workrooms that occupy the two wings of the building as well as between them and the central circulation space,"[58] thus making heterotopia virtually synonymous with Foucault's "heterotopias of deviance," and equating the key function of heterotopias with that of rationalisation and the emergence of regularised spaces as producers of forms of social categorisation – something that only occupies a very small fraction of Foucault's "Of Other Spaces" text. Foucault's text instead covers many kinds of heterotopias in traditional society and of several different types, involving illusion and crisis as much as deviance.

Teyssot thus collapsed Foucault's concept of heterotopia into Foucault's discourse on taxonomy and the epistemic shift from the classical to the modern brought about by the reorganisation of systems of knowledge. In regards to Borges's "Chinese Encyclopedia" (Figure 11.4), which Foucault used to illustrate the idea of a heterotopia in *The Order of Things*, and which Tafuri took as naming simply the impossible spaces made possible by language that can momentarily invert the existing order, Teyssot showed more interest in the form of the list itself, or we might say the grid of the table or the logic of regularisation that govern emerging systems of knowledge from the

17th century through the end of the 18th) in opposition to the Renaissance, which preceded it, and the modern age from which we are about to 'emerge'. In attempting to reconstruct the classical episteme, Foucault's analysis turns on three cognitive axes: namely, 'speaking (Language)', 'classifying (Life)' and 'exchanging (Labour)', which in the modern age comprises philology or linguistics, biology and economics but in the Classical Age were known respectively as 'general grammer', 'natural history' and 'analysis of wealth'.

The 400 pages of *The Order of Things* sets forth the problem of the discontinuity, or disjunctions, between one particular system of ordering and the next. Foucault demonstrates that there can be no transition (in the sense of 'evolution' or 'progress') between, for example, the natural history of Buffon or Linnaeus—still related, as it was, to the task of a *mathesis universalis*, as a science of universal order—and modern biology (from Cuvier onward) where the concepts 'history', classification, structure and 'table' are replaced by anatomy, organism and series. Science, as a cognitive practice, encounters epistemological 'obstacles' at certain moments, the resolution of which is achieved through 'ruptures', that constitute *events*. It was the anti-evolutionist and anti-positivist thinking of Gaston Bachelard which introduced these notions of discontinuity to the history of science in France. For Bachelard and for his successor Georges Canguilhem (for the important influence of Canguilhem on Foucault, see bibliography, Section II) every science generates, at each moment of its history, its own truth criteria. While Bachelard's epistemology is historical, Canguilhem's history of science is epistemological: to set an analysis of the object and the 'ruptures' in cognitive organization against the subject and its *continuity* is—for Foucault—'to achieve a form of historical analysis able to take into account the subject's position in the network of history'. The 'truth' of a science occasions an 'irruption', and it is the discovery of a number of such occurences in simultaneous fashion that allows Foucault to define the episteme. Nevertheless, the fact, as Canguilhem notes, that *not all* the sciences are taken into accont by Foucault poses, paradoxically, a doubt with respect to the epistemological existence of the 'Classical episteme': the Foucaultian edifice gives no place to the relative *continuity* of physics from, for example, Newton to Maxwell. It is perhaps for this very reason that the term episteme is relatively little used in his subsequent writings (further to this observation, see bibiography, Section III). However, the aim and scope of Foucault's work is not so much to construct a universal system of knowledge as to

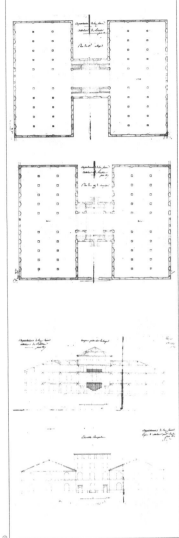

Figure 11.3 Bicetre Prison by Louis Pierre Baltard (1816), from "Heterotopias and the History of Spaces" in *A+U* no. 121 (1980), 64–71

Image Courtesy of A+U Publishing Co., Ltd

classical age onwards. In this sense, Teyssot saw the very form of the encyclopaedia as a historical matter, as an instrument of knowledge and a space that defined the birth of modernity. It was this system of categorisation and spatial internment of the parts above all that produced what he referred to as "heterotopic separation."[59]

ETEROTOPIE E STORIA DEGLI SPAZI

di Georges Teyssot

All'inizio de *Le parole e le cose,* Foucault cita una «certa enciclopedia cinese» di Jorge L. Borges, dove venivano elencati gli animali del mondo: «gli animali si dividono — egli dice — in:

a) appartenti all'Imperatore;
b) imbalsamati;
c) addomesticati;
d) maialini di latte;
c) sirene;
f) favolosi;
g) cani in libertà;
h) inclusi nella presente classificazione;
i) che si agitano follemente;
j) innumerevoli;
k) disegnati con un pennello finissimo di peli di cammello;
l) eccetera;
m) che fanno l'amore;
n) che da lontano sembrano mosche».

Questa classificazione che ovviamente non può che far sorridere per la sua incongruenza e per il suo carattere eteroclito, permette a Foucault di iniziare un discorso sui modi di organizzare le «cose» in un dato periodo storico; perfino l'incongruenza della successione alfabetica che uno può rilevare leggendo un dizionario o un'enciclopedia come un romanzo, è più logica dell'incongruenza di questa classificazione, dove struttura del-

Figure 11.4 Jorge L. Borges's "Chinese Encyclopedia" cited by Foucault in the preface to *The Order of Things* and reproduced by George Teyssot in "Eterotopie E Storia Degli Spazi" *Il Dispositivo Foucault* (CLUVA, Veniezia, 1977)

Image Courtesy of Cluva Libreria Editrice

With this interpretation of heterotopia as an instrument in a historical process of social modernisation, Teyssot compared Borges's list to the categorisation of different kinds of deviance in the town of Caen as described by Jean-Claude Perrot, a study discussed by Foucault in his 1977–1978 Collège de France lectures. Even though, in reality, the various social functions being categorised within the town were not literally ordered in a regularised spatial or geometrical grid of any kind but were rather dispersed haphazardly around the town, Teyssot placed them into an imagined literal grid in his own diagram (Figure 11.5), to make his point clearer and to emphasise that what was at stake was simply categorisation and separation, more than spatial relations of contiguity or threshold – which were the main theme of Foucault's "Of Other Spaces."

Foucault did indeed link heterotopia to power in his brief remark in that text, writing that, when entering a heterotopian place, one is usually "constrained, as in the case of entering a barracks or a prison, or else one has to submit to rites and to purifications."[60] Yet, this one sentence comprises only a small proportion of the text which is concerned with far more than power, and as Foucault's life-long partner, Daniel Défert argued, making a similar criticism of Teyssot's interpretation of heterotopia, is concerned with the "embeddedness of spatiality in the totality of human existence: the Heterotopia and discontinuity of lived temporalities, the thresholds of life."[61] In Teyssot's 1977 interpretation, however, in the context of attempting to demonstrate the usefulness of Foucault's thought for new practices of architectural history to his Venetian colleagues in which one might better understand architecture's role in underlying historical processes of modernisation and rationalisation, he argued that heterotopia was primarily and exclusively a concept linked to architecture's relationship to discipline. As Teyssot put it: "A clear idea of this phenomenon of a 'spatially discontinuous ground' is essential for an understanding of the structure of spaces fixed by modern society,"[62] and "one of the principal objectives of ... [this] research" was the analysis not of "monumental visibility, but the inscription in space of many regulatory and autoregulatory apparatuses, in sum, 'heterotopias'."[63]

Conclusion

This chapter has traced two interpretations of Foucault's concept of heterotopia in architecture through the interconnected writings of Manfredo Tafuri and George Teyssot between 1968 and 1980, which constitute an early phase in the reception of the idea of heterotopia among architects and architectural historians, theorists and critics. This tracing has revealed a larger set of political antagonisms both in society at large and the field of architecture in particular. At the level of society at large, Tafuri and Teyssot occupied different positions with respect to the fate of the Left and the most appropriate strategy for progressive politics. Tafuri was more aligned with Cacciari and held some reservations about the turn of politics towards a politics of language or a politics of culture; a politics that adopted the strategy of manoeuvring within the more invisible structures, subjectivities and mechanism of desire of the social body. Like Cacciari,

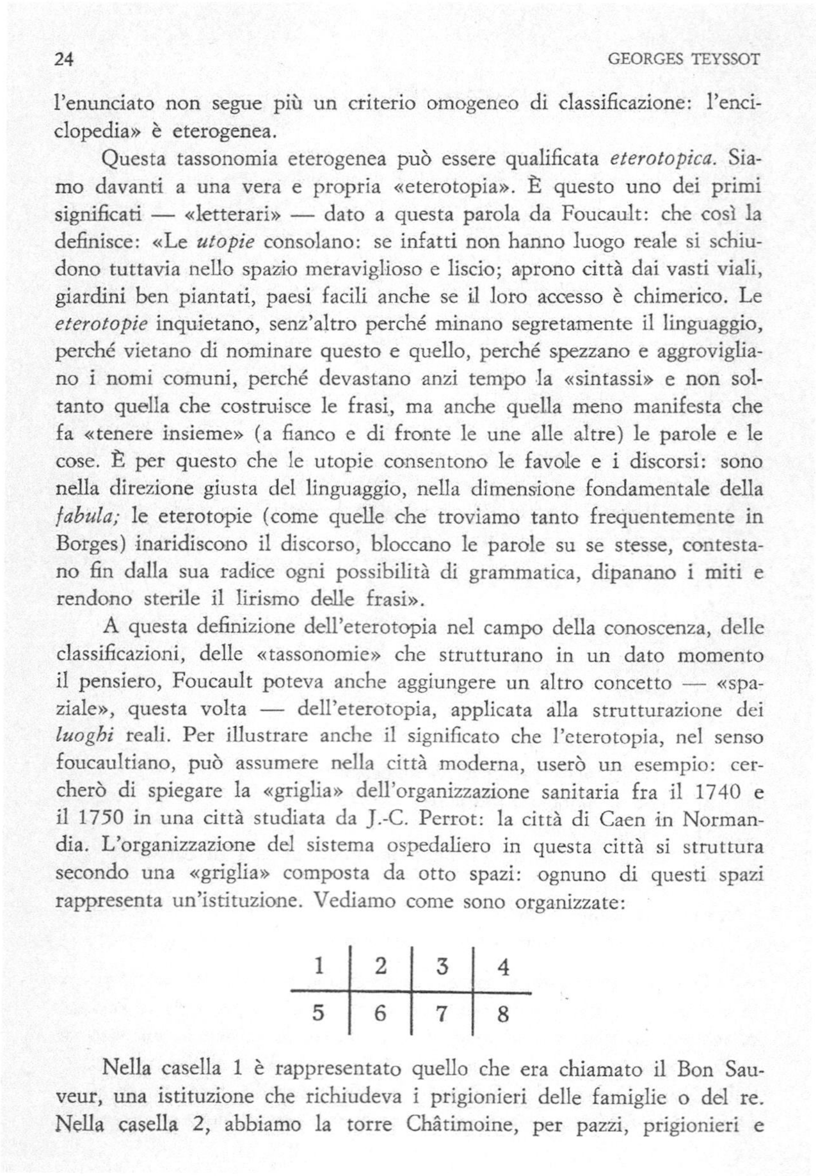

24 GEORGES TEYSSOT

l'enunciato non segue più un criterio omogeneo di classificazione: l'enciclopedia» è eterogenea.

Questa tassonomia eterogenea può essere qualificata *eterotopica*. Siamo davanti a una vera e propria «eterotopia». È questo uno dei primi significati — «letterari» — dato a questa parola da Foucault: che così la definisce: «Le *utopie* consolano: se infatti non hanno luogo reale si schiudono tuttavia nello spazio meraviglioso e liscio; aprono città dai vasti viali, giardini ben piantati, paesi facili anche se il loro accesso è chimerico. Le *eterotopie* inquietano, senz'altro perché minano segretamente il linguaggio, perché vietano di nominare questo e quello, perché spezzano e aggrovigliano i nomi comuni, perché devastano anzi tempo la «sintassi» e non soltanto quella che costruisce le frasi, ma anche quella meno manifesta che fa «tenere insieme» (a fianco e di fronte le une alle altre) le parole e le cose. È per questo che le utopie consentono le favole e i discorsi: sono nella direzione giusta del linguaggio, nella dimensione fondamentale della *fabula;* le eterotopie (come quelle che troviamo tanto frequentemente in Borges) inaridiscono il discorso, bloccano le parole su se stesse, contestano fin dalla sua radice ogni possibilità di grammatica, dipanano i miti e rendono sterile il lirismo delle frasi».

A questa definizione dell'eterotopia nel campo della conoscenza, delle classificazioni, delle «tassonomie» che strutturano in un dato momento il pensiero, Foucault poteva anche aggiungere un altro concetto — «spaziale», questa volta — dell'eterotopia, applicata alla strutturazione dei *luoghi* reali. Per illustrare anche il significato che l'eterotopia, nel senso foucaultiano, può assumere nella città moderna, userò un esempio: cercherò di spiegare la «griglia» dell'organizzazione sanitaria fra il 1740 e il 1750 in una città studiata da J.-C. Perrot: la città di Caen in Normandia. L'organizzazione del sistema ospedaliero in questa città si struttura secondo una «griglia» composta da otto spazi: ognuno di questi spazi rappresenta un'istituzione. Vediamo come sono organizzate:

1	2	3	4
5	6	7	8

Nella casella 1 è rappresentato quello che era chiamato il Bon Sauveur, una istituzione che richiudeva i prigionieri delle famiglie o del re. Nella casella 2, abbiamo la torre Châtimoine, per pazzi, prigionieri e

Figure 11.5 George Teyssot's diagram of the grid of eight institutional spaces of sanitation in the town of Caen in "Eterotopie E Storia Degli Spazi" *Il Dispositivo Foucault* (CLUVA, Veniezia, 1977)
Image Courtesy of Cluva Libreria Editrice

Tafuri remained wedded to politics as a visible and public struggle over the political institutions of state and economic power.

At the level of architecture, Tafuri and Teyssot occupied different positions within the field of architectural history, theory and criticism, with respect to the fate of the political role of architecture in their own time. Tafuri was caught up in a theoretical engagement with the fate of the architectural avant-garde and the possibility of its continuation in the present moment through an architecture committed to the critical use of architectural language. His interest in the possibilities of architectural design, composition and linguistic meaning as a critical instrument, indicated a residual hope – despite his remarks about dispelling such hopes – in the possibility of the singular architectural object and its author to speak. For Teyssot, by contrast, perhaps imbibing Foucault's posthumanist sentiment more fully than Tafuri, if one was interested in the political role of architecture, one had to look not to any singular building or author, but to architecture as a distributed typological fabric; a machine deployed by state functionaries concerned with legal regulations and categories of knowledge.

Tafuri and Teyssot's positions on the politics of architecture, furthermore, implied different methodological approaches to architectural history, theory and criticism. Tafuri was interested in Foucault's work, but he was less interested in Foucault as a historian and more interested in Foucault as a philosopher of language. By contrast, Teyssot could be described as more properly moving towards the development of a more Foucauldian mode of architectural history. This difference can be signalled by the fact that where Tafuri engaged with singular authors such as a Piranesi, a Stirling or a Rossi and dramatised the larger narrative meaning of his histories through the psychological conditions of anguish experienced by this or that author. Teyssot's histories orbited less around subjects and singular objects and more around everyday spaces or instruments of modern life, from water and gas supplies to suburban homes and lawns. This methodological difference charts something of architectural history's shift from its alliance with theory, criticism and neo-avant-garde practices in the 1970s and 1980s to a more anonymous, materialist and empirical mode of historicism; one more closely aligned with the fields of history of science or science and technology studies.

These differences between Tafuri and Teyssot both in terms of politics more generally and in terms of the political role of architecture more specifically are also interconnected. Tafuri's residual hope in architecture as able to communicate as a singular authored object was likely linked to his view of politics as a battle over the institutions of power that remained hierarchical, public and visible. Politics for Tafuri was an explicit struggle over the more consequential symbolic spaces of privileged contestation. It was in a sense, always the politics of princes, of the city, and of significant projects that would draw him ever more towards the history of the Renaissance. Teyssot, by contrast, had shifted away from the visible terrain of monuments and authors, towards a conception of architecture as a distributed field of typical and everyday spaces. In this sense, Teyssot's interpretation of heterotopia as synonymous with the concept of discipline was more aligned with what Foucault's work represented politically in Europe during the 1970s. The political meaning of Foucault's work in these years was, like that of Deleuze and Cacciari, bound up with the larger history of Left in these years after the mid-century crisis of orthodox Marxism. The political meaning of Foucault's work was aligned with the shift from the early classical Marxist focus on the economic means of production and the control of state institutions towards the New Left's focus on forms of oppression that operated through subjectivity, desire, social practices, habits and cultural expressions.

These divergent readings of heterotopia offered by Tafuri and Teyssot were historically intertwined within the period from the 1970s through the 1980s. There were many architects, especially in the epicentres of avant-garde culture such as New York, who were especially interested in Tafuri's interpretation of heterotopia. Take, for instance, Diana Agrest and Stan Allen who both adopted it.[64] Tafuri's Piranesi remained an inspirational force for architects wishing to practice and theorise the political possibilities of contemporary architecture. Tafuri's interpretation of the meaning of Foucault's concept circulated widely in design schools and among practicing architects for this reason. Yet, simultaneously, in the increasingly professionalising field of architectural history and theory, as doctoral programs began to expand, there were many architectural historians who were interested in Teyssot's interpretation of heterotopia because it suggested a means for the historian to operate on a theoretical plane, in dialogue with contemporary practitioners, and equally engaged with the writings of so-called post-structuralist writers emanating from Paris. Yet, it also enabled them to ween history off its alliance with theory and practice and transform it into an independent professional field in an increasingly academicised environment. Take, for instance, Reinhold Martin, a student of Teyssot at Princeton University who followed Teyssot's lead in interpreting Foucault's concept of heterotopia.[65]

This history of Foucault's concept of heterotopia is less a history that reveals the inherent meaning of Foucault's concept than it is a history that traces its negative shadow on the historical field around it: examining how architects reacted to it, how they fought over it, how they distorted it or how they took inspiration from it, and for what reasons. The word "architecture" is of course the name we give to concrete material things like buildings or the equally material and technical practices of surveying, measuring, drawing, documenting and constructing. Yet, it is also the word we use to name the discursive field of ideas and meanings of the architectural discipline; a discipline that is as much an intellectual formation as it is a practical formation. These ideas and meanings are always nested in larger fields of ideas that are part of a larger cultural, political, economic and historical terrain. Architecture as a discourse has a long history of receptivity to the latest concepts and ideas emerging in other fields. For this reason, it is constituted by a constant external and internal dialogue and one that both reflects and projects a larger world outside of architecture.

Notes

1 Peter Johnson, "Unravelling Foucault's 'Different Spaces'", *History of the Human Sciences*, vol. 19, no. 4 (2006), 75–90.
2 Michel Foucault, *Les Mots et les Choses, une archéologie des sciences humaines* (Paris: Éditions Gallimard, 1966), translated into Italian as Michel Foucault, *Le parole e le cose: un 'archeologia delle scienze umane*, translated by Emilio Panaitescu (Milan: Rizzoli, 1967) and into English as *The Order of Things: An Archaeology of the Human Sciences* (New York: Pantheon Books, 1970).
3 Manfredo Tafuri, "Architecture as Indifferent Object and the Crisis of Critical Attention", in *Manfredo Tafuri, Theories and Histories of Architecture* (New York: Harper & Row, 1980), 79–103. Originally published

in Italian as Manfredo Tafuri, "L'architettura come 'oggetto trascurabile' e la crisi dell'attenzione critica", in *Teorie e storia dell'architettura* (Bari: Laterza, 1968).
4. Manfredo Tafuri, "Introduction", in *Theories and History of Architecture* (New York: Harper & Row, 1980), 80.
5. Tafuri, *Theories and History*, 80.
6. Tafuri, *Theories and History*, 92–96.
7. Manfredo Tafuri, "G.B. Piranesi: L'architettura come utopia negativa", in *Angelus Novus*, no. 20 (1971), 89–127, later republished under a revised title and changes as "'The Wicked Architect:' G. B. Piranesi, Heterotopia, and the Voyage", in *The Sphere and the Labyrinth*: Avant-Gardes and Architecture from Piranesi to the 1970s, trans. Pellegrino D'Acierno and Robert Connolly (Cambridge, MA: MIT Press, 1987), 29.
8. Tafuri, "'The Wicked Architect'", 29.
9. Manfredo Tafuri, "L'Architecture dans le Boudoir. The Language of Criticism and the Criticism of Language", *Oppositions*, no. 3 (May 1974), 38–62.
10. Michel Foucault's inaugural lecture, "L'ordre du discourse" was delivered on 2 December 1970. It was published the following year in French as the book *L'ordre du discourse: Leçon inaugurale au Collège de France prononcée le 2 décembre 1970* (Paris: Gallimard, 1971). Tafuri cited from this French publication. The first English translation was published as "The Discourse on Language" as an appendix in Michel Foucault, *The Archaeology of Knowledge* (New York: Pantheon Books, 1972).
11. Tafuri, "L'Architecture dans le Boudoir", 38.
12. Tafuri, "L'Architecture dans le Boudoir", 41.
13. Tafuri, "L'Architecture dans le Boudoir", 55.
14. Manfredo Tafuri, "Lettura del testo e pratiche discursive", in *Il Dispositivo Foucault* (Venice: Cluva, 1977), 39.
15. Tafuri, "L'Architecture dans le Boudoir", 55.
16. Tafuri, "L'Architecture dans le Boudoir", 56.
17. Tafuri, "L'Architecture dans le Boudoir", 38. Citing Michel Foucault, *L'Ordine del discorso* (Turin: Einaudi, 1972), 19.
18. Manfredo Tafuri, "Ceci n'est pas une ville", *Lotus International*, no. 13 (December 1976), 10–13.
19. Michel Foucault, "Preface", *Order of Things* (Abingdon: Routledge, 2001), pp. xvii–xix.
20. Manfredo Tafuri, "Ceci n'est pas une ville", *Lotus International*, no. 13 (December 1976), 11.
21. Tafuri, "Ceci n'est pas une ville", 11.
22. George Teyssot and Paul Henninger, "One Portrait of Tafuri", *ANY*, no. 25–26 (2000), 8–9.
23. Tafuri, "The Wicked Architect", 40.
24. Michel Foucault, "The Confession of the Flesh" (1977) in *Power/Knowledge Selected Interviews and Other Writings*, ed. Colin Gordon (Harvester Press, 1980), 194—228.
25. On this history, see the forthcoming edited volume by Moritz Gleich and Anne Kockelkorn, titled *Habitat and Equipment: Architecture and urban research with Michel Foucault, 1975–77*.
26. Stuart Elden and Jeremy W. Crampton, eds., *Space, Knowledge and Power: Foucault and Geography* (London: Ashgate, 2007), 72.
27. See Perrot, Michelle, "L'espace maudit et l'homme-machine", in *A.M.C*, no. 30 (1973), 16–18; *Recherches*, no. 3 (CERFI); Francois Fourquet & Lion Murard, *Les Equipments du Pouvoir: Territoires et Equipements Collectifs* (Paris: Union Generale d'Editions, 1976); Bruno Fortier, *L'espace institutionnel de l'architecture entre 1750–1850* (Paris: CORDA, 1976); *Les Équipements sanitaires* (Fontenay-sous-Bois: CERFI 1976).
28. See Michel Foucault, Blandine Barrett Kriegel, Anne Thalamy, Francois Beguin and Bruno Fortier, *Les machines a guerir (aux origines de l'hopital moderne)* (Bruxelles: Pierre Mardaga, 1976), Michel Foucault and Bruno Fortier *Politics of Space in Paris at the End of the Ancien Regime* (CORDA/DGRST, 1976) and Michel Foucault (ed.) and Francois Beguin *Politiques de l'habitat" (1800–1850)* (Paris: CORDA, 1977).
29. The publication of the Spanish translation of Foucault's "Of Other Spaces" text was announced in the very first issue of *Carrer de la Ciutat* (November 1977), 5–9. Il Dispositivo Foucault was reported on in *Carrer de la Ciutat*, no. 1 (January 1978), an article "La arquitectura en Théleme" offering critical commentary was published by Josep Muntañola I Thornberg, *Carrer de la Ciutat*, no. 6 (January 1979), 3–4. Foucault's "Of Other Spaces" text was then published *Carrer de la Ciutat* 1 (January 1978), 5–9.
30. Francois Dosse, *Gilles Deleuze and Félix Guattari: Intersecting Lives* (New York: Columbia University Press, 2011), 285. See also Marco Assennato, "Il Dispositvo Foucault", *Il 68 Che Verra*, eds. Michela Maguolo and Peppe Nanni (Venezia: Edizioni Engramma, 2018), 117–135; and Alessandra Ponte, "Molecular Revolution in Aula Magna", in *Radical Pedagogies*, eds. Beatriz Colomina, Ignacio G. Galán, Evangelos Kotsioris and Anna-Maria Meister (Cambridge, MA: MIT Press, 2022).
31. Sandro Mezzadra, "Beyond the State, Beyond the Desert", *The South Atlantic Quarterly* (Fall 2011), 991; and Franco "Bifo" Berardi, "First Bifurcation: 77 the Year of Premonition", in *Precarious Rhapsody: Semiocapitalism and the Pathologies of the Post-alpha Generation* (New York: Autonomedia, 2009), 25.
32. Claude Lefort, *Democracy and Political Theory*, trans. David Macey (University of Minnesota Press, 1988) and Mario Tronti, *Sull'autonomia del politico* (Milan: Feltrinelli, 1977).

33 Mezzadra, "Beyond the State", 989.
34 Franco "Bifo" Berardi, "First Bifurcation: 77 the Year of Premonition", in *Precarious Rhapsody: Semiocapitalism and the Pathologies of the Post-alpha Generation* (New York: Autonomedia, 2009), 19.
35 Gilles Deleuze, *Deleuze: Saggi, colloqui, interviste* (Cosenza: Lerici, 1976). Later published in English in Gilles Deleuze, *Foucault* (University of Minnesota Press, 1988), 1–44. Tafuri's discussion of this source appears in Tafuri, *The Sphere and the Labyrinth*, fn. 18, 306.
36 Gilles Deleuze, "A New Cartographer", in *Foucault* (University of Minnesota Press, 1988), 24.
37 Deleuze, "A New Cartographer", 25.
38 Deleuze, "A New Cartographer", 27.
39 Deleuze, "A New Cartographer", 27.
40 Massimo Cacciari, "Il Problema Del Politico in Deleuze e Foucault (Sul Pensiero di 'autonomia' e di 'gioco')", *Il Dispositivo Foucault* (Venice: Cluva, 1977), 61, trans by author.
41 Tafuri, "Lettura del testo e pratiche discorsive", 39, trans by author.
42 Tafuri, "Lettura del testo e pratiche discorsive", 40, trans by author.
43 Tafuri, "Lettura del testo e pratiche discorsive", 40, trans by author.
44 Tafuri, "Lettura del testo e pratiche discorsive", 40, trans by author.
45 Tafuri, "Lettura del testo e pratiche discorsive", 43, trans by author.
46 Tafuri, "Lettura del testo e pratiche discursive", 43, trans by author.
47 Tafuri, "Lettura del testo e pratiche discorsive", 43–44, trans by author.
48 Tafuri, "Lettura del testo e pratiche discorsive", 45, trans by author.
49 Manfredo Tafuri, "Il 'progetto' storico", *Casabella*, 429 (October 1977), 11–18. Reprinted in Manfredo Tafuri, "The Historical Project", in *The Sphere and the Labyrinth: Avant-Gardes and Architecture from Piranesi to the 1970s* (Cambridge, MA: The MIT Press, 1990), 5.
50 Tafuri, "The Historical Project", 9.
51 David Stewart, "Why Foucault", in *Architecture and Urbanism*, vol. 10, no. 121 (October 1980), 105.
52 IERAU was founded in 1971 by Bernard Huet and integrated into the UP8 (Paris-Belleville School of Architecture). Georges Teyssot's publication *Les bâtiments civils en France et la planification du Mans* (Paris: DGRST, 1973) was the third in their list of publication. He later collaborated with Marco De Michelis between 1976 and 1977 on a further project on "architecture of social democracy" published as *Les Conditions historiques du projet social-demorate sur l'espace de l'habitat* (Corda, 1977).
53 Georges Teyssot. Pers. Comm. March 9, 2020.
54 See Georges Teyssot, "Citta-servizio. La produzione dei Batiments civils in Francia (1795–1849)", *Casabella*, no. 424 (April 1977), 56–65; and Georges Teyssot and Paolo Morachiello, "State Town: Colonization of the Territory during the First Empire", *Lotus*, no. 24 (1979). Foucault's Collège de France lectures between 1975 and 1976 were published under the titles of *Society Must Be Defended* and his lectures between 1977 and 1978 were published under the title *Security, Territory, Population*.
55 See George Teyssot and Bruno Fortier, "Birth of Public Buildings; The Logic of Public Buildings: Notes for the History of a Project; and, The Town and Public Buildings: Architectural Production of Public Buildings, 1795–1848", *Architecture Mouvement Continuite AMC*, no. 45 (May 1978), 79–94.
56 Teyssot's text was translated into English and published as "Heterotopia and the History of Spaces" in *A+U*, no. 121 (1980), 64–71. It was also advertised in a forthcoming Spanish translation in *Carrer de la Ciutat* in 1980 though this never took place.
57 Georges Teyssot. Pers. Comm. March 9, 2020. Those who did present at the conference included, Bruno Fortier, Jacques Guillerme, Jean-Claude Perrot, Christian Devillers, Bernard Huet, Robin Evans, Renzo Dubbinia, Paolo Morachiello, Giandomenico Romanelli, Ennio Concina, Donatella Calabi and Manfredo Tafuri.
58 George Teyssot, "Heterotopias and the History of Spaces", *A+U*, (1980), 87.
59 George Teyssot, "Heterotopias and the History of Spaces", *A+U*, (1980), 87.
60 Michel Foucault, "Of Other Spaces" (1967) trans. Lieven De Cauter and Michiel Dehaene, in Lieven De Cauter and Michiel Dehaene, *Heterotopia and the City: Public Space in a Postcivil Society* (London: Routledge, 2008), 21.
61 Daniel Défert, "Foucault, Space, and the Architects", *Documenta X* (Kassel: Hatje Cantz Verlag, 1997), 280.
62 George Teyssot, "Heterotopias and the History of Spaces", *A+U* (1980), 85.
63 George Teyssot, *Le macchine imperfette. Architettura, programma, istituzioni nel XIX secolo* (Rome: Officina Edizioni, 1980), 11.
64 Diana Agrest, "The City as the Place of Representation", *Design Quarterly*, no. 113–114 (1980), 8–13 and Stan Allen, "Piranesi's 'Campo Marzio': An Experimental Design", *Assemblage*, no. 10 (December 1989), 70–109.
65 Reinhold Martin, "Borges and Piranesi", *Oz*, vol. 14 (1992), 10–14.

Chapter 12

Interruptions

A form of questionable fidelity

Doreen Bernath

This chapter proposes 'interruptions' as a necessary part of a collective, within a temporal assembly of different actors, producers and agents that are expected to work together. If the intention of the collective is to honour the productive differences between these forms of work, then it is precisely where the need for gaps, mismatches and incongruous adjacencies becomes important. Rather than being smoothed over by an imposed uniformity, continuity or authority, deliberate staging of interruptions enables the manifestation of such noisy, polyphonous gathering, which exposes the inadequacy of a dominant form or a singular interpretation. Thus, the question of fidelity, being faithful to a certain common cause, is transposed into a constructed situation of complicit infidelity. In this chapter, these situations are played out in three cases – 'an interrupted image,' 'an interrupted meal' and 'an interrupted way.' These collective yet complicit apparatuses present, on the one hand, parts with diverging actions that refuse to sum up to a whole; and on the other hand, disruptive counter-actions that provide the opportunity to override given norms, thus allowing alternative voices and opinions, a way out.

In a larger sense, the production of theory as a discursive, collective practice carries with it a questionable fidelity. This duty of provocation, expanding to works of research and criticism, resists the expectation of being a faithful ally of other practices; instead, the relation is that of both love and betrayal. Every act of insight, imagination and innovation possible in architecture is a trace of such transgression, intentional deceit and treacherous exposure between the work of thinking and the work of doing between theory and practice. This is where what is said and not said, the visible and the hidden, the mark and its erasure, constitute the relation of complicity behind

Doreen Bernath

movements of conservation and revolution that shaped what we now know as architectural histories.

An interrupted image

When Gabriele Basilico takes a shot of the Pantheon in Rome in 2010, half covered by scaffolding and diminished amongst ordinary pedestrians, 250 years after Piranesi's etching of the same monument ruining in time, can we learn something new about it?[1] Basilico captured a moment when the Pantheon's perfect and permanent presence was disrupted (Figure 12.1). Maybe the Pantheon would have wished to put up a sign, 'no photographs.' The effect of partial obscuring and distortion – which can be disputed as more or less beautiful or more or less profound – complicates what the Pantheon means to us.

In her exploration of the notion of 'erasure,' Teresa Stoppani describes it as a project in its own right, requiring a determination, a decision, towards the object that it erases, both the presence and absence of it.[2] Far from a simple act of removal, to erase involves a complex process of adding and effacing, producing new connotations by changing the 'face.' The Pantheon here had been temporarily 'effaced' by both the presence of the scaffolding, the unexpected show of fragility and by Basilico's decision to frame it through his photo-*graphy*: the image has double-crossed itself, and the

Figure 12.1 Veduta del Pantheon, by Gabriele Basilico, 2010
Permission obtained from Archivio Gabriele Basilico (in Italian, from Giovanna Calvenzi, see below correspondence)

symmetry of the gaze is broken by the asymmetry between the exit and the return. The Pantheon is both there and not there, itself and not-quite-itself; it 'exited' when partially obscured from view, and subsequently, it is never the same when it 'returned' into full view either in other images or in other instances of visits.

This double-edged process of effacement interrupts the supposed continuity between object, medium and subject, and it interrupts the assumed correlation between a work of photography and its meaning. Walter Benjamin repeatedly discusses the importance of such deliberate 'interruptions' in a work, from theatre, film, radio, photography to writing, to reveal and be critical of 'conditions of actions' and 'organising functions.'[3] He praises how the technique of 'montage' interrupts the continuity of action or drama and prevents the work from simply reproducing stimulations and consumables. To prevent such blindness, the creator of the work must not only make visible the organising, or operative, function of the work to the audience, therefore turn them from passive spectators into active collaborators, but also open the work up to interruptions by other creative forms and techniques. Benjamin demonstrates this resistance through instances when John Heartfield's 'photo-collages' interrupt the passive status of a book cover to turn the face of a book, over and above the content of the book, into a political instrument, and when 'songs' by actors-chorus interrupt the dramatic actions in Bertolt Brecht's epic theatre.[4]

This instance of interruption, in Benjamin's critical framework, resists complacency and produces astonishment. It is not enough, as Benjamin daringly put forward in the 1930s, to judge a work simply by adhering to the concept of commitment. It is not enough to commit to certain revolutionary causes, yet being complacent at the level of producing work. This is why he criticises photographic works by both Henri Tracol, who faithfully belonged to the short-lived communist front in France and photographed proletariat activities, and Albert Renger-Patzsch, who travelled throughout rural and industrial areas of Germany to produce revealing images of poverty and exploitation, as part of the so-called 'New Objectivity' movement in photography.[5] Their images, which submitted to the given production apparatus without exposing or changing it, too easily turned depiction of human misery, and the struggle against misery, into objects of consumption and themes of entertainment.

Underlying the need to question the apparatus of production, as well as the relation between producers and spectators-turned-collaborators, is the transformative necessity of 'betrayal,' which "consists in an attitude which transforms [the revolutionary intellectual], from a supplier of the production apparatus, into an engineer who sees his tasks in adapting that apparatus...." Benjamin makes reference to Louis Argon to emphasise the hinge of disloyalty, of going against a context of origin, a set of personal relations, acquired skills and values which altogether define the person in the first place, which is necessary for such functional transformation to achieve the 'quality' of work over and above 'commitment.'[6] This hinge of infidelity in both the apparatus of production and the intellectual commitment is manifested at such constructed moments of interruption in the work; thus, infidelity becomes functional and operative. It allows the work to be doubted, that is, to make bare the gaps and incongruous elements as opportunities of re-thinking and re-acting. It allows multiple perspectives, opinions and voices to co-exist and contradict. It may be full of faults and laughter; it resists becoming a complete, perfect and reproducible product.

There is one recent theatre work which exemplifies a continuation of the Benjaminian and Brechtian effort in tearing down the complacency in the apparatus of production. Katie Mitchell's direction of *Kristin, after Miss Julie* in 2011, based on August Strindberg's play *Fröken Julie* (1889), transformed the stage into a live film set.[7] The presence and movement of camera crews, cables and lighting equipment, switching of channels between different camera views, close ups and doubles, constructed scenes and editing, technicians manipulating and synchronising sound effects, were all laid bare to the audience, who also witnessed the play as a film through live streaming on the overhead cinema screen. Mitchell described the intention to re-examine Strindberg's characters, stereotypical of his time, "as if they had been grown in a Petri dish and were being looked at under a microscope."[8] This laboratory-like analogy is evident in both the technical resolution of live filming on stage and the presentation of multiple versions of the same scene to the audience.

During the play, the protagonist Kristin appears as: first, an actual person on stage but only partially visible (present but not filmed); second, by means of a double also present on stage (filmed live); third, as an image on the projected screen in full, closed up and detailed view through the camera; and finally, as conjured through simulated sounds of her actions by technicians at the front of the stage (Figure 12.3). One

Figures 12.2 and 12.3 Kristin, after Miss Julie (2011), directed by Katie Mitchell and Leo Warner, adapted from August Strinberg's play from 1889, in collaboration with Schaubühne Berlin, produced and performed at Festival d'Avignon

Photograph by Christophe Raynaud de Lage

character in manifold, occupying four or more different locations on stage and distracting one another in competition for attention, breaking all prior expectations of a smooth theatrical or filmic experience. The way that the audience is invited to witness and scrutinise all aspects of this dismantled production shatters the pretence of any singular interpretation of the story and its characters and, furthermore, demands a much more involved attention from the audience to make sense, each potentially with a different conclusion, of what is going on across this manifold.

With the help of the vivisected techniques and thus the penetrating gaze of the audience-collaborators, Mitchell reveals Kristin's opaque self by bringing attention to lesser, peripheral and subconscious details, multiplied and enlarged through the apparatus of the production.[9] From beside, beneath and behind the scenes, shifting between being conscious or not conscious of the camera, the audience or the whole dance of equipment and technicians, new 'Kristins' emerge in midst of this collective yet interrupted apparatus. From Mitchell's laboratory, grafting character specimens between Petri dishes, the 'lens' moves now to the noisy feast by Anthropocene servomotors on Oligocene creatures.

An interrupted meal

Resin from plants, which gradually fossilises into amber, is produced as a kind of trap to repel or attract insects and fungi, friends or enemies. In Pierre Huyghe's recent video work *De-extinction* (2014), the camera places itself at a microscopically close range to the amber, not quite yet but tempted to be caught, such that its searching eye focuses, moves, refocuses, all within this tiny confinement, to the effect of re-animating some very dead insects in a very dead piece of stone.[10] The camera feasts on the amber which is full of insects frozen in time; the self-recorded soundscape hauntingly captures the way it targets, bites, tears and devours each fragment of bodies, fleshing the ancient stone. Adrian Searle has remarked on the hunger for flesh and blood permeating from this "amplified soundtrack of whirrs and jolts from the camera's servos" that continuously "focuses and refocuses on a glutinous mass of 30 million-year-old amber… including what is apparently the oldest known example of copulating mosquitos," comparing it to the tanks in the same exhibition where live mosquito larvae dance "among the fish and the lily roots, before emerging as adults to fly off in search of blood."[11]

Our science lessons have constructed for us a historicised relationship with amber, fossils and immortal flies, but none of which involves the noise of a microscopic camera. The amazement created back in 1878 when David Hughes' carbon microphone picked up and amplified a fly's footsteps is here interjected by Huyghe by picking up the camera's 'footsteps' while capturing the fly's footsteps, so to speak.[12] The audio patterns are intuitively recognisable, based on experiences not of the science of fossils but more immediately of noises of familiar photographic equipment that rotate, slide and track. The handheld artificial eye makes noises that speak of the dynamics of its interior, the producing mechanism, and at the same time, it occupies the attention of our visual field, the produced image. Previously, we had only seen the latter; here, in *De-extinction*, we hear the former while seeing the latter.

The hidden apparatus combines mechanisms of phonographs and cinematographs, which Friedrich Kittler has described as two technologies that have enabled us to store "time as a mixture of audio frequencies in the acoustic realm and as the movement of single-image sequences in the optical."[13] This ability to arrest "daily data flow in order to turn it into images or signs," as Kittler exposes, threatens the scientific continuum of time and brings what is dead back to life again. By revealing the mechanical sound of the camera, that is, the audible control of the invisible cameraman, Huyghe disrupts the dormant status of the 30-million-year-old amber to offer a glimpse of not only a new kind of fluidity for both the substrate of amber and the bodies swimming in it but also of the viewer as proxy cameraman that can carry on after the film ends the adventure within the amber, now synchronised with the actual time of a new navigator with a prosthetic eye.

'In the beginning was the noise,' which, according to Michel Serres's parables, brings "an interruption, a corruption or a rupture of information."[14] The noise of the camera here becomes the 'third person' that upsets the balance and disrupts the original feast, that is, the consumption of those 'natural images' in text books of biology and evolution and in popular science television shows. There is nothing natural about the images of our biological world, as all have been as artificially produced as political images from the aforementioned 'New Objectivity' movement in photography so much objected to by Walter Benjamin. Rather than questioning the given visuals by means of visual criticisms, the interruption that surprises us and changes our relation with dead insects is the noise. It is the noise – the sign of perpetual parasitic relation, and the sign of threats, betrayals and errors – that creates the system; and it is the noise that changes the system.[15] The correspondence between the aural trace of the producing mechanism and the produced image is deliberate and uncanny, inducing our imagination in its calibration. The artificiality of biology is part of our biology; the relation is changed by the parasitic noise, and such that, we reorganise our role to become a co-producer of our natural knowledge.

It is inherent to technology to make itself invisible, to become a precisely sealed and concealed 'black box,' which Bruno Latour describes as technology's "characteristic form of mini-transcendence," as if all occurring by magic.[16] Latour goes on to say, resonating with the ubiquitous noise in Serres' model of the parasite, that it is only magic insofar as it is performing; the magic breaks down when it is not performing, making visible the cascade of contingencies, the inadequacies within techno-complexity, when encountering an obstacle, a problem, an error. Our biology lessons have been presented to us with such aura of magic, such that the technology of constructing the 'natural' necessarily remains invisible. It is already a cliché – a form of magic achieved through mini-transcendence – that the plethora of media reinforces a smooth continuum of photo-real images of nature, animals, plants, planet(s), environment and ecological systems. This is accompanied by audio tracks of yet another smooth continuum of sounds made by protagonists of the natural show, altogether fabricating a beautiful fantasy of certain originary primordial jungles or oceans, and of expected scenes of cycles of life.

The appearance of the noise of technology breaks the magic, shifting our relation to technology from a mode of transcendence to a mode of imminence according to Latour, as a result of a deliberate, inappropriate change in the audio domain from performing organisms in front to the servomotor mechanism behind.[17] More distractingly, Huyghe's noise is about a machine that copies what we do, as an aural analogy of what our eyes do, as much as we believe that the artificial eye has a correspondence with natural vision, or rather, a cultured vision. Our machines, our technology, is 'intersubjective.'[18] In this model of relations, that oscillates with variable stability, subjects turn into objects, in such ways that we turn into cameras and cameras in turn feast on the insects in stone. We become complicit in this interruption, overriding one fable with another fable or science's anthropomorphism.

'The system works because it does not work,' warns Serres as he dismantles the dialectical basis – subject-object, positive-negative, friend-enemy, victor-victim, predator-prey – of our relations, observing that "as soon as we are two, we are already three or four," or more.[19] Inclusions and exclusions are shifting nebulously, without reciprocation, only a change of system, either when the gift from the host has been exhausted by the parasite, or when another parasite appears, supplanting the first. It took the construct of a 'faulty' situation, a camera that makes a noise, contrary to the desire for the perfect, silent camera, as a new parasite that enters the picture and creates a new order. Our meal of biology has been interrupted, and now, we are invited to join in with Huyghe, the host that opened the door to a new intruder that changed the order of relations, alarmed or relieved by a different set of noises to feast on flies and cameras. The noise moves on, from that of a camera's footsteps around flies, to a folly in the gap between two streams of elevated traffic of a flyover.

An interrupted way

In 1971, in Vienna's prominent urban space in front of St. Stephan's cathedral, to the shock of local conservative shop owners, a scene of 'free' architecture of play unfolded. While Coop Himmelblau inflated four giant footballs to invite city dwellers to a spontaneous urban game, the other radical Viennese practice Haus-Rucker-Co installed a 'Walking School,' which was an obstacle course of 60 meters in length that offered participating pedestrians chances to experience 'balance shifts,' 'haptic walking' and expansion of 'consciousness at the very bottom.'[20] (Figure 12.4)

This piece of temporary architecture, caught between the impression of being inviting and fun, and being seriously obstructing due to its size and location, was intended as a form of resistance to the loss of walking spaces in the city centre to the flow of traffic and vehicle parking. In a gesture to reconquer urban spaces for the pedestrian, Haus-Rucker-Co disrupted normal behaviours and routines, which then were relocated, reassembled and intensified in the production of a new pedestrian experience. The Walking School played on the increasing impossibility to walk in cities by, first, mocking street obstacles that interrupted people's ways, then second, staging gaps in the obstacles as invitations to those with arousing curiosity to walk onto and

Figure 12.4 Walking School (1971), project by Haus-Rucker-Co
Photograph by Gert Winkler

into the construct. Pedestrians temporarily recruited by the Walking School would be both reassured yet shocked by this juxtaposition, as transitions between routine and staged walks had been deliberately dramatised. Those who entered the stage of unexpected walks were looked on by passers-by as if they had become a new troop of actors, attempting to act out another normal walk, but stimulated by the unusual circumstances of waving grounds, level changes, surprising tactility and barriers. As the festival of *fussgangerzone* hoped, citizens of Vienna may not walk the same after this, and in turn they may expect a different kind of future for their urban spaces.

It is obvious how, throughout their periods of engagement, participants may remain undecided whether this was normal or abnormal. They might feel strangely familiar or playfully unfamiliar in the Walking School, which further blurred given boundaries of expected behaviours. Those who embraced undecidability as a moment of opportunity at such moments of interruptions did, in the depth of their subconscious being, give way to a new expectation. The installation produced a switch at a fundamental level: obstacles are noises in the system, which in turn change the system.

Assemble, the Turner Prize winning architectural collective, tells a new 'fairy tale' for a folly they created between and beneath a flyover: "it is the home of a stubborn landlord who refused to move to make way for the motorway, which was subsequently built around him, leaving him with his pitched roof stuck between the East and Westbound lanes"[21] (Figure 12.5). The construct presents abundant signs of a 'home' that embodies this fairy tale: an exaggerated pitched roof that pokes its top just above the horizon of the flyover traffic, a mock brick façade, corner and base coursing details reminiscent of Victorian terraces and a house-like arrangement of doors and windows. Yet, all of these appear imprecise and disjointed. These details have been deliberately

Interruptions

Figures 12.5 and 12.6 Folly for a Flyover (2011), project by Assemble
Photograph by David Vintiner. Permission obtained from Assemble Studio

staged, driven by Assemble's intention to reclaim 'the future of the site by re-imagining its past.'

A cross between an actual theatre for performative activities and a fictional theatre conjuring the fairy tale of a leftover house, Assemble took the liberty of stretching the physical and experiential gaps between the actual and fictional aspects of the project. These home/house-like details appear as playful surprises, without logical links to how the building is actually made; it is clearly not a house with loadbearing brick wall. The analogy to 'home' is also contrary to its function since the folly is a thoroughly public building: a café, workshop and canal boat trips base by the day, and by night, it hosts film-screenings, theatres, talks and performances (Figure 12.6).

The gaps as a result of such questionable relevance are obvious. The rough and patchy pseudo brick construct somehow holds together the invented myth of a leftover home from the past. These details are not random but deliberately portrayed as a scene of discontinuity – a *designed* discontinuity – carrying within its assembly ostensible truth values between the contesting realities: the reassurance of a familiarity that came from a cultural norm shared by its audience, the strange siting of the work, the work as a material production and the work's critical opinions. The presence of *true-to-life* or *having-been-there* details, yet seemingly 'superfluous,' 'futile,' 'useless' or 'insignificant' in relation to the main plots or narratives of the work, according to Barthes, pose a resistance to meaning.[22]

Barthes argues that the construction of *verisimilitude*, in classical cultures where we inherited structures of rhetorics, 'is never anything but *opinable*: it is entirely subject to (public) opinion… in verisimilitude, the contrary is never impossible, since notation rests on a majority, rather than on the absolute, opinion.'[23] Barthes goes on to contrast this 'opinable truth' with the more recent obsession over 'concrete reality' because 'what is alive cannot not signify – and vice versa,' as a crucial difference between the ancient mode of verisimilitude and modern realism.[24] From literary realism to 'objective' history, as Barthes further expands, the imperative of realism has driven the development of techniques, works and institutions that endeavour to 'authenticate the real,' such as 'journalistic/reportage photography,' 'exhibitions of ancient objects' and 'tourism of monuments and historical sites.' By such *reality effect*, which depends on the employment of 'referential illusion,' opens up a radical mode of modern verisimilitude.

The city of Rouen, in Barthes' attempt to demonstrate a modern mode of verisimilitude through the analysis of Flaubertian narrative, is caught up in a realistic imperative in *Madame Bovary*. Yet, as we find out in other passages, Flaubert's seemingly realistic description becomes an analogy of a painting. This contradictory mix of both fantasy and objectivity can be related to Brecht's insistence that the actress actually does carry the laundry basket with wet laundry so that "her hip would have the right movement."[25] The epic theatre as a special mechanism in the production of reality effect retains such duplicity of denoting *and* signifying reality, by which the artificiality of reality and its truth value would become apparent. This directly echoes, as discussed earlier, Walter Benjamin's demand for a work to make available to its audience the gaps between constructed realities as a way to elevate it from the question of commitment to the question of critical quality. This is why Brecht's epic theatre, politically motivated to expose the problem of spectacles and dramatisation of his days, would reject elaborate scenographic sets and rely on a few simple props to restore the capacity of the 'actor,' along with the 'audience-as-actor,' as a way into and as a way out of 'verisimilitude.'

Assemble's staging of the 'house' for a public project exemplifies such a mode of referential plenitude, where paradoxically, the truth of the illusion lies between the attempt of all details "to *denote* the real directly, [but] all that they do – without saying so – is *signify* [the real]."[26] The truthful status of the illusion is relieved from the structure of representation of the discipline of architecture, the source of judgment and negotiating opinions or larger discourses on the planning and design of private or public spaces. The folly is where the notion of a modern verisimilitude, as further interpreted by Menachem Brinker, can be understood as a believable mirage of reality that is negotiated between a certain rhetorical structure of the art form and the expectations of its audience.[27] Neither interested in debating situations of domestic dwellings nor significances of public spaces, Assemble's folly project by stealth embraces the ambivalence at a common sense level grounds of what can or cannot be an architectural site, and what kind of behaviour can or cannot be imagined or even permitted. Questions of marginalisation, appropriateness, legality, identity and otherness, the imagination of very-real-conditions of interstitial lives so commonly taken for granted in contemporary modes of 'reality' journalism, are staged here through verisimilitude to its audience, which are then invited to bestow new opinions.

The reality effect of the folly achieved through the constructed discontinuity between the illusion of a home and the actuality of an unexpected public insertion in a problematic infrastructural leftover space provides the ground for Assemble's critique. The Folly for a Flyover project approximates an architectural 'epic theatre' by conjuring verisimilitudes yet interrupting the smooth communication of the reality-effect. All who visit the folly would enjoy, yet not be fooled by, the playful mockery of its façades and construction; it quickly dismantles the fiction, materially and functionally, and offers a counter-subversion by a new possibility of a public 'homeliness.' Visitors, suspended between assurance and astonishment, inevitably partake in 'reworking both the history and future of a site.' One can start to doubt the permanence of neglect as a result of the flyover, the impossibility of a new identity for such a faulty space and the passivity of urban inhabitants to action. The folly, as an instigator of such aporia, as Jacques Derrida would tempt us to think, has opened up a new collective thinking and action.

Notes

1 These two images of the Pantheon, 250 years apart, are: Giambattista Piranesi's etching 'Veduta del Pantheon d'Agrippa oggi Chiesa di S. Maria ad Martyre', da *Vedute di Roma* (1760) and Gabriele Basilico's photograph 'Veduta del Pantheon' (2010). See 'postcard' about Rome and the Pantheon as a double dialogue – between Giambattista Piranesi and Gabriele Basilico, and between Teresa Stoppani and Doreen Bernath – published in 'Gabriele Basilico: Postcards', *The Journal of Architecture*, vol. 24, no. 8 (2020), 1164–1166.
2 Stoppani, Teresa, 'Material and Critical: Piranesi's Erasures', in *Mobility of the Line: Art, Architecture, Design*, ed. Ivana Wingham (Basel: Birkhäuser, 2013).
3 Benjamin, Walter, 'The Author as Producer', *Understanding Brecht*, trans. Anna Bostock (London, New York: Verso, 1998). Address at the Institute for the Study of Fascism, Paris, 27 April 1934 and first published in *New Left Review* 1/62, July–August 1970.
4 'Brecht has coined the phrase "functional transformation" (*Umfunktionierung*) to describe the transformation of forms and instruments of production by a progressive intelligentsia – an intelligentsia interested in liberating the means of production and hence active in the class struggle'. Benjamin, 'The Author as Producer', in *Understanding Brecht*, 93–95.
5 Benjamin, 'The Author as Producer', in *Understanding Brecht*, 93–95.
6 'The revolutionary intellectual appears first of all and above everything else as a traitor to his class of origin.' Benjamin, 'The Author as Producer', 101–102.

7. Katie Mitchell's production of *Miss Julie* was in collaboration with Schaubühne, Berlin and was premiered on 25th September 2010. The use of sound and live video images were explored earlier in Mitchell's earlier production of *The Waves* (2006), adapted from Virginia Woolf's novel written between 1929 and 1931.
8. Tom Cornford, 'Willful Distraction: Katie Mitchell, Auteurism and the Canon' in *The Theatre of Katie Mitchell*, ed. Benjamin Fowler (Oxon, New York: Routledge, 2019).
9. Mitchell is well known to employ and expand an approach developed by Konstantin Stanislavski, who believed in the importance of a certain psychological accuracy in acting individual characters. Cornford, 'Willful Distraction'.
10. This work was shown as part of the 'In. Border. Deep.' exhibition at Hauser & Wirth, London, 2014.
11. Adrian Searle, 'Monkey waiters and axolotls: the disconcerting art of Pierre Huyghe', exhibition review, Adrian Searle encounters in Art section of *The Guardian*, published online 17 Sep 2014. https://www.theguardian.com/artanddesign/2014/sep/17/pierre-huyghes-exhibition-hauser-and-wirth-encounters-review [accessed 2 Nov 2019].
12. Friedrich A. Kittler, *Gramophone, Film, Typewriter*, trans. G. Winthrop-Young, G. and M. Wutz (Stanford, C: Stanford University Press, 1999), 102.
13. Kittler, *Gramophone, Film, Typewriter*, 3.
14. Michel Serres, *The Parasite*, trans. Lawrence R. Schehr (Baltimore, MD and London: Johns Hopkins University Press, 1982), 3, 13.
15. Serres, *The Parasite*, 10–12.
16. Bruno Latour, *An Inquiry into Modes of Existence. An Anthropology of the Moderns*, trans. Catherine Porter (Cambridge, MA: Harvard University Press, 2013), 207–215.
17. Bruno Latour, *We Have Never Been Modern*, trans. Catherine Porter (Cambridge, MA: Harvard University Press, 1993), 29–37.
18. Serres, *The Parasite*, 8.
19. Serres, *The Parasite*, 12–14.
20. Victoria Bugge Øye, 'When Architecture Took to the Streets (and the Laboratory)', *Contemporary Art Stavanger Journal*, Built Environments section, 10 June 2018. https://www.contemporaryartstavanger.no/when-architecture-took-to-the-streets-and-the-laboratory/ [accessed 15 Nov 2019].
21. The project description of 'Folly for a Flyer' is available on Assemble's website: https://assemblestudio.co.uk/projects/folly-for-a-flyover [accessed 15 Nov 2019].
22. Roland Barthes, 'The Reality Effect' (appeared in *Communications* in 1968), *The Rustle of Language*, trans. Richard Howard (New York: Hill and Wang, 1986), 141–148.
23. Barthes, *The Rustle of Language*, 147.
24. Barthes, *The Rustle of Language*, 146–147.
25. Roland Barthes quoted in D. Fleming and D. Sturm, *Media, Masculinities and the Machine* (New York: Continuum, 2011), 154.
26. Barthes in Fleming and Sturm, *Media, Masculinities and the Machine*, 148.
27. Menachem Brinker, 'Verisimilitude, Conventions, and Beliefs', *New Literary History*, vol. 14, no. 2, On Convention: II (Winter 1983), 253–267.

Part IV
The welfare state

Chapter 13

Constructed landscapes for collective recreation

Victor Bourgeois's open-air projects in Belgium

Marie Pirard

Victor Bourgeois, architect, urbanist, teacher and founding member of the CIAM, was a key figure in Belgian modernism. However, his work, especially from the 1930s and the post-war period, has been disregarded by historians and critics of the past decades like Albert Bontridder, Geert Bekaert or Pierre Puttemans. The architect is considered as influential for his writings and thoughts. But his built work is deemed too dogmatic, showing an obsessive wish of organisation.[1] More recently, Iwan Strauven, in a PhD about Bourgeois, has brought some nuance to the discourse by reconnecting Bourgeois's theory and practice and pre-and post-war works. Nevertheless, the leisure-oriented projects studied in this chapter were still neglected by Strauven. Only some of them are briefly addressed in his thesis, presented as projects where architectural composition didn't matter and where Bourgeois mainly emphasised the importance of realising a social program, indicating a shifting moment in the architect's career, where urbanism took place over architecture.[2] These considerations will not be denied (as the dogmatic aspect of Bourgeois's work will appear in the fourth section). But they will be put momentarily aside, in order to recompose another narrative from these marginal projects and their cultural and political context. Indeed, highlighting this part of Bourgeois's career constitutes above all an opportunity to explore the construction of a modernist proposition for collective life, in close relationship with the public-sector contractor and rooted in a landscape approach.

DOI: 10.4324/9781003118985-17

Marie Pirard

Political backgrounds and leisure projects

In the beginning of the 1930s, Belgium was severely affected by the Great Depression. Unemployment and the lowering of living conditions became major political topics while social tensions were exacerbated, leading to violent movement of strikes.[3] Beside wage claims, unions called for the reduction of working hours in order to regulate over-production, to reduce unemployment and to redistribute the positive effects of the rise of productivity.[4] A 1936 law provided six annual days of paid vacation to Belgian workers, arguably motivated by the wish to dissipate class tensions.[5] Simultaneously, the Inter-war period saw the emergence of a movement of protection of nature, supported by scientists like the doctor René Wynants. He called for 'climatic reserves' which weren't only dedicated to preserve biodiversity but were also judged as necessary places of recreation to regenerate the physical and moral health of the workers. Inspired by the German cult of the body, sports and holidays in the nature were presented as a necessary "antidote to the industrial civilization".[6] From unions as well as from the naturist movement, the right for leisure was not to be seen as an opposition to the industrialisation but rather as an internal tool to counterbalance its negative effects regarding health, social cohesion and social justice.

Bourgeois's projects were developed in close relationship with this double discourse in which leisure was presented as a hygiene-oriented social claim. In 1937, he simultaneously started to work as technical advisor for the Ministry of Public Health[7] that had launched an investment campaign called "the crusade for health"[8] and to collaborate with the OREC (office for national recovery), an institution that attempted to operationalise Henri de Man's policy of economic regulation, often compared to the US new deal.[9] The existence of leisure programs in such policies demonstrates the role it played for unions and leftist politics as a tool to find a new economic and social balance. Yet, in both institutions, recreative projects were marginal interventions, on the fringes of investments in engineering infrastructures like the development of drinking water network, river embankments and construction of new roads and canals.[10]

As advisor for the Ministry of Public Health, Bourgeois designed, among others, the master plan for a beach in Hofstade, in the suburbs of Brussel and an unbuilt touristic dam in St-Hubert, in the Southern rural part of the country. Both projects exemplify the state ambition to provide public infrastructures that could shape the leisure of the working-class population, for a day off in Hofstade or for the summer break in St-Hubert. Both projects allowed people to swim, to do sports or relax in large wooded parks. But, beyond the appearance of healthy natural sites, they also share the particularity to be largely artificial. In Hofstade, the site was a former sand quarry whose operation was linked with the creation of railway embankments. Holes left on the site were naturally filled with water and transformed into an artificial pond spontaneously reused by local people for swimming.[11] The master plan aimed at organising the site, including its access and surroundings, in order to improve but also to supervise and clean it up. Influenced by his experience in Hofstade, Bourgeois designed a dam in St-Hubert in order to create an artificial reservoir of about ten hectares in a region where swimming

Figure 13.1 The beach in Hofstade
Source: postcard, editor: L'Heembeekoise, s.d.

opportunities were judged missing. The infrastructure was supposed to attract tourists and to support the development of a leisure centre at its shore, including hotels, a casino, an open-air theatre, a campground and sports fields. But, if in Hofstade, the quarry was a given aspect of the project, in St-Hubert, Bourgeois regarded voluntarily the tools of an industrial process as an inspiration for a leisure-oriented purpose, which was precisely supposed to break with the pressure of the industrial everyday life. These two man-made sites transformed into recreative infrastructures reveal the gap that existed between the ideology transmitted by the public sector of a return to a 'pure an untouched nature' and the actual construction of sites that led to a domesticated nature, artificially adapted for leisure purposes.[12]

In 1937, the OREC launched a special commission for the recovery of the Borinage declining mining region. Bourgeois got involved by designing a master plan for 12 'playgrounds' or recreational areas.[13] They included sports fields, swimming pools or open-air schools and were often surrounded by new housing units. Half of the projects were partly constructed, with, most of the time, Bourgeois as an architect. They were not only merely recreative programs but also aimed at creating civic centres that could support the transformation or the extension of the public space of the villages. In Frameries, he developed a housing complex organised around a large oval-shaped recreative area. A few kilometres away, in Hornu, he integrated a new school, a small open-air theatre and a playground in the centre of the village.[14] Both projects introduced a network of 'green spaces' into the existing structure of the villages. The networks consisted in a series of outdoor rooms dedicated to open-air functions, using topography or vegetation as guidelines.

Marie Pirard

In Frameries, the central playground was divided in several sports fields by large terraces. In Hornu, the garden around the city hall, the open-air theatre and the playground were enclosed by lines of trees. These networks of outdoor rooms were not closed systems; they opened up views towards the industrial landscape, with a special focus on the typical leftover forms from the coal industry, that is, slag heaps, that Bourgeois wanted to turn into parks. In Frameries, the recreational area was on the axis of the two nearest heaps, while others, scattered in the countryside, could easily be spotted by looking between the buildings.[15] In Hornu, Bourgeois enlarged the street beside the church and implanted the school building in a line on the north of the plot in order to open a perspective from the centre of the village to the slag heap located behind the school.[16] These industrial leftovers were not only offered a new status as public green spaces but also envisioned as an extension of the traditional public space. The consolidation of the existing settlements, following Bourgeois's ideas, had to be done by adding new civic and leisure-oriented functions but also, quite surprisingly, by re-linking the villages with their industrial heritage.

Quarry, dams and slag heaps were opportunities found by Bourgeois while working on leisure programs in the context of the early industrialisation of Belgium which, in his own words, had transformed the country into "an extraordinary amalgam of industry, ports, waterways, railways and inhabited centres."[17] He criticised this unregulated transformation, but simultaneously enhanced it by re-using the industrial leftovers or copying the tools of industrial infrastructures like in St-Hubert. Why such an attitude? And how could it support the development of leisure? Opportunism could

Figure 13.2 Housing complex and recreational area in Frameries (the slag heaps are partly visible at top right)
Source: postcard, editor: CIM, s.d.

be one valid answer, as industrial leftovers were already abundant and as public funds were then mostly assigned to infrastructural projects. Nevertheless, this pragmatic assumption was not the only one, as it will be highlighted in the next section.

Earth architecture: an industrial 'détournement'

During the war, Bourgeois wrote "Charleroi, region for urbanism" (Charleroi, terre d'urbanisme), a book that gathered several studies of the industrial city (realised, among others, for the 4th CIAM[18]). Throughout the text, the spatial features introduced in the first section of the chapter resurface, as if Bourgeois assembled all his recent leisure-oriented propositions in this theoretical project for his hometown: slag heaps turned into parks, artificial swimming lakes, open-air theatre and sport stadium were all provided. While explaining the construction of these propositions, Bourgeois gave us a clue concerning his fascination for the industrial landscape:

> (…) the stadium would be mostly dig in the ground. Why not making more often an earth-architecture, as allowed by the present-day technique? From now, architects have only slightly modified the ground relief (…); engineers were more dynamic. Remember the trenches of the Albert canal. With the use of shovels, everything is possible. (…). Earth- architecture will come to the rescue to equip the region of Charleroi; as already mentioned, we have to remove or convert no mountains but at least slag heaps and to create "windscreen" embankments; we will have to dig the open-air theatre and the lake. The shape of the stadium will be given by shovels. The matter is not anymore to make an architecture with facades, more or less independent from the stadium itself. We recommend a rigorously unified composition, whose interest lies, like for a sculpture, in the ground modeling. Every part of this piece: the places to play and run, the bleachers for spectators, roads and parking lots – those neglected aspects of the older stadium – collaborate to create a sportive architecture, unified, simple as well as emotional. And if the artificial landscape created by the stadium and its surrounding – because it is more about that than about buildings – integrates harmoniously the natural landscape, the goal will be completely achieved.[19]

The architect was not only fascinated by industrial constructions (as a result) but also inspired by the industrial way of transforming the whole environment (as a process). Beyond an early attitude of 'adaptive reuse' of industrial leftovers, Bourgeois claimed for the update and the extension of architectural tools. Distancing himself from the traditional way of regarding buildings (locked in the academic issue of the composition of the façade and the social prestige with which it was traditionally associated), he highlighted new technological possibilities allowed by mechanic shovels that architecture should appropriate. Bourgeois didn't give up architectural questions but rather challenged and blurred the border between architecture and landscape, in an ambition to

Figure 13.3 The recreational forest in the South of Charleroi including pedestrian and cycling paths, an artificial swimming lake (bottom left), a stadium (centre) and an open-air theatre (right)

Source: © CIVA, Brussels, Fonds Bourgeois

create a new kind of spatiality (or a new monumentality), while trying to give meaning to the artificiality of the Belgian landscape.

However, these 'artificial landscapes' supported a very different purpose than industry, as the architect assigned them exclusively to public leisure programs. Without apparent irony, he subverted man-made industrial sites to address a topic related to the reform of working conditions (the reduction of working hours) and promoted the creation of natural recreational areas, while encouraging the use of the mechanical shovel, a machine that is commonly associated with the exploitation of soils and the deterioration of landscapes. Through a strategy of 'detournement' of industrial tools, he deeply rooted the reformist program of leisure in the system within which the reform had to occur, suggesting a soft internal reform rather than a revolutionary one. In short: improving and counterbalancing the industrial life with the industrial tools.

From the cult of the machine to the cult of manual labour

Bourgeois's projects could then be seen as heroic ones, embodying social vocation, landscape quality and even the promise to reconcile the society with the machinist era and its influence on the environment. Yet, exploring the construction of a case study

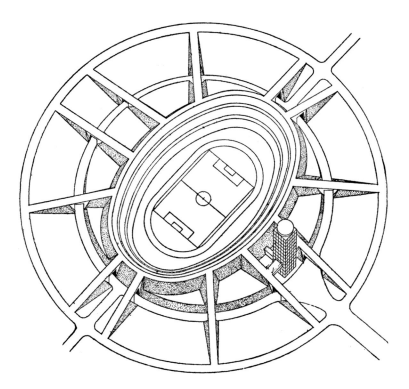

Figure 13.4 Axonometric view of the stadium for Charleroi
Source: © CIVA, Brussels, Fonds Bourgeois

in Antoing reveals a more ambiguous process. In an 1941 interview modestly titled "Urbanism as a savior: sanitation and planning of Antoing" (l'Urbanisme sauveur: l'assanissement et l'aménagement d'Antoing),[20] Bourgeois expounded a top-down, paternalist and spatially determinist point of view: the country under German occupation had to be rebuilt to be saved. Its reconstruction, led by architecture and urbanism, would support the expression of a new social order and would create jobs first by itself and then by creating new economic opportunities.

In this dogmatic context, Bourgeois developed a meaningful example of earth-architecture consisting in transforming a stone quarry into a playground (with sport fields, a school and an open-air theatre). The bottom of the quarry had to be drained and flattened in order to accommodate the programs. The projects thus implied huge earthworks, with about 300,000 m^3 of earth handled, but shovels weren't put at work, they were replaced by manual labour. A working camp was organised by the association 'the volunteers of work' (les volontaires du travail), which welcomed young unemployed man in order to avoid their deportation and forced labour in Germany.[21] In the context of war, the project missed the opportunity of technological modernisation creating a large amount of unspecialised simple jobs. From a faith in progress, the project's ideology shifted towards the valorisation of manual labour as a moral and

Marie Pirard

hygiene-oriented value, similar to the cult of the body expressed in the open-air programs the workers were digging for.

The ambiguity found in the process of construction is also noticeable in the landscape architecture itself. Bourgeois tried to emphasise the industrial past and the romantic decor of the site by re-using the old lime kiln as backstage for the theatre. But despite that, while comparing the pictures before and after the intervention, what emerges is an impression that the site had been severely domesticated, and that almost nothing of the rough atmosphere of the industrial leftover was kept. The expression of

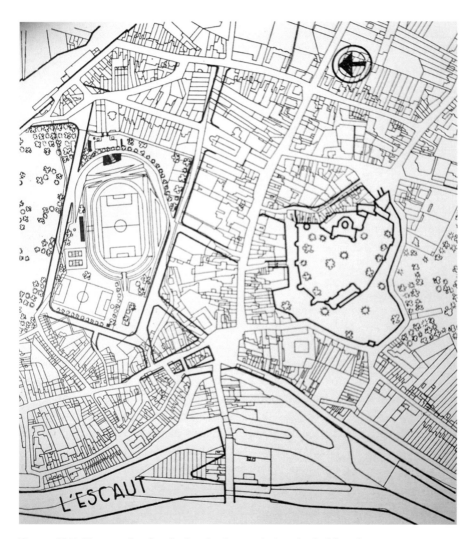

Figure 13.5 Master plan for the 'sanitation and planning' of Antoing
Source: © CIVA, Brussels, Fonds Bourgeois, retrieved from Flouquet, P.-L. (1952)

a social reform seems difficult to find here, arguably overwhelmed by Bourgeois's first ambition: sanitation and planning, leading to a rational but quite inexpressive project that most of the time goes unnoticed.

An oxymoron between industrial tools and recreation in nature

Despite their incompletion, limitations and ambiguity, Bourgeois's projects depict well the complex vision of leisure of his time. They addressed a large range of ambitions from emancipation and social cohesion to paternalism and dissipation of class tensions, from reform of the working conditions to pro-nature and hygiene-oriented considerations. From all these interpretations, an assumption emerges clearly: that leisure was not anymore to be considered as a luxury free time reserved to an elite but had a central role to play in the new social life. In a discourse that can be intellectually rooted in Durkheim's French school of sociology, leisure had been assigned to the role of reinforcing solidarity and collective life in the industrial context that was deemed responsible of a general fragmentation of the beliefs and values of the citizens.[22] Bourgeois was thus looking not merely for a new architectural expression bound with leisure but more generally for the basis of a new collective life. In doing so, he echoed Giedion's 1944 text: "the need for a new monumentality," which claimed for the reconquest of a monumental expression transcending functionality in order to offer people a way to spatially represent their social, ceremonial and community life.[23]

In accordance to Giedion who noticed that the architects of the 20th century had mainly searched this expression in references to market halls, factories or great exhibitions buildings ('naked and rough but true') instead of in the traditional monumental edifices, Bourgeois proposed to focus on industry to create a new kind of monumentality. However, he didn't focus on industrial buildings but on industrial landscapes, as he believed that industrialisation had not only transformed the way building was constructed but had also impacted the whole environment. By using shovels, a tool that allows to quickly transform a landscape, Bourgeois urged architecture to adapt itself in order not to be overwhelmed in scale and significance by the radical engineering transformations of the environment. On the other hand, his particular focus is also explained by the programs to which he was confronted: open-air infrastructures, where few buildings but a lot of topographical interventions and plantations were to be provided. These programs pushed him to a landscape approach because they were based on the idea that the new collective life had to rely on outdoor activities in contact with a revitalising nature.

Bourgeois's blurred approach, at a crossing point between architecture, landscape architecture and urbanism may explain that his unclassifiable projects have been neglected by later historians. But, it is also what made them innovative. As argued by David H. Haney, the modernist movement demonstrated an ambivalent attitude towards industrialisation: concurrently inspired by new technologies as a tool for progress and driven by the ambition to counterbalance the 'evils of the industrialised landscapes' while discussing the topics of new settlement patterns or land reform.[24] Bourgeois's interdisciplinary work allowed him to conciliate these two opposite terms. By suggesting the use of the 'naked and rough' industrial features in order to build a new landscape, he actually combined a belief in the industrial progress and a wish to reform its negative effects through a new relationship with the nature.

> We are beginning to transform the surface of the earth. We thrust beneath, above, and over the surface. Architecture is only a part of this process, even if a special one. Hence there is no "style," no proper building style. Collective design. A fluid transition of things.[25]
>
> (Giedion, 1928)

Notes

1. Puttemans, 1974, p. 137; Bekaert & Strauven, 1971.
2. Strauven, 2015, pp. 332–333.
3. Storck & Ivens, 1933.
4. Bonneuil & Fressoz, 2013, p. 188; Cross, 1993.
5. Gosseye & Heynen, 2013, pp. 53–54.
6. Rahir, 1931, pp. 111–118.
7. Strauven, 2015, p. 524.
8. Charlier, 2010, p. 91.
9. Vanthemsche, 1982, p. 339; Flouquet, 1937, pp. 1177–1178.
10. de Man, 1936.
11. Carton de Wiart, 1941, pp. 103–105.
12. Gosseye & Heynen, 2013, pp. 61–68.
13. Bourgeois, 1938a, p. 12.
14. Bourgeois, 1937, pp. 1179–1181.
15. Bourgeois, 1938b, p. 1.
16. Bourgeois, 1940, pp. 3–9.
17. Bourgeois, 1933, p. 46.
18. Bourgeois, 1933, pp. 46–47.
19. Bourgeois & de Cooman, 1946, pp. 51–53.
20. Gilles, 1941, pp. 20–25.
21. Bauchau, 1941, pp. 26–28.
22. Lafortune, 2004, pp. 15–19.
23. Giedion, 1944.
24. Haney, 2001, p. 149.
25. Giedion, 1928.

References

Bauchau, H. (1941). Les volontaires du travail. Reconstruction, 11, 26–28.
Bekaert, G., & Strauven, F. (1971). La construction en Belgique 1945–1970. Bruxelles: Confédération nationale pour la construction.
Bonneuil, C., & Fressoz, J-B. (2013). L'événement anthropocène. La terre, l'histoire et nous. Paris: Le seuil.
Bourgeois, V. (1933). 4me congrès international d'architecture moderne, extrait du rapport sur l'urbanisme en Belgique. L'émulation, architecture et urbanisme.
Bourgeois, V. (1937). L'Urbanisation pratique en Hainaut, le plan d'urbanisation et de verduration de la commune de Hornu. Batir, 54, 1179–1181.
Bourgeois, V. (1938a). Pouvoirs publics devant l'architecture et l'urbanisme. l'Equerre, 1, 11–14.

Bourgeois, V. (1938b) International Federation for Housing and Planning. Planning recreation. Paper presented at the International Housing and Town Planning Congress Mexico.

Bourgeois, V. (1940). La nouvelle école du centre à Hornu. l'Ossature métallique, 1.

Bourgeois, V., & de Cooman, R. (1946). Charleroi, Terre d'Urbanisme. Bruxelles: Art et Technique.

Carton de Wiart, X. (1941). Hofstade-Plage ou les délices du Brabant. Touring club de Belgique, 7, 103–105.

Charlier, S. (2010). Une histoire des plaines de jeux en Belgique. Le cas de la « Reine Astrid » à l'Exposition internationale de l'Eau à Liège en 1939. Art&fact, 29, 91–101.

Cross, G. (1993). Time and Money: The Making of Consumer Culture. New York: Routledge.

de Man, H. (1936). Les travaux publics et la résorption du chômage. Bruxelles: Ministère des travaux publics.

Flouquet, P.-L. (1937). Réveil de la Wallonie, Interview de M.Merlot, Ministre des travaux publics et de la résorption du chômage. Batir, 54, 1177–1178.

Flouquet, P.-L. (1952). Victor Bourgeois : architectures 1922–1952. Bruxelles: Editions Art et technique.

Giedion, S. (1928 (translation: 1995)). Building in France, Building in Iron, Building in Ferroconcret (J. Duncan Berry, Trans.). Los Angeles: The Getty Center for the History of Art.

Giedion, S. (1944). The Need for a New Monumentality. In New architecture and city planning. New-York: Philosophical library.

Gilles, P. (1941). L'urbanisme sauveur, l'assainissement et l'aménagement d'Antoing. Reconstruction, 11, 20–25.

Gosseye, J., & Heynen, H. (2013). Campsites as Utopias? International Journal for History, Culture and Modernity, 1(1), 53–85.

Haney, D. (2001). "No House Building without Garden Building!" ("Kein Hausbau ohne Landbau!"): The Modern Landscapes of Leberecht Migge. Journal of Architectural Education, 54(3), 149–157.

Lafortune, J.-M. (2004). Introduction aux analyses sociologiques du temps hors travail, fondements théoriques et enjeux sociaux du temps libre, du loisir, du jeu et du sport. Québec: Presses de l'université du Québec.

Puttemans, P. (1974). Architecture moderne en Belgique. Bruxelles: Marc Vokaer.

Rahir, E. (Ed.) (1931). Réserves naturelles à sauvegarder en Belgique. Bruxelles: Touring Club de Belgique.

Storck, H., & Ivens, J. (Writers). (1933). Misère au borinage.

Strauven, I. (2015). Victor Bourgeois 1897–1962: radicaliteit en pragmatisme, moderniteit en traditie. Universiteit Gent. Faculteit Ingenieurswetenschappen en Stedenbouw, Université Libre de Bruxelles. Faculté d'Architecture La Cambre-Horta.

Vanthemsche, G. (1982). De mislukking van een vernieuwde economisch politiek in België vóór de Tweede Wereldoorlog : de OREC (Office de Redressement Economique). Revue belge d'Histoire contemporaine, 2–3, 339–389.

CIVA, Brussels, Fonds Bourgeois:

P-1937.07 Lac d'Altitude à Saint-Hubert. CIVA.

(1937). Plan d'aménagement de la Plage d'Hofstade. CIVA.

(1937). Plan d'urbanisme pour le centre de la commune de Hornu. CIVA.

(1937–1959). Plaine de jeux de la cité Louis Pierard à Frameries. CIVA.

(1937–1940). La nouvelle école du centre de Hornu. CIVA.

(1949–1955). Cité Louis Pierard à Frameries. CIVA.

Chapter 14

Vienna's Höfe

How housing builds the collective

Alessandro Porotto

The housing projects carried out in Vienna during the Interwar period, usually grouped under the name 'Red Vienna,' were executed in light of a precise architectural model: the *Hof*, loosely translated as 'superblock' or 'large courtyard block.'

This model was at the core of planning policies and new dwelling initiatives, a reaction to both the accelerated metropolitan growth and an acute housing shortage (Blau, 1999). To the Viennese, housing started to become a public utility and part of a wider and multifaceted social view, being thus considered a fundamental element to the construction of the city (Tafuri, 1980). The attention and responsibility of planners, architects and politicians focused on housing working class and impoverished members of the urban environment, challenging and redefining the role of professionals involved in the projects.

The *Höfe* embodied both an architectural idea and a vision of society, which were founded on a 'living together' model. This collective dimension takes spatial form through the design of the courtyard's layout and exterior spaces.

According to the guidelines presented in the City's programmatic booklets, exterior spaces play a fundamental role in the *Hof* design. For instance, in order to achieve significant open space devoted to collective uses, courtyards in new municipal housing projects were asked to exceed the traditional 15% of land allotted to open space and to aim instead towards 50% (Gemeinde Wien, 1929: 54). Architecturally and typologically, the *Gartenhof* [courtyard garden] in Vienna became the main spatial principle to orient the design (Hardy, 1934).

However, the guidelines for courtyards did not provide specific criteria or standards, focusing instead on addressing expected qualities. The housing policy

Vienna's Höfe

guidelines stressed the need for ornamental gardens, for the allowance of sufficient area for all to receive as much sunlight [and ventilation] as possible, for the provision of play areas for children, rest areas for adults, room for planting and even for ice rinks. The guidelines claimed that such design approach resulted in courtyard-facing apartments –with pleasant views of lawns, hedges and trees – being more sought after than apartments overlooking the street (Gemeinde Wien, 1929: 44). Implicitly, these characteristics stress use by inhabitants and link collective living with the spatial features and equipment.

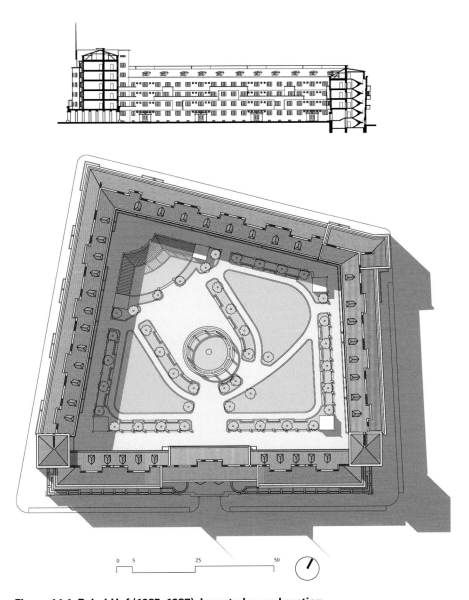

Figure 14.1 Bebel-Hof (1925–1927), layout plan and section
© Alessandro Porotto

Consequently, the collective dimension of the *Hof* can be traced back to the urban morphology and design of the courtyard. These elements highlight *how* the architectural elements employed were able to produce the project's collective dimension, and *why*, even today, they should be considered as inspiring suggestions for collective housing design.

Spatial principles of the large courtyard

Due to rapid urban development and speculative activities in Vienna during the 19th century, the opportunities for parks or green space extensions were limited (Auböck, 1975). In contrast to many European cities at the time (Bauer, 1934), where urban planning was based on the garden city or *Trabantenstadt* [satellite city] – each positing an intrinsic relationship between housing and nature, with the *Siedlungen* [settlements] in Frankfurt, conceived by Ernst May, being the most outstanding initiatives (Porotto, 2019) – Vienna did not adopt such strategies for urban development. Instead, the *Hof* model allowed the city to 'look for green space' (Auböck, 1975: 61).

Indeed, the large courtyard allows nature to enter the city directly rather than being consigned to an empty space within the urban fabric. As a result, a new conception of the urban landscape emerges that is related to the form of the courtyard and the role of vegetation. These features allow *Höfe* to be intricately interwoven with the historic city. It is no coincidence that, when writing on the Viennese complexes, Werner Hegemann appreciated their variety, detail, urban character and the "ingenious way in which the plans of the blocks are related to existing streets and open spaces" (Hegemann, 1938: 93).

The model of the courtyard block has a long tradition in Vienna's history (Bobek and Lichtenberger, 1966; Fabbri, 1986). It was endowed with a precise theoretical frame by two Viennese masters: Camillo Sitte and Otto Wagner. In 1910, Wagner described the apartment block as far more appropriate for modern life than the suburban detached houses (Wagner, 1912). Sitte theorised that "the *sanitary greenery* should not be found amidst the dust and noise of the streets, but rather in the sheltered interior of large blocks of buildings, surrounded on all sides" (Collins and Collins, 1986: 319). According to these ideas, the recreational greenery of the courtyard could serve many other functions such as playgrounds and even markets. Sonne (2009: 77) writes that "what Sitte proposed [...] was nothing less than opening the formerly private ground of the urban block to the public—a strategy which later became important for the large *Höfe* of Red Vienna."

It is possible to outline some essential aspects of the *Hof* model: first, the typology of the large courtyard defines both the built fabric and the open spaces of the city; second, the courtyard is linked to the public street, but defines a more intimate space; third, its inner space is considered a part of the urban green space system.

In order to address the hygienic and social problems of *Mietkasernen* [tenement blocks], the *Höfe* propose a concrete solution by providing natural light and ventilation to the dwellings and offering the inhabitants a place for socialisation – not possible in speculative buildings occupying up to 85% of the plot. Furthermore, access to the stairwells is always granted from the inner space of the block, offering a spatial continuity between the public space of the street, the collective one of the courtyard and the private dimension of dwellings. In this perspective, the *Hof* literally defines collective space as halfway between public and private: it realises Sitte's idea of attributing public use to gardens within the block as an architectural model.

The strength of the Viennese garden and courtyard block designs also stems from the city's longstanding culture and education, dating back to the beginning of the 20th century, in which nature is framed as an integral part of the housing project (Schmidt, 1993). The majority of Red Vienna architects were trained at Otto Wagner's Academy (Pozzetto, 1979) and focused on "strong relationships between the interior and the exterior, through arcades, loggias, viewpoints […]." In addition, student works were investigative in their employment of various configurations of the exterior space, using "designed trails, […] divided garden areas and numerous structures […], such as arbours, benches and lattices […]" (Auböck, 1995: 294). For this reason, *Höfe* display a high degree of formal integrity between the buildings and the courtyard gardens.

Components of large courtyards: pedestrian paths

Fundamentally, the *Hof* always provides a peripheral path into the courtyard, connecting, at regular distances, the access to the stairwells [*Stiegen*] that lead to the apartments or other collective facilities. This could be considered the first main element designed in order to facilitate collective socialisation within the *Hof*.

This system is evident in the Bebel-Hof designed by Karl Ehn in 1925–1927, in which the main path along the courtyard perimeter gives access to the stairwells, while other paths in the middle of the courtyard shape the garden areas (Figure 14.1). Due to the presence of only one main gateway from the street to the courtyard, these paths build a more protected and intimate area. The inhabitants, living with access to different stairwells and sharing common facilities, come to identify this space with their community life.

In the Schüttau-Hof, designed by Alfred Rodler, Alfred Stutterheim and Ludwig Tremmel in 1924–1925, four entryways provide direct access from the street to two inner courtyards (Figure 14.2). This structure suggests that it is possible to cross the block through the collective space of the courtyard, which also connects two adjacent public streets. Consequently, the space was also designed for the neighbourhood inhabitants to use the collective space as a pedestrian passage in order to move within the urban fabric near the riverbank of the Danube. At the same time, the inner spaces of the courtyard are arranged to ensure circulation, by means of paths connecting the entryways and leisure areas, and of gardens in the concavities created by the central building.

Within *Höfe* courtyards in general, pedestrian paths are spatially conceived and architecturally treated in order to increase the opportunities for inhabitants to socialise and collectively share the same place – whether on the scale of the block, or, as it is often the case, of the neighbourhood.

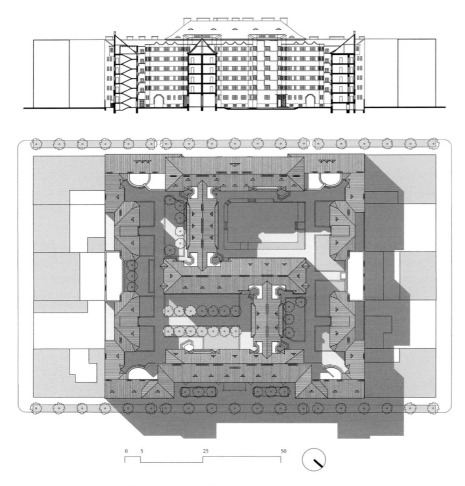

Figure 14.2 Schüttau-Hof (1924–1925), layout plan and section
© Alessandro Porotto

Components of large courtyards: greenery

Unlike the *Siedlungen* in Frankfurt, where row-houses' gardens were designed with a rational and botanical approach by landscape architects (Haney, 2010), Viennese *Höfe* adopted layered principles to design the green areas in the courtyard.

Gardens separate the pedestrian path from the leisure areas, usually placed in the middle of the courtyard. Therefore, they have a functional character of separation as well as of architectural ornamentation: their arrangement fits perfectly the idea of the architectural 'construction' of exterior space. In most cases, this procedure employs architectural principles to the size and position of the trees, with the design of greenery aiming to reinforce the axes of symmetry and increase visual impact with regard to the façades.

This configuration is visible in the Karl Seitz-Hof, designed by Hubert Gessner in 1926–1933, which highlights the paths between courtyards and leisure areas

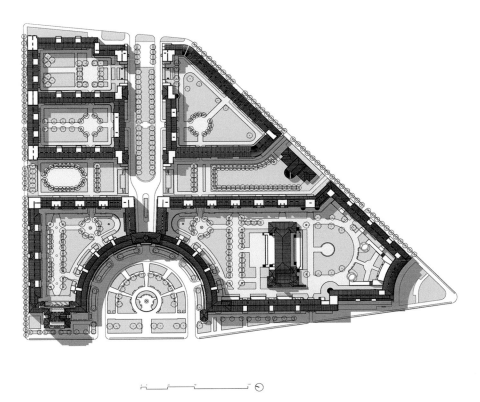

Figure 14.3 Karl Seitz-Hof (1926–1933), layout plan.
© Alessandro Porotto

through tree sequences following the symmetry lines of the layout. The *Hof* consists of a series of seven courtyards, arranged along a central artery that departs from the semi-circular square overlooking the main street (Figure 14.3).

The courtyards are linked by sequences of passages, producing a porosity that is sustained throughout the variations of the different exterior spaces. The greenery 'builds' this spatial permeability, with large trees giving emphasis to the common areas and paths that vary according to the courtyard shapes. In the same way as the building, vegetation is also conceived as an architectural element.

Originally intended to be a project based on the garden city model, Karl Seitz-Hof's green areas should not be seen as contradicting this first intention. As Gessner explained:

> I would like to point out that I think of the garden city in a very different way from what is commonly heard. I am not building a garden city so that each house has its own garden, but so that the houses are inside a park.
>
> (Kristan & Gantenbein, 2011: 264)

In the Bebel-Hof, the courtyard design was also an architectural issue of major importance (Figure 14.1). From the main entryway to the courtyard, the first axis brings one to the playground in the middle of the space, which is surrounded by a circular concrete

Alessandro Porotto

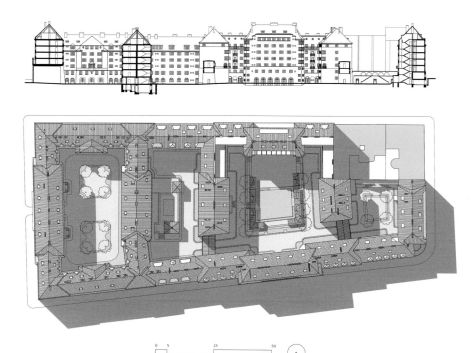

Figure 14.4 Fuchsenfeldhof (1922–1925), layout plan and section
© Alessandro Porotto

pergola; the second axis starts from the middle to reach the northwest corner of the complex, where a second collective pergola has been built in connection to the playground. In the first case, one sees the axis of symmetry of the layout; in the second case, it is the bisector of the angle. The role of trees and greenery is to mediate the transition between the two and to give consistency to the variations of garden shapes.

The Bebel-Hof courtyard has been, from a spatial and scenic point of view, precisely designed. The project adopts solutions that refer to the artifices of the Baroque period (Weihsmann, 2002).

The arrangement of the various components in these cases reinforces the hypothesis that the courtyard was conceived on the principles of public park design (Blau, 1999). Indeed, it is no coincidence that the architects of these two *Höfe* – Hubert Gessner and Karl Ehn – studied at the Wagner Academy.

Components of large courtyards: leisure areas

The third component of the *Hof* collective space consists of common playgrounds and leisure areas. These elements are always integrated into the paths and gardens system that is located in the central part of the courtyard. The equipment of these areas lends the entire *Hof* its collective character.

From the previous examples, it is possible to observe that this equipment consists of furniture dedicated to recreation and socialisation, such as benches, pergolas, plant and flower pots, street lamps, sculptures and fountains. This equipment shapes the courtyard with architectural variations determined by different types of daily life use.

In addition, the leisure areas are in direct relationship with other collective facilities integrated within the built volume – for instance, *Kindergärten*, collective laundries, neighbourhood libraries and common rooms.

This is evident in the Fuchsenfeldhof (Figure 14.4), the first building entirely conceived as a *Hof* according to the city's planning guidelines (Fuchs, 1923). Designed in 1922–1925 by Heinrich Schmid and Hermann Aichinger, students at the Wagner Academy, the ground floor of four linked courtyards establishes an interaction between public, collective and private spaces, accommodating many facilities and functions. The main central courtyard with swimming pool and equipped leisure areas is one of the most outstanding examples of collective living and daily usage. The *Hof* typology at Fuchsenfeldhof introduced a new spatial and functional quality into the urban district by incorporating public elements into the residential fabric.

The apparently simple organisation of the *Hof* entails a complex system of different elements and facilities that overlap to define a multi-functional space for collective use (Monterumisi and Porotto, 2018). By analogy, *Höfe* courtyards have the qualities of an 'open-air living room' (Mang, 1993), a definition that clearly synthesises the model's spatial character, usage and collective status. Associating the courtyard with the largest and most important room of the apartment summarises the relationship between the 'outside' and the 'inside' of *Höfe*: the different leisure areas of the courtyard space are designed to be the extension, in a communal perspective, of the dwellings.

Components of large courtyards: urban layouts

Observing the provided examples, it is possible to note that, while each *Hof* has unique morphological specificities and layout variations, the principles and typical elements previously discussed are always adopted. These elements do not change according to courtyard size and, more importantly, built density. Fuchsenfeldhof (built density: 3.23; land occupancy: 59%) and Karl Seitz-Hof (built density: 1.27; land occupancy: 28%) are characterised by a sequence of connected courtyards, but their densities diverge; Schüttau-Hof (built density: 2.69; land occupancy: 52%) completes a pre-existing high-density urban block, providing two narrow garden courtyards in contrast to the adjacent buildings; Bebel-Hof shapes only one large courtyard space, reducing significantly the density (built density: 1.89; land occupancy: 42%). Such quantitative data actually represent a concrete operational instrument between the city and housing scales.

Höfe negotiate with the pre-existing urban fabric and the master plan of the city, being able to integrate urban elements and building a real part of the city. The urban concept is determined by a unitary organisation. *Höfe* combine spacious inner courtyards, connections to the public street, services necessary for daily life, stairwells accessible from the courtyard and balconies or loggias overlooking the courtyard, while at the same time increasingly reducing the land occupation coefficient and urban density.

Figure 14.5 Plan of Vienna (2019), showing the position of *Höfe*
© Alessandro Porotto

These urban layout components have a remarkable impact on the structure of the city. The courtyard layout is the generating principle of a system of collective spaces that connect the different parts of the city, thanks to the intricate interconnectedness in the structure of the interventions (Figure 14.5).

Vienna's Höfe

Figure 14.6 *Höfe*, archival pictures of the collective courtyards (clockwise order): Bebel-Hof, Schüttau-Hof, Karl Seitz-Hof and Fuchsenfeldhof
© Wiener Stadt- und Landsarchiv – WStLA

Figure 14.7 *Höfe*, pictures of the current state of the collective courtyards (clockwise order): Bebel-Hof, Schüttau-Hof, Karl Seitz-Hof and Fuchsenfeldhof
© Alessandro Porotto

In contrast to the fact that the *Höfe* are often considered as solitary and autonomous elements within the urban fabric (Tafuri, 1980), the principles of *Hof* layouts generate a degree of urbanity that aims not only to improve real urban conditions but also to extend its collective dimension throughout the city.

Conclusions

The old photos of the Viennese *Höfe* demonstrate the positive impacts of the large courtyard layout on the collective life, particularly in the depiction of children playing in a space adequate to their activities – which is in contrast to the infamous restriction of the speculative *Mietkasernen*, where children had no space to play in the dwellings or in the yards (Figure 14.6). These images indicate the essential role of the courtyard in the very identity of its community: due to its spatial quality and facilities, its inhabitants identified themselves with 'their *Hof.*' Thanks to these positive results, the concept and character of the *Hof* also inspired some remarkable collective housing initiatives in other countries, which were executed in the 1930s – for instance, the square projects by Maurice Braillard in Geneva, Quarry Hill Flats (1934–1938) in Leeds and other municipal housing examples in England. Even some housing initiatives in United States present a direct connection to the Viennese cases.

Visiting *Höfe* today (Figure 14.7) means remarking on their capability to produce, through the architectural design of the large courtyards, a collective vision of society (Porotto, 2019). This capacity to adapt the main principles of the *Hof* model to actual situations and to invent different solutions to reach the same goals allowed *Höfe* to preserve to this day their collective character in the courtyard space. *Höfe* courtyards spatially embody social equality, even though society and living needs have changed through time. They did not implement pre-set quantitative standards, but aimed to build spaces that could accommodate social uses (Porotto, 2019).

In recent years, *Höfe* have been renovated, adapting easily to contemporary living requirements. Most of the facilities and common equipment in the courtyard have been preserved, but, in some cases, they have been substituted. Still, even though the water pool in the Fuchsenfeldhof, for instance, is presently used as a playground, the transformed elements have not altered the collective character.

Höfe demonstrate that the collective space is not a mere autonomous function. Rather, it is linked to the interaction strategies that take into account the complexity of components within the urban scale, by means of a relationship with elements of the public space and of domesticity that increase opportunities for sharing the space of daily life use.

For these reasons, the Viennese urban and housing policies probably achieve one of the most remarkable results for collective housing in Europe. Although *Höfe* were designed and built almost a century ago, they offer key suggestions for today's housing initiatives. Indeed, we have recently been observing in Europe the progressive crisis of the social concept and architectural connotation of the 'collective.' As sociologists Norbert Elias and Zygmunt Bauman claim, in our individualistic society, the collective dimension of the city and common living becomes even more crucial (Secchi, 2013).

Today, the *Höfe*'s heritage is one of the long-lasting impact concerning social housing policies in Vienna (Wien & Wohnen, 2014). Indeed, Höfe's dwellings are still today managed for social housing purposes by the municipality. Consequently, they continue to entail a vision for living together and to promote collective life within the contemporary city.

Bibliography

Auböck, M. (1995). "Zur Gartenarchitektur der Otto-Wagner-Schule und ihrer Zeit". *Die Gartenkunst*, 7(2), 291–297.
Auböck, M. (1975). *Die Gärten der Wiener*. Wien: Jugend und Volk.
Bauer, C. (1934). *Modern Housing*. Boston: Houghton Mifflin.
Blau, E. (1999). *The Architecture of Red Vienna 1919–1934*. Cambridge, London: MIT Press.
Bobek, H., Lichtenberger, E. (1966). *Wien. Bauliche Gestalt und Entwicklung seit der Mitte des 19. Jahrhunderts*. Graz-Köln: Hermann Böhlaus Nachf.
Collins, G. R., Collins, C. C. (1986). *Camillo Sitte: The Birth of Modern City Planning*. New York: Rizzoli.
Fabbri, G. (1986). *Vienna. Città capitale del XIX secolo*. Roma: Officina Edizioni.
Fuchs, G. A. (1923). *Der Fuchsenfeldhof*. Wien: Wiener Magistrat.
Gemeinde Wien (1929). *Die Wohnungspolitik der Gemeinde Wien: Ein Überblick über die Tätigkeit der Stadt Wien seit dem Kriegsende zur Bekämpfung der Wohnungsnot und zur Hebung der Wohnkultur*. Wien: Gesellschafts- und Wirtschaftsmuseum.
Haney, D. H. (2010). *When Modern Was Green. Life and work of landscape architect Leberecht Migge*. London; New York: Routledge.
Hardy, C. (1934). *The Housing Program of the City of Vienna*. Washington, DC: The Brookings Institution.
Hegemann, W. (1938). *City Planning Housing*. Vol. III. New York: Architectural Book Publishing Company.
Kristan, M., Gantenbein, G. (2011). *Hubert Gessner: Architekt zwischen Kaiserreich und Sozialdemokratie 1871–1943*. Wien: Passagen.
Mang, B. (1993). "Grünräume im Roten Wien". In Öhlinger, W., (ed.). *Das rote Wien 1918–1934*. Wien: Eigenverlag de Museen der Stadt Wien.
Monterumisi, C., Porotto, A. (2018). "Why Can't We Live Together? Stockholm and Vienna's Large Courtyard Blocks". In Day, K., Cairns, G. (eds.). *Global Dimensions in Housing. Approaches in Design and Theory from Europe to the Pacific Rim*. Faringdon, Oxfordshire: Green Frigate Books.
Porotto, A. (2019). *L'intelligence des formes: Le projet de logements collectifs à Vienne et Francfort*. Genève: MētisPresses.
Pozzetto, M. (1979). *Die Schule Otto Wagners*. Wien-München: Verlag Anton Schroll.
Schmidt, S. (1993). "Gärten im Roten Wien/The gardens in Red Vienna". *Topos*, 2, 92–99.
Secchi, B. (2013). *La città dei ricchi e la città dei poveri*. Rom-Bari: Laterza.
Sonne, W. (2009). "Dwelling in the Metropolis: Reformed Urban Blocks 1890–1940 as a Model for the Sustainable Compact City". *Progress in Planning*, 72, 2, 53–149.
Tafuri, M. (1980). *Vienna Rossa. La politica residenziale nella Vienna socialista*. Milano: Electa.
Wagner, O. (1912). "The Development of a Great City". *Architectural Record*, 31, 485–500.
Weihsmann, H. (2002). *Das rote Wien. Sozialdemokratische rchitektur und Kommunalpolitik 1919–1934*. Wien: Promedia.
Wien, S., Wohnen, W. (2014). *Gemeinde baut: Wiener Wohnbau 1920-2020/Residential construction in Vienna 1920–2020*. Wien: Holzhausen.

Chapter 15

Learning from Loutraki

Thermalism, hydrochemistry and the architectures of collective wellness

Lydia Xynogala

Writing in 1842, Frederick Strong noted that "no country in the world possesses a greater abundance of mineral waters than Greece, nor is there any country in which they are less known" (Strong 1842). A century later in 1930, *The New York Times* noted that:

> Modern Greece wants cash. She has discovered that archaeologists, architects, historians, poets, professors, teachers, students and dreamers are very respectable people. But they do not spend money fast enough. So Greece has cast envious eyes on the gold which flows in Monte Carlo.
>
> (*The New York Times*, 1930)

These two comments record significant moments for Greece; the first describes the period when the analysis of water, soil and terrain mapping leads to a scientific understanding of the country's landscape and resources. Thermalism, the therapeutic use of hot water springs, was initially advocated in scientific literature[1] by doctors and chemists and later described by travel writers.

The second moment records the efforts of the Greek state to turn those thermal springs into international tourist destinations for hydrotherapy and leisure. Loutraki, a seaside town in the Peloponnese, is a significant case study; it became one of the biggest and most popular centres for hydrotherapy in Greece. This chapter examines a the political and economic forces behind Loutraki's thermal architectures in the first half of the 20th century.[2] The towns' architecture and urban life was a product of the scientific and environmental movement that ultimately gave rise to new societal forms. The proponents of thermalism were among those in Greek society that wanted to become 'European': adopting scientific and medical standards along with urban attributes, attitudes and aesthetics.

Loutraki became the testing ground for a range of ideas and aspirations: using specific buildings; the scientific discourse permeated politics, city planning, tourism and ultimately, the collective social structures of Loutraki. Doctors made concrete suggestions and directly addressed the built environment. They advocated for projects which were later constructed, transforming this quiet seaside town into a hydrotherapy centre with diverse forms of leisure. The impact of this bathing infrastructure extended through the Second World War and into the post-war society.

Thermalism

While Hippocrates[3] is considered the father of thermal medicine and hydrotherapy in Antiquity, very few of the locations known to the Ancient Greeks were in use in

Figure 15.1 **Poster produced by the Greek Organisation for Toursim (EOT) heavily promoting Greece through Loutraki. The hydrotherapy building with its colonade at the foot of the mountain**
http://www.gnto.gov.gr/el/posters#ad-image-0 (accessed September 15, 2018

modern times. Thermalism emerged as scientific discourse only in the second half of the 19th century[4] after Greece was recognised as an independent Nation State (1832). The Bavarian Prince Otto became the first King of Modern Greece,[5] and his arrival saw an influx of academics and scientists into the newly established universities. King Otto was accompanied by his military pharmacist, the Bavarian Chemist Xaver Landerer who became a pivotal character in the development of thermalism[6]; he was the first modern doctor to visit Loutraki. He wrote about the therapeutic properties of its water inspiring other doctors to conduct further studies.[7] A broader legal and institutional framework[8] followed that promoted thermalism through state-funded benefits.

Loutraki and its waters

Loutraki is uniquely located between the Corinthian Gulf Sea and the dense pines of the Gerania Mountains to the north. In Antiquity, it was called *Therme* and was known for its thermal springs[9]; which, according to myth, were a preferred bathing location for the Olympian gods and Spartan warriors.[10] The geologic features of the area[11] generate waters, rich in sodium, calcium, magnesium, potassium, sodium and radon. The waters aid digestion, kidney stones and other gastroenterological ailments as well as muscular ones such as sciatica. Until the end of the 19th century, only a few patients from nearby villages visited the springs; there was little infrastructure for hydrotherapy or accommodation;[12] but, in the early 20th century, a steady upgrade in the hydrotherapy infrastructure and accommodation was prompted by numerous scientific publications.[13]

Doctors and buildings, chemists and landscapes

Doctors prescribed Loutraki's waters as cure to their patients; through chemical analyses, field observations and examinations, they affirmed its healing properties. Dissatisfied with the poor treatment conditions and state of the buildings, they urged the government and municipality to invest in infrastructure. At the same time, the Austrian Customs agency Lloyd brought international visitors to the town helping to further spread its healing reputation (Dritsas, 200). Archives record the recommendations made to architects and urban planners by doctors. This medical community, educated in Europe, shared a collective aspiration Loutraki to compete with European spa towns of the time.[14]

In 1880, Dr Georgios Vafas described a village, with its 20 buildings, as rather 'unremarkable' with 'dire' facilities.[15] Unlike central European spa towns, Loutraki lacked clean accommodation and entertainment. The hydrotherapy centre, a small stone building, was very dark and poorly ventilated.[16] Vafas argued for treatment improvement and blamed the authorities for the spring's bad conditions, the patients for not complaining and the doctors for not speaking out.[17] He believed that the town had potential and advocated for new buildings with specific interiors.[18] He proposed that the architects study similar spa buildings in Europe and identified the need for a new bathhouse[19] with a range of treatments, a drinking fountain, tubs and a large swimming pool. Finally, he made suggestions for entertainment in the form of boat excursions and mountain walks and new roads with flowering trees and gardens.

In 1891, despite significant scientific progress,[20] there was still no accommodation[21] suitable for patients (Dalezios). Doctors lobbied for the town to become a 'pleasurable temple of Asclepius,' and by 1902, a new bathhouse,[22] far superior to the old one, with clean marble tubs and a means for patients to regulate the water according to doctors' orders was built, but there was little hope in rivalling European spa towns.[23] Some writers urged the mayor to plant trees and even made requests for a pianist in the main square. Critiquing the lack of entertainment, they identified the need for a central building, a type of casino, describing its rooms in great length.[24] In 1926, one doctor described Loutraki as "emerging and foaming in the caress of the Corinthian wave."

> Only the Greek has not yet felt the shock of the endless natural beauty, and for this reason delays and delays to help the magnificent divine gift through works that reflect the needs of today's social explosion and to make Loutropolis not only centers of welfare, health, tranquility but also a profitable source for the Greek society and the State.[25]

The gardens, boulevards and urban planning of European bath towns were seen as the main contributors to the success of treatment (Sioris),[26] but not all doctors were in agreement about the incorporation of entertainment and leisure.[27]

Earthquake and reconstruction

Building activity was still slow until 1928 when an earthquake hit Korinthos with devastating results. Constructed with poor building materials, Loutraki was completely destroyed. A major reconstruction fund was set up; the Organisation for the Rehabilitation of Earthquake Victims (AOSK) was tasked to rebuild Loutraki with new plans for hydrotherapy facilities and a casino. Profits from these projects would aid the earthquake victims (Dritsas, 202). AOSK measured destroyed buildings and determined their reconstruction value accordingly (Kranidiotis, 68). Funding was provided for re-building the exact area and volume with earthquake-proof structures. A peculiar set of transactions[28] laid the ground for rebuilding Loutraki in the 1930s (Kranidiotis, 69); the newly built town was based on an urban grid[29] punctuated by open spaces designed to comply with all "scientific guidelines" (*Loutraki Review*, 23). The master plan divided the new urban grid into residential and hospitality zones. This urban plan followed the logic of the aquifer's view: thermal and mineral water sources. The residential zone would be built near the mineral water whilst hotels were near the thermal water sources; urban typologies followed water types. A new municipal park in the north coast was formed

Figure 15.2 Colonnade in the new municipal hydrotherapy centre
Kranidiotis, p. 20

from the earthquake's remnants; rubble from demolished buildings and land from the receded hill.

Taking the waters, buildings for water

In 1932, AOSK announced a bid for the construction of a municipal hydrotherapy centre (Technika Hronika, 1932). Statistics collected by the Ministry of Tourism in the 1940s showed Loutraki as the place with most visitors with an annual number of 12,000[30] (Zografos 41). The new hydrotherapy centre (1934) was praised in tourist guides as the "latest statement of art and science" and was frequently visited by the Prime Minister. In 1932, the architect Leonidas Bonnis built a new[31] positherapy building to house the municipal source.[32] The circular building with narrow openings throughout its perimeter had a large gallery with intricate mosaics and water emerging from a rock.[33] The mosaics portrayed Mother Earth with a kore waiting among granite pillars and flashes of gold. The positherapy building featured in tourism campaigns by EOT and advertisements for mineral water becoming the landmark of modern Loutraki. Numerous other bath houses were constructed[34] some with natural spring sources emerging in their interior, others providing light therapy, electrotherapy and massage. The popular Karantanis private bath building was a meeting point, event space and art exhibition venue; water was the trigger of social activities.

During the 1930s and 1950s, ownership of the springs was divided between public agencies and private interests.[35] Monitored, quantified, measured and studied, water was the Loutraki's precious commodity. The municipality recorded numbers of bathers, water volume consumed or exported. Publications reference statistics such as "113.719 glasses of water consumed in 1954"[36] (Kranidiotis 55). In one year, 2,094,999 bottles of water were exported from Loutraki (Kranidiotis 57). Water triggered a new industry, exemplified by the Karantanis factory (1963) which bottled mineral water, sodas and fruit juices and was the first of its kind in Greece. Architects Sthenis Molfesis and Thymios Papayiannis designed the three-storey factory to accommodate machinery, refrigerators, a loading bay and garage and to allow visitors to admire its state-of-the-art equipment and production.[37]

A decade of Leisure

In 1930, an urban development competition envisioned Loutraki becoming "not just the Queen of Loutropolis for the Balkans and the East but also one of the most excellent Loutropolis of the world" through advertising, new buildings and infrastructure. The same year, the Casino opened in a former villa and became a landmark during the Interwar period. The *Loutraki Review*, a weekly magazine on the casino activities captures life in the 1930s,[38] comparing traffic in the casino to that of San Remo and Monte

Figure 15.3 View showing the rapid construction that took place after the earthquake
https://www.loutraki365.gr/blog/post/arthro-kosmima-gia-loytraki (accessed 1 October 2019)

Carlo and carrying reports on notable hotel guests,[39] horse races and social scandals. A weekly column dedicated to future projects reported on British interests in a scheme to build parks, luxury hotels, a new casino, bathhouses, theatre and new transportation which didn't progress but was reviewed by Greece's Prime Minister.[40] The *New York Times* article[41] referred to above captured the entrepreneurial spirit and excitement of the decade. Titled *A Monte Carlo for Corinth, Famous Greek City hopes to Outrank Rival as the World's Centre of Gambling*, it popularised the idea of Greece as 'the latest challenger' to the reigns of Monte Carlo.[42]

The casino's management organised dancing nights, concerts at the beach, swimming competitions, fireworks and theatre plays featuring renowned actors. There were jazz bands, luxury cars arriving from Athens and fashionable crowds in the bustling restaurants. Resembling the nightlife of international resorts, the casino ended "the boredom and monotony of life in the Loutropolis" (*Loutraki Review* 45). A vibrant music scene with exotic rhythms of Argentinian orchestras or the fashionable band 'lucky boys' entertained visitors from Egypt, the President of the Greek Parliament and other prominent political figures. An electricity company begun its operation, and the city was fully illuminated, "something that the Athenians must be jealous of" (*Loutraki Review* 45).

Newly built hotels[43] were reasonably priced, with fully furnished, well-ventilated rooms, with names such as Hotel Kosmopolit[44] to reflect their European aspirations. Loutraki's growth led to new transportation networks; repairs to the connecting highway, new railway connections with luxury train cars and even hydroplanes, which greatly reduced the trip from Athens. Previously only be reached by steamboat,[45] car or bus, this frequency of routes reflects the steady influx of affluent visitors. However, the city suffered from high taxation resulting in high accommodation costs equal on par with spa towns abroad. The casino owner asked the Prime Minister to lower taxes, aid tourism and invest in new buildings: a grand hotel that would house the casino along with a theatre, cafe, brewery, patisseries, dancing centre and room for concerts.

Collective life

Before 1939, guides described Loutraki as the "Queen of Greek Loutropolis" (Zografos 67) in stark contrast with the gloomy picture painted in the past. The brightly lit town had numerous bathhouses, majestic buildings, squares, tree-lined streets, amusement centres, luxury hotels and restaurants,[46] many smaller cafes and beerhouses, concerts, excursions to the pine forest and sea and constant visitors. Writers concluded that Loutraki had become a first-class therapeutic and entertainment destination for Greek and international visitors. All this was brought to a standstill with the outbreak of the Second World War; when Loutraki's was designated, a hospital centre and thermalism infrastructure was appropriated to heal war victims. Unlike the neighbouring Corinth, Loutraki mostly escaped the Luftwaffe bombings.[47] Second World War was followed by the Greek Civil War; it ended in 1949 and the thermalist activities of the town resumed. By 1953, there were six hydrotherapy complexes with 161 baths and 3 kiosks

Figure 15.4 The Karantanis bottling factory completed in 1963 with the mountain as backdrop
Archives of the architect Thymios Papayiannis

for positherapy. In those facilities, public and private hydrology doctors were available for consultations. With over 70 seaside hotels[48] of all categories – many incorporating thermal springs and bath facilities – Loutraki was bustling in the summer months.[49]

Factories[50] produced sweets, sodas and bottled mineral water[51] and a local newspaper, cinemas and public lectures sparked its intellectual and artistic life. Athletic clubs for water polo, football, volleyball and basketball were established (Vlahakis 41). Guides from the 1950s refer to Loutraki as a "very clean town with majestic buildings" (Kranidiotis 55). Statistics from post-war years demonstrate a steady increase of visitors and, in 1950, record numbers.[52] A 1951 report[53] by EOT summarised the effort and investment laid into the Loutraki facilities and called for long-term programming in combination with securing funding for future works.

Conclusion: learning from Loutraki

Venturi and Scott Brown claim in *Learning from Las Vegas* that "learning from the existing landscape is a way of being revolutionary."[54] Learning from the natural landscape in Loutraki triggered an industry centred on healing and leisure, radically transforming the town. From rock to water to spring to town.

Lydia Xynogala

Figure 15.5 Cover of the *Loutraki Casino Review*, a weekly magazine covering the social life of the town in the golden 1930s era. The subtitle reads: Scientific, Critique, Social

> We architects who hope for a reallocation of national resources toward social purposes must take care to lay emphasis on the purposes and their promotion rather than on the architecture that shelters them…Sources for modest buildings and images with social purpose will come, not from the industrial past, but from the everyday city around us, of modest buildings and modest spaces with symbolic appendages.[55]

wrote Venturi et al. In Loutraki, natural resources were first written about, then documented, analysed, extracted and finally exploited. This process was then manifest in buildings of various types, sizes and aesthetics. The State envisioned the well-being of society through bathing and simultaneously promoted the national resources for tourism. Modest buildings were erected first which were suited to this social purpose, buildings for luxury, gambling and leisure followed.

The concept of Thermalism which came from doctors and chemists was translated into numerous urban, architectural, industrial, landscaping projects during the 1930s and 1950s. Primary sources such as medical treatises, tourist guides, weekly journals and advertisements demonstrate how these projects sparked the interest in health tourism, and how the post-earthquake projects had a rippled effect onto social, artistic, intellectual and political circles. Many aspired to a 'European' Greece, but how the town should supplement health treatments with amusements divided opinion. Loutraki embraced amusement, but the 'leisure'-centred approach brought seasonal unemployment and a dependence on casino visitors rather than an all-year-round health tourism. Some writers argue that the decline of interest in hydrotherapy was a result of a paradigm shift to the beach culture in the next decades (Dritsas). The advent of pharmacology and surgery further overshadowed the need for natural cures. Doctors shifted their prescriptions from curing waters to newly discovered drugs or performed surgeries. Loutraki's experience was mirrored in many of the spa towns of Pre-war and Post-war period in Greece.

For Loutraki, the earthquake provided an opportunity to build a new city, one that embraced scientific and European-centric ideals. Notions of leisure in the post-war era changed and the original identity and spirit of Loutraki and its landscape faded. In the dance between the Apollonian and Dionysian natures of the city, detoxifying and being intoxicated, the latter prevailed.

Notes

1. Medical literature from the 19th century demonstrates an increasing interest from doctors and chemists to document the hydro chemical and curing properties of the various springs throughout Greece (Kostidi 19).
2. The state not only funded hydrotherapy centres, parks and kiosks but also insurance benefits for the population to use them.
3. Throughout his work, and in his treatise "Airs, Waters, Places," he identified the therapeutic properties of various natural waters and advocated for their use in curing diverse illnesses. Hippocrates categorized the natural spring sources and systematically recorded the diseases over which they had beneficial effects.
4. Slowly, it rippled from the scientific circles and permeated the public interests through advertisements and articles in popular magazines and newspapers.
5. King Otto was keen on creating the first Thermal Baths in Greece and commissioned the architect Theofil Von Hansen to build the first hostel and baths in the island of Kythnos (1836–1857).
6. As the first regular professor of Chemistry and of Botany at the University of Athens, he sparked interest on the Greek natural resources and their potential. An avid writer and traveller, he assembled large mineral collections and wrote books on the hydro chemical properties of natural springs across Greece. He urged the state to build better infrastructures to welcome visitors in the said locations. Landerer started a larger movement that was not confined to scientific circles but rippled out into the wider political and social milieu. He published his findings in Greek and international publications, disseminating his knowledge to doctors, patients and scientists. These texts became a reference point for other foreign authors who wrote guides about Greece, its landscapes and environmental resources.
7. The Department of Thermal Springs in 1918 is a direct outcome of these scientific publications.
8. In 1920, the legislative framework for the institutionalization of thermal springs and balneotherapy was created sponsoring research work in various scientific disciplines. In 1931, a comprehensive search recorded all thermal springs of the country.
In the following three decades, all thermal natural resources were registered. State agencies such as the General Chemistry of the State, the General Secretariat of Tourism and the Department of the Thermal Resources of the Greek National Tourism Organization were established. By 1950, all sources were managed by the Hellenic Tourism Organization (EOT).
9. The historians Xenophon and Pausanias both wrote about its thermal springs.
10. Xenophon writes in Hellenica IV that, after the battles, the Spartan soldiers retreated there and bathed in thermal water.
11. Charoneion Sousakion is a cave from which hydrosulphur gas and carbonated acid comes out (Dalezios). On its route down from the mountain, the water of the Gerania Mountains is naturally filtered through the various rocks, a process that is due to its trace elements, the most important of which is magnesium, which helps the heart, nerves and heart function and increases metabolism.
12. In 1855, Loutraki had its first and very modest wooden bathing facilities with ten tubs.

13 In 1866, Landerer publishes his findings on the mineral springs. In 1874, the wooden bathhouses are replaced by stone buildings. In 1898, the doctors Christomanos and Damvergis publish their treatises on Loutraki and more follow over the next years.
14 I should also note that references to European SPA towns are not only made to compare the infrastructure, hotels and bathing facilities but also the quality of waters. Greek waters are often declared to be equal or superior to those of European mineral springs.
15 From the Loutraki village until the foot of the mountain, there is a row of houses along the bay. The last one is the hydrotherapy building. Ten to twelve houses that belong to villagers are rented out to patients. There is also a larger building, which used to be the Loutraki-based agency of the Austrian Lloyd, has been turned into a hotel with a few small repairs/renovations.
16 The bathhouses which are situated towards the seaside have small rooms and the spring comes out of the floor. Due to their small size, patients are even allocated slots during nighttime to use the baths between 12 and 3 am!
17 He believed that hydrotherapy in Loutraki due to its current state brings no benefit or cure. In contrast, there is evidence that waters of a similar composition in Europe have great healing action in a range of illnesses. "The power of these waters is manifest tenfold if they were in another country or even in Greece but under different conditions… The Waters of Loutraki can be very beneficial to the Greek Society because they have properties that can heal or improve a variety of conditions very common in Greece." (Georgios Vafas 1880, p.48) Blames the negligence of the State, doctors, patients and private owners for the deplorable living conditions next to the spring which lacks basic conditions of hygiene. He believes that it is our (the doctors) responsibility to advise those who administer the healing springs of Loutraki that they have to work in order to ensure the pleasant conditions equivalent to those of Europe" (Vafas).
18 Commenting on the current small architecture and interior partitions of the existing houses, he acknowledges that this typology is widespread in Greece. However, for rented accommodation to house patients, this typology is not suitable and cannot be profitable. "There is the need for a large house if you would like to name it hotel or however you would like to call it."
19 "The bathhouse would have to be built from scratch, any repairs on the existing are a waste of money."
20 In 1891, 12 geological studies of various locations around Greece were undertaken.
21 The only appropriate room according to his opinion is at the former Lloyd Steamboat agency that has been converted into a hotel. He records 2137 visitors in 1891.
22 Οδηγός των εν Λουτρακίω λουομένων, υπό Αλεξάνδρου Γ. Δευτεραίου. 1902 Guide for Loutraki Bathers by Alexandros Deuteraios. Athens 1902.
23 "We cannot demand from Loutraki neither the scientific perfection of Carlsbad building nor its magical promenades nor the numerous theaters and the excellent concerts…for this we need millions and time" (Deuteraios 30).
24 This building would need a reading room with main European and Greek with dedicated rooms to read the newspapers, ballgames, concerts, dances or comedies and also one for shooting. The making of such centre would present a significant cost, but its contribution will be really important to the bathing population (Deuteraios, 33).
25 Sioris.
26 "All the civilized nations and especially those leading in culture, foremost demonstrate their bath towns. Vichy, Baden-Baden, Carlsbad; aside from their therapeutic springs, they also demonstrate the investment and human inspiration in works such as gardens, boulevards and tree-lined streets. Thanks to these works good life and satisfaction peek to the maximum ideal limit. The matter of natural beauty of Greece is unsurpassable. The laced coastline of Greece, the intoxicating, the endless, the sun-drenched. Close to which lay our alkaline springs is beyond competition and the Lido of Venice, the Abazia of Italy, Nice or Monte Carlo, all pale in comparison. Loutraki and Aidipsos have been blessed with a scandalous favour by the Creator. (Athanasios Nikitas Sioris Patra 1926 p.23)
27 As one doctor writes:
for many, a visit to Loutropolis is considered a social obligation, or a social demonstration. If the excursions, Casinos, dance gatherings, allow it the visitors go to the bathhouses and gather to the spring to chat rather than for Therapeutic purposes. The Loutropolis today have to stop to be considered amusement centers and to be recognized as centers for restoration of health.
(Labrinopoulos 101)
28 Building owners were issued a written order to collect the funds at the bank. The beneficiary of these notes could transfer the ownership. Villagers who owned a demolished hut in the countryside would go to Loutraki and sell these orders at a discount. Their buyers would collect a sum of money from the bank and construct a larger building in town.
29 The new city plan was composed of 7 parallel roads and 13 intersecting streets running perpendicular to the sea was punctuated by four main squares.
30 There are 180,000 baths recorded. The competing bath town Aidipsos comes second with 9,000 visitors a year.
31 It replaced a wooden kiosk with its architecture reminiscent of European spa towns.
32 Later, its operation passed to EOT and was the home of the state-owned spring.

33 Mosaics were created by the artist Stefanos Xenopoulos and his students.
34 Two bath buildings became prominent in the town life: The Oikonomou Bath which housed an old source from 1870 and the very popular Karantanis Bath whose source was the richest in volume (Vlahos).
35 In 1940, there are different ownerships of the thermal springs: the municipality owns the main spring with three other private owners. Karantanis, Oikonomou and Protopapas (Zografos). By 1953, there are four owners of the sources, the municipal source, EOT source, Karantanis and Oikonomou (EOT).
36 In 1951, 644,630 glasses, 1,566,598 in 1952 and 1,967,277 in 1953.
37 Publications of the time praise the coordination and precision with which it was designed and executed: "the whole construction was carried out with considerable precision as the machines, which had been ordered from Germany, would arrive preassembled and allowed no variation in dimensions" (Technika Chronika 1963, p. 4).
38 The *Loutraki Review* gives a really broad insight into all aspects of life of the city that extend beyond the casino. It is also sold in Athens, establishing a direct news reel of the happenings of Loutraki into the Greek capital.
39 The hotels Pigai, Pallas, Karelion and Akti are referenced.
40 The negotiations with the British club fail as they request insurance coverage from the Greek Government in the case of earthquake or domestic unrest and that their funds will be secured. In return, they provide guarantee of the capital from one of the largest English banks. The insurance from earthquake is something that the Greek President cannot provide. The Prime Minister states that if he had that capacity, he wouldn't lease Loutraki to foreigners but would distribute the funds to the earthquake victims. The deal is then off.
41 Published in 2 November 1930.
42 "The ancient and honorable city of Corinth has been aroused from her centuries of slumber and designated as the site where a glittering casino will rise above the blue waters- a casino that will outdo Monte Carlo in games of chance, surpass the Lido as a fashionable bathing resort and challenge the spas of Europe in effecting 'cures'...Corinth claims curative waters that out-rate Carlsbad, Evian, Bad Ems and other 'cure' places. Add to all this, the proposed casino of Corinth – not the eighth wonder of the world, but the first! The casino and other buildings are to overlook both the Gulf of Corinth and the Gulf of Aegina…it will offer all latest games and amusements from baccarat to bull fights." *The New York Times*, 7 November 1930.
43 One of the few buildings still standing after the earthquake was the five-story Hotel "PALLAS" built in 1923.
44 During World War II, it became bomb shelter due to its particular structural strength.
45 Steamboat Manna.
46 Pigai, Karelion, Marion, Palmyra, Theoxeneia, Akti, Plaza, Delphi, Sesis.
47 The Corinth Strait was completely destroyed by bombs towards the end of the war.
48 Providing a total of 1976 rooms or 3,233 beds.
49 Loutraki 1955 has 1,041 rooms and 1,984 beds and 710 homes available for rental.
Statistics of visitors before and after the Second World War (Kranidiotis).
(1931) 6.746, (1932) 7.000, (1933) 9.874, (1934) 11.629 (1935) 10.479 (1936) 10.948 (1937) 7.835 (1939) 8.324 (1950) 14.167 (1951) 13.243 (1952) 10.363 (1953) 8.172 (1954) 9.350.
50 Kazino, Peukaki, Hraio.
51 Karantani, Dimitropopoulou, Kazino.
52 Visitors starting with 14,000 and again a slow decrease over the subsequent years. All data in this section are from the EOT report 1951–1953.
53 This report, like the ones from the years 1949, 1950 and 1951, aims to present the picture of all the movement in the Loutropolis and thermal springs of Greece over a three-year period. In a dedicated chapter, EOT also includes full scientific data of the thermal springs with detailed tables of the chemical characteristics of the waters and the healing properties in the main Loutropolis. The report contains a summary of the geographic location of each Loutropolis, the transportation means to get to them and in a special table, the existing bathing and hotel infrastructures so that any interested party can obtain all necessary information.
54 Venturi Scott Brown, Learning from Las Vegas, p. 3.
55 Venturi Scott Brown, Learning from Las Vegas, p. 155.

Bibliography

Agar, Jon, and Crosbie Smith. *Making Space for Science: Territorial Themes in the Shaping of Knowledge*. Springer, 2016.
Anderson, Susan C., and Bruce H. Tabb. *Water, Leisure and Culture: European Historical Perspectives*. Berg, 2002.

Dalezios, Orestis. Ιαματικά Λουτρά της Ελλάδος (Mineral Waters of Greece). Athens, 1891.
Dambergis, A.K. Περί των εν Λουτρακίω ιαματικών και φρεατιαίων υδάτων. (On the healing waters of Loutraki). Athens, 1899.
Deuteraios, Alexandros. Οδηγός των εν Λουτρακίω Λουομένων Guide for Loutraki Bathers. Athens, 1902.
"Die Heilquellen in Griechenland. Beschreibung Der Heilquellen von Patradgik … - Xaverios Landerer - Google Books." Accessed November 10, 2018. https://books.google.com/books?id=O4xfAAAAcAAJ&pg=PA23&dq=Beschreibung+d.+Heilquellen+Griechenlands&hl=en&sa=X&ved=0ahUKEwjA9LD-f3NLfAhXnnuAKHV6EADYQ6AEIKjAA#v=onepage&q=Beschreibung%20d.%20Heilquellen%20Griechenlands&f=false.
Du thermalisme traditionnel au tourisme de santé =: Von der traditionellen Badekur zu modernen Formen des Gesundheitstourismus = From traditional spa tourism to modern forms of health tourism. Publications de l'AIEST, vol. 30. St-Gall, Suisse: Editions AIEST, 1989.
"Efymeris (Newspaper), Archives" https://srv-web1.parliament.gr/display_doc.asp?item=43286&seg
Ελληνικός Οργανισμός Τουρισμού (ΕΟΤ, National Tourism Organisation).
E.O. T, Loutropolis 1951–1952–1953 (Bath towns 1951 – 1952 – 1953). Athens, 1953.
Emmanouil Emmanouil. To Loutrakion Kai at Ydata tou, (Loutraki and its waters). Athens 1927.
Frederick Strong. *Greece as a Kingdom.* Longman, Brown, Green, and Longmans, 1842. Accessed October 1, 2018. http://archive.org/details/greeceasakingdo01strogoog.
Hippocrates. *On Airs, Waters and Places.* Library of Alexandria, 2007.
Kostidi, Melpomeni. "The Medical Discourse on Greek Spas from the Mid-Nineteenth Century to the Early Twentieth Century." *Postgraduate Journal of Medical Humanities*, 3 (2016): 52–70.
Kranidiotis Tourist Guide. Loutropoleis (Bathtowns). Athens, 1955.
Labrinopoulos, G.L. Ta Loutra (The Baths). Athens, 1908.
"Landerer." Accessed February 12, 2019, http://jupiter.chem.uoa.gr/pchem/lab/landerer.html.
Landerer, Xaverios. *Die Heilquellen in Griechenland. Beschreibung der Heilquellen von Patradgik, Aidipso und den Thermopylen.* Literarisch-artistisches Institut, 1837.
Lekkas, Nikolaos. Ai 750 Metallikai Pigai tis Ellados (The 750 Mineral Springs of Greece). Athens, 1938.
Loutraki Casino Review. Επιθεώρησις του καζίνου Λουτρακίου : επιστημονική, κριτική, κοινωνική (Loutraki Review), multiple issues, 1930–1931, Loutraki.
Panousis, Spilios. Ta Ydata tou Loutrakiou, (The Waters of Loutraki). Athens, 1929.
Pyla, Panayiota Ioanni. *Landscapes of Development: The Impact of Modernization Discourses on the Physical Environment of the Eastern Mediterranean.* Aga Khan Program at the Harvard Graduate School of Design, 2013.
Sioris, Athanasios Nikitas. Άι Ιαματικαι Πηγαί της Ελλάδος (Thermal Springs of Greece). Athens, 1926.
Strong, Frederick. Greece as a Kingdom. Longman, Brown, Green and Longmans London, 1842.
The New York Times. A Monte Carlo for Corinth, Famous Greek City hopes to Outrank Rival as the World's Centre of Gambling, November.
Vafas, Georgios. Meleti epi town Metallkwn Idatwn tou Loutrakeiou (Study of the Mineral Waters of Loutraki). Athens, 1880.
Venturi, Robert. Denise Scott Brown and Steven Izenour, *Learning from Las Vegas.* MIT Press 1972.
Vlahakis, Nikos. Loutraki Perahora. Athens, 1971.
Vlastos, Miltiadis and Papapioannou Nikolaos. Praktikos Odigos tou Louomenou: Loutrotherapeia Krinotherapeia Iamatikai Pigai tis Ellados (Practical Guide for the Bather). Athens, 1930.
Zografos, Panagiotis. Ai en Elladi prwtai Iamatikai Pigai. Loutraki, Aidipsos, Kaiafas (The first thermal springs of Greece, Loutraki, Aidipsos, Kaiafas). Athens, 1940.

Chapter 16

BiG: Living and working together

Meike Schalk, Sara Brolund de Carvalho and Helena Mattsson

> We searched for a rather different way to live where we could have both a private home and also a series of common rooms. We saw daily cooperation as a base for community building/togetherness, a better environment for our children to grow up in, to save material resources as well as a possibility to have a more fun and richer life. We decided to investigate what such housing might look like.

In April 2019, the authors of this chapter held a 'witness seminar' at the Swedish Centre for Architecture and Design – ArkDes in Stockholm with the group BiG.[1] BiG is short for 'Bo i Gemenskap' and translates to Living in Community. BiG is a multi-disciplinary collective that has been researching and promoting collective housing since 1976 both as a housing typology as well as an infrastructure of social support and care. Besides their crucial influence on collective house models in Sweden, BiG's work has received little international attention. One reason for this may be that, in the early days, the group published mostly in Swedish, although they travelled and presented their work internationally. Another reason is perhaps the group's unusual composition including ten practicing architects, planners and activists as well as researchers, all women.

Today, the BiG group has six active members: Ingela Blomberg, Kerstin Kärnekull, Gunilla Lundahl, Ann Norrby, Inga-Lisa Sangregorio and Sonja Vidén with backgrounds in architecture, urban planning, art history and journalism. The purpose of forming a group around the topic of collective housing is described by its members in their common statement above, published on their homepage.[2] This chapter looks

Figure 16.1 Illustration by Inger Blomgren Larsson from the publication 'Vi bor för att leva' [We dwell for living]

Byggforskningsrådet 11:1980

at the collaborative practice of BiG and their collective housing concept. It foregrounds the 'witness seminar' as a method for participatory research which the authors who are part of a research collective themselves, explore in their practice.[3]

The BiG model and concept

Although they never presented themselves as a feminist group, BiG had a strong connection to the Swedish feminist movement of the late 1960s and 1970s and organisations such as Grupp 8. They were also connected to grassroots organisations and associations that aimed to increasing inhabitants' influence on local planning, such as Byalagrörelserna [village community movements], and cultural actors that promoted self-organisation and practices of commoning on a neighbourhood level like Aktion Samtal [Action Dialogue]. In order to spread information and make 'Living in Community' as tangible as possible to an interested audience and collective housing enthusiasts, the group developed a collective housing model which illustrated their concept of a 'small collective house.' This particular housing concept, the BiG model, became the basis for around 50 collective houses that have been built in Sweden since the late 1970s.

In 1980, a dollhouse-sized physical model was shown at the Boplats 80 exhibition which was organised by the Swedish Association of Architects in the park Kungsträdgården in Stockholm. It consisted of a 1930s housing typology retrofitted to a small collective house in the scale 1:12, to fit dollhouse furniture, which accommodated a number of small private flats and several large common rooms for a range of different purposes. It demonstrated the economic relationship between private and common rooms in the equation of apartments dedicating 10% of their average size to common use. The opportunities that would arise from this were exemplified in a large dining room, a common room, laundry, sauna, TV room and a workshop when 15 apartments would share space. It showed that a group of 40 apartments would, beside these, even have access to a library, textile workshops, a table tennis and a playroom. But the most important community room in the BiG model was the large kitchen and the dining area emphasising the social dimension of cooking and eating together.

BiG promoted an ideal size of 'the small collective house' organised from the activities within, with between 15 and 50 individual small flats including individual kitchens, several large shared spaces and a schedule for common cooking and meals. Regarding ideal sizes, BiG member Inga-Lisa Sangregorio writes:

> it all depends on what the residents want to do together and how they organise. In several medium sized blocks with about twenty-five flats, the residents say that another ten households would have been welcome. On the other hand, there are buildings with fewer flats where the residents think they have found their ideal size.[4]

Central to the BiG model was the possibility to have both access to community while at the same time to be able to close ones' own apartment door; "We had a common vision, to live in one's own apartment, to be able to close one's door, and to organise food together. Well, this was my own motivation. Not so much ideology in all this. This came later. This was the base for me", witnessed Ingela Blomberg.[5] Kerstin Kärnekull expands "… it was this, to have one's own flat and at the same time to have the common which benefitted both the children and the adults … and where one was not so confined." Kärnekull explains that their collective housing model was different from self-organised life in individual communes as they existed at the time in some, previously posh, larger villas in suburbs.[6] BiG's collective housing was not only about residents sharing a house, but it was also thought of as a visionary model for future living on a broader scale which addressed all areas of housing production, developers, policymakers and politicians as well as prospective inhabitants.

> We really wanted to contribute with something that was possible to accomplish for real, therefore, we understood that the only way forward in Sweden in the 1970s and 1980s was to find forms to collaborate with the large actors, the municipal housing companies, and not try to start a cohousing project, where the group is the owner. We didn't either had own capital but wanted to live with tenancy. Imagine, we have been going on for almost 45 years![7]

Färdknäppen, a different house

Färdknäppen is a typical BiG concept house which has received international attention in research projects and publications lately.[8] It has 43 one to three-room apartments

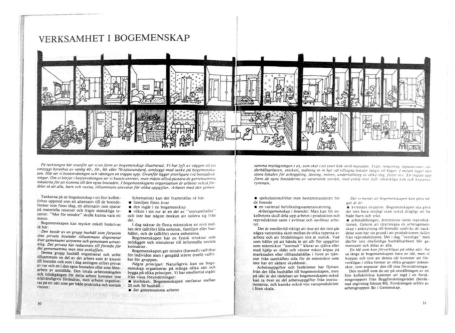

Figure 16.2 A spread in the Boplats 80 [Living Place 80] exhibition catalogue showing BiG's model. Boplats 80 was meant as a follow-up of the famous 1930s Stockholm Exhibition

Figure 16.3 BiG's model, 'Ett litet kollektivhus' [A little collective house], at Boplats 80
Photo: BiG

and approximately 350 square meters of common area, and it was the first of eight of a new type of collective house for people in the 'second half of life'; people over 50 and without children.[9] The project was started in 1987 by seniors who were concerned about their living conditions as they grew older. The collective house, which was built in 1993 and is owned by a municipal housing company, was designed with the participation of future inhabitants. The outcome of this collaboration was tailored private apartments, a novelty in municipal housing in Sweden at the time, with access to common rooms to support social togetherness and greater independence from the municipal services for older people.

The common area is flexibly planned for a variety of activities: a library with TV and a computer, a weaving room, laundry room, common dining room and kitchen, a room for woodwork and a garden accessible from the dining room. On the top floor, there is an all-purpose room with a fireplace and an adjoining open-air roof garden. There is a recycling area at the ground floor with a shelf for donations. All refundable bottles are collected, and the money is donated to charity. The basement includes individual storage rooms and collective pantry/food storage rooms plus a recreational/ exercise room and a sauna. There is a small office which can be used by everyone, equipped with a computer, scanner, copying machine and office supplies. There are also three small guest rooms available to out-of-town guests.[10] Färdknäppen's abundance of programs in one single house comes close to contemporary co-housing projects. It was unusual, at the time, due to its focus on a particular group, middle-aged and elderly residents. In contrast to co-housing projects which are mostly self-funded and with resident-owned flats, Färdknäppen's flats are rental.

BiG was not the first collective housing model in Sweden that led to realised projects. BiG was building upon a strong tradition of collective housing and debates on living collectively in Sweden which had begun with early modernism. The 1935 collective house in John Ericssonsgatan in Stockholm by the social reformer Alva Myrdal and architect Sven Markelius is well known. Collectivity is expressed here in private flats of minimum size and basic common functions such as a common dining hall and a crèche which were serviced. This project was examined critically by the American urban historian Dolores Hayden in her well-known article "What would a non-sexist city be like? Speculation on housing, urban design, and human work" of 1980 for its focus on collective benefit for the residents of the house instead of taking a broader perspective and including the neighbourhood.[11]

BiG refers to even earlier examples of one-kitchen housing projects such as the 1906 Hemgårdens Centralkök (The Home Yard Central Kitchen) in Stockholm which was originally conceived for working women. A few more buildings of this type were realized in the 1910s and 1920s.[12] But most of the collective houses were built in Sweden between the 1930s and 1950s primarily based on the idea of sharing services. BiG managed to launch the idea of a 'second wave' of collective housing based on labour distribution among the residents rather than the distinction between employees and residents.[13] While earlier examples were more oriented towards needs, for example, of working women, or utopian or reformist projects, the BiG model expresses specific values about 'living together' which went beyond the sharing of resources and spaces.

Meike Schalk et al.

BiG's witness seminar

Several of BiG's members have been successful individually as researchers and writers within the field of housing research. However, as a group, they remain largely unknown among a younger generation of planners and architects who are working with cohousing concepts. Despite BiG's strong influence on the collective housing discourse in the 1980s and 1990s, the group is barely present in the recent and current Swedish planning and architectural history writing. Through the witness seminar, we wanted to bring to the foreground their collaborative practice and their work as simultaneously visionary and applied. Paradoxically, their practice is both marginalised in the Swedish context and has had a major impact on Swedish planning through the BiG model and their publications from the 1980s and the 1990s. Consistent with the methods of witness seminars, all members of BiG were asked to prepare a short statement. The statements were responding to questions concerning their initial goals and personal motivations, reflections regarding how attitudes towards collective housing have shifted in the last decades and thoughts on specific achievements in terms of their influence on Swedish building politics and policies.

Although the witness seminar was announced on ArkDes' homepage and open to everyone interested in the subject, the audience consisted mostly of especially invited scholars, planners, architects and long-term residents of collective houses. Several of the guests posed questions as well as gave an account on historical shifts which framed BiG's work in a new way. The dialogue with the audience broadened the view on BiG as it reflected the narratives of the witnesses through supporting,

Figure 16.4 Witness seminar with BiG, from left to right: Kerstin Kärnekull, Ingela Blomberg, Gunilla Lundahl, Inga-Lisa Sangregorio, Ann Norrby and Sonja Vidén at The Swedish Centre for Architecture and Design, April 2019
Photo: Mariette Parling

complementing or sometimes contesting statements, creating arguments, enhancing discussion and thus contributing to shared new knowledge.

To study a group that has been active for more than four decades together with its members and an audience demands a certain curatorial approach. Archival research and interviews can 'unpack' heterogeneous stories but often cannot bring out the specific, layered forms of information, where a complexity of knowledge is embedded in the groups' collective experiences. The witness seminar drew a picture of a truly entangled and collaborative way of thinking and working concerning, for example, questions of authorship, but also how BiG members' personal life situation had a large impact on their view on the social interaction provided by collective housing. Topics such as aging and societal political changes were framed in relation to shifting building regulations and the introduction and withdrawal of governmental building support throughout the years, all intertwined with personal life stories of changing social situations due to having children, or the lack of children, of marital status, of health issues, work load, etc.

BiG's legacy

> We have not invented something new but have put ideas together. We put words to common wishes of many. We wrote a program for it.[14]

Most of BiG's members have previously and simultaneously been part of other groups and associations; collective work has always been fundamental to their thinking and production mode. Although in retirement-age today, the BiG group is still active, does recurring study visits to collective houses all around the world and lectures and publishes within academia as well as in popular science media.

It was first in 2000 that English translations of some of BiG's works appear, namely the booklet *Collaborative Housing in Sweden*.[15] It was authored by the planner and journalist Inga-Lisa Sangregorio, but it builds on previously published material by the whole group. The booklet presents principles of collaborative housing in Sweden. It gives examples of how concepts have turned real in practice narrated through stories from inhabitants where they motivate their choice for collaborative housing. Although only two of BiG's members, Sonja Vidén and Ingela Blomberg, are actually architectural researchers, many of BiG's works appeared "[w]ith the support of The Swedish Council for Building Research (and a lot of our own time)," and "many research reports and books were produced as well as many case studies and study visits in Sweden and in Europe were conducted. This in return resulted in new articles, lectures and new contacts."[16]

In their publications, the group seldom addresses only a small audience of academics, but their mission was to disseminate and spread practically oriented knowledge on collective housing to as many professional architects, administrators and future residents as possible.[17] BiG produced hands-on material such as manuals including rules and policies, case study research, environmental argumentation and personal

Figure 16.5 Some of the many publications written by BiG and individual members
Photo: Action Archive

reflections as well as fictional diary entries. BiG's work can be seen as a 'practical activism' from within intended to construct collective models for a future habitat.

> Their work demonstrates a new attitude towards activism and feminist strategies in the field of architecture, moving from a critique of power structures to instigating real changes within these power structures. Through their positions as writers for widely circulated magazines and newspapers, and as occupants of central positions in the Swedish Association of Public Housing Companies as well as in the Swedish Association of Architects, they had the capability to change reality.[18]

BiG's practice shows that collectivity and living in community are influenced by legal frameworks, divisions of labour and the planning and designing of adequate common rooms. Collectivity and community do not necessarily mean the same thing: while sharing spaces, tools and services can be described as collective uses, creating community requires greater care, the provision of spaces and the investment of free time.[19] The importance of an infrastructure of common rooms was debated at the BiG witness seminar. A long discussion on the need to look more into their history in Swedish Housing and Planning ended with Kerstin Kärnekull stating: "common rooms are in themselves an almost unresearched field. Who will take on this next research question?"

Notes

1. A witness seminar is a form of oral history approach often used in contemporary history research. Witness seminars have been performed at the Institute of Contemporary British History since 1986 and the Institute for Contemporary History at Södertörn University, in Sweden, since 1998. The BiG witness seminar was organised by Sara Brolund de Carvalho and moderated by her together with Helena Mattsson.
2. http://www.boigemenskap.se/boigemenskap.se/Forskargruppen_Bo_i_Gemenskap.html (accessed 1 December 2019). Translation by the authors.
3. Action Archive is an association founded by the authors in 2013 pursuing participatory historical research.
4. Inga-Lisa Sangregorio, *Collaborative Housing in Sweden* (Borås: The Swedish Council for Building Research, T1:2000), p. 11. See also BiG-gruppen and Elly Berg (eds), *Det lilla kollektivhuset. En modell för praktisk tillämpning* [The small collective house: A model for practical application], Byggforskningsrådet T14:1982, and Gunilla Lundahl and Inga-Lisa Sangregorio, *15 kollektivhus: en idé förverkligas* [Fifteen collective houses: an idea put into practice], Byggforskningsrådet T9:1992.
5. Ingela Blomberg, at the witness seminar, 12 April 2019.
6. Kerstin Kärnekull at the witness seminar, 12 April 2019.
7. Kerstin Kärnekull in an email to Sara Brolund de Carvalho, 19 May 2020.
8. See, for example, Michael LaFond, Thomas Honeck, Institute for Creative Sustainability, Experimentcity, *Cohousing Cultures: Handbook for Self-organized, Community-oriented and Sustainable Housing* (Berlin: Jovis Verlag, 2012) discussing nine very different examples of cohousing cultures in practice, among them Färdknäppen in Stockholm. See also Naoko Imami, "The Possibility of Collective Housing for the Elderly – A Case Study of Hyogo Reconstruction Collective Housing", J-STAGE home, *SOSHIORO*, 53(3) (2008–2009).
9. Dick Urban Vestbro, "Cohousing in Sweden, History and Present Situation" (2014), *kollektivhus.nu*, http://www.kollektivhus.nu/pdf/SwedishCohousing14.pdf (accessed 31 October 2019).
10. Färdknäppens homepage, http://fardknappen.se/in-english/ (accessed 31 October 2019).
11. Dolores Hayden, "What Would a Non-sexist City Be Like? Speculation on Housing, Urban Design, and Human Work", *Signs: Journal of Women in Culture and Society* 5(3) (1980), pp. 170–187.
12. Ingela Blomberg and Kerstin Kärnekull, "Do-It-Yourself: The Stony Road to Cohousing in Sweden", in *Built Environment* 45(3) (2019), pp. 280–295.
13. Helena Mattsson, "Shifting Gender and Acting Out History: Is there a Swedish Postmodern-feminist Architecture?", in *Feminist Futures of Spatial Practice: Materialisms, Activisms, Dialogues, Pedagogies, Projections*, eds. Schalk, M., Kristiansson, T., Mazé, R. (Baunach: AADR/Spurbuchverlag, 2017), 289–300.
14. Ingela Blomberg at the witness seminar, 12 April 2019.
15. Inga-Lisa Sangregorio (2000).
16. http://www.boigemenskap.se/boigemenskap.se/Forskargruppen_Bo_i_Gemenskap.html (accessed 31 October 2019).
17. See Ingela Blomberg and Kerstin Kärnekull, *Bo i Gemenskap, Bygga seniorboende tillsammans – en handbok* [Living in community, building senior housing together – a handbook] (Stockholm: Svensk Byggtjänst, 2013); and Kerstin Kärnekull, Ingela Blomberg, Bengt Ahlqvist and Nathan Large, *Äldres boende i Tyskland, England, Nederländerna och Danmark* [Housing for the elderly in Germany, England, The Netherlands and Denmark] (Stockholm: Svensk Byggtjänst, 2013).
18. Helena Mattsson (2017), 294.
19. See Meike Schalk, Sara Brolund de Carvalho, Helena Mattsson and Beatrice Stude, "Introduction: From Collective to Common Rooms. The Swedish and the Viennese Model", in *Caring for Communities*, eds. M. Schalk, S. Brolund de Carvalho/Action Archive + Stude, B. (Stockholm: Action Archive Publishing, 2019).

References

BiG-gruppen and Elly Berg (ed.), *Det lilla kollektivhuset. En modell för praktisk tillämpning* [The Small Collective House: A Model for Practical Application], Byggforskningsrådet T14:1982. Bo i Gemenskap. http://www.boigemenskap.se/boigemenskap.se/Forskargruppen_Bo_i_Gemenskap.html (accessed 1 July 2019).

Boplats 80: en idéutställning om boendet, Kungsträdgården Stockholm 23 maj-18 september 1980 [Living place 80: an idea exhibition about housing, Kungsträdgården Stockholm 23 May – 18 September 1980] (Stockholm: SAR, 1980). [exhibition catalogue].

Meike Schalk et al.

Dick Urban Vestbro, "Cohousing in Sweden, History and Present Situation" (2014), *kollektivhus.nu*, http://www.kollektivhus.nu/pdf/SwedishCohousing14.pdf (accessed 31 October 2019).

Dolores Hayden, "What Would a Non-sexist City Be Like? Speculation on Housing, Urban Design, and Human Work", *Signs: Journal of Women in Culture and Society* 5 (3), 1980, 170–187.

Färdknäppen, http://fardknappen.se/in-english/ (accessed 31 November).

Gunilla Lundahl and Inga-Lisa Sangregorio, *15 kollektivhus: en idé förverkligas* [Fifteen Collective Houses: An Idea Put into Practice], Byggforskningsrådet T9:1992.

Helena Mattsson, "Shifting Gender and Acting Out History: Is there a Swedish Postmodern-Feminist Architecture?", in *Feminist Futures of Spatial Practice: Materialisms, Activisms, Dialogues, Pedagogies, Projections*, eds. M. Schalk, T. Kristiansson, and R. Mazé (Baunach: AADR/Spurbuchverlag, 2017), 289–300.

Inga-Lisa Sangregorio, *Collaborative Housing in Sweden* (Borås: The Swedish Council for Building Research, T1, 2000).

Ingela Blomberg and Kerstin Kärnekull, *Bo i Gemenskap, Bygga seniorboende tillsammans – en handbok* [Living in community, building senior housing together - a handbook] (Stockholm: Svensk Byggtjänst, 2013).

Ingela Blomberg and Kerstin Kärnekull, "Do-It-Yourself: The Stony Road to Cohousing in Sweden", *Built Environment* 45 (3), 2019, 280–295.

Kerstin Kärnekull, Ingela Blomberg, Bengt Ahlqvist and Nathan Large, *Äldres boende i Tyskland, England, Nederländerna och Danmark* [Housing for the elderly in Germany, England, The Netherlands and Denmark] (Stockholm: Svensk Byggtjänst 2013).

Meike Schalk, Sara Brolund de Carvalho, Helena Mattsson, Beatrice Stude, "Introduction: From Collective to Common Rooms. The Swedish and the Viennese Model", in *Caring for Communities*, eds. M. Schalk and S. Brolund de Carvalho. Action Archive + Stude, B., (Stockholm: Action Archive Publishing, 2019).

Michael LaFond, Thomas Honeck, Institute for Creative Sustainability, Experimentcity, *Cohousing Cultures: Handbook for Self-organized, Community-oriented and Sustainable Housing* (Berlin: Jovis Verlag, 2012).

Naoko Imami, "The Possibility of Collective Housing for the Elderly – A Case Study of Hyogo Reconstruction Collective Housing", J-STAGE home, *SOSHIORO*, 53 (3), 2008–2009.

Part V
Autonomy and organisation

Chapter 17

Design precepts for autonomy

A case study of Kelvin Hall, Glasgow

Jane Clossick and Ben Colburn

The way that architects design public buildings has an impact on people's capacity to exercise their autonomy. Using an exploration of the architecture of Kelvin Hall, a public building in Glasgow, and interviews with its project architect, this chapter investigates the relationship between Clossick's 'depth structure' architectural theory of spatial relationships, and Colburn's philosophical theory about the nature and value of autonomy. The two ideas, autonomy and depth structure, can be brought together usefully to offer pointers to designers of public places.

We begin by setting out the core theory: the value of autonomy, the design precepts it implies and the idea of depth structure. Then a discussion of the case study: Kelvin Hall, a mixed-use public building in Glasgow. We offer a worked example of a depth structure that fosters autonomy and suggest a design toolkit and useful vocabulary. The case study shows how the configuration of internal boundaries in Kelvin Hall generates a depth structure which exemplifies the design precepts and thereby allows people to flourish to their fullest potential and exercise their ethical right to autonomy.

Autonomy

Autonomy is an ideal of the self-authored life. That's Joseph Raz's phrase.[1] Colburn has developed and extended this theory.[2] On his view, the autonomous life is on where a person decides for herself what is important and lives her life in accordance with those values. The autonomous life is characterised by three conditions, on Colburn's view:

DOI: 10.4324/9781003118985-22

endorsement, independence and responsibility. In endorsement, one has some goals, values, ambitions and preferences which (perhaps implicitly) set out a pattern of contentment for one's life.[3] With independence, those endorsements must not be covert: that is, they must be explained by things which would not make us repudiate them if we became aware of them. That rules out, for example, manipulation or malign influence which works only because we are not aware of it.[4] With responsibility, the autonomous person actively and successfully shapes their life in line with their values. That means that your life must go as you wish and you must be the one who makes it so, by exercising responsibility, both in the sense that you make it so (i.e., your decisions explain the way your life goes) and that you bear the consequences.[5] Turning from what it means to be autonomous to the question of how we help people live that way, it is worth emphasising the following important design precepts which follow from the theory just summarised. If we seek to make design choices which support people in living self-authored lives, we need to attend to these precepts in our architectural and urban practice.

Self-directedness and clarity

The responsibility condition tells us that it matters that people's lives are explained by their own judgements, decisions and actions. That means trying to arrange things so that people can live according to their decisions about what is valuable without needing constantly to negotiate or engage in transactions with people on whose discretion they depend. This doesn't mean that people have to be isolated or avoid interaction with others: we are social beings, and we mostly self-author in cooperation with other people. But those interactions must be clear and non-arbitrary, if they are to respect the individual's responsibility for how their life goes and thereby to contribute to their life being autonomous as a whole.

   The term 'autonomy' might make you think that this is about giving the individual maximal freedom of choice without interference. But that's not so! A range of choices is often important for autonomy. But what usually matters more than the size of this range is that it is clear, in several ways: that the choices are significant, that they are distinct, the individual can know what their meaning will be for them given their values without unreasonable difficulty. Without this clarity, it is hard for someone to know how to pursue their values, which threatens the responsibility condition. It also makes it more likely that their choices and actions are explained covertly, by factors which – if only they were not opaque – they would repudiate; so, lack of clarity also threatens the independence condition.

   There is a third precept which we think is also important: anti-perfectionism, which requires that the architect avoids making judgments on people's behalf about what it is valuable or important for them to do. But both the underpinning theory and the design implications here are complicated, so for reasons of time, we set it aside for now and concentrate on self-directedness and clarity.

   Architects are aware of these precepts, although not in these terms. Karen Pickering, one of the architects who worked on Kelvin Hall (our case study below), describes how they fostered self-directedness by giving users the information upfront to form a 'mental map,' as though, in doing so, the building itself has an attitude of friendliness towards its users.

> Karen: We always design a building where you can have a clear mental map. So, you arrive at the building, you know where the front door is, and you know where to go. And you can see the different spaces. I think that's the key thing about it being accessible for everybody, it's not an intimidating building, you feel like you can walk in and nobody's going to stop you. You can go in for a coffee, you can just go on and have a wander and have a look at the Scottish Screen Archive ... it's friendly and it feels safe.

Karen also understands the importance of clarity. As she indicates, accessibility is not only physical but it is also psychological.

> Karen: The key thing for us was, you arrive in the building, and you can see where everything is. If you're in the gym you can see people doing all their weight stuff, and then the big window here, you can see people on their running machines. We put these big windows in, so that people can see what's going on inside. It makes it more accessible to ordinary people, saying "now I can see what's going on in the Kelvin Hall."

The precepts give us a kind of rough-and-ready design specification for how one might respect and foster autonomy in spatial design: we want to secure the conditions of autonomy, and attending to the precepts of self-directedness and clarity is a good way to do it.

Depth

Suppose that you think that individual autonomy (in Colburn's sense) is important, and that you therefore want to build our precepts into your design practice. What, practically, does that mean for someone shaping our environment, including individual spaces/places and the urban environment more generally? We think that a key part of the answer, at least for public buildings such as Kelvin Hall, is to offer a navigable depth structure.

Depth structure is Clossick's term for the landscape of boundaried sociospatial zones within which the social life of human beings takes place.[6] Peter Carl defines depth as the capacity of the city to accommodate a wide variety of settings, each with its own character and direction: the way a building or block structures the "fruitful coexistence of formal and informal life."[7] The landscape of zones which comprise the depth structure in public places is one mechanism by which humans are able to structure and control our social life, by making decisions about which zones to enter and by acting on implicit information about how to behave.[8] By social life here, we mean all human life, not just that which directly involves interaction with other people. As social animals who live in large groups, all human life is social life, even if our social energies may temporarily be focussed on attaining aloneness. A navigable depth structure which offers clarity lets us make these kinds of social choices in a self-directed way.

A depth structure, shown in the diagram in Figure 17.1, is composed of zones, thresholds and boundary conditions.[9] Usually, you will find a series of zones in a building

Jane Clossick and Ben Colburn

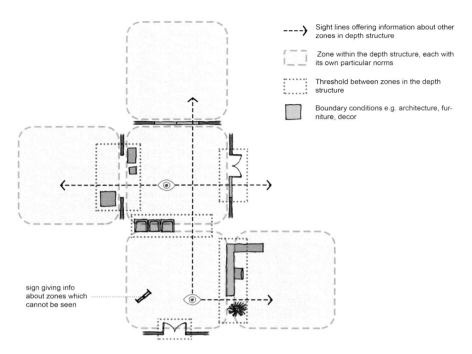

Figure 17.1 Diagram of a typical depth structure
Drawn by J. Clossick

or block, adjacent to one another, each with its own differing set of norms, decorum and behavioural expectations. Zones may accord with rooms, but not necessarily. At the edges of the zones are thresholds, defined by physical boundary conditions. The boundary conditions can include architectural elements, furniture or objects, lighting, colours, textures, human gatekeepers and signage. Differences in norms in each zone may be radical or subtle, but people with typical psychological traits usually adhere firmly to shared assumptions about what behaviour is expected in each zone, and about which individuals exhibit the appropriate characteristics to permit entry.

Karen describes the zones in the depth structure of Kelvin Hall:

> Karen: The Scottish Screen Archive wanted to go at the back of the building, that was the first piece of the jigsaw. Obviously, the entrance and the café and reception have to be at the front. And then Glasgow University didn't mind being at the back and upstairs because they weren't public facing. And then the academics from the Hunterian, they're in their ivory tower right at the back in that little penthouse. Everybody just naturally found their space.

People use the clues available to them via architecture and other corporeal phenomena about the organisation of the depth structure to control the way they carry out their social life in public places. Few would be able to articulate this process verbally because it is based in embodied or tacit knowledge. Dalibor Vesely has called this embodied conversation between people and their environment which helps them decide how to behave and where to go the 'communicative space' of architecture.[10]

Karen explains the communicative nature of the threshold of the front door in her buildings:

> Karen: I think the key thing is the front door. Sometimes in architecture you might want to be a bit more, I don't know, subtle? A bit more, oh kind of, intriguing? But I think the main thing is making a very big and obvious front door. The bigger the better, and that is actually more inviting for people. So, if you get the front door right, then you've got 80% of getting people to feel comfortable and happy in the building.

There are several different kinds of information communicated by a depth structure: decorum, location of thresholds and information about other zones. Decorum: the norms, the expected behaviour and individual characteristics required to enter a zone. Thresholds: their location is communicated by the boundary conditions, enabling people to decide whether to cross a particular threshold from one zone to the next. Other zones: information is communicated via sight lines, signage and gatekeepers about zones deeper in the structure, so people know what other options are available and can choose whether to pursue them.

Using a combination of architectural features, movable objects and signage, designers can create public buildings which exhibit the clarity to enable the self-directedness which is core to autonomy.

Kelvin Hall

Kelvin Hall is an example of a building with clarity in its depth structure which enables self-directness for its users. Kelvin Hall in Glasgow was built in 1926–1927 as an exhibition venue and has been undergoing refurbishment since 2014 by architects Page\Park (a render by Page\Park of their design for Kelvin Hall is shown in Figure 17.2). Phase 1, the extension which we are examining here, was completed in 2016. The refurbishment is a partnership between Glasgow Life, the University of Glasgow and the National Library of Scotland. Kelvin Hall is now a cultural centre, with access to collections, temporary displays, teaching and research, alongside a fitness centre. Entry to Kelvin Hall is free, and it is a public building, although the fitness centre requires a paid subscription. Each of these uses occupies a separate zone, connected by a long and wide spinal corridor which Karen calls 'the avenue' down the centre of the plan.

The case study shown in Figures 17.3–17.6 considers the clarity of the three types of depth structure information communicated by the architecture: decorum, the location of thresholds and information about other zones. The sequence examines moments of transition between some of the zones: between the street and the foyer; between the foyer and the café; between the reception and the avenue and between the avenue and the sports centre. For each, features which create clarity are tabulated; the thresholds and sightlines to other zones are identified in plan; and boundary objects are photographed.

Figure 17.2 Kelvin Hall Phase 1, architect's render
Reproduced with kind permission of Page\Park. For more information about Kelvin Hall, see https://pagepark.co.uk/project/architecture/kelvin-hall/

Kelvin Hall is a building that works well for its users. The reason we suggest is its architecture clearly communicates three core types of knowledge: location of thresholds, decorum of zones and information about other zones. It communicates this information through its architectural features: doors and openings; walls and wall finishes; fixed and movable furniture and objects; floors and ceilings and their finishes; gatekeepers; signage and sightlines between zones.

Because it communicates its depth structure clearly, Kelvin Hall epitomises the autonomy-minded design precepts we discussed earlier. In relation to clarity, the combination of zones and clear boundaries at their thresholds makes it easy to see what your distinct options are, where you must go and what you must do to pursue each one. It helps to make those options distinct (both by transparently indicating what they are – the sports hall is different to the repository – and by using difference in surface, lighting and signage). The clarity results in self-directedness because it allows people to navigate without depending on mediation or instruction, without seeking permissions from gatekeepers: overall, people will just follow the norms without needing intervention.

Kelvin Hall is exemplary on both clarity and self-directness and was designed purposefully by the architects to be so. Karen even managed to persuade the clients to spend more that strictly necessary to achieve them:

> Karen: You walk along the avenue and you can see into the sports halls, you can see into the gym. We made them big openings - we could have made them solid walls – and those openings were expensive because it's fire glass. You then get to the end [of the avenue] and you can see the big video screen of the libraries. You walk through the building and you know there are lots of different things going on.

Although they can't necessarily articulate it verbally, architects know what they are doing and when they design successful depth structures. The terms 'depth structure,' 'boundary conditions' and 'clarity' may prove normatively useful for architects like Karen in

Design precepts for autonomy

making the argument to clients for the value of autonomy-minded design. Obviously, the way that it works here is very particular to this building and to the combination of cultural, academic and leisure activities it contains. But the idea that these precepts are important rules of thumb to keep in mind to protect and promote autonomy in our architectural design and thereby to help people live lives of well-being that they shape for themselves.

Main Entrance

Between the street and the entrance to the building. Two zones, the inside and the outside, and at the threshold of are a number of boundary conditions so threshold doesn't have a clear boundary line, but extends from the paving slabs outside, through the doors to the point where the floor becomes polished concrete. Although anyone can walk in off the street, some activities which would be acceptable on the street (e.g. begging) would be strictly prohibited inside and this prohibition would be enforced by the gatekeepers.

Feature	Type	Details
Door	Threshold location / decorum	Two sets of automatic doors, opens when approached, with a porch in between.
Walls	Threshold location	Extruded dark beam running across the entrance to the corridor.
Floor	Threshold location	Outside: municipal paving slabs (street), to specialised paving slabs (directly outside entrance) to a coir mat (in the porch) to polished concrete to the interior.
Ceiling	Decorum	No ceiling outside, internally there is a glass ceiling.
Signs	Information about other zones	List of all the public facilities available within; opening times of the different parts of the building. .
Gatekeeper	Decorum	Although no gatekeeper at the door, the reception staff have clear view..
Sight lines	Information about other zones	Clear view from outside through glass walls through to foyer and cafe. Once through the door, there is also a clear view down the avenue to the rest of the building.

Polished concrete floor signifies threshold

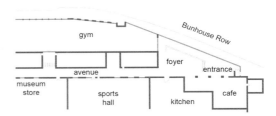

Main entrance from Bunhouse Row

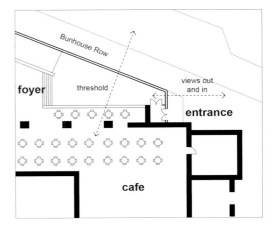

Figure 17.3 Analysis
Drawn by J. Clossick

Jane Clossick and Ben Colburn

Cafe / Foyer

Between foyer (which sells sports goods), and the Kelvin Hall Cafe. At threshold is slight blurring of precise location of boundary because cafe furniture spills out into foyer. Anyone can enter the cafe provided they purchase food or drink, or if they sit at one of the tables - people use the tables to work. Cafe staff do not prevent people from sitting at the tables to work unless the cafe is full of people who want to eat or drink. Unlike the reception area, people do not stand in

Feature	Type	Details
Door	Threshold location	Very large (>3m wide) openings to cafe from foyer.
Walls	Threshold location / decorum	Changes from cast concrete (reception) to white render and timber panelling - muffling sounds in cafe.
Floor	Threshold location	Changes from grey terrazzo (reception) to timber, although the reception floor continues to approx. 2m into cafe area.
Signs	Decorum	Free standing sign and menu - signs about cafe. No signs to other zones.
Objects/ furniture	Threshold location	Bins to cafe entrance. Chairs and tables inside cafe. Cafe entrance and location of serving hatch is marked with a free standing drinks fridge and with racks containing leaflets for local activities.
Lighting	Threshold location	Cafe has low level hanging light fittings, foyer has ceiling mounted lights.
Gatekeeper	Decorum	Cafe staff in serving hatch.
Sight lines	Information about other zones	Clear view from the cafe into the reception area, out to the street, towards the main entrance.

Threshold with cafe staff as gatekeepers

Signs as boundary objects at cafe entrance

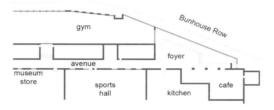

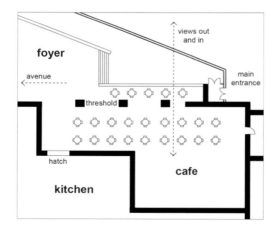

Figure 17.4 Analysis
Drawn by J. Clossick

Design precepts for autonomy

Foyer / Avenue

Between the reception and the corridor which leads into to the sports centre entrance, the University of Glasgow Hunterian collection, conference suite and the National Library of Scotland. Threshold is simple, demarcated with a number of boundary indicators. Only people who intend to access one of the functions of the building will cross this threshold, although anyone can do so.

Feature	Type	Details
Walls	Threshold location	Changes from timber panelling behind reception desk, to white painted plaster in avenue. Dark painted stripe across the ceiling and part way down the wall indicating threshold.
Ceiling	Threshold location	Dark brown extruded beam running across entrance to avenue.
Signs	Information about other zones	On wall, with list of zones in building, also inside corridor showing the location of the sports hall. Two free standing signs showing temporary T-rex exhibition (right) and info about the National Library of Scotland (left).
Objects	Decorum	Demountable barrier, which can prevent access to avenue.
Gatekeeper	Decorum	Reception staff, but we entered the avenue and no one challenged us.
Sight lines	Information about other zones	Clear view from the cafe into foyer, out to the street and towards the main entrance. Clear view to the sports hall and down avenue.

Reception desk and view down avenue

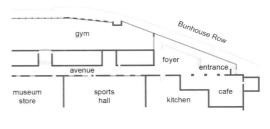

Sign as information and boundary object

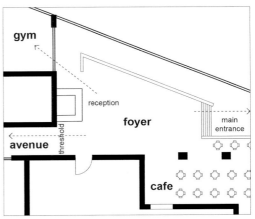

Figure 17.5 Analysis
Drawn by J. Clossick

Avenue / Glasgow Club

Threshold between corridor which runs through the centre of the building and the entrance area to the gym and sports centre, the Glasgow Club. It is a barrier formed by card entrance gates. The sports club is accessible only by staff and by those who pay a subscription. There are clear sight lines between the corridor and the sports centre, through glass walls and windows to the avenue, so there is clarity about other zones in the building, enabling individuals using it to understand what's happening in adjacent zones.

Feature	Type	Details
Walls	Threshold location	Wall colour changes dramatically, the sports centre colour is orange
Fixed furniture	Decorum	The threshold is marked by metal and glass card-operated barriers/gates
Ceiling	Threshold location	The ceiling drops above the gates, there is a light well above
Lighting	Threshold location	There is natural light falling from the roof behind the barriers, to the corridor side the light comes from recessed strip light
Gatekeeper	Threshold location / decorum	Automatic gates require clients to tap a pass to enter the gym
Sight lines	Information about other zones	There is a clear view from the corridor through the class doors into the gym, through glass walls into the sports hall to the opposite side of the corridor

View from avenue to sports hall

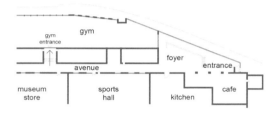

Card gates as boundary objects

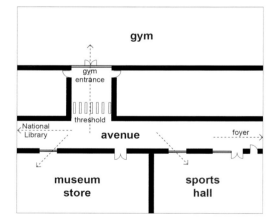

Figure 17.6 Analysis
Drawn by J. Clossick

Notes

1 Joseph Raz, *The Morality of Freedom* (Oxford: Clarendon Press, 1986).
2 Ben Colburn, *Autonomy and Liberalism* (New York: Routledge, 2010).
3 Colburn, *Autonomy and Liberalism*, pp. 25–26.

4 Colburn, *Autonomy and Liberalism*, pp. 26–31; Ben Colburn, 'Authenticity and the Third-Person Perspective', in *Autonomy, Authenticity, and Multiculturalism*, ed. by G. Levey (New York: Routledge, 2015), pp. 121–141.
5 Colburn, *Autonomy and Liberalism*, pp. 31–32.
6 Jane Clossick, 'The Depth Structure of a London High Street: A Study in Urban Order' (London: Metropolitan University, 2017).
7 Peter Carl, 'Type, Field, Culture, Praxis', *Architectural Design*, 81.1 (2011).
8 The claim that spatial boundaries exist and reflect the cultural matrix of social conventions, values and norms has been claimed by numerous authors, key examples include Lewis Mumford, *The Culture of Cities* (San Diego, CA: Harcourt Brace & Company, 1996); Erving Goffman, *The Presentation of Self in Everyday Life* (Doubleday, 1959); E Clark, 'Order in the Atoni House', in *Right and Left: Essays in Dual Symbolic Classification* (London: The University of Chicago Press, 1973); Amos Rapoport, *House Form and Culture* (Englewood Cliffs, NJ: Prentice-Hall, 1991).
9 Jane Clossick, 'Depth Structures in High Street Publics: The Sociospatial Ordering of three Tottenham High Road Case Studies' (Forthcoming, 2020).
10 D. Vesely, *Architecture in the Age of Divided Representation: The Question of Creativity in the Shadow of Production* (Cambridge, MA: MIT Press, 2004).

References

Carl, Peter, 'Type, Field, Culture, Praxis', *Architectural Design*, 81.1 (2011), pp. 38–45.
Clark, E., 'Order in the Atoni House', in *Right and Left: Essays in Dual Symbolic Classification* ed. by R. Needham (London: The University of Chicago Press, 1973).
Clossick, Jane, 'The Depth Structure of a London High Street: A Study in Urban Order' (London Metropolitan University, 2017).
Clossick, Jane, 'Depth Structures in High Street Publics: The Sociospatial Ordering of three Tottenham High Road Case Studies' (Forthcoming, 2020).
Colburn, Ben, *Autonomy and Liberalism* (New York: Routledge, 2010).
Colburn, Ben, 'Authenticity and the Third-Person Perspective', in *Autonomy, Authenticity, and Multiculturalism*, ed. by G. Levey (New York: Routledge, 2015), pp. 121–141.
Goffman, Erving, *The Presentation of Self in Everyday Life* (Doubleday, 1959).
Mumford, Lewis, *The Culture of Cities* (San Diego, CA: Harcourt Brace & Company, 1996).
Rapoport, Amos, House Form and Culture (Englewood Cliffs, NJ: Prentice-Hall, 1991).
Raz, Joseph, *The Morality of Freedom* (Oxford: Clarendon Press, 1986).
Vesely, Dalibor, *Architecture in the Age of Divided Representation: The Question of Creativity in the Shadow of Production* (Massachusetts: MIT Press, 2004).

Chapter 18

Calcutta, India

Dover Lane – a cosmo-ecological collective life of Indian modernity

Dorian Wiszniewski

Following the first and second partitions of Bengal, in 1905 and 1947, respectively, Hindu East Bengalis, even if not particularly religious, were faced with the urgency to re-house themselves in West Bengal. Many of the areas in South Calcutta were built for the exiled East Bengali middle classes by Bengali builders in what was then wetlands or 'jungle' on Calcutta's urban margins. Built without architects, but nonetheless evidencing commitment to collective cultural expression and aspirations, the streets accommodated individual family plots whilst bearing testimony to a shared economic and social enterprise. They were built with deep generational knowledge of the environmentally sensitive basis of tropical construction, with understanding of traditional cultural values but also the necessity to remodel them for the changed circumstance of the new communities. These factors establish these houses and streets as representative of a unique Indian architectural modernity.

Although the specific artefacts and arrangements of these houses show clear understanding of western paradigms, they are of a specific Bengali and Indian tropical modernity, but also a cultural modernity arising from being steeped in the patterns emerging from the humanities of the *Bengal Renaissance*. It is no accident, then, that from the layout of the streets, the specific arrangement of buildings, the spaces within and between each building, right through to the name-plate fonts (some of which name the owners and their occupations in both Bengali and English), these streets carry the confident sonority and rhythm of a well-educated literary society of modest means but with generosity and optimism of spirit towards a new collective, architectural and urban life.

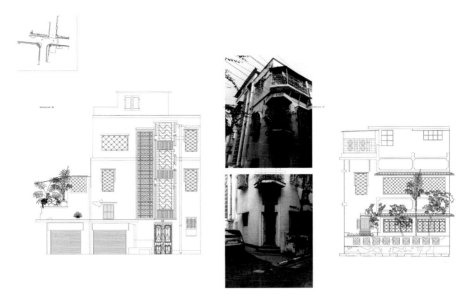

Figure 18.1 North East Corner of Prasad Mukherjee Road, Kalighat area intersection, a 'Bangal's' house

Drawing Credit: Sabrina Syed drawn from a survey by Adam Brown and Findlay McFarlane, January 2018, University of Edinburgh, M Arch 2017–2019, Parasituation [Calcutta/Kolkata]

Indian humanism leading to the modest architecture of Indian modernity

What constitutes modernity must be distinguished from the merely modern and the frequently prejudiced memory of Modernism. Modernity, speaks of radicality or at least progressivism. Traditional values in 19th and 20th-century Indian Calcutta were affected as much by the reactions to being colonised as the prejudices and actions of the colonisers. Departure from many cultural traditions was enforced by the colonisers, for example: at one end of the scale, the partitioning of India; and at the other end of the scale, the infilling of many Bengal ponds and the dispersal of those communities that relied upon them. However, it was also deemed necessary to change some traditions by the colonised; for example, the *Brahmo Samaj* was developed as a non-theistic form of Hinduism from the early 19th century by Raja Ram Mohan Roy, an early figure of the *Bengal Renaissance*, and upheld by the Tagore family.

So, in terms of modernity, it is not so much that these streets of Indian Calcutta are evidently formally, politically, culturally or even socially radical. Their progressivism is subtle and nuanced – it grew primarily from an intellectual radicalism that had a gradual effect on the material reality of Calcutta, particularly in the developing trajectory of modernity in middle-class Indian homes over the 19th and first half of the 20th century. Society progressed but seemed not to need such a radical image of the home to communicate its advances. These examples of Indian modernity simultaneously hold something of traditional values whilst confidently pointing to a future of

Dorian Wiszniewski

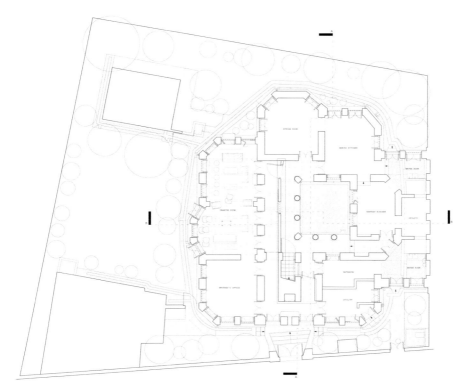

Figure 18.2 Ground Plan of Sukanya Mitra's House, a 'Ghoti's' house, 3 Peary Row, Maniktala, North Calcutta, built 1905. The Drawing Room is on the left side of the plan

Drawing Credit: Adam Brown and Findlay McFarlane, University of Edinburgh, M Arch 2017–2019, Parasituation [Calcutta/Kolkata]

community development over different magnitudes and types of social and civic interactions. The streets of Ballygunge and Kalighat propose a way of life that offers both multi-generational family retreat and generous and progressive Indian sociality in the environmental specificity of the Bengal 'jungle/forest' and wetlands and cultural para-urban situation (more than sub-urban) adjacent to Calcutta's colonial city.

Indian humanism as building/s and the embedding of cosmo-ecological collective life

Literary invocations of environmental humanism are evident in the works of Rabindranath Tagore,[1] which most of the *Bhadralok* and *Bhadramahila* of Calcutta would have on their bookshelves.[2] In parallel, the building trades that shaped the material reality of Bengali homes demonstrated a further environmental sensitivity. The trades had developed over multiple generations in pre-colonial India and reached a particular flourish in the economic boom of colonial Calcutta. Despite having no Indian architects, the boom gave opportunity for the early emergence of commercial building contractors and contractor-developers who could coordinate the vast and abundant array of cultural/craft skills available locally and across India. Sadly, these trades are now disappearing; some seem already to have disappeared, for example, there appear to be no skilled workers able now to make the traditional 'Laal' red-oxide floors. The trades evident in the areas of this study are many:

Ordinary and specialist mineral painters and decorators;

Painted sign-writers and **enamelled metal sign makers**, each of whom called upon the skills of avant-garde Bengali typographers who had been busy over several generations throughout and after the Bengal Renaissance designing fonts for books, newspapers and posters (including Satjavit Ray, who worked as a graphic designer prior to being a film maker[3]);

Ceramicists;

Glass-workers;

Laal cement flooring specialists (the famous but ever disappearing red-oxide floors);

Cast-iron ventilation grille manufacturers;

Lime plaster specialists, sculptors and formers, who, as well as making flat panel coats to brick walls also made, for example, hand rails, "rawks,"[4] drainage channels, tanks, sinks and moats;

Joiners;

Metal fabricators, for beams (Figure 18.4), railings and screens;

Furniture makers and cabinet-makers, who also made hard-wood panelled doors, door-sets and the hard-wood adjustable louvered window shutters, originally painted Calcutta Green but now all sorts of colours;

Brick-workers and clay-workers (mostly all buildings in Calcutta are made of brick, and the usual floor construction involves clay tiles spanning between timber joists to receive the mix for 'bagra' lime floors and 'laal' cement finishes); and the **Jaggerry Makers**[5] and other organic product alchemists who added their boiled sugar cane and toddy palm tree juice to the various cocktails of sand, broken bricks, clay-dust, lime cement, fruits, herbs and egg-whites to make the various coats of wall plasters and build-ups for waterproof flat roofs.[6]

Looking at the traditional methods of preparing plaster, we can see that they are precise and well-practised, but they read as much like cookery recipes as projects of building science; they are both poetic and scientific, in place and of the place:

> Take fifteen bushels [60 x pecks, where 1 peck equals 2 dry gallons] of fresh Pit-Sand, well sifted: Let it be moistened or slack'd with Water in the common manner, and so laid two or three Days together. Then dissolve 20lbs of *Jaggery*, which is course Sugar (or thick Molasses) in Water, and sprinkling this Liquor over the Mortar, beat it up together till all be well mixed and incorporated, and then let it lie by in a Heap. Then boil a Peck of Gramm (which

is a Sort of Grain like *Tare*, or between that and a *Pea*) to a Jelly, and strain it off through a course Canvas, and preserve the Liquor that comes from it. Take also a Peck of *Myrabolans* [cherry plums], and boil them likewise to a Jelly, preserving that Water also as the other; and if you have a Vessel large enough, you may put these three Waters together; that is, the *Jaggery*-Water, the *Gram*-Water, and the *Mirabolan*. The *Indians* usually put a small Quantity of fine Lime therein, to keep their labourers from drinking of it …

Having your Mortar thus prepared, as is before described, you must separate some of it, and to every half Bushel, you are to take the White of five or six Eggs, and four Ounces of Ghee (or unsalted Butter) and a Pint of Butter-Milk, beaten all well together: Mix a little of your Mortar with this, until all your Ghee, Whites of Eggs, and Butter-Milk be soaked up; then soften the rest well with plain fresh Water, and so mix all together, and let it be ground, a Trowel full at a time, on a Stone with a Stone-Roller, in the same manner that Chocolate is usually made, or ground in England.[7]

These buildings and their lime-based constructions could breathe. The building fabric acts like the tropical ecology they sit within: a building as much as jungle foliage "soaks, blows, seeps, osmotes, and transpires its way to ever-extending holdings of wetness, holdings that eventually become the ocean that reconnects with the wind."[8] There were hardly any inorganic products in Indian buildings. Only the rush towards a democratic India in the competitiveness of the modern world saw a move towards reductive concrete practices of the modern temperate West.

The Indian humanism that establishes, maintains and promotes this rich interweave between craft and literary communities was developed over time – multi-generational time. Through recurrent seasonal fluctuations, the Indian builders knew not only how to build buildings but also how and when to maintain them. It was an ongoing practice. Recurrent painting of lime-washes over cracks will allow lime plaster to self-heal, working recurrent chemical reactions between top-coats and substrates. These trades were once ubiquitous as was the sensibility of environmental consciousness.

Throughout, Indian literature references human relationships bound up in environmental relationships. There are deep ties between environmental rhythms, language rhythms, the landscape, the streets, the buildings, building sciences, domestic sciences and human relationships. Community rhythms, both everyday practices and embedded literatures (buildings and texts), are environmental rhythms, cosmo-ecological rhythms, within which the 'home' (*oikos* in Greek) and the 'world' (*kosmos* in Greek) were reciprocally inscribed. Tagore's famous novel *Ghare Baire* (Home and the World – literally, something like 'in the room outside of the room') points the way towards a developing modernity in India. It is a rich, dialogically propelled and political–philosophical examination of many existential and metaphysical themes at stake in a progressive India as it moves from archaic traditions and 'superstitions' to an unpredictable but necessarily different rational future.

Figure 18.3 Sukanya Mitra's House, Drawing Room, 3 Peary Row, Maniktala, North Calcutta, January 2017

Photo Credit: Sukanya Mitra

Indian humanism as urbanism, literature, culture and environmentalism

The urbanity of South Calcutta seems to allude more to the Bengal 'village' than colonial or European city: it is an urbanity set in pre-existent landscape, within a deep cultural and environmental context that has developed in relation to what is available in the landscape and a consequent clearly defined series of artisanal skills and traditions. The Bengali village has a form of urbanity specific to the widely different environmental conceptions between *India* and *Sindhu*. Elaborating from Anuradha Mathur and Dilip da Cunha, India is conceptual, emotional, ideological and political. Sindhu is everyday reality and *cosmo-ecological* – literally holding the rain-drop in its expression.[9] Mathur and da Cunha offer us a clarification of the subtle but fundamental environmental and ecological difference between India and Sindhu. They suggest:

> If in India, a surface inscribed with a drainage network of rivers, canals, pipes, gutters, reservoirs, and dams awaits the water of the monsoon, in Sindhu, a plethora of holdings awaits its wetness. These holdings, which

extend from high in the atmosphere to deep in the earth, transform dramatically each monsoon. The air thickens, the soil fills, and flora and fauna come to life and thrive for a period before receding.[10]

The Bengal collective life understands these environmental rhythms and works within them. The literature of Bengal is full of allusions to them, from Kalidasa's 4th-century Sanskrit *Cloud Messenger* to Rabindranath Tagore's early 20th-century essay, *The Religion of The Forest*, written in English, where he pre-affirms Mathur's and da Cunha's position:

> in the level tracts of Northern India men found no barrier between their lives and the grand life that permeates the universe. The forest entered into a close living relationship with their work and leisure, with their daily necessities and contemplations. They could not think of other surroundings as separate or inimical.[11]

Tagore goes on to say more about this unity between the human and non-human world in the 7th-century Sanskrit literature of the poet Banabhatta, even suggesting that it is architecture that operates as mediation:

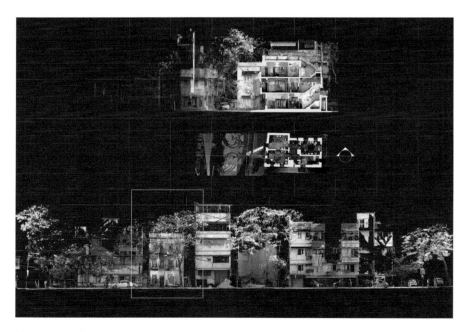

Figure 18.4 Section, Plan and Elevation of Z's Precinct, Dover Lane, Ballygunge, Calcutta, January 2019. Note: all houses are individual on individual plots, no repetitions. Lidar scans and drawing credit: Paul Pattinson, M Arch tutor 2018–2019 and PhD Architecture By Design candidate, University of Edinburgh. With thanks to Rajesh Sen, owner and proprietor of Z's Precinct, for allowing full access

A poet of a later age, while describing a hermitage in his Kadambari, tells us of the posture of salutation in the flowering lianas as they bow to the wind; of the sacrifice offered by the trees scattering their blossoms; of the grove resounding with the lessons chanted by the neophytes, and the verses repeated by the parrots, learnt by constantly hearing them; of the wild-fowl enjoying *vaishva-deva-bali-pinda* (the food offered to the divinity which is in all creatures); of the ducks coming up from the lake for their portion of the grass seed spread in the cottage yards to dry; and of the deer caressing with their tongues the young hermit boys. It is again the same story. The hermitage shines out, in all our ancient literature, as the place where the chasm between man and the rest of creation has been bridged.[12]

Conclusion

This chapter suggests that people of the South Calcutta streets (as Indians and Bengalis everywhere in Calcutta had done so for generations) work within these Sindhu rhythms. The rhythms are evident in language, music, film and, therefore, also in their buildings and community practices.[13] In the colonised world of India, the home changed. It developed in knowledge of a wider world, changing over the different phases of the "pre-Saidian Orientalism"[14] of the *Bengal Renaissance* where family relations and traditions are upheld in some ways but transformed dramatically in others as the old and new India found different ways to negotiate with the newly discovered epistemological inclinations of the West. There was a rapid growth of education in Indian- and English-speaking humanities, spreading and accelerating in each subsequent generation as they moved from wealthy to modest middle-class economic status. The independence movement developed, reaching critical levels after the 1889–1890 famines, the first Partitioning in 1905 and the *Jallianwala Bagh* massacre in Amritsar in 1919. The *Swadeshi* movement took hold. Political shifts were tumultuous but always held in the grip of deep-seated environmental and cultural rhythms. The *bhadralok* and *bhadramahila* became less the principle characters of romantically idealistic privileged life-styles raised to prominence in colonised India to develop more as adjutants and emissaries of a new forward-thinking political and culturally informed India.[15] Through necessity but following an already established trajectory towards modernity, the East Bengali first- and second-phase 'refugee' women went out to work in economic co-existence with men; they were refugees without refugee status but, as envoys of a newly configured set of urban relations, necessarily pioneered some of these cultural revisions.[16]

The modest 'village' architecture of the South Calcutta streets departs from the interiority of the estates and courtyard houses of the wealthy and exclusive *Zamindars* from 150 years previously and in which Tagore lived, the grandeur of the large mansions/bungalows of the relatively wealthy, a life-style set by colonials within large gardens in the suburban 'white-town,' or the intense overlapping working- and living-environments of the courtyard blocks of tenements that house multiple families of varied economic means found in the dense urbanity of *Burra Bazaar* in 'Black Town.'

Rather, they offer side-by-side assemblage of individual family plots of well-educated, fourth-, fifth- or sixth-generation *bhadralok* and *bhadramahila* of modest means, with patios, balconies, bay windows and roof terraces wrapping round tree-lined streets, "houses rising out of the pavements,"[17] houses rising out of the 'jungle.' Many of them place *rawks* at their entrances to encourage and accommodate the very Indian and Bengali tradition of *adda*,[18] where people speak as much about the recurring rhythms of Sindhu, which take on different degrees of wetness throughout the six seasons,[19] as the ever-changing culture, politics and economics of urban life in Calcutta. These informal conversations can go on for hours at a stretch. This extended street discourse seems to be either cause or symptom of Amartya Sen's *The Argumentative Indian*. Sen says, "Prolixity is not alien to us in India. We are able to talk at some length … We do like to speak."[20] However, importantly, Sen also argues that this tendency towards loquacity and the long history of heterodoxy in India are also the bases of "democracy as public reasoning." The streets of South Calcutta, then, in terms of people, place and as a projection of Indian modernity, seemed set to recurrently dramatise the rich exchange between traditional and new conceptions and physical expressions of home in an equally developing view of the world.

Notes

1. Tagore understood his privileges and the need to modernise society. He was a technological and cultural progressive not a romantic idealist – see Amartya Sen, chapter 5, Tagore and His India, *The Argumentative Indian*, 2006, pp. 89–120. Also, Amit Chaudhuri, 'Triumphant Eclecticism', *Outlook India*, May 7, 2006. https://www.outlookindia.com/website/story/triumphant-eclecticism/231146.
2. *bhadra* = gentle, *lok* = men, and *mahila* = women/ladies.
3. See Ray's cover illustration to Jibananda Das' poetry book, *Banalata Sen* (Calcutta: Signet Press, 1952).
4. *rawks* are steps built into the street-walls, frequently around house entrances, for people to sit and exchange in conversation.
5. A molasses like sugary block made from sugar cane and toddy palm tree pulped, juiced and concentrated.
6. See William Jones, 1809, and Pyke and Halley, 1731–1732.
7. Pyke and Halley, pp. 231–233.
8. Anuradha Mathur and Dilip da Cunha, A Clash of First Natures, in Dorian Wiszniewski, *Argufying Calcutta: Parasituation* [Kolkata] (Wedge Publications: Edinburgh, 2019), pp. 151–158.
9. indhu = raindrop, thus, Sindhu is translated as ocean of raindrops, *ocean of wet*ness. Anuradha Mathur and Dilip da Cunha, ibid. p. 152.
10. Ibid.
11. Tagore, Rabindranath, *The Religion of The Forest*, I, para. 10. http://tagoreweb.in/Render/ShowContent.aspx?ct=Essays&bi=72EE92F5-BE50-40D7-AE6E-0F7410664DA3&ti=72EE92F5-BE50-4A47-6E6E-0F7410664DA3.
12. The Religion of The Forest, II, para. 3.
13. For example, in the Ballygunge area, the Dover Lane music Festival and Conference have been running in the month of January from 1956.
14. See Bashabi Fraser, 2017, p. 17, but also Subrata Dasgupta, 2007.
15. For a more elaborated notion of the *bhadralok*, see Wiszniewski, *Argufying Calcutta*, pp. 7–8.
16. Babashi Fraser in conversation with Dorian Wiszniewski, September 2019.
17. Sumana Mukherjee, 2015.
18. *adda* refers to informal conversations between people, that can go on for hours at a stretch – at street corners, roof-tops, cafes, markets and living rooms. Sen argues that this tendency towards loquacity and the long history of heterodoxy in India are also the bases of "democracy as public reasoning." Sen, *The Argumentative Indian*, pp. 3–33.
19. Vasant Ritu – Spring; Grishma Ritu – Summer; Varsha Ritu – Monsoon; Sharad Ritu – Autumn; Hemant Ritu – Pre-winter; and Shishir or Shita Ritu: Winter.
20. Sen, *The Argumentative Indian*, pp. 3–33.

References

Akhter, ASM Maswood, Text Within a Text: The Shaping of Sunetra Gupta's 'Memories of Rain', *Journal of the Asiatic Society of Bangladesh* (Hum.), Vol. 60, No. 1 (2015), pp. 17–34.

Chakrabarty, Dipesh, Remembered Villages: Representation of Hindu-Bengali Memories in the Aftermath of the Partition, *Economic and Political Weekly*, Vol. 31, No. 32 (August 10, 1996) pp. 2143–2145; 2147–2151.

Chaudhuri, Amit, 'Triumphant Eclecticism', *Outlook India*, e-magazine (https://www.outlookindia.com/website/story/triumphant-eclecticism/231146), 07.05.2006, accessed 07/02/2019 13.07.

Chaudhuri, Amit, *On Tagore, Reading The Poet Today* (New Delhi: Viking by Penguin, 2012).

Chaudhuri, Amit, *A Strange and Sublime Address* (London: Oneworld Publications, 2015).

Dasgupta, Subrata, *The Bengal Renaissance: Identity and Creativity from Rammohun Roy to Rabindranath Tagore* (Delhi: Permanent Black, 2007).

Dasgupta, Keya, *Mapping Calcutta, The Collection of Maps at The Visual Archives of The Centre for Studies in Social Sciences, Calcutta Archive Series 2* (Calcutta: Centre for Studies in Social Sciences, Calcutta, September, 2009).

Dimarco, Danette and J. Sunita Peacock, The Bhadramahila and Adaptation in Meera Syal's and Gurnder Chadha's 'Bhaji on The Beach,' *Mosaic: An Interdisciplinary Critical Journal*, Vol. 41, No. 4 (December 2008), pp. 161–178 (University of Manitoba).

Fraser, Babashi, Tapati Mukherjee and Amrit Sen, eds., *Scottish Orientalism and The Bengal Renaissance* (Edinburgh: Luath Press, 2017).

Ghosh, Deepanjan, Why is South Calcutta Losing its Buildings? *The Concrete Paparazzi*, Monday 13 July 2015, http://double-dolphin.blogspot.com/2015/07/why-is-south-calcutta-losing-its-buildings.html

Guha-Choudhury, Archit Basu, Engendered Freedom: Partition and East Bengali Migrant Women, *Economic and Political Weekly*, Vol. 44, No. 49 (December 5–11, 2009), pp. 66–69 (Economic and Political Weekly).

Jones, William, Communicating Sundry Queries Proposed by Him to William Jones Esquire, Civil Engineer of Calcutta, Relative to the Principles and Practice of Building in India, with His Answers to the Same, *Transactions of the American Philosophical Society*, Vol. 6 (1809), pp. 375–383. Published by: American Philosophical Society.

Kalidasa, *Meghaduta; or Cloud Messenger; a Poem, In The Sanskrit Language: by Çálidása*, trans. Horace Hayman Wilson (Calcutta: Black, Parry and Co, 1814).

Kaviraj, Sudipta, The Sudden Death of Sanskrit Knowledge, *Journal of Indian Philosophy*, Vol. 33, No. 1 (February 2005), pp. 119–142 (Springer).

Mukherjee, Sumana, Living and Dying on Dover Lane, *LiveMint*, 11.07.2015, https://www.livemint.com/Leisure/pTmpWXINhTRvD5Pu7bdxmJ/Living-and-dying-in-Dover-Lane.html

Pyke, Isaac and Edmund Halley, The Method of Making the Best Mortar at Madras in East India; Described in a Letter from the Honourable Isaac Pyke, Esq; Governor of St. Helena, to Edmund Halley, L. L. D. Reg. Astr. Vice-President R. S. and by Him Communicated to the Royal Society, *Philosophical Transactions (1683–1775)*, Vol. 37 (1731–1732), pp. 231–235 Published by: Royal Society.

Roy, Lily, Tagore's views on the Religion of the Forest and Relationship of Man and Nature, *International Journal of Research and Analytical Views*, Volume 5, No. 3 (July–September 2018).

Sen, Amartya, *The Argumentative Indian, Writings on Indian Culture, History and Identity* (London: Penguin, 2006).

Sen, Amarya, Positional Objectivity, *Philosophy & Public Affairs*, Vol. 22, No. 2 (Spring, 1993), pp. 126–145 (Wiley).

Tagore, Rabindranath, Home and the World (Ghare Baire), in *Classic Rabindranath Tagore Complete and Unabridged* (Haryana: Penguin, 2011), pp. 669–799.

Tagore, Rabindranath, *The Religion of The Forest*, http://tagoreweb.in/Render/ShowContent.aspx?ct=Essays&bi=72EE92F5-BE50-40D7-AE6E-0F7410664DA3&ti=72EE92F5-BE50-4A47-6E6E-0F7410664DA3

Wiszniewski, D., *Argufying Calcutta: Parasituation [Kolkata]* (Edinburgh: Wedge Publications, 2019)

Chapter 19

The city of ragpickers

Shaping a faithful collective life during *les trente glorieuses*

Janina Gosseye

The development of Europe's welfare states began as a gradual motion in the late 19th century as a reaction to processes of modernisation and accelerated in the mid-20th century following the massive destruction wrought by two world wars. Caught between American corporate capitalism and Soviet communism, the welfare state concept offered a specifically European answer to Cold War politics. In many countries on the continent, this resulted in the construction of new bureaucracies aimed at facilitating the redistribution of wealth, knowledge and political power. The planning of the built environment was one of the key areas in which welfare states in Europe sought to achieve their ambitions of redistribution, particularly during *les trente glorieuses* – a period bookended by the end of the Second World War and the arrival of the 1970s energy crisis.[1]

Housing for all was high on the agenda, and across Europe, the state became a key actor in the delivery of accommodation. In some countries, this occurred through the provision of subsidies to individual families, while in others, universal housing was promoted through the construction of social housing by corporations and local authorities. However, state intervention in the built environment during *les trente glorieuses* was not limited to housing, it also included buildings for health, education and leisure to cater to the whole community. Apart from schools, universities and hospitals, the modern ideal of a 'healthy mind in a healthy body' also prompted the construction of a new leisure infrastructure, such as youth clubs, swimming pools and cultural centres to channel the social energy of the masses towards healthy recreation. This government intervention in Europe's maturing welfare states has been well-documented.

Less well-documented are the building initiatives undertaken by other welfare state actors. To achieve the desired overhaul of everyday life that was destined to result in a more fair and equitable society, all welfare state regimes relied on a so-called 'welfare mix' – on interactions between various social institutions and orders.[2] The basic social orders are the community, the market, the state and the third sector, and the social institutions generally associated with these four social orders are households, private firms, public agencies and voluntary associations or non-profit associations, respectively.[3] Europe's various welfare state regimes relied on interactions between these different institutions, which means that apart from the state, also private (for-profit actors) and voluntary and non-profit organisations adopted key roles. In Europe's various welfare state regimes, built environment experts collaborated not only with major business interests, such as construction companies and property developers, but also with the third-sector actors, such as NGOs and voluntary organisations. While scholarship on the interactions that occurred between the market and governments in Europe's various welfare state regimes has increased in recent years,[4] not much research has been done on the built/urban contributions that were made by other actors, particularly those belonging to the third sector.

Religious welfare organisations constituted a large portion of this third sector. By proclaiming the equal value of each human being and promoting the idea of equality, the religiousness of communities had long impelled citizens to help the ill and the poor in order to secure their own salvation. According to German sociologist Franz-Xaver Kaufmann, it is no coincidence that the Christian occident became the cradle of the modern welfare state.[5] In the second half of the 20th century, as Europe's various welfare state regimes matured, religious welfare associations operated alongside (and at times in collaboration with) the state and the market to promote social equality. To do so, they not only built churches and chapels, but also houses, schools, holiday camps, homes for children, men and women, hospitals, child care facilities, community centres, etc.

This chapter takes a first step in exploring how religious associations contributed to the building of post-war European welfare states. It highlights some of the activities of Emmaüs, an organisation that was founded in France in the late 1940s by Catholic priest and Capuchin friar Abbé Pierre. In the post-war decades, particularly from the mid-1950s on, Emmaüs built thousands of homes in France for *les hommes sans toit* (or 'homeless people') as well as communal facilities. Documenting and examining some of the organisation's activities near Nice, this chapter reveals how religious welfare associations contributed to building the post-war welfare state and demonstrates how the architectures that these organisations produced sought to shape collective life.

Emmaüs and the development of the French post-war welfare state

In January 1946, seeking to restore and ultimately revolutionise the economy after the war, the French government set up the Commisariat Generale du Plan. The main priority of this newly founded commissariat was economic post-war recovery. To this end, in 1947, it initiated a Five Year Plan, which, by 1952, had increased France's gross national product by 39% (in comparison with 1946). However, in prioritising industrial recovery and growth, the first Five Year Plan blatantly neglected other problems, most notably housing. By the time that the first Five Year Plan had completed (in 1952), the housing stock in France was still in very poor shape, and the situation was particularly dire in the larger urban centres. In the Paris region, for instance, as late as 1950, 85% of the housing units pre-dated the First World War.[6] Moreover, 40% of all housing units were overcrowded, and a fifth of all families lived in a hotel or hostel.

Over the following decade, migratory movements and demographic phenomena further exacerbated the situation: the baby boom, increased life expectancy, a reduced mortality rate, the mass exodus from the countryside to the towns and the influx of French citizens returning from North Africa following decolonisation all increased the demand for affordable housing in the country.[7] Accordingly, the second plan that the Commisariat Generale du Plan launched in January 1953 – the so-called 'Courant Plan' – placed great emphasis on housing construction and set out to build 240,000 houses per year. However, the housing policies that the government implemented to achieve this goal continued to be based on tax incentives designed to encourage economic agents to invest in the housing sector. As a result, initial progress was slow and the need for housing remained acute. It was around this time that Emmaüs stepped into the limelight.

Founded in the late 1940s by Abbé Pierre, Emmaüs devoted itself to addressing the needs of the homeless, while at the same time pressuring the government to continue with their own proactive measures to solve the housing crisis in post-war France. The winter of 1953–1954, which was particularly harsh, became a turning point for the organisation. During the night of 3 January 1954, a three-month-old baby froze to death in the abandoned shell of a public bus in Paris. In response to this drama, Abbé Pierre wrote a letter to the Minister of Reconstruction, inviting him to attend the baby's funeral. The Minister, Eugène Claudius-Petit complied with this request[8] and, in early February 1954, committed the government to creating 12,000 'emergency and transit housing sites' offering cheap, basic homes for those in need. This was not only the start of a more sincere commitment from the government towards solving the housing crisis but also the impetus that propelled the rise of Emmaüs. During *les trente glorieuses* – a period plagued by a continuous shortage of and a large demand for new dwellings[9] – the French housing stock grew by 50% and housing conditions significantly improved.[10] To achieve this aim, the government worked closely together with private (for-profit) companies as well as with voluntary organisations, such as Emmaüs.

From the founding of the organisation in the late 1940s, Abbé Pierre had constructed temporary homes for those in need; initially, in his own garden, and then on any land the organisation could obtain.[11] At the end of January 1954, following an outpouring of public support (after the baby's death), Emmaüs established its own public limited social housing company, which immediately became involved in the government programme to create the aforementioned 12,000 emergency and transit housing sites.[12] Not only did it buy plots of land to initiate the construction of such housing, but some local councils also entrusted Emmaüs with the task of building these accommodations for

The city of ragpickers

them. In the region of Paris alone, 6,000 emergency or transit homes were to be built. Emmaüs' contribution to this effort was celebrated in the Christmas 1954 edition of its magazine *Faim & Soif*, which featured an overview of the organisation's activities in and around Paris, and which boasted that: "… only the completed or under construction sites [amounting to] 1,500 housing units, are included [in this overview], but next year, more sites will be opened, which will increase Emmaüs' assets to 3,000 units."[13]

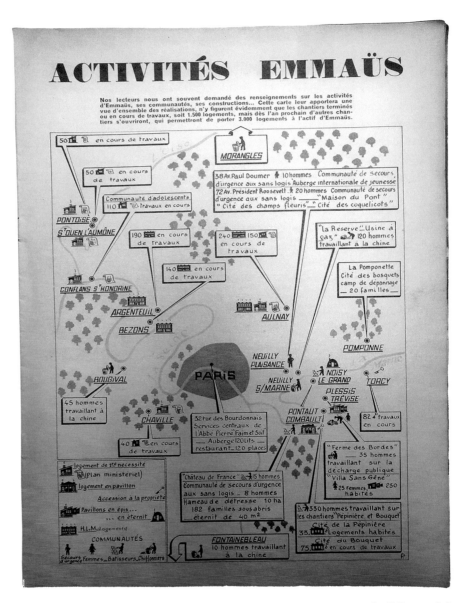

Figure 19.1 Infographic published in December 1954, showing the building activities of Emmaüs in and around Paris

'Activités Emmaüs', *Faim & Soif* 6, n.p.

The way in which the organisation raised funds to construct such housing was through 'ragpicking'; by collecting unwanted items for resale. As one of the organisation's brochures announced: "We don't have any money [and] we don't ask for it. But help us by getting rid of everything that irritates you; cloths, metals, paper, clothing, furniture, bottles, etc."[14] Those who joined Emmaüs became known as Emmaüs companions or Emmaüs ragpickers.[15] They were charged with carrying out an activity of recovery and recycling of second-hand objects that were not only donated to the organisation but also actively collected to ensure the economic sustainability of the movement. The social economy that sustained these Emmaüs communities – or 'Ragman's Cities' as social historian Boris Simon called them[16] – brings to mind the utopian communities that emerged in the early 19th century, such as the Phalanstère Fourier (1808) or the Familistère de Jean-Baptiste Godin (1846). In line with such utopian communities, Emmaüs also consciously strove to build social institutions in their newly established housing sites, such as teaching centres, nurseries, laundrettes, meeting rooms, libraries, chapels and churches.[17] In 1955, Emmaüs founded one such new (utopian) community in Saint-André de Nice. Here, Swiss architect Rainer Senn played an important role in giving shape to this settlement's social institutions and (more broadly) its collective life.

Emmaüs in Nice: shaping collective life in the city of ragpickers

Early in 1955, a community of Emmaüs ragpickers and builders was established in Saint-André, a municipality in the French Alpes Maritimes, just north of Nice. The settlement, called 'La Cerisaie,' was located on municipal land[18] between two small roads servicing the village of Abadie, in a valley "covered with brambles, grasses and trees, at the bottom of a small torrential stream."[19] Shortly after its establishment, Emmaüs commissioned Swiss architect Rainer Senn to construct a chapel on the grounds. In August 1955, Senn had visited several building sites of the Emmaüs companions around Paris, to – in his own words – "learn what our future can expect from these men."[20] This is likely how contact between Senn and the Emmaüs organisation was first established.

When Senn was commissioned to design the chapel for La Cerisaie, few other buildings existed on site. There were a few makeshift dwellings, and some sheds and tents under which piles of rags and other recyclables were collected. The construction of the chapel was thus as a founding act for the new settlement – an expression of the Emmaüs' desire to do more than merely build emergency shelters for those in need. It was a first step in building a community. Pierre Tarteaut, the leader of La Cerisaie, told Senn that with this chapel, he wanted to create "a place where members of the community could gather to listen to the word of God … [a place that would] reunite in a circle his Companions whom society had rejected and to give them back the protection of a community."[21]

Senn responded by designing a compact chapel with a square plan measuring just eight metres square. It was covered by a pyramid-shaped roof towering six metres overhead, which was held aloft by four large wooden beams that extended beyond the perimeter of the space. The walls were clad with recycled wood, and the top of the pyramid was covered in roofing felt. One of the requirements of Emmaüs was that the chapel could be built without scaffolding or the need for skilled labour. And so, the building was erected by three men – two Spanish companions who were living at the new settlement and the young Swiss architect Rainer Senn. Together, they completed the build in two weeks for a cost of 50,000 French francs, as had been requested by Emmaüs. Describing the building process in a 1956 issue of the periodical *Das Werk: Architektur und Kunst*, Senn offered some insights into the relationship between the community of ragpicker-companions that was established at La Cerisaie and the local municipality and its inhabitants. He writes:

> On the second evening, shortly before we wanted to erect the four main beams, the mayor of the community came and complained that we were taking too much of his land. … We waited until dusk fell and then went on with our work. The next evening the main construction was complete. Then the priest of the village came to visit our work and was very much in agreement with it. That secured our cause. The next Sunday the villagers took a look at our new building and expressed themselves very sympathetically. Thus, the concerns of the mayor were dispelled.[22]

Soon after its completion, Senn's chapel received international acclaim in the world of ecclesiastical architecture; mostly for the way in which it formulated a low-cost yet highly refined response to contemporary appeals that echoed throughout the Catholic Church to construct houses *of* God rather than grand shrines *to* God. Indeed, contrary to many other churches and chapels that were constructed at the time, the

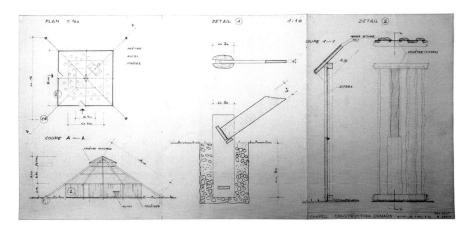

Figure 19.2 Plans for the Emmaüs chapel at 'La Cerisaie' by Rainer Senn
Rainer Senn collection, gta archive, Zürich (Switzerland)

Figure 19.3 Construction of the chapel at 'La Cerisaie', October 1955
Rainer Senn collection, gta archive, Zürich (Switzerland)

one in Saint-André had a very intimate almost domestic feel which it owed not only to its small size, but also to its materiality and to the way in which light was admitted into the building. The two main sources of light were the lantern at the top of the chapel, and several vertical slits in the walls where timber boards had been omitted. Furthermore, in response to Tarteaut's request, the chapel was designed in such a way that it quite literally gathered the community of ragpickers in a circle around the altar, which was a simple concrete-block table with a timber top set directly on the soil.

In September 1958, the community of ragpickers at Saint-André counted 20 companions. By this time, several permanent dwellings had been erected on site, and Senn was commissioned to add to the building stock by designing a house with two apartments. This building was very simple, even traditional in its design and layout. It had a low-pitched roof, white-washed walls, and both apartments were organised around a central 'living room' core onto with three bedrooms and the kitchen cum bathroom opened up. This building was not as innovative as the chapel that Senn had designed for La Cerisaie a few years earlier and also less modern than other housing developments that Emmaüs commissioned for some of the other communities of ragpickers that cropped up across France since that fateful night in January 1954.

Conclusion

By early 1957, 18 Emmaüs communities were up and running in France. Many of these were located in the vicinity of Paris, but there were also quite a few further afield; not

The city of ragpickers

Figure 19.4 The chapel at 'La Cerisaie', photographed in October 1955
Rainer Senn collection, gta archive, Zürich (Switzerland)

only in Nice, but also in Rouen, Marseilles, Rennes, Évreux and Limoges, to name just a few.[23] In setting up such 'cities of ragpickers,' Emmaüs did not shy away from architectural and urban experimentation. Aspiring to alleviate the housing crisis, the organisation welcomed spatial innovation and often initiated design competitions to elicit new ideas in affordable domestic design *and* community organisation. As a result, Emmaüs collaborated with several prominent post-war practices, such as Candilis-Josic-Woods, who, in 1954, were commissioned to design the Cité de l'Étoile, a large housing estate in Bobigny, which is documented in a 2014 book by architectural historian Richard Klein.[24] And yet, in spite of such scattered fragments of information that hint at the important role that organisations such as Emmaüs played in post-war Europe, scholarship on the contributions of religious welfare associations to urban development during *les trente glorieuses* remains limited.

    This chapter thus seeks to set an agenda. Beginning to document some of the (lesser-known) projects of Emmaüs, it hopes to highlight the need for a more thorough and holistic examination of the impact that religious welfare associations had on the development of the post-war built environment – one that not only considers their ecclesiastical work but also their other building programmes. Doing so will offer greater insight into the different ways in which different actors shaped collective life – through architecture and urban design – during *les trente glorieuses*.

Notes

1. Mark Swenarton, Tom Avermaete and Dirk van den Heuvel, 'Introduction,' in Mark Swenarton, Tom Avermaete and Dirk van den Heuvel (eds.), *Architecture and the Welfare State* (London and New York: Routledge, 2015), 1–23.
2. Victor Pestoff, 'Third Sector and Co-operative Services: An Alternative to Privatization,' *Journal of Consumer Policy* 15 (1992): 21–45.
3. Wolfgang Streeck and Philippe Schmitter, *Private Interest Government: Beyond Market and State* (London: Sage, 1985).
4. Examples include: Janina Gosseye and Tom Avermaete (eds.), *Shopping Towns Europe 1945–1975: Commercial Collectivity and the Architecture of the Shopping Centre* (London: Bloomsbury Academic, 2017); Janina Gosseye, 'The Janus-faced Shopping Centre: The Low Countries in Search of a Fitting Shopping Paradigm,' *Journal of Urban History* 44, 5 (2018): 862–886; Janina Gosseye, '"Uneasy bedfellows" Conceiving Urban Megastructures: Precarious Public–private Partnerships in Post-war British New Towns,' *Planning Perspectives* 34, 6 (2019): 937–957; Tim Verlaan, 'De in Beton Gegoten Onwrikbaarheid van Hoog Catharijne: Burgers, Bestuurders en een Projectontwikkelaar 1962–1973,' *Stadsgeschiedenis* 7, 2 (2012): 183–205; Tim Verlaan, *De Ruimtemakers: Projectontwikkelaars en de Nederlandse Binnenstad, 1950–1980* (Nijmegen: Vantilt, 2017); Tim Verlaan, 'Producing Space: Post-war Redevelopment as Big Business, Utrecht and Hannover 1962–1975,' *Planning Perspectives* 34, 3 (2019): 415–437.
5. Franz-Xaver Kaufmann, 'Christentum und Wohlfahrtsstaat,' *Zeitschrift für Sozialreform* 34, 2 (1988): 65–89.
6. Tom Avermaete, *Another Modern: The Post-war Architecture and Urbanism of Candilis-Josic-Woods* (Rotterdam: NAi Publishers, 2005), 42.
7. Axelle Brodiez-Dolino, *Emmaus and the Abbé Pierre: An Alternative Model of Enterprise, Charity and Society* (Paris: Presses de la Fondation Nationale des Sciences Politiques, 2013), 119.
8. Boris Simon, *Abbé Pierre and the Ragpickers of Emmaus* (New York: P.J. Kenedy & Sons, 1955), 3.
9. Avermaete, *Another Modern*, 114.
10. Brodiez-Dolino, *Emmaus and the Abbé Pierre*, 69.
11. 'L'Album d'Emmaüs,' *Faim & Soif* 6, n.p.; 'Naissance d'Emmaüs', *Faim & Soif* 6, n.p.
12. Brodiez-Dolino, *Emmaus and the Abbé Pierre*, 69.
13. Original quote: 'n'y figurant évidemment que les chantier terminus ou en cours de travaux, soit 1.500 logements, mais dès l'an prochain d'autres chantiers s'ouvriront, qui permettront de porter 3,000 logements à l'actif d'Emmaus.' Source: 'Activités Emmaüs,' *Faim & Soif* 4, 13.
14. Original quote: 'Nous n'avons pas d'argent, nous ne vous en demandons pas. Mais aidez-nous en vous débarrasant de tout de qui vous embarrasse. Chiffons, métaux, papiers, vêtements, meubles, bouteillers, etc.' Leaflet held in folder 260-01-7, Rainer Senn collection, gta archive, Zürich (Switzerland).
15. Joël Ambroisine, 'Les Communautés Emmaüs en Europe,' *Revue Internationale de l'Économie Sociale* 332 (April 2014): 74–92.
16. Boris Simon, *Ragman's City* (London: The Harvill Press, 1957).
17. Brodiez-Dolino, *Emmaus and the Abbé Pierre*, 73.
18. Rainer Senn, 'Kapelle der Chiffonniers d'Emmaüs,' *Das Werk: Architektur und Kunst* 43, 2 (1956): 34.
19. 'A "Emmaüs,"' booklet narrating the establishment of the 'La Cerisaie' settlement, held in folder 260-01-7, Rainer Senn collection, gta archive, Zürich (Switzerland).
20. Original quote: 'pour apprendre ce que notre avenir peut attendre de la part de ces hommes.' Source: 'Saint-André de Nice,' *L'Art Sacré*, 'Les Églises Récentes de France II – A la Recherche d'un Plan' 5-6 (January-February 1957): 24.
21. 'Original quote: 'un lieu où les communautaires se réuniraient pour écouter la parole de Dieu … de réunir à nouveau en un cercle ses Compagnons que la société avait rejetés et de leur redonner la protection d'une communauté: de la communauté chrétienne.' Source: 'Saint-André de Nice,' *L'Art Sacré*.
22. Original quote: 'Am zweiten Abend, kurz bevor wir die vier Hauptträger aufrichten wollten, kam der Bürgermeister der Gemeinde und beschwerte sich, daß wir doch zuviel von seinem Land in Anspruch nähmen. Was wollten wir machen? Wir warteten ab, bis die Dämmerung hereinbrach, und fuhren dann weiter mit unserer Arbeit. Am nächsten Abend stand die Hauptkonstruktion. Dann kam der Priester des Dorfes, besichtigte unser Werk und war sehr damit einverstanden. Und damit war unsere Sache

gesichert. Am nächsten Sonntag nahmen die Dorfbewohner einen Augenschein von unserem neuen Bau und äußerten sich sehr wohlwollend. Damit waren auch die Bedenken des Bürgermeisters zerstreut.' Source: Rainer Senn, 'Kapelle der Chiffonniers d'Emmaüs,' *Das Werk: Architektur und Kunst* 43, 2 (1956): 34.
23 Brodiez-Dolino, *Emmaus and the Abbé Pierre*, 74–77.
24 Richard Klein, *La Cité De L'étoile à Bobigny : Un Modèle De Logement Social : Candilis, Josic, Woods* (Paris: Créaphis, 2014).

Chapter 20
Visions of Ecotopia

Meredith Gaglio

In the April 1976 edition of *RAIN: Journal of Appropriate Technology*, its editors, architect Tom Bender, community organiser Lane de Moll, author and activist Steve Johnson, and solar engineer-cum-economist, Lee Johnson, presented four posters based on the key aspects of the American Appropriate Technology, or AT, Movement: 'Dollar Power,' 'Make Where You *Are* Paradise,' 'Good-bye to the Flush Toilet' and 'Ecotopia.' The latter, a double-sided poster composed by illustrator Diane Schatz, offers a compelling entry point for discussing the ideal, appropriate technology, or AT, based city – a self-sufficient, decentralised community, reliant upon sustainable practices that could reverse the environmental, economic and social degradation of the US.

Through text and image, the poster synthesised the diverse components of appropriate community design, which *RAIN*'s editors introduced each month in their groundbreaking journal. From apprentice learning and geodesic dome-covered rooftop gardens to community credit unions and putt-a-cabs, 'Ecotopia' demonstrated the healthy future that could be achieved by the implementation of ecologically and socially responsible methods of AT.

In the US, the appropriate technology movement emerged in the late-1960s from a countercultural desire to reform Establishment policies and amend traditional American consumerist and technocratic values. Based on the practice of 'intermediate technology' theorised by German-British economist E.F. Schumacher, American AT was a grassroots approach to development, which relied upon alternative technological methods to prevent the further environmental, social, economic and cultural decline of the nation.

Visions of Ecotopia

Figure 20.1 'Ecotopia'
Poster from *RAIN: Journal of Appropriate Technology* 2, no. 6 (April 1976), drawn by Diane Schatz

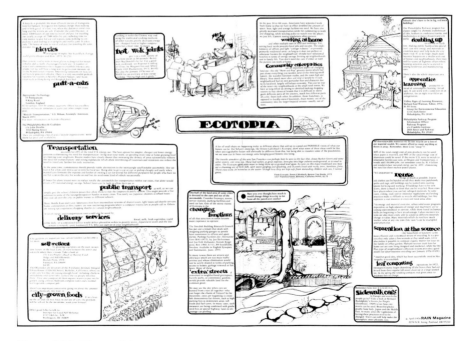

Figure 20.2 'Ecotopia'
Poster from *RAIN: Journal of Appropriate Technology* 2, no. 6 (April 1976), drawn by Diane Schatz

Appropriate technologists defined 'technology' in such a way that social issues blended with traditionally technological ones to create a holistic vision of a new, utopian society; at times, they called these the 'software' and 'hardware' of AT practice. The former included, for example, decentralised and community-led education, health care, economic and communications systems, while the latter incorporated what we might today describe as sustainable building, transportation, energy production and agricultural practices. The AT movement borrowed theories from a variety of disciplines – some countercultural and others not – in order to develop its own, singular internal logic.

E.F. Schumacher introduced the concept of 'intermediate technology' in an article, "How to Help Them Help Themselves," published in the British newspaper, *The Observer*, in August 1965. Informed by his experience as an economic advisor to the governments of Myanmar and India in the 1950s and 1960s, "How to Help Them Help Themselves" laid out what the economist believed to be a more prudent development strategy for rapidly industrialising nations such as those that he had recently visited. During his travels, the economist observed that "developing countries [were] suffering from the twin disease of growing unemployment and mushrooming metropolitan slums, which [was] placing their social and political fabric under an intolerable strain."

His plan sought to remedy both aspects of the disease by promoting small-scale, inexpensive, regional industries reliant upon production processes that required minimal skill, depended upon scant financing and utilised local materials.[1] Around such industries, Schumacher envisioned, self-reliant cohesive districts would form, developing independently of one another in a socially and economically healthful way. Eight years later, in his influential text, *Small is Beautiful*, the economist built upon that concept. He highlighted the integral nature of intermediate technology by situating the technological concept within a larger and more complex socio-economic framework, which incorporated the aspects of ecology, non-violence and socialism.

Prior to the publication of Schumacher's book, it is unclear how many American countercultural thinkers had read the relatively obscure 1965 article, "How to Help Them Help Themselves." A great number were likely introduced to his ideas when countercultural guru Stewart Brand included an excerpt of Schumacher's essay, "Buddhist Economics," in his influential *Whole Earth Catalog*.[2] At that point, the 54-year-old economist definitively joined the constellation of social, political and economic theorists who framed the thought process of early American appropriate technologists.[3] "Buddhist Economics," as it was presented in the *Whole Earth Catalog*, focused less on the economic development of non-Western nations than the fuller versions of the article found in *Asia: A Handbook* (1966) and the British magazine *Resurgence* (1968). Instead, it concentrated primarily on issues of technology and materialism, that is, to say, the conception that small, non-violent technological solutions had been suppressed by Western mass-production methods, which may have resonated more deeply with the *Catalog*'s self-reflective American readership.

Stripped of its focus on the 'developing' world, Schumacher's work offered solutions to Western overdevelopment that resonated with nascent appropriate technologists, who, as countercultural youth, condemned the social, economic and ecological pollution wrought by irresponsible corporate and government technocrats. Practitioners of AT, many of whom were inspired by Brand's holistic approach, began to generate their own microcosms of knowledge – more topical but equally complex. Schumacher was central to this galaxy, even if his texts during the late-1960s had not yet explicitly integrated ecological concepts and were, moreover, not intended to reflect the political realities of post-war America. Appropriate technologists thus supplemented the economist's literature with that of other contemporary thinkers, including R. Buckminster Fuller's *Operating Manual for Spaceship Earth*, Murray Bookchin's *Post-Scarcity Anarchism* and Ivan Illich's *Tools for Conviviality*, which informed their Western practice.[4]

Another countercultural voice that influenced AT advocates was the author Ernest Callenbach, whose seminal novel, *Ecotopia: The Notebooks and Reports of William Weston*, clearly influenced the title of *RAIN*'s poster. In the book, published in 1975, Callenbach envisioned a new, ecologically oriented North American nation, the result of the imagines 1980 secession of Washington, Oregon and Northern California from the US. *Ecotopia*, Callenbach explained, "was based on the assumption that a critical mass of people could come to see that their survival and happiness depend upon giving at least as much weight to the biological bottom line as to the economic one."[5] This fantastical nation inspired the book's first readers, many of whom were, in effect, ideological counterparts to Callenbach's Ecotopians. The architect, Tom Bender, for example, praised *Ecotopia* as "more like a kit than any Utopia I've read – or like a ten-year plan" for creating a brighter future.[6] Callenbach did, indeed, create a comprehensive universe. His detailed explanations of Ecotopia's government, labour practices, transportation, health care and economy were complemented by thoughtful descriptions of its environmentally based spirituality, sexual mores, philosophy and other folkways.

Through its decade-long run,[7] *RAIN* circumscribed a similar universe, albeit one focused on appropriate technology, within the pages of each issue. The magazine featured an extensive, categorised list of AT books, organisations and other resources, each with a brief written caption by the editors describing its significance. Interspersed within these annotated lists were philosophical essays, political commentary and in-depth discussions of topics ranging from the economic value of trash and basics of composting toilets to the United Nations Conference on Discrimination Against the Indigenous Populations of the Americas and the history of androgyny. The purpose of their work, according to the so-called Rainmakers, was "to share with people information that [was]: workable…novel…successful… practical… perceptive… loving/humorous… integral…cosmic…down-to-earth…fitting…appropriate… sane… infertilating… hopeful…[and] encouraging": in compiling such material, the journal made a significant step in creating a cohesive network of appropriate technologists in the US. At that time, there was a dearth of communication networks available to appropriate technologists, and practitioners of AT "were hungry for news of each other's projects and for leads to often-obscure books and magazines being published in their areas of interest."[8]

While *RAIN* never reached the popularity of the *Whole Earth Catalog* and, indeed, exists in very few libraries today, it did develop between 1974 and 1979, when its original editors departed, from a local, countercultural magazine to what the journalist

Raymond Mungo called a 'mythological publication' that reached far beyond environmental firebrands to professional architects, ecologists and even government officials.[9] For its readership, the monthly publication provided a dynamic, often prescient and remarkably expansive characterisation of the AT Movement. Their journalistic aim was not to present an objective view of AT, per se, but rather to introduce the complexities and contradictions of the Movement.

In one of their first articles in *RAIN*, Bender and de Moll explained, "Our ability to develop a culture that can endure beyond our own lifetimes depends upon our coming to a new understanding of what is desirable for a harmonious and sustainable relationship with the systems that support our lives" and went on to elaborate upon the concepts of AT through a series of pairings that juxtaposed current Western approaches and more 'appropriate' strategies, such as 'Stewardship, not progress,' 'Responsibilities, not rights,' 'Betterment, not biggerment' and 'Tools, not machines.' When the editorial staff became more political in 1978 – criticising recent government support of AT while at the same time recognising its necessity – the effort revealed their confidence in the holistic network they had helped build in the preceding years and their philosophical commitment to reevaluation and change. The Rainmakers' capacity to maintain the journal's core message while also clearly demonstrating flexibility and self-criticism was, perhaps, its most extraordinary quality, and through their actions, AT practitioners nationwide could confidently move forward as a united, yet free-thinking alliance.

Despite Bender's praise of Callenbach's work, the inclusive vision of Ecotopia presented in *RAIN* was at a smaller scale, owing more to Schumacher's essays in *Small is Beautiful* than the Californian writer. *RAIN*'s utopian kit was less explicit than that of the novel; the editorial staff expressed its model society via the books, organisations and essays it selected for inclusion in the magazine. In addition, unlike Callenbach's, their utopian society was placeless, in order to emphasise the commonalities among appropriate technologists, regardless of regional specificity. Analogous to the ideological network RAIN was constructing at the time in the pages of the journal, the conception of an ideal community the journal advanced from October 1975 forward presented readers with the practical AT mechanisms to realise changes in their own neighbourhoods.

In the centre of the 'Ecotopia' poster, the Rainmakers explained its purpose:

A lot of small changes are happening today in different places that add up to a good and POSSIBLE vision of what our future can be. Diane Schatz's drawings, like Ernest Callenbach's *Ecotopia*, show what some of these ideas could be like when put together. Our future will obviously be different from this, but being able to visualise some of the possibilities we see now can help focus our energy onto bringing good futures into being.[10]

The single Callenbach quote they chose to include described "the bucolic atmosphere of the new San Francisco," namely the creeks and "charming series of little falls, with water gurgling and splashing, and channels lined with rocks, trees, bamboos, [and] ferns" that had replaced Market Street and other major thoroughfares.[11] Ecotopians cultivated this pastoral environment by eliminating the subterranean culverts which had previously rerouted these natural streams underground. Since public transportation had largely replaced individual automobiles in Ecotopia, such innovative, ecological urban planning strategies abounded. Despite RAIN's follow-up question, "Have you ever thought how much it would change things in a city to let loose all the paved-over creeks?," Bender, de Moll, Johnson and Johnson's vision was more grounded than Callenbach's fictional one and represented the overarching ideological principles of appropriate technologists nationwide. Their more practical approach emerged in Schatz's poster, which focused on four significant aspects of appropriate community technology: transportation, work, food and recycling.

To some extent, RAIN's Ecotopia was transportation-centric – many of its ideas either depended upon or contributed to the reduction or elimination of automobile traffic in American communities. Since transportation, according to the editors, "account[ed] for twenty-five percent of U.S. energy use" in the mid-1970s, it was a key facet of any appropriate design scheme. In 1977, they noted:

> We are only beginning to realize that transportation represents a *cost* of society and is therefore something to be minimized rather than maximized. What we really want is to be in good places, with good people, doing good things, and feeling good about it. These things can usually be gotten more easily directly than with transportation.[12]

Minimising any sort of travel was ideal, and their suggestions for appropriate modes of work and tourism spoke to this, but the Rainmakers knew that it was an untenable proposition in 1970s America. Thus, the editors suggested a tripartite, grassroots plan of action utilising existing resources and technologies. In their own communities, appropriate technologists might make a small difference through bicycling, using public transportation and perhaps even establishing local 'rent-a-car' systems, which would give community members access to vehicles without the need for personal ownership. In Schatz's image, the end effects of such appropriate transportation practices appeared; the large-scale reduction of individual automobiles repurposed streets and alleyways as greenspace, bike paths and community gardens, encouraged density and variety in neighbourhoods and rendered parking garages obsolete, as one can see on the right-hand side of the image. "We may see a day when cars are banned from cities all together," the poster mused, "Who can forget the charm of Venice?"[13]

Energy-efficient alternative transit methods were superior to private automobiles but could not alone, the editors anticipated (despite their Venetian reverie), engender the systemic change that a holistic AT society required. Johnson and Johnson first alluded to the appropriateness of certain types of movement patterns in an essay on networking featured in the eighth issue of *RAIN*; in the piece, they speculated that computer technology, properly implemented as a tool for connecting people, might become a "substitute for transportation in an energy-conserving society," allowing individuals to "work at home through communication," which, in turn, would reduce wasteful commuter traffic and encourage neighbourhood development.[14] In late-1975, however, the group moved away from work-related telecommunication solutions, the implementation of which, even if such technology existed at the time, would require a significant capital investment and strong interest on the part of mainstream Americans. Still, the concept of working from home or in one's own neighbourhood remained appealing to the group. 'In the past 30 to 40 years,' the editors explained on the poster:

> Americans have separated work from home so that we have in effect doubled the amount of space, heat, light and sewage facilities we need. We have also greatly increased transportation needs for commuting to work and shopping, while needing police to watch over the places we just left.[15]

Rezoning residential neighbourhoods to allow for small offices, cottage industries and other community enterprises would enliven neighbourhoods, according to the Rainmakers, giving each "its own particular flair and character due to its localized, largely self-reliant economy."[16] Contrary to many other discussions of AT transportation, which concentrated solely upon the substitution of a particular technology, such as the automobile, for a more energy-efficient, economical one, such as a public bus or bicycle, *RAIN*'s presentation of the topic questioned the appropriateness of transit entirely, recognising the holistic implications of appropriate community design.

From this perspective, the home or apartment became the key microcosmic unit of successful community planning, quite fittingly, since the meaning of *oikos*, the Greek root of ecology, itself means house. Self-reliance, another term emboldened on the Ecotopia poster, was not only important at a neighbourhood level, but for individuals and families as well. RAIN specifically encouraged gardening – in window boxes, rooftop greenhouses and backyards – as a way to cultivate self-sufficiency while at the same time rejecting the hyperindustrialised, energy-intensive, socially oppressive processes of American agribusiness. Recycling, too, began in the home, where waste materials could be composted for the garden, old clothes could be repurposed as quilts and rugs, and decaying neighbourhood buildings could either be renovated, ideally through sweat equity loans, into new community or office space or could provide salvage materials for other architectural enterprises. "*All* non-renewable resources we do not recycle are a loss of our material wealth," the poster reminded readers. "We cannot afford to waste anything or throw it away. Remember, there is no 'away'!!"[17] Here, the Rainmakers reminded readers that conservation involved far more than reducing the use of fossil fuels: they would need to evaluate all of their consumptive practices to truly reform society.

To this end, it was impossible for *RAIN* to address every facet of appropriate technology on the back side of the poster. Schatz's vision, with its rooftop windmills, credit union and solar equipment store provided an image of a potential AT utopia, as did other offerings in *RAIN*'s Special Poster Issue, but still they could not present the breadth of an appropriately designed community. Absent from the drawing were, for example, appropriate modes of health, education, communication and economics. Moreover, portraying the underlying conceit that synergistic actions of people across neighbourhoods and regions would be necessary to effect synthetic change was beyond the pencil's capacity. AT community building involved citizen participation, cooperation and the foundation of informational networks in addition to the interventions shown in the illustrated Ecotopia.

In an article entitled "Towards a Federation of Ecotopian Nations," which appeared in the journal's second volume, the editors expressed their anticipation that readers, inspired by the journal, might assemble their own grassroots lists and indices: these regional versions of *RAIN* would further disseminate the 'good word' of appropriate technology within local communities, constructing a sort of macro-cosmic web of small-scale coalitions and, eventually, Ecotopian communities. Steve Johnson had described *RAIN*'s ideal network as a system of personal connections in which:

> (1) it feels like everybody knows everybody else (especially weird and nice when great leaps of time and geography exist between people), (2)… everything is related to everything else, (3)… there are an equal number of people that you know so well you refer to them in conversations like old familiar sweaters, (4)… you find out about things before you see them in print, (5)… [and] you know, by some kind of double time mental calculations – within minutes, whether or not someone is part of your network, karass, or karma.[18]

This vision revealed the microcosmic intention of *RAIN* but, at the same time, indicated the potential for synergistic growth across the nation. For RAIN, Ecotopia was more abstract and ideological than Callenbach's fictional society, and yet, Bender, de Moll, Johnson and Johnson saw its practical merits. They hoped that, someday, such communities would exist across the US.

In one of Lee Johnson's final essays, published before his editorial departure in January of 1979, the Rainmaker provided a concise summary of AT advocates' trajectory during the previous decade.

> [Print tools such as *RAIN*] reflect the kind of purposeful, feedback-to-the-system that began for us in the noisy 1960s, when we knew or *felt* we knew what we didn't like about society but didn't really have much of a positive agenda beyond some faint inklings here and there.
>
> Well presto-chango! We're *still* mouthing off about what's not going to work in America, but we've also been writing, designing and building some damn good stuff that has led a whole bunch of us… onto new paths that feel better than the old.[19]

RAIN became a great organising force in the campaign to realise small, simple, sustainable and non-violent technologies throughout the US. In so doing, the publication created an effective network of organisations, individuals and ideas that defined the path of AT in the years that followed. *RAIN* was a dynamic and holistic work that educated its diverse readership and, its original editors believed, presented a secure ideological foundation for the practice of appropriate technology and the creation of Ecotopias to come. In a farewell letter published in the journal, de Moll and Bender, who had decided to leave the cooperative to more directly engage their local community in the coastal town of Manzanita, wrote, "We have been with *RAIN* for four years, helping share new patterns that are emerging and becoming real around us. It has been an exciting time, and one which has been successful far beyond what most people could then conceive"; despite this accomplishment, they noted that the time had come for a second generation of appropriate technologists with new visions for a sustainable future to direct the magazine's progress.[20]

The second and third generations of editors introduced fresh content to *RAIN* during its second decade, widening the subjective scope of the magazine to include less traditional AT issues, such as feminism and Native American activism; at the same time, they also were forced to sustain the weakening Movement in defiance of Reagan-era policies. Overwhelmed by such a task, and with the earnest belief that the national AT structure *RAIN* had helped create would safeguard itself, the editors gradually diminished the geographical scope of the journal, shifting its focus to the Pacific Northwest. The conceptually dissonant expansion and contraction of the intranational Ecotopian network the former Rainmakers built in the mid- to late 1970s revealed a crisis of purpose in *RAIN* and, in many ways, signalled a crisis within the AT Movement itself.

Perhaps, Callenbach's *Ecotopia* was, as Bender wrote, a 'utopian kit' or 'ten-year plan' for appropriate technologists, but it also depended upon a violent factionalism, a radical decentralisation that he and many other AT advocates were unwilling to accept, favouring instead a more synergistic, peaceful transfer of power. As we know, in the US, "a critical mass of people [never came] to see that their survival and happiness depend[ed] upon giving at least as much weight to the biological bottom line as to the economic one," and with neither cohesive grassroots activism nor progressive government policy following the election of Ronald Reagan in 1980, RAIN's ultimate Ecotopian vision failed to manifest.

Notes

1. E.F. Schumacher, "How to Help Them Help Themselves," *The Observer*, August 29, 1965.
2. For more information on the history of the *Whole Earth Catalog*, see Kirk's *Counterculture Green* (footnote 4), and for additional readings on the relationship between the counterculture and American architecture, see Greg Castillo's edited volume, *Hippie Modernism: The Struggle for Utopia* (Minneapolis: Walker Art Center, 2015), Caroline Maniaque-Benton's *French Encounters* (footnote 2), Simon Sadler's "An Architecture of the Whole," (*Journal of Architectural Education* (2008): 108–129), and Felicity Scott's *Architecture or Techno-Utopia* (Cambridge, MA: MIT Press, 2007).
3. It is probable that the founders of the American Appropriate Technology Movement, including the editors of *RAIN* and members of the New Alchemy Institute, were already exposed to the work of Schumacher prior to the publication of "Buddhist Economics" in the *Whole Earth Catalog*. However, for many others, this text would have been an introduction to Schumacher's work.
4. Texts such as Rachel Carson's *Silent Spring* (1962), Aldo Leopold's *A Sand County Almanac* (1949) and Percival and Paul and Percival Goodman's *Communitas: Means of Livelihood and Ways of Life* (1947) were all certainly significant to the ideological development of the AT Movement in the United States, but these were seldom directly mentioned in the literature of AT proponents, whereas the work of Bookchin, Fuller, and Illich often appeared.
5. Ernest Callenbach, "Author's Afterword" in *Ecotopia: The Notebooks and Reports of William Weston* (Berkeley, CA: Banyan Tree Books in assoc. with Heyday, 2014), 170.
6. Tom Bender, "In Ecotopia's Big Woods," *RAIN* 2, no. 1 (September/October 1975): 3. *Rain*'s editors frequently used the term "ecotopia" during its early years. Moreover, its anniversary issue began with an article entitled, "The Magazine from Ecotopia: A Look Back at the First RAIN Decade."
7. In 1984, the editors of RAIN eliminated "appropriate technology" from the title. Although the magazine continued in some form for many years afterwards, I will primarily discuss the group's work from 1974 through 1984.
8. Ibid., 6.

9. Raymond Mungo, "Sunshine and Oregon Rain," *New Age* 2 (November 1976): 46.
10. "Ecotopia" poster, *RAIN* 2, no. 6 (April 1976).
11. Ibid.
12. RAIN, *Rainbook: Resources for Appropriate Technology* (New York: Schocken Books, 1977), 123.
13. Ibid.
14. Johnson and Johnson, "Roughdraft IV: Networking," *RAIN* 1, no. 8 (May 1975).
15. "Ecotopia" poster, *RAIN* 2, no. 6 (April 1976).
16. Ibid.
17. Ibid.
18. S. Johnson, "Networks," in *Rainbook*, 70. Kurt Vonnegut invented the term "karass" in his 1963 novel, *Cat's Cradle*, describing *karasses* as "teams that do God's Will without ever discovering what they are doing" (Vonnegut, *Cat's Cradle* (New York: Delacorte Press, 1963), 2.)
19. L. Johnson, "With a Little Help from Our Friends," *RAIN* 4, no. 10 (August/September 1978): 5.
20. Bender and de Moll, "Letting Go," *RAIN* 5, no. 10 (August/September 1979): 18.

Part VI
Practice and life

Chapter 21

Intraventions in flux

Towards a modal spatial practice that moves and cares

Alberto Altés Arlandis and Oren Lieberman

> "What if neither skin nor self were the starting point for the complex inter-relational matrix of being and worlding? Being and worlding depend on the activity of reaching-toward."
>
> (Manning, 2013)

We have introduced elsewhere the notion of 'intravention' which, qualitatively different from 'intervention,' carries with it the understanding that we are always already within and connected. It suggests the need to inhabit a situation throughout time (in the ever-present now) in order to become knowingly part of it and implies a performative approach that focuses on the transformative character of practices, privileging what a thing does over what a thing looks like (Altes and Lieberman, 2013). Intravention speaks of engaged presence, attention and care: a respectful and responsible 'mode' or attitude which proceeds in relation with what happens. In order to 'intravene,' those involved (not always or only human) adjust and attune to what happens around and through them, and this makes them situated. We conceive intraventions as a mode of 'situated architecture'.

    We are approaching the development of this notion through a closer look at its dynamic dimensions and a care for movement that we believe can help us develop forms of responsible practice with respect to co-existence, commons and collectives. Situatedness, we claim, has never been about static or fixed conditions, but rather about a form of constant open attention which engages with what is going on, with what happens, always in motion. Intraventions are not static; to emphasise intraventions-in-flux is to think through the moving components and dimensions which

DOI: 10.4324/9781003118985-27

Figure 21.1 Final state of a two-week improvisatory design and construction workshop with TU Delft students which led to the production of a public space including a public sauna, two adjacent volumes hosting a changing room, wood storage, chill-out and back stage rooms and a performance stage/public dance floor, in an area called Hiedanranta, in the outskirts of Tampere (Finland)

Photo A. Altés

already exist within the notion of 'intravention,' to help us develop engaged spatial practices and caring modes.

We believe in the power of intraventional work to inform processes in which architectural practices emerge from the relations developed through inhabitation understood as moving along (Ingold, 2011) and to question static descriptions of urban space and understandings of place as extension (Norberg-Schulz, 1971).

To inhabit a place as moving along is not simply to be somewhere, on top of a specific geographical location, but to be attentive to what happens, to what is in flux; it means to be alert to our very natures as being in flux, to be attuned to the relations and movements which traverse and co-constitute the presences involved, including ours. Much has been written and designed on the basis of understandings of place and home as a circumscribed, bounded-off entity, organised around a centre (as represented in Norberg-Schulz's diagrams published in "Existence, Space and Architecture," implying a self which is 'originally' oriented towards the home (Norberg-Schulz, 1971, p. 19) Instead, situated architecture locates architectural production (not *in* or *on top* of places) but *within* 'situations.' A situation is a site and a moment, a field of relations, an intra-acting assemblage of matter and movement, including place-related dimensions, what we normally refer to as the land, and also organisms and their activities, atmospheres and many other things. The notion of situation is imbued with a sense of openness

Figure 21.2 Initial steps in a 48-h improvisatory design and construction process leading to the construction of a small Finish sauna equipped with a stone fire place and activated through the combined efforts of its users who would need to flip it in order to make it receive the heat accumulated in the stones once the fire was put out after burning for hours

Photo A. Altés. Design: Sami Rintala, Joar Nango, Roger Mullin, Håvard Arnhoff and Alberto Altés

and ongoing-ness, opposed to ideas of solidified, frozen or essential understandings. (It is nevertheless possible to speak of 'the state of the situation': as the conditions, namings, structurings and distributions that co-determine it and the ways in which it is governed or can be 'entered.')

While Norberg-Schulz's understands identity as 'rooted' in its orientation to a (central) place, which presupposes an ideal subject "[…] we can characterize as essentially colonizing, enlightened, white, straight, male and able-bodied" (Norwood, 2018, p. 12), Edouard Glissant's notion of 'relational identity' emphasises ongoing-ness and the circulation of lives which are different and in-formation (Glissant, 1997):

> Relational identity is linked not to a creation of the world but to the conscious and contradictory experience of contacts among cultures. It is produced in the chaotic network of 'Relation' and not in the hidden violence of filiation. It does not devise any legitimacy as its guarantee of entitlement, but circulates, newly extended; it does not think of a land as a territory from which to project toward other territories but as a place where one gives-on-and-with rather than grasps.
>
> (Glissant, 1997, p.144)

We don't live in 'space' or 'place' understood as extension, and we can't help but find ourselves in the midst of situations, always evolving. They move, we move along. And thus, we must consent, in Glissant's words, 'not to be a single being.' We should drop any assumptions about what human (and non-human) bodies can or must be or do and engage in understanding all forms of life as modes, as modalities of embodiment, emerging relationally from the various intra-actions our common existence is made of.

In 'Queer Phenomenology,' Sara Ahmed interrogates the ways in which something or someone gets relegated to the background, revisiting Husserl's work table and thinking through the ways in which his focus on the table is only possible through the suppression/relegation of children, wife, cleaner, maker of the table, as well as other things. She speaks thus of the notion of 'orientations,' which involve different ways of registering the proximity of objects and others. They shape not only how we inhabit space, but how we apprehend this world of shared inhabitance as well as who or what we direct our energy and attention towards – not only how the table gets relegated to the background but how we might be able to think about the fact that the table might have a background too. She writes:

> The work of inhabitance involves orientation devices; ways of extending bodies into spaces that create new folds, or new contours of what we could call liveable or inhabitable space. If orientation is about making the strange familiar through the extension of bodies into space, then disorientation occurs when that extension fails. Or we could say that some spaces extend certain bodies and simply do not leave room for others.
>
> (Ahmed, 2006, p. 11)

Now, our engagements (with)-in situations involve our choices/decisions to bracket things in and out of the always on-going activity and environment/organism relations, which is not only about orientation and disorientation but also about 'attention.' Exploring and learning, understood after James Gibson as the 'education of attention,' means to progressively develop more and more skilled abilities to detect the affordances of the environment and the differences that make a difference. We need to approach attention in multiple ways: as listening, as caring, as waiting, as being present, as going along. And as Tim Ingold would have it, as 'longing,' in the precise sense of stretching a life along a line; a 'longitudinal' understanding of attention. (Ingold, 2013) To attend, ad-tendere, is to tend-toward, to stretch toward and 'attendre' in French means 'to wait.'

> The kind of attention we pay actually alters the world: we are, literally, partners in creation. This means we have a grave responsibility, a word that captures the reciprocal nature of the dialogue we have with whatever it is that exists apart from ourselves.
>
> (McGilchrist, 2009, p. 5)

Care brings in an ethical dimension to attention by approaching it not as a cognitive process oriented towards understanding, but as a way of restoring (things) to presence, and not in order to become aware of, but to draw us into correspondence with the world. Through the education of attention, a combination of care and curiosity, and what Donna Haraway proposed to term 'feminist objectivity,' we can develop the kind of 'situatedness' we imagine constitutes the core of 'intraventions-in-flux' and other responsible practices: "Feminist objectivity is about limited location and situated knowledge, not about transcendence and splitting of subject and object. It allows us to become answerable for what we learn how to see" (Haraway, 1988, p. 583).

Situatedness and movement

What interests us are the always-in-flux yet distinctive boundary-making cuts which are made through modes of movement, as bodies – understood as members of an array of ecologies – meet and become intimate. All kinds of things, human and non-human, meet in a situation, and as they go on moving, they clash or establish links, or act together or in concert… and produce effects. These enactments are just such boundary-making cuts, and the terms and conditions of a situation are further defined through/in them, even though movement goes on. Movement is always already there. Nevertheless, the world of spatial making and discourse is full of what is understood to be stable, at rest, immovable even: theories, practices, materials and constructions which appear to be fixed – but, in relation to what exactly? This is indeed the crux of flux: does what we understand to be in-flux determine what we understand to be stable? Or is it the other way around? Or is it a dialogical dance? Perhaps, a more useful term instead of stability would be 'duration.' We use duration to refer to the apparent reliability of patterns and rhythms (choreographies) of intra-action which appear as stable phenomena, including histories, bricks, walls, relationships, houses and other things. We could say, with Karen Barad, that specific boundary-making cuts 'hold,' to a great extent due to the duration or repetition (relative stability) of the intentions and characteristics of the apparatuses involved in making them possible (Barad, 2007, pp. 93, 146). In her seminal essay 'Situated Knowledges: The Science Question in Feminism and the Privilege of Partial Perspective,' Donna Haraway explained it this way:

> […] bodies as objects of knowledge are material-semiotic generative nodes. Their boundaries materialize in social interaction. Boundaries are drawn by mapping practices; 'objects' do not pre-exist as such. Objects are boundary projects. But boundaries shift from within; boundaries are very tricky. What boundaries provisionally contain remains generative, productive of meanings and bodies. Siting (sighting) boundaries is a risky practice.
> (Haraway, 1988, p. 595)

If we speak about collectives of people coexisting with each other, with non-humans, materials and constructions, this duration of seeming stability is always that of movement, a movement which, paradoxically perhaps, holds stuff together. A number of things are 'holding' together within an intra-acting cut, as situated. There are dimensions of the situation which rest or depend on previous situations, and on things which brought things to where they are now, and yet, things go on moving. It is our task to approach situations with a curiosity and a care that allows us to pay attention to the ways in which accounts of what happens are constructed, to the ways in which what is being constructed is also simultaneously in movement and to the ways in which this movement and these arrangements 'hold' in duration.

Rather than understanding spatial practice as stable and immobile (as it's often been the case with the notion of place), we propose to focus on a caring attention to both what holds or endures (within its own emergent becoming) and to what is in flux: situatedness and movement. And because of our attention to movement, because we experience our actions within spatial research, education and practice as 'moving,' we are moved to articulate ways in which we might be able to both think through and take part in making and enabling the patterns, rhythms and modes in which 'spatial things' last or endure. We are starting to refer to spatial intra-actions – people, constructions, non-humans, words and materials in moving relations – as 'situated choreographies'.

Situated choreographies

Situated choreographies are also boundary-making apparatuses; space and movement-inclined ones. In a similar way to that of Karen Barad's notion of intra-action, which "[...] involving a specific material configuration of the 'apparatus of observation', enacts an agential cut [...] effecting a separation between 'subject' and 'object'" (Barad, 2003, p. 815), situated choreographies establish the conditions of a cut which co-determines the kinds of things and materials that will be moved and how and through what modes of engagement. If, for Barad, the agential cut "enacts a local resolution within the phenomenon of the inherent ontological indeterminacy," and therefore, "[...] relata do not pre-exist relations; rather, relata within-phenomena emerge through specific intra-actions" (Barad, 2003, p. 815), in our architecture-making engagements, situated choreographies enact cuts which guide steps for spatial and collective intra-action that enable the emergence of architectures, which are not preceded by authorised projective representations, but result instead from the attentive, in-flux investments and care of participants, meeting and acting in-formation and in movement.

The movement we speak of, this always moving, boundary-making and cutting motion, is movement of bodies moved in relation, of cells always on the move, of contingent mobilities of needs and desires. It is the movement of life: material flows and flows of conscious awareness. It is not movement understood as speed or transportation, not as displacement in relation to time, but rather, the movement of becoming, and the movement of bodies intra-acting with other bodies.

In 'Relationscapes: Movement, Art, Philosophy,' Erin Manning describes relational movement: "Think walking with a lover, or dancing tango. Walking relationally means: when you walk into the hole, you walk – with. Walking-with is more than taking a step, it is creating a movement" (Manning, 2009, p. 29). Walking-with, doing things with, becoming with others implies an invitation to shared intimacy. There seems to be a dimension of intimacy within intra-action. Things intra-acting become not only connected but somehow close, and the intimacy of intra-actions speaks both of closeness and affect: the cut brings things incredibly close together through its enactment of differentiation. Intra-actions are intimate as they are proximate. They encourage emergent care and moments of endurance, which unfold through the inhabitation of the space and time of the cut. The bodies involved in this closeness are not just human bodies but the bodies of things, materials, regulations, structures or other organisms.

This post-human understanding of intimacy can be further expanded through the notion of kin, if kin is understood as an open bond. Kinship is thus not predefined, but emerging within the specificities of a singular cut, that is, it's not necessarily about brotherhood, fatherhood or other societal belief systems but emerges with/through beams, rivers, trees, skateboarders, others… In Haraway's words, it is not kin but 'oddkin,' that is, "we require each other in unexpected collaborations and combinations, in hot compost piles. We become-with each other or not at all" (Haraway, 2016, p. 4).

The kinds of cuts which situated choreographies enact do not only include and invite proximity and kinship, but they necessarily therefore exclude. This exclusion is nevertheless not unethical. Being inclusive as an ethical stance is not opposed to exclusion: the very act of phenomena coming into being, that is, boundaries being created as articulations and delineations of some 'thing,' is driven by an enabling care for the specificities of the situation. "The concept of complementarity makes clear that for Barad, when one apparatus instantiates a particular world another is necessarily excluded. It is in these cuts and through these boundary-making practices that Barad's ethical contribution is to be found" (Hollin et al. 2017, p. 932).

The intimacy and situatedness we have been thinking through and their encouragement of open forms of kin require of us not only a disposition to collaborate in unexpected ways, but a willingness to stay put, to hold on and to 'hold our own,' to endure… which speaks of another understanding of time. A better name for this kind of time, might be, as mentioned above, duration. And situated duration is essentially not about chronological or measured time, but about time in-formation or what the Greeks referred to as 'kairos.' Kairos referred initially to "a vital or lethal place in the body [...] susceptible to injury and [...] requiring special protection" (Sipiora et al., 2002, p. 2), its meaning evolving later towards an idea of 'due measure' and the sense that there is a best moment to achieve this just measure. As opposed to the uniformity and linearity of 'chronos,' 'kairos' emerges thus as the time of 'opportunity.' And in the measuring of the opportunity, "the situational factor is paramount" (Cahn, in Sipiora et al., 2002, p. 9).

Nevertheless, kairos is not just some kind of subjective time as opposed to the objectivity of the clock's time but carries with it a sense of situated objectivity additional to, and perhaps also grounded in its experiential and qualitative dimensions. Although kairic time "is made up of discontinuous and unprecedented occasions, instead of identical moments within 'a causally related sequence of events' [...] [and] therefore, marks opportunities that might not recur, and moments of decision [that make it] interpretive, [and] situational" (Benedikt, 2002, p. 226), kairos emerges also in relation to the order of actual happenings and the attention we may or may not pay to them, which bring in a sense of objectivity and engagement.

In a similar way in which thinking situatedness with Haraway is helpful to question the solidifying and fixing effects of the loaded 'context,' kairic time affords us the possibility to engage with more actually in-flux and moving understandings of movement.

> Whereas in the active-passive common sense model, time and space are located as stable signifiers into which the body enters, within a relational model, space and time are qualitatively transformed by the movements of the body. The body does not move into space and time, it creates space and time: there is no space and time before movement.
>
> (Manning, 2007, p. xiii)

Movement as we see it is not about displacement throughout measured time, or about speed, but "can only be felt" (Manning, 2014, p. 36).

Intraventions in flux are non-cynical practices of care which interrogate methodologies and embrace the modal. They think through movement, emphasise attention and foreground the way(s) in which we are moved (by things), questioning the usual understanding of movement as a property of subjects. Movement is something that happens to us rather than an identified 'us' performing it.

We might say 'collectives collecting' happens, as Spinoza's 'nature naturing' (natura naturans) does. The implication would be that there is something in human 'nature' which drives us together to form groups, an implication borne out by anthropologists and sociologists. But if we side on that of 'pure immanence' (Deleuze, James, etc.) and Haraway's and Barad's cuts, we do so with an understanding that architecture is a participant in distributions of ecologies of boundary-making practices and can make differences, in collaborations with other 'kin': collectives move, are moved, congeal and dissipate. The joy of being-with exceeds any 'natura naturans,' any natural inclinations of the human species to form groups; it is not about mobile architectures, it's about architecture(s) of love: "it ends with love, exchange, fellowship. It ends as it begins, in motion" (Halberstam, 2011, p. 5).

References

Ahmed, Sara (2006) *Queer Phenomenology: Orientations, Objects, Others* (Durham, NC; London: Duke University Press).
Altes, Alberto and Lieberman, Oren (2013) *Intravention, Durations, Effects: Notes of Expansive Sites and Relational Architectures* (Baunach: Spurbuchverlag).
Barad, Karen (2003) Posthumanist Performativity: Toward an Understanding of How Matter Comes to Matter, *Signs: Journal of Women in Culture and Society*, vol. 28, no. 3 (Chicago, IL: The University of Chicago).
Barad, Karen (2007) *Meeting the Universe Halfway: Quantum Physics and the Entanglement of Matter and Meaning* (Durham, NC; London, Duke University Press).
Benedikt, Amelie Frost (2002) On Doing the Right Thing at the Right Time: Toward and Ethics of Kairos, in Sipiora, Philip and Baumlin, James S. (eds.) *Rhetoric and Kairos: Essays in History, Theory and Praxis* (Albany: State University of New York Press).

Glissant, Edouard (1997) *Poetics of Relation* (Ann Arbor: The University of Michigan Press).

Halberstam, Jack (2011) The Wild Beyond: With and for the Undercommons, in Harney, Stefano and Moten, Fred (eds.) *The Undercommons: Fugitive Planning & Black Study* (New York: Minor Compositions, Autonomedia).

Haraway, Donna (1988) Situated Knowledges: The Science Question in Feminism and the Privilege of Partial Perspective, *Feminist Studies*, vol. 14, no. 3.

Haraway, Donna (2016) *Staying with the Trouble: Making Kin in the Chthulucene* (Durham, NC; London: Duke University Press).

Hollin, Gregory et al. (2017) (Dis)entangling Barad: Materialisms and Ethics, *Social Studies of Science*, vol. 47, no. 6, pp. 918–941 (Sage Journals).

Ingold, Tim (2011) *Being Alive: Essays on Movement, Knowledge and Description* (New York: Routledge).

Ingold, Tim (2013) *Making: Anthropology, Archaeology, Art and Architecture* (London; New York: Routledge).

Manning, Erin (2007) *Politics of Touch: Sense, Movement, Sovereignty*, (Minnesota: University of Minnesota Press).

Manning, Erin (2009) *Relationscapes: Movement, Art, Philosophy* (Cambridge, MA; London, UK: The MIT Press).

Manning, Erin (2013) *Always More Than One: Individuation's Dance* (Durham, NC and London: Duke University Press).

Manning, Erin and Brian Massumi (2014) *Thought in the Act: Passages in the Ecology of Experience* (Minneapolis, London: University of Minnesota Press).

McGilchrist, Ian (2009) *The Master and His Emissary: The Divided Brain and the Making of the Western World* (New Haven, CT; London: Yale University Press).

Norberg-Schulz, Christian (1971) *Existence, Space & Architecture* (London: Studio Vista Limited).

Norwood, Brian E. (2018) Disorienting Phenomenology, Log 42 (New York: Anyone Corporation).

Sipiora, Philip and Baumlin, James S. (2002) *Rhetoric and Kairos: Essays in History, Theory and Praxis* (Albany: State University of New York Press).

Chapter 22

Ethics of open types

Davide Landi

A characteristic of the 21st century for some societies is the establishment of better healthcare systems, a reduction in infant mortality and a growing number of adults living longer. However, these accomplishments can have a downside. For example, people are living longer, and therefore, there has been an increase in age-related conditions such as dementia. At the same time, societies are becoming more aware of the potential increase in demand for high-dependency-related services and their impact upon health and social care budgets. Additionally, difficulties in defining a clear dividing line between normal ageing and pathological ageing have led to stigmatisation and segregation of older adults as a social and economic burden. These societal changes have informed only a few architectural examples that attempt to adopt innovative care models. If we consider architecture as a practical and conscious answer to a posed unconscious problem, these few architectural examples set the basis for a theoretical contribution to architecture through a typological analysis. They are 'open types' which expand the nascent theoretical discourse on 'open architecture.'

This chapter describes and empirically explores the Rudolf in Helsinki as an open type example. The Rudolf is a senior home with a population of 18 young adults with mental impairments; 50 older adults with later stages of dementia; 52 older adults with early stages or no mental or physical impairments and four young adults/university students. By welcoming a renewed investigation of Aristotelian ethics, open types promote multi-disciplinary, collaborative and socially inclusive design principles and thereby order as a result. Consequently, the analysis will introduce an approach to ethics that is concerned with the notion of dwelling that emphasises the value of the

Figure 22.1 Photograph of the Rudolf in Helsinki
By Davide Landi

common. This allows a work of architecture and ageing to reject their medicalisation while to reveal new forms of collective life.

Historically, ethics was underpinned by primary questions, for instance, questions concerning the limitations of personal liberties and interests against communal one. They embraced the notion of goodwill and thereby to do actions that aim for good outcomes. Inevitably, this established a contradiction. On the one hand, ethics investigated universal shared principles, duties and obligations. On the other hand, they attempted to preserve an individual state of mind. Consequently, ethics and ethical questions frame an equilibrium between individual and communal existences.[1] In this, architecture becomes an ethical problem. It is about how to be in the world, to live and thereby how to dwell.[2,3]

Contemporary culture has posed profoundly new challenges.[4] The term culture refers to all the unself-conscious agents and challenges, which are latent in our contemporaneity.[5] A striking example is the different socio-demographic and economic landscapes (i.e. improved but stagnant economies, a reduction in infant mortality, a growing number of adults living longer and better health care systems). Nevertheless, they have downsides, long term and high-dependency care services expenditures are spiralling,[6] and older adults are subject to stigmatisation and segregation patterns for the sake of efficiency and performance.[7,8] As a consequence, there is a clear debate around the necessity to improve not only our built environment for an aged society but also a 'social model of ageing' rather than a medical one.[9,10] This debate, through a typological analysis, sets the basis for architecture to make a theoretical contribution,[11] which will broaden on "open architecture"[12] or in this case "open types."[13] This exploratory chapter, therefore, examines the Rudolf© Senior Home in Helsinki as an open type revealing its ethical impact. Open types are a term introduced by Landi[14] which frames the use of collaborative and socially inclusive design principles; it imposes a multi-disciplinary, collaborative and socially inclusive order as a result.[15,16] Open types imply a consciousness of inhabitants in dwelling.[17]

With no constraints, the Rudolf© Senior Home as an open type aims to put together the different and the possible. In this sense, duties and justice are homogenously distributed among its inhabitants, and thereby mutations are absorbed and digested. Consequently, this process becomes ethical and capable to generate new forms of collective life.

On theories and practices of the ethics

Ethics takes into consideration the modalities and the possibilities in addressing our lives according to virtuous and good principles. These are connected with the idea of living morally.[18,19] Nowadays, the ethical quest is again a central aspect of our lives which are underpinned by a new socio-economic matrix. Over time, theorists and historians of ethics have more comprehensively identified different facets that constitute the subject. Smith,[20] for example, groups ethics in two main theoretical categories: "Normative and Non-normative Theories."[21,22] The *Virtues*, instead, are central to this chapter. Aristotle, for example, abundantly investigated it in his treatise on virtues. Curzer[23] proposes a contemporary interpretation of these virtues. In this, the character and consciousness of a subject are central to moral action.[24,25] Virtues, therefore, becomes an alternative to more pragmatic normative ethics.[26] It can thus be suggested that 'to be ethical is to be human,' and thereby, ethical questions hold the right to inform human nature.[27]

As ethical questions shape human nature, the spatial consistency of ethics can be found in architecture. Architecture combines aesthetically with symbolic meanings and social values. It becomes a collection of different practices, while buildings and cities are containers of human dignity and thereby an expression of civilisation.[28,29] Consequently, architecture has a multi-layered system of ethical implications. Law and construction standards inform the minimum design requirements, and ethics provides a more robust framework that directly affects human values.[30] Illies and Ray,[31] for example, identify six relevant areas that concern architecture and ethics, i.e.

> the morally acceptable and unacceptable nature of building; issue on professional behaviours and interaction during the planning design and construction phase; the impact of building on nature; the impact of the health and safety of those who use the building; the sociological influence in human behaviour; and the furnishing of symbolic and cultural meaning.

Ethics of open types

Figure 22.2 Block layout by Davide Landi

In this, architects, design processes and buildings are the three leading figures that are underpinned by ethics in architecture.[32] Consequently, it is helpful to comprehend the ethics of professional bodies peculiar to this study more roundly.

First, architecture is a profession. Besides building regulations and laws, an architect as a professional embodies certain kinds of responsibilities and values.[33,34] Architects, therefore, embrace an ethical reasoning process which is underpinned by critical reflections and lifelong learning. However, architects as proponents of a comprehensive profession must not take decisions, which are only suggested by pure ethical theories. They instead must adopt a "moral imagination."[35] In this regard, Dewey's philosophical pragmatism helps to expand the discussion around "moral imagination."[36] It informs an intelligence, which is keen on experimentations and seeing what is known and understood in new ways. In this, new forms of education take place.[37,38] Brenner et al.[39] describe "moral imagination" as a "critical imagination." It embodies strongly intellectual and political values to produce a totally diverse type of built environment (e.g. The Mauri-Ora philosophy and design thinking and practice).[40]

Second, professional caregiving, as well as architecture, is a profession that, since 1889, implies a university curriculum, which is combined with training.[41,42] In particular, professional caregiving for older adults/dementia sufferers is a long-life learning experience whose practice is parallel to the discipline of psychiatry. Inevitably, the practice of caregiving is continuously subject to ethical decisions. It is grounded in the interaction with others. Ethical theories and a person's psychosocial and professional development (i.e. comprehension of patients' situations, emphatic and communication skills), therefore, are the tools that support ethical decisions.[43,44] In this, therapeutic relationships are the core of care models that focus on patients' well-being.[45,46] Consequently, professional caregivers embody characteristics of being emotionally and ethically sensitive, which are counterbalanced by more pragmatic ones such as clinical decision-making and risks management.[47]

A robust legal framework regulates both professions and their ethics. The National Council of Architectural Registration Boards adopted a code of conduct, which acted as guidelines for professional codes of national professional organisations such as the American Institute of Architects (AIA) or The Royal Institute of British Architects (RIBA).[48,49] In the same vein, the legal framework in professional caregiving is the Nurses and Midwives code of conduct (NMC).[50] The architectural and caregiving legal frameworks imply professional sanctions in case of misconduct.[51,52]

Open city, open architecture and open types

A simplistic zoning and single-use development approach still prevail amongst our urban and architectural landscape, originating in the 20th-century Fordism model and underpinned by the necessity of economic performance and efficiency.[53] A critique of these urban strategies is clearly nothing new in sociology and architecture. In the 1960s, Jane Jacobs critically evaluated the urban impacts of a process driven by diversity and density. The findings allowed Jacobs to frame later the notion of the "open city."[54] Over time, Richard Sennett has criticised zoning and single-use development policies and the city that results from their application – the 'closed city.' Referring to Jacobs' work, Sennett has speculated on the notion of 'open city' as an urban strategy. Nevertheless, Sennett's writings showed a lack of examples of 'open systems' at the architectural scale.[55] This lack in forms of open architecture described above is robustly investigated at various points in the work of the historian Esra Akcan. In her book *Open Architecture*, she engages with the analysis of speculative projects such as Tange's Tokyo Bay Project (1960) and collective projects such as IBA-1984/1987 in Berlin. If the former embeds principles of flexibility and adaptability; the latter is underpinned by theories of transnational solidarity, collectivity and collaboration, plurality and democracy, expansion of social citizenship and human rights, and multiplicity of meanings.[56] The nature and scale of Akcan's analysis leads to a question concerning types of open architecture, which are prior to open forms of Architecture. As authors such as Rossi have shown, the typological analysis provides a powerful tool for the translation of a society's articulation into a work of architecture.[57] Consequently, the critical potential of types is related to situations of social rupture. Whether oppositional or conciliatory towards a specific situation of social rupture, only the agency of architects informs types' critical deployment.[58] In this, open types are for the 'both-and' instead for the 'either-or' of their critical potential to promote multi-disciplinary, collaborative and socially inclusive design principles, and thereby order. In this particular study, open types propose an alternate order of older adult's long-term care facilities.[59] To illustrate this, the following section empirically untangles the Rudolf senior home as a case study.

Learning from the Rudolf© senior home: the open type

The Helsinki Department of Youth launched the three-year project: 'A Home that Fits' (i.e. Oman Muotoinen Koti) in February 2015. It attempted to find a new housing solution for homeless young adults with design becoming a tool to suggest effective social strategies.[60,61,62]

Three different projects were proposed. First, a seasonal housing project. Second, a communal housing project in existing empty apartment buildings. Third, the Rudolf senior home project. Four students were accommodated in a nursing home for older adults with different levels of physical and mental impairments. The first and second project came to an end in December 2017, while the Rudolf senior home project is the only one to continue.[63,64]

Thinking

The Rudolf © in Helsinki is a senior home. Designed by the Housing Department of the City of Helsinki, the Rudolf© is underpinned by the Finnish derivative of international functionalist movement thinking.[65]

Due to a lack of economic resources, the Home that Fits' manager opened up the decisional process to policymakers to get the right senior home and the right permissions, after to young adults.[66] Their selection process started on the web (i.e. Facebook©) and was followed by group, and individual interviews for young adults do not have an academic or professional background in health or social care.[67,68,69]

The role of the 'A Home that Fits' designer became a facilitator of the project between its core ideas and the different subjects involved.[70]

In this, the Rudolf© aimed to preserve its principles and values (e.g. togetherness, avoiding prejudices, ensuring security, equality and quality in the care provision while preserving residents' privacy and their capacity to do what they are still able to do).[71,72]

Making

The Rudolf© was completed in 1974. It was first a social housing complex which gave shelter to Helsinki citizens who presented socio-economic difficulties. It embodies many characterising features of the international functionalist movement, its architectural forms and materials.[73]

The Rudolf© became a senior home in the 1990s to accommodate older adults with difficult socio-economic background, and the Helsinki Health Care Department took over its management. In this, the Rudolf© went through first a refurbishment process according to the spatial and accessibility requirements of the Finnish Land Use and Building Act for long-term-care facilities (e.g. the number of internal staircases were reduced, or alternative paths were proposed by introducing ramps or wheelchair lifts).[74,75,76] It was further refurbished in the early 2000s to increase the number of communal areas (e.g. a restaurant and a gym open to the public) and to fulfil additional accessibility requirements for young and old adult with mental impairments.

The Rudolf© has 124 residential units. They are one or two-room units with an average size of 23–46 square metres with private kitchens which are rarely used to maximise collective meals (i.e. couples of 15/16 square metre residential units were joined together).[77,78]

The 124 residential units are distributed with two five-storey residential blocks: the west and east blocks. A green area which is composed by a 'formal garden' (i.e. it is used for recreational and collective activities) and a 'wild garden' (i.e. it is a piece of existing woods) connects the two blocks. It is open to the public (e.g. community members doing jogging). The gardens, therefore, are central in residents' social life, sensorial experience and thereby well-being.[79] The main entrance is at the centre of the east block. Inside, there is no reception desk, although it is a welcoming space with benches, armchairs and tea table. In addition, the interior design of spaces such as decoration, second-hand furniture and colours is the outcome of an ongoing collaboration between residents, both older adults and young adults, and the professional staff working at Rudolf©.[80,81]

Nevertheless, the Rudolf© has still substantial physical limitations such structural columns in the middle of rooms, and thereby some of the residential units were left unoccupied.[82,83]

Living

The Rudolf© accommodates a total of 124 residents who come mainly from the Helsinki city area. Only 3% are international resident.[84] The care is provided through 91 professional caregivers and 20 retired Finnish volunteers who help professional caregivers in field trips, barbecues and sometimes assist them in caretaking duties.[85,86]

In 2015, the Rudolf © in Helsinki opened up the traditional care model and residential setting to initially three then four young adults/students. In exchange for a very affordable accommodation, the young adults/students give to the Rudolf© between 3 and 5 hours per week for social work. There are no guidelines about how to behave; youngsters, for instance, are not informed about the health conditions of older residents. They could do what they feel to do such as baking and going to music concerts. In this, young adult/university students spend conventionally one year.[87,88] However, this innovative housing solution might have some implications. Two of the students, for example, could not effectively contribute to the Rudolf© due to personal problems.[89,90]

In the beginning, therefore, these activities were not regulated by any contract or tenancy agreement. It was a reciprocal exchange between the different groups' inhabitation of the senior home underpinned by a trust, responsibilities and 'principles

Ethics of open types

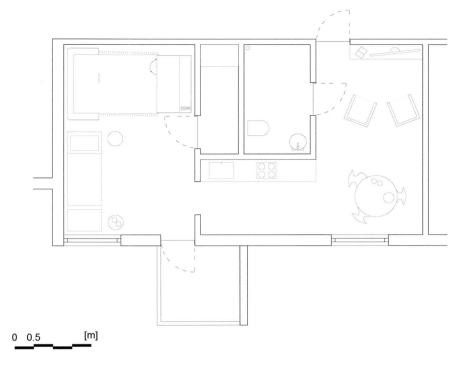

Figure 22.3 Flat plan by Davide Landi

of goodwill.' Afterwards, the one-year stay was officialised with a contract in which the volunteering contribution and its number of hours were stated with a possible extension to a second-year stay. In addition, the manager asked younger residents to have a diary of the activities as a record while using social networks such as Instagram© to record their volunteering digitally.[91]

The Rudolf© implies some lifestyle changes for young residents, although it has positive effects on them as well the older residents' well-being and independence.[92,93,94]

The open type and its ethical dilemmas

The Rudolf© as an open type that emphasises the value of the collectivity. It rejects passive architectural settings, whereas it embraces active ones. It accommodates alternate experiences far from well-known experiences, which are peculiar to older adults' long-term care facilities. The Rudolf©, for instance, opened up standard older adults long-term care models to engage in care provision diverse groups of professional and informal care providers such as volunteers, community/social workers and young-adult residents. They are invited to contribute and collaborate informally.[95] The Rudolf© senior home has a robust relational pattern between young adult and older residents such as baking cakes, drawing, painting, reading newspapers and books, going to concerts and having parties together.[96] Whilst they represent just an additional informal

267

layer that defines a new paradigm of care, professional caregivers are still crucial for sharing their expertise.

Inevitably, this may imply an additional effort and expenditure of physical and psychological resources for professional caregivers and the economic and clinical risks management.[97] The episode at the Rudolf© of two young adult resident who could not effectively contribute to the innovative model is an outstanding example. Interviews from the Rudolf©,[98,99] however, confirmed that the presence of volunteers and other age groups living in the two facilities have a positive impact on the well-being of caregivers and older adults.

The Rudolf©, therefore, serves as architectural settings in which people with different ethnic, economic, demographic and social backgrounds could bridge together. These have been active elements, major basins for the production and circulation of values underpinned by diversity. The Rudolf© as an open type is an architectural stage to access these values and thereby alternate ways of their consumption.[100] Differences and displacements become synonymous of growth and the creation of an inclusive identity.[101]

It can thus be suggested that the contemporary socio-economic matrix which considers an ageing population and an increasing dementia rate confirm the immediate necessity in opening the ethical dialogue to a broader audience.

These alternate ethics with a clear Aristotelian reference encourages complex, equal and propositional synergies (i.e. Aristotle's virtue of friendliness).[102] Inhabitants, therefore, would be free from the risks of prescriptive environments.[103] In this, the open type does not simply tear down the wall between different socio and age groups, and it also fosters a sociological work between them. This sociological work is rooted in the awareness of the others, whilst it refuses the unification and simplification of the diverse, which instead generates misunderstandings.[104] Consequently, the architects, professional caregivers and inhabitants are equally central figures in this social work by producing the richness instead of the efficiency of the relationships. For example, these figures' collaborative and participatory contribution in the adaptation process of the case studies crystallises a renewed version of the ethics. These figures accomplish their social responsibility beyond conventional professional and societal domains. In this, the design paradigm is deeply questioned.[105]

Nonetheless, it is important to acknowledge the necessity of members/inhabitants' consciousness to ethics, its duties and justice to properly accomplish the virtue. If Dewey framed this consciousness as "moral imagination,"[106] Aristotle defined it as practical wisdom. It is "the knowledge of which acts are right."[107] Only then, ethics and being ethical means being human.

The open type, therefore, not only proposes an alternate way of conceiving ethics beyond professions bodies that gather back some of the ethics which have been eroded,[108] but it also appeals to the necessity of a renewed consciousness of inhabitants of a work of architecture and thereby of a city. This is a new ethic, the ethics of the open type.

The Rudolf may propose a new form of communal and individual life not yet consistently present in Western countries. This form of architecture, however, unveils design principles that respond to the typological problem in contemporary culture. It suggests a different attitude towards ethics. They concern the notion of inhabitation and thereby the ethics of the open type to reclaim Aristotelian investigations on the theme beyond the ethics of professional bodies. However, this implies a certain kind of responsibilities for inhabitants who may require a renewed consciousness of ethics, its duties and justice. To this end, the open type may inform future care, living and design practices and must be politically and economically supported by institutions and governments.

Acknowledgements

Dr Grahame Smith.

Notes

1. Barry Wasserman, Patrick J. Sullivan, and Gregory Palermo, *Ethics and The Practice of Architecture* (New York: John Wiley and Sons, Inc., 2000).
2. Karsten Harries, *The Ethical Function of Architecture* (Cambridge, MA: MIT Press, 1997).
3. Christian Illies, and Nicholas Ray, *Philosophy of Architecture* (Cambridge: Cambridge Architectural Press, 2014).
4. Richard Sennett, *Together. The Rituals, Pleasure and Politics of Cooperation* (London: Penguin Book, 2012).
5. Christopher Alexander, *Notes on the Synthesis of Form* (Cambridge, MA: Harvard University Press, 1973).
6. European Union, ed., The 2015 Ageing Report. Economic and Budgetary Projections for the 27 EU Member States (2010–2060) (Brussels: European Commission, 2015).
7. Becca R. Levy, "Age-Stereotype Paradox: Opportunity for Social Change," *The Gerontologist, 57*(S2) (2017): 118–126.
8. Liat Ayalon, "Perception of Old Age and Ageing in the Continuing Care Retirement Community," *International Psychogeriatric 27*(4) (2015): 611–620.
9. Jeremy Myerson, ed., *New Old* (London: Design Museum, 2017).
10. Giovanna Borasi, and Mirko Zardini, eds. *Imperfect Health: The Medicalisation of Architecture* (Zurich: Lars Muller Publishers, 2012).
11. Aldo Rossi, *The Architecture of the City* (Cambridge, MA: MIT Press, 1982).
12. Esra Akcan, *Open Architecture: Migration, Citizenship, and the Urban Renewal of Berlin-Kreuzberg by IBA-1984/87* (Basel: Birkhauser GmbH, 2018).
13. Davide Landi, "Open Typology as Heterotopia: A Comparative Analysis between Gojikara Mura in Nagakute (Japan) and Humanitas in Deventer (Netherlands)," *The International Journal of Design in Society 12*(3) (2018): 41–71.
14. Davide Landi, "'The Open Typology': Towards Socially Sustainable Architectural and Care Types." *Architecture_MPS 16*(1) (2019): 1–18.
15. Kevin Hetherington, *The Badlands of Modernity: Heterotopia and Social Ordering* (London: Routledge, 1997).
16. Landi, "Open Typology as Heterotopia: A Comparative Analysis between Gojikara Mura in Nagakute (Japan) and Humanitas in Deventer (Netherlands)," 41–71.
17. Martin Heidegger, *Poetry, Language, Thought* (New York: Harper and Row Publishers, 1971).
18. Wasserman, Sullivan, and Palermo, *Ethics and The Practice of Architecture*.
19. Steven Fesmire, *John Dewey and Moral Imagination. Pragmatism in Ethics* (Indianapolis: Indiana University Press, 2003)
20. Grahame Smith, *A Practical Introduction to Mental Health Ethics* (London: Routledge, 2017): 93.
21. Fesmire, *John Dewey and Moral Imagination. Pragmatism in Ethics*.
22. Smith, *A Practical Introduction to Mental Health Ethics*.
23. Curzer, Aristotle and the Virtues.
24. Smith, *A Practical Introduction to Mental Health Ethics*.
25. Ann Gallagher, "Dignity and Respect for Dignity – Two Key Health Professional Values: Implications for Nursing Practice," *Nursing Ethics 11*(6) (2004): 587–599.

26 Fesmire, *John Dewey and Moral Imagination. Pragmatism in Ethics.*
27 Smith, *A Practical Introduction to Mental Health Ethics*, 5.
28 Wasserman, Sullivan, and Palermo, *Ethics and The Practice of Architecture.*
29 Julienne Hanson, "Morphology And Design: Reconciling Intellect, Intuition, And Ethics In The Reflective Practice Of Architecture" (Proceedings of the 3rd International Space Syntax Symposium, Atlanta, GA, May 7–11, 2001).
30 Jane Collier, "The Art of Moral Imagination: Ethics in the Practice of Architecture," *Journal of Business Ethics 66* (2006): 307–317.
31 Illies and Ray, *Philosophy of Architecture*, 59.
32 Wasserman, Sullivan, and Palermo, *Ethics and The Practice of Architecture.*
33 Ariel Guersenzvaig, "Design and Ethics" (Lecture at ELISAVA – Barcelona School of Design and Engineering, Barcelona, Spain, March 7, 2018).
34 Nicholas Ray, ed., *Architecture and its Ethical Dilemmas* (London: Routledge, 2005).
35 Collier, "The Art of Moral Imagination: Ethics in the Practice of Architecture": 316.
36 Fesmire, *John Dewey and Moral Imagination. Pragmatism in Ethics.*
37 Fesmire, *John Dewey and Moral Imagination. Pragmatism in Ethics.*
38 Ray, ed., Architecture and its Ethical Dilemmas.
39 Neil Brenner, Peter Marcouse, and Margit Mayer, eds., *Cities for People, Not for Profit* (London: Routledge, 2012): 130.
40 Amanda Yates, "Mauri-Ora: Architecture, Indigeneity, and Immanence Ethics," *Architectural Theory Review* (2016): 261–275.
41 Smith, *A Practical Introduction to Mental Health Ethics.*
42 Martin Woods, "Nursing Ethics Education: Are We Really Delivering the Good (s)?" *Nursing Ethics 12*(-1) (2005): 5.
43 Mary C. Corley, Ptlene Minick, R.K. Elswick, and Mary Jacobs, "Nurse Moral Distress and Ethical Work Environment," *Nursing Ethics 12*(4) (2005): 381.
44 Katharine V. Smith and Nelda S. Godfrey, "Being a Good Nurse and Doing the Right Thing: a Qualitative Study," *Nursing Ethics 9*(3) (2002): 301.
45 Smith, *A Practical Introduction to Mental Health Ethics.*
46 Mary C. Corley, "Nurse Moral Distress: A Proposed Theory and Research Agenda," *Nursing Ethics 9*(6) (2002): 636.
47 Smith, *A Practical Introduction to Mental Health Ethics.*
48 Ray, ed., Architecture and its Ethical Dilemmas.
49 Wasserman, Sullivan, and Palermo, *Ethics and The Practice of Architecture.*
50 Smith, *A Practical Introduction to Mental Health Ethics.*
51 Wasserman, Sullivan, and Palermo, *Ethics and The Practice of Architecture.*
52 Smith, *A Practical Introduction to Mental Health Ethics.*
53 Ricky Burdett and Deyan Sudjic, eds., *The Endless City* (London: Phaidon, 2008).
54 Jane Jacobs, *The Death and the Life of the Great American Cities* (New York: Random House, 1961).
55 Richard Sennett, *Building and Dwelling. Ethics of the City* (London: Penguin Books, 2018).
56 Akcan, *Open Architecture: Migration, Citizenship, and the Urban Renewal of Berlin-Kreuzberg by IBA-1984/87.*
57 Rossi, The Architecture of the City.
58 Adam Himes, "The Embedded Politics of Types: Sedad Hakki and the Turkish House," *The Journal of Architecture 24*(6) (2019): 756–774.
59 Landi, "'The Open Typology': Towards Socially Sustainable Architectural and Care Types": 1–18.
60 Rudolf Senior Home "WELCOME TO RUDOLF SENIORS HOME!" (Speech, Rudolf Senior Home, Helsinki, Finland, June 25, 2018).
61 Designer interviewed by the author, Helsinki, Finland, June 23, 2018.
62 CityLab, "This Helsinki Suburb Is Offering Millennials Cheap Rent to Live in a Senior Center," CityLab, https://www.citylab.com/equity/2015/12/helsinki-laajasalo-millennials-senior-home-studio-rent/418134/ (Accessed April 12, 2018).
63 Manager interviewed by the author, Helsinki, Finland, June 25, 2018.
64 The Holding Project, "A Home That Fits - Experimental Housing Approaches," The Holding Project, https://www.theholdingproject.co.uk/single-post/2017/06/15/A-Home-That-Fits---experimental-housing-approaches (Accessed April 12, 2018).
65 Michael Dobbins, Alvar Alto, Aulis Blomstedt, Kaija Siren, Heikki Siren, Aarno Ruusuvuori and Reima Pietila, "The Achievement of Finnish Architecture: Social Responsibility and Architectural Integrity," *Perspecta 8* (1963): 3–36.
66 Manager interviewed by the author.
67 Manager interviewed by the author.
68 The Guardian, "Why Young People are Renting Rooms in a Helsinki Care Home," *The Guardian*, https://www.theguardian.com/society/2017/jun/21/young-people-renting-rooms-helsinki-care-home (Accessed April 12, 2018).

Ethics of open types

69 Eoghan Macguire, "Young People Given Cheap Rents in Finnish Seniors Home," *CNN*, https://edition.cnn.com/2016/01/21/europe/helsinki-seniors-home-oman-muotoinen-koti/index.html (Accessed April 12, 2018).
70 Designer interviewed by the author.
71 Manager interviewed by the author.
72 Rudolf Senior Home "WELCOME TO RUDOLF SENIORS HOME!"
73 Dobbins, Alto, Blomstedt, Siren, Siren, Ruusuvuori and Pietila, "The Achievement of Finnish Architecture: Social Responsibility and Architectural Integrity," 3–36.
74 Designer interviewed by the author.
75 Department of Housing and Building, Decree on Accessible Buildings, 2005, Ministry of the Environment, Helsinki.
76 Agi, "Mettereste il Nonno a Vivere con un Senzatetto? A Helsinki lo Fanno," https://www.agi.it/estero/helsinki_giovani_senzatetto_case_di_riposo_anziani_affitto-1901231/news/2017-06-26/ (Accessed April 12, 2018).
77 Department of Housing and Building, Decree on Accessible Buildings.
78 Designer interviewed by the author.
79 Resident interviewed by the author, Helsinki, Finland, June 25, 2018.
80 Resident interviewed by the author.
81 Professional Caregiver interviewed by the author, Helsinki, Finland, June 25, 2018.
82 Professional Caregiver interviewed by the author.
83 Resident interviewed by the author.
84 Manager interviewed by the author.
85 Professional Caregiver interviewed by the author.
86 Rudolf Senior Home "WELCOME TO RUDOLF SENIORS HOME!"
87 Manager interviewed by the author.
88 Resident interviewed by the author.
89 Professional Caregiver interviewed by the author.
90 Manager interviewed by the author.
91 Manager interviewed by the author.
92 Stories, "Why These Millennials Live in a Retirement Home," 2016, Stories, March 3, 2016, video, 3:08. https://www.youtube.com/watch?v=Xiofjk9rYAM (Accessed April 12, 2018).
93 Professional Caregiver interviewed by the author.
94 Resident interviewed by the author.
95 World Health Organisation (WHO), *Dementia. A Public Health Priority* (London: World Health Organization, 2012).
96 Resident interviewed by the author.
97 Manager interviewed by the author.
98 Resident interviewed by the author.
99 Professional Caregiver interviewed by the author.
100 Brenner, Marcouse, and Mayer, eds., *Cities for People, Not for Profit*.
101 Mohsen Mostafavi, ed., *The Ethics Of The Urban: The City And The Space Of The Political* (Zurich: Lars Muller Publishers, 2017).
102 Curzer, Aristotle and the Virtues.
103 Sennett, Building and Dwelling. Ethics of the City.
104 Sennett, Building and Dwelling. Ethics of the City.
105 Wasserman, Sullivan, and Palermo, *Ethics and The Practice of Architecture*.
106 Fesmire, *John Dewey and Moral Imagination. Pragmatism in Ethics*.
107 Curzer, Aristotle and the Virtues: 293.
108 Ray, ed., Architecture and its Ethical Dilemmas.

References

Agi. "Mettereste il Nonno a Vivere con un Senzatetto? A Helsinki lo Fanno." Agi. https://www.agi.it/estero/helsinki_giovani_senzatetto_case_di_riposo_anziani_affitto-1901231/news/2017-06-26/.
Akcan, Esra. 2018. *Open Architecture: Migration, Citizenship, and the Urban Renewal of Berlin-Kreuzberg by IBA-1984/87*. Basel: Birkhauser GmbH.
Alexander, Christopher. 1973. *Notes on the Synthesis of Form*. Cambridge, MA: Harvard University Press.
Ayalon, Liat. 2015. "Perception of Old Age and Ageing in the Continuing Care Retirement Community," *International Psychogeriatric 27*(4): 611–620.
Borasi, Giovanna and Mirko Zardini, eds. 2012. *Imperfect Health: the Medicalisation of Architecture*. Zurich: Lars Muller Publishers.
Burdett, Ricky and Sudjic, Deyan, eds. 2008. *The Endless City*. London: Phaidon.

Brenner, Neil, Marcouse Peter, and Margit Mayer, eds. 2012. *Cities for People, Not for Profit*. London: Routledge.
CityLab "This Helsinki Suburb Is Offering Millennials Cheap Rent to Live in a Senior Center." CityLab. https://www.citylab.com/equity/2015/12/helsinki-laajasalo-millennials-senior-home-studio-rent/418134/.
Collier, Jane. 2006. "The Art of Moral Imagination: Ethics in the Practice of Architecture." *Journal of Business Ethics 66*: 307–317.
Corley, Mary C. 2002. "Nurse Moral Distress: A Proposed Theory and Research Agenda." *Nursing Ethics 9*(6): 636.
Corley, Mary C., Minick Ptlene, Elswick R. K., and Mary Jacobs. 2005. "Nurse Moral Distress and Ethical Work Environment." *Nursing Ethics 12*(4): 381.
Curzer, Howard J. 2012. *Aristotle and the Virtues*. Oxford: Oxford University Press.
Department of Housing and Building. 2005. *Decree on Accessible Buildings*. Helsinki: Ministry of the Environment.
Design Stories from Helsinki. "Tackling Youth Homelessness with Design Experiments: A Home That Fits." https://www.muotoilutarinat.fi/en/project/a-home-that-fits/.
Dobbins, Michael, Alto Alvar, Blomstedt Aulis, Siren Kaija, Siren Heikki, Ruusuvuori Aarno and Reima Pietila. 1963. "The Achievement of Finnish Architecture: Social Responsibility and Architectural Integrity." *Perspecta 8*: 3–36.
European Union, ed. 2015. *The 2015 Ageing Report. Economic and Budgetary Projections for the 27 EU Member States (2010–2060)*. Brussels: European Commission.
Fesmire, Steven. 2013. *John Dewey and Moral Imagination. Pragmatism in Ethics*. Indianapolis: Indiana University Press.
Gallagher, Ann. 2004."Dignity and Respect for Dignity – Two Key Health Professional Values: Implications for Nursing Practice." *Nursing Ethics 11*(6): 587–599.
Guersenzvaig, Ariel. 2018. "Design and Ethics." Lecture at ELISAVA – Barcelona School of Design and Engineering, Barcelona, Spain, March 7.
Hanson, Julienne. 2001. "Morphology And Design: Reconciling Intellect, Intuition, and Ethics in the Reflective Practice Of Architecture." Proceedings of the 3rd International Space Syntax Symposium, Atlanta, GA, May 7–11.
Harries, Karsten. 1997. *The Ethical Function of Architecture*. Cambridge, MA: MIT Press.
Heidegger, Martin. 1971. *Poetry, Language, Thought*. New York: Harper and Row Publishers.
Hetherington, Kevin. 1997. *The Badlands of Modernity: Heterotopia and Social Ordering*. London: Routledge.
Himes, Adam. 2019. "The Embedded Politics of Types: Sedad Hakki and the Turkish House." *The Journal of Architecture 24*(6): 756–774.
Illies, Christian, and Nicholas Ray. 2014. *Philosophy of Architecture*. Cambridge: Cambridge Architectural Press.
Jacobs, Jane. 1961. *The Death and the Life of the Great American Cities*. New York: Random House.
Landi, Davide. 2017. "Towards New Architectural and Urban Typologies: Thinking, Making and Living as a Post Occupancy Evaluation Method." *Conscious Cities Journal 3*.
Landi, Davide. 2018. "Open Typology as Heterotopia: A Comparative Analysis between Gojikara Mura in Nagakute (Japan) and Humanitas in Deventer (Netherlands)." *The International Journal of Design in Society 12*(3): 41–71.
Landi, Davide. 2019. "'The Open Typology': Towards Socially Sustainable Architectural and Care Types." *Architecture_MPS 16*(1): 1–18.
Levy, Becca R. 2017. "Age-Stereotype Paradox: Opportunity for Social Change." *The Gerontologist 57*(S2): 118–126.
Macguire, Eoghan. "Young People Given Cheap Rents in Finnish Seniors Home." *CNN*. https://edition.cnn.com/2016/01/21/europe/helsinki-seniors-home-oman-muotoinen-koti/index.html.
Markus, Thomas A. 1993. *Building and Power*. London: Routledge.
Mostafavi, Mohsen. 2017. *The Ethics of the Urban: the City and the Space of the Political*. Zurich: Lars Muller Publishers.
Myerson, Jeremy, ed. 2017. *New Old*. London: Design Museum.
Ray, Nicholas, ed. 2005. *Architecture and its Ethical Dilemmas*. London: Routledge.
Rossi, Aldo. 1982. *The Architecture of the City*. Cambridge, MA: MIT Press.
Royal Institute of the British Architects (RIBA). 1963. *Plan of Work for Design Team Operation*. London: RIBA.
Rudolf Senior Home. 2018. "WELCOME TO RUDOLF SENIORS HOME!." Speech, Rudolf Senior Home, Helsinki, Finland, June 25.
Sennett, Richard. 2012. *Together. The Rituals, Pleasure and Politics of Cooperation*. London: Penguin Books.
Sennett, Richard. 2018. *Building and Dwelling. Ethics of the City*. London: Penguin Books.
Smith, Grahame. 2017. *A Practical Introduction to Mental Health Ethics*. London: Routledge.
Smith, Katharine V., and Nelda S. Godfrey. 2002. "Being a Good Nurse and Doing the Right Thing: a Qualitative Study." *Nursing Ethics 9*(3): 301.
Stories. "Why These Millennials Live in a Retirement Home." 2016. Stories, March 3, 2016. Video, 3:08. https://www.youtube.com/watch?v=Xiofjk9rYAM.

The Guardian. "Why Young People are Renting Rooms in a Helsinki Care Home." *The Guardian*. https://www.theguardian.com/society/2017/jun/21/young-people-renting-rooms-helsinki-care-home.

The Holding Project. "A Home That Fits – Experimental Housing Approaches." The Holding Project. https://www.theholdingproject.co.uk/single-post/2017/06/15/A-Home-That-Fits---experimental-housing-approaches.

Wasserman, Barry, Sullivan Patrick J., and Gregory Palermo. 2008. *Ethics and The Practice of Architecture*. New York: John Wiley and Sons, Inc.

Woods, Martin. 2005. "Nursing Ethics Education: Are We Really Delivering the Good (s)?" *Nursing Ethics 12*(1): 5.

World Health Organisation (WHO). 2012. *Dementia. A Public Health Priority*. London: World Health Organization.

Yates, Amanda. 2016. "Mauri-Ora: Architecture, Indigeneity, and Immanence Ethics." *Architectural Theory Review 21*(2): 261–275.

Chapter 23

The Age of Ecology in the UK

Penny Lewis

The Age of Ecology (1968–1974) was short-lived; it began with the post-war boom and ended with the adoption of the environmentalism into the mainstream in the mid-1970s.[1] The relationship between architecture, ecology and counterculture in this period is a thriving area of scholarship in the US; in the UK, it has attracted less attention despite the fact that Reyner Banham, John McHale and The Independent Group are seen as key players in the early discourse (Vidler 2008). This chapter speculates on the links between those members of the Independent Group concerned with architecture and the discussion on ecology and urban theory.

One of the first mentions of ecology among post-war British architects appears in Alison and Peter Smithson's memo in preparation for the 1956 CIAM meeting in Dubrovnik. It sets out the task:

> to formulate some way of thinking which would consider the problem of urbanism as an entity, as a unique form of human association at a particular time and in a particular place. This might be termed the ecological concept of urbanism,
>
> (Yale School of Architecture 2006)

Drawing on the ideas of the ecology movement and the thinking of individuals such as German émigré, EA Gutkind, the Smithsons used the term 'ecology' to capture the organic nature of their evolving approach to urbanism. Their language was reminiscent of the vitalist texts produced by 19th-century ecologists such as Ernst Haeckel,[2] it

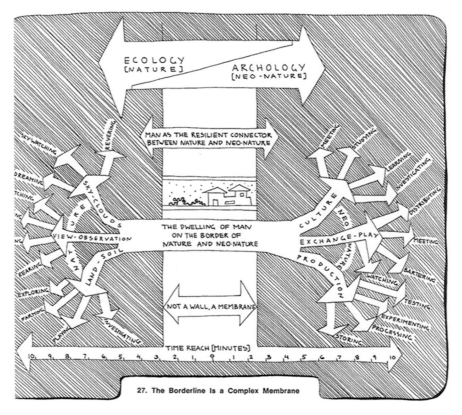

Figure 23.1 Image taken by author from Arcology – the City in the Image of Man
Published by MIT Press, New York (1970)

provided a new way of describing modern urban life using biological analogies to capture the complexity of post-war social relations.

This tendency to draw on biological analogies to describe architectural forms and processes was not new,[3] but the term ecology is used in this post-war period to express a very specific meaning in relation to urban design. These ecological approaches to urban questions emerged in the late 1960s on the back of a loss of belief in progress recorded by Gideon.[4] By the mid-1970s, the high-water mark of the so-called Age of Ecology, the ecology movement was associated with anti-car and anti-development campaigns,[5] while ecological thought started to make an impact on both the architectural profession and the schools.[6]

Ecology is an interesting discipline because it sits on the boundary of science and society; it is a science addressing the inter-relationship of living creatures, and as such, "it has never been far removed from the messy, shifting, hurly-burly world of human values" (Worster 1992, XIV). Any crossover between biological and social thought or tendencies to use naturalistic metaphors to describe social patterns of behaviour provide fertile ground for ecological thinking (Rampley 2017). While nature has historically been understood as something to be either tamed or emulated (MacNaugthen and

Urry 1998) with the emergence of ecology as a Popular idea in the post-war period, we are encouraged to see life in terms of cycles of natality, growth, reproduction, death and entropy. If Enlightenment thought gave rise to the idea of public life as something that worked against natural cycles and human biology (Arendt 1998), post-war ecology represented an early attempt to recalibrate our understanding of human activity and social life.

In the process of developing a new approach to the discipline, post-war architectural thinkers explored a range of ideas including ecological and systems theory. The conventional history of these two decades tends to focus on the debate between modernism and historicism or functionalism and formalism, but Jencks suggests that we can see this period as one in which the influence of ecological thinking was high (or even pulsating) (Gugger and Macaes Costa 2014). 'Systems theory' a cultural outlook in which social questions and science were both understood as 'networked, system-based, and feedback driven'[7] (Martin 2003) also made an impact on the architectural imagination. Correspondence between Nobert Weiner, the father of cybernetics, and Sigfried Giedion, is cited as evidence of the strong intellectual parallels between an interest in computer technology and networks and the need for a broader or holistic approach to the natural and built environment.[8]

In 2008, Vidler's lecture 'Whatever happened to ecology?' attempted to explain why environmentalism (and ecology in particular) captured the imagination of the schools and the professional bodies in the US and the UK in the 1960s.[9] He looks at the work of Buckminster Fuller and his influence on Reyner Banham and John McHale, both associated with the Independent Group. According to Vidler, the reason ecology dropped off the agenda was because the profession became embroiled in an internecine debate about the tension between form and function that would evolve into the discourse on post-modernism. There is some truth in this analysis – but the limitation of this understanding is that it ignores the tensions within ecological thought.[10]

Alison and Peter Smithson's CIAM 1956 memo built on the discussion of 'habitat' (an ecological concept) that emerged in the CIAM meeting at Doorn in 1954. This manifesto-like 'instruction to groups,' written on a single page of foolscap, suggested that CIAM needed "some way of thinking which would consider each problem of urbanism as an entity, as a unique form of 'human association' at a particular time and in a particular place" (Architecture 2006). They argued that: "Urbanism considered and developed in the terms of the Charte d'Athenes tends to produce 'towns' in which *vital* human association are inadequately expressed." They rejected the analytical method favoured by CIAM which relied on technical data to inform urban design decisions and supported an appreciation of context that involved comprehension of human association and an appreciation of every community as a 'particular total complex.' This new approach was called an 'ecological concept of urbanism.'[11]

Their aspiration was to develop a new modernist language that transcended the narrow rhetoric and instrumentalism of the Athens Charter, their interest in sociology, their enthusiasm for the imagery of mass consumerism and their interest in the ordinary and everyday objects and aspects of life is well-recorded. Their interest in the environment in the later part of their careers is evident in *Climate Register: Four Works* by Alison and Peter Smithson (Climate Register: Four Works 1994) which looks at 'the environmental resonances' in their earlier work, but this idea of ecological urbanism is worth deconstructing.[12]

Erwin Anton Gutkind, a Berlin Jew, resident in London between 1935 and 1956, was particularly influential in the development of the thinking of the Independent Group (Avermaete 2003). Gutkind provided a direct relationship to the first generation of European Modernists. He had worked for the Berlin building firm, Gruppe Nord for ten years on the design of German Siedlung in the 1920s and was a member of the so-called 'Ring of Ten' (Taut brothers, Hans Poelzig, Eric Mendelsohn, Ludwig Hilberseimer, Otto Bartning, Martin Wagner and Walter Gropius) who met at Mies van der Rohe offices. In 1933, Gutkind fled Berlin for Paris, then London; in 1956, he moved to the University of Pennsylvania until his death in 1968. While, in London, Gutkind published a number of planning books; *Creative Demobilisation* (1943), *Revolution of Environment* (1946), *Our World from the Air* (1952), *Man and his Environment* (1952), *Community and Environment* (1953), *A Discourse on Social Ecology* (1953) and *The Expanded Environment* (1953). He came into close contact with the MARS group, the English branch of the CIAM in the mid-1950s.

In a letter to the group from 1953, he wrote:

> I am glad that at long last the Athens Charter has been recognised as what it is in reality, namely an utterly useless and nonsensical salad of meaningless phrases. It has nothing whatever to do with LIFE, for it neglects the greatest reality, the human beings whom it degrades to functions of the Functions on which it purports Town Planning to consist.[13]
>
> (Avermaete 2003, 255)

The book that accompanied the letter *The Expanded Environment* (1953) explores dwellings and landscapes and tries to identify structural principles or patterns in these settlements. He was particularly interested in the street as a historic form that guides development and as the realm of communal or shared activity.

At the Princeton Conference (1955), Gutkind argued; "something like a new discipline is needed, which for want of a better name might be called 'social ecology.'" This attempt to provide an intellectual framework for thinking about man and the environment draws on many disciplines. In particular, the Birdseye view, or 'synoptic' approach allows for this new unity of thought, he argued.[14] It "demands the appreciation of the whole nexus of relations in every detail and of the creative potentiality of every detail within the whole." This aspiration for a holistic or total approach was also echoed in the work of his contemporary Moholy-Nagy who argued that the main lesson we can learn from animal ecology is the need for studying human communities as a whole and in their total relationship to their physical and social environment (Anker 2005).

Gutkind's adoption of ecology appears to be driven by an aspiration to create new institutional frameworks that could prevent the reoccurrence of war rather than more conventional environmental concerns about resource depletion or overpopulation. In *Creative Demobilisation* (1943), he argued that a new generation needed to address problems in a new way. Ostensibly, the book is about planning, but the argument is that the struggle against totalitarianism and for democracy must be underpinned by a global outlook. "The shrinking of the world is a matter of primary importance," he writes:

> spiritual and material intercourse is increasing in time and space on an unprecedented scale. The outcome of this forces us to face the problem of a world administered as one coherent unit and to make the best use of the resources which Nature and Man have put at our disposal... Domestic reconstruction is the fundamental counterpart of international cooperation and vice versa.
>
> (Gutkind 1943, ix)

For the young members of CIAM, an interest in a holistic approach to planning was particularly compelling. According to Tafuri:

> At the start of the 1960s came a widespread dissatisfaction with the traditional instruments for the control and shaping of the environment... architects reacted against the new limits imposed by administrative bodies in charge of the various sectoral plans... To broaden the scope and capacity of architecture to deal with the problem of the total environment seemed to call for going well beyond the principles inherited from CIAM.
>
> (Tafuri and Co 1976, 363)

Herbert Read's used the foreword to Gutkind's *Creative Demobilisation* to highlight the tension associated within the idea of a total environment.

> Planning has become the catchword of our age; not merely, one suspects, because it is a necessity inherent in our historical situation, but also because it offers many people a welcome escape from the ambiguities of political action. It is the 'scientific' attitude in social relations, and to be scientific in our days is as good as being moral.
>
> (1943)

For Read, freedom should drive progress and morality rather than science and technocracy, and he cautions against planning that imagines that people can be 'handled like docile cattle.' Both Read and Gutkind's are keen to stress that "a social relationship cannot be set up at the command of some authority or other, however enthusiastic it might be. It must grow" (Gutkind 1943, xiii).

The relationship between planning, instrumental thought and the complexity of social life underpins the discussion on post-war reconstruction. The tension between planning and the spontaneous social interaction of an urban population is evident in many forms. Gutkind tended towards a psychological approach arguing that mankind was estranged from nature in a way that earlier societies based on local settlements, local materials and vernacular techniques were not. "In these settlements the I-Thou relationship between man and nature is reciprocal. In modern society nature becomes it and is objectified," wrote Gutkind (Avermaete 2003). This aspect of Gutkind's thought can be seen in the Team X memorandum and the later work of the Smithsons; despite the fact that they looked to sociology as much as psychology for guidance. Ecology suggests a more complex and meaningful set of relations than the simple set of procedures associated with instrumental planning.

It is this tension which gave rise to the idea of planning as an organic or ecological rather than technical process and this tension which led to a shift in the architectural imagination to social questions. It may explain the manner in which ecology slipped off the architectural agenda after 1974 (Vidler 2008). While Vidler might be right about the introverted nature of architectural discourse in the 1960s, it seems far more likely that ecology fell off the architectural agenda because it was not able to address the social contradictions of the time.

The tensions are played out more explicitly in the US in Jane Jacobs' highly influential book *The Death and Life of the Great American City* (1961). Although Jacobs is not often described as an ecologist, in the foreword to the 1971 edition, Jacobs describes how, when writing the book, it became clear to her she was engaged in the study of the ecology of cities.

> By *city ecology* I mean something different from, but similar to natural ecology. A natural ecosystem is defined as composed of physical, chemical and biological processes active within the space-time unit of any magnitude...A city ecosystem is composed of physical, economic, ethical processes active at any given time within a city and its close dependences.[15]
>
> (Jacobs 1992)

Jacobs is not the first person to use the expression ecology to describe social activity rather than natural systems, but the emphasis she places on processes rather than things is reflected in today's ecological discourse. She writes: "It does not do to focus on things and to expect them to explain much in themselves, processes are always at the essence" (Jacobs, 1992, 1).

For Jacobs, there are two eco-systems: one created by nature and the other by human beings. Their common features are that they both require diversity to be sustained, that diversity develops organically over time and that it consists of components that are 'interdependent' in 'complex' ways. Some of these components can be overlooked but are vital to the whole. According to Jacobs, the more there are niches for diversity of life and livelihoods, in either system, the greater its carrying capacity for life. These diverse activities allow for mutation and hybridity. Jacobs attempts to strike a balance between an appreciation that natural and human eco-system are fragile and easily disrupted and that stability is an illusion, while at the same time capturing the resilience of human beings and natural systems.

John McHale, who wrote two books in the early 1970s on these issues, tried to resolve these contradictions. Like Buckminster Fuller, McHale believed in new technology but with the caveat that only a global institutional framework that took power away from the individual (and the nation) could deliver this realm of freedom. At the same time, he makes the point that people interested in systems tend to undermine the possibility of the individual autonomous action.[16] In this context, McHale develops the idea of 'Man Plus,' the natural human with scientific elements that improve his capacity to deal with the conventional problems thrown up by nature. "Until recently our technological systems were hardly considered as an organic part of ecology; hence little attention was given to this aspect of their function" (McHale, 1970, 246). For McHale saw a continuity between the romanticism in Shelley's Frankenstein, the concern about the automation of human life expressed by the Deutche Werkbund and the Modern Movement and argued for a new relationship to nature in which human innovation and technology was embraced as part of the natural condition rather than being understood as a source of alienation.

Reyner Banham was also forced to address these tensions. The Utopie Group's intervention at Banham's Aspen Design Conference in 1970 may provide one of the clearest explanations for the eclipse of ecology in architecture. In the open letter held in the Getty Archives, Baudrillard lays out his critique on behalf of the 'French group' Utopie in a robust polemic in which Banham is not spared (Spencer 2016). "Professor Banham has clearly shown the moral and technical limits and the illusion of Design and Environment practice," says Baudrillard. For Baudrillard, the 'Environment' is a myth, and environmentalists are 'boy-scout idealist' with a naïve commitment to a 'hygienic nature.' Utopie described the conference's approach as a hoax in which architects as 'acting like medicine men' pretending that they could cure social ills by building. For the radicals in Utopie, the international establishment were using the environmental question in order to naturalise or normalise the economic conditions and to marginalize discussions on social inequality. "It is not by accident that all Western governments have now... launched this new crusade and try to mobilise people's conscience by shouting apocalypse."[17]

For Utopie, 'Design and Environment' was not an idea thrown up spontaneously, but an idea generated to coincide with an economic and political crisis. After Aspen, Banham had planned to take on the role of director of undergraduate studies at University College London. Llewellyn Davies had renamed the architecture and planning department the School of Environmental Studies. Banham created a foundation course for a Master's in professional environmental disciplines. A flexible curriculum with courses relating to the man-made environment would address a range of environmental questions including architecture. Banham hoped to recruit community activists who wanted to develop their understanding of the political and institutional systems behind local social inequality and environmental damage. However, the relationship between the environmental and social agenda was not without its problems. The left environmentalist, Murray Bookchin, argued that ecological problems had, through their adoption by mainstream politicians, become 'de-socialised'; "Be they Ethiopian children or corporate barons, all people are held to be equally culpable in producing the current ecological problems" he explained (Bookchin 2005).

In conclusion, it appears that the ecological imagination in the 1950s and 1960s played some role in the development of thinking about the city and the relationship between planning, authority and the people. This discourse was cut short and placed in the back burner because it was understood as being in opposition to questions of social justice. Ecological thinking remained low key for about three decades and then re-emerged in the wake of the discourse on sustainability towards the end of the millennium. However, some of the ideas and language developed in the age of ecology continue to influence the way in which we discuss building and environment today. In particular, the early discussion about networks and systems has been developed by leading ecological exponents who argue that human society should be seen as one part of the web of natural relations nature (Lovelock 1988) and that human knowledge' as something that is fluid, operating beyond the rigid categories of classical science. Ecological thought relies on "dialectical, open-ended terms to characterise the ebbs and flows, nuances and subtleties and the ambiguities of environmental politics" (Jamison, 2001). Perhaps, the most important insight from the exploration of ecology in the UK in the 1950s–1970s is not simply to build a historiography of green ideas but to improve our understanding of the discourse on modern planning and post-war reconstruction and to understand how something as intangible as the question of political accountability shaped the architectural imagination.

Notes

1. Jamison in *The Making of Green Knowledge* (2001) maps these high points in ecological thinking; the Age of Ecology 1968–1974 emerged with post-war expansion and consumerism and ended with US Government sponsorship of Earth Day.
2. Haeckel's books were translated into English by the Rationalist Press Association and sold for two shillings (Bramwell 1989) and at the end of the 19th century were as popular as the works of Darwin and Marx. Haeckel coined the term ecology in 1866 in *Generelle Morphologie*, a thesis on the way that biological entities operate within systems (Haeckel 1866). In the early part of the 20th century, Haeckel joined with others to form the Monist League and linked his biological research to political, social and spiritual questions and a critique of Cartesian thought. He argued that standard dichotomies of rational thought, such as 'mind versus matter,' were unhelpful in understanding complex systems and relationships and that we should look at things holistically. Monism emerged as a framework to understand the world in terms of one single reality linked to a singular vital life force; Lukács described it as 'religious atheism' (Lukács 1980) (Proctor 2006, 148).
3. Forty's overview of the changing attitudes to nature in architectural thought outlines shifts in thinking about art and nature since the Enlightenment (Forty 2000). His schema begins not with Kant but with Johann Wolfgang von Goethe (1749–1832) and his understanding of art (and architecture) as 'second nature.' For Goethe, the study of anatomy and plant morphology guided the artist to an approach that transcends the mechanistic qualities of the natural sciences. He argued that architecture was animated by the vital forces of mankind (Forty 2000). Early proponents of modernism tended to reject nature as a source of formal or material expression. Forty describes how nature disappeared from the architectural discourse with the onset of modernism and only to reappear in the late 1960s.
4. At the end of the 1960s, the critiques of modernisation and the Modern Movement started to gain momentum. One important shift underpinning the development of critical approaches to conventional ideas of Modernist urbanism was a lack of enthusiasm for the idea of progress. Sigfried Giedion reported in the introduction to Mechanisation Takes Command (1948): "Now after the Second World War, it may well be that there are no people left, however remote, who have not lost their faith in progress. Men have become frightened by progress, changed from a hope into a menace. Faith in progress lies on the scrap heap, along with many other devaluated symbols" (Giedion 1948, 715)
5. In Peter Hall's *Cities of Tomorrow*, 1994 Blackwell Publishers, Oxford, UK and Cambridge USA page 312. Hall writes that, in Stockholm, despite the fact that the ecological movement was 'at its height' in the early 1970s, a 'liberal totalitarian' approach to city planning prevailed while the critics of large-scale urban redevelopment programmes were unable to win the argument confronted by the efficiency of the city's public transport and road systems.
6. At Berkeley and other schools in the US, 'environmental studies' had replaced conventional names at several schools including Berkeley (Ockman, 2012).

7 Systems theory was developed after Second World War from a new understanding of society and science in which were both understood to be 'networked, system-based, and feedback driven' (Martin 2003, 8). Correspondence between Nobert Weiner, the father of cybernetics, and Siegfried Gideon, the leading modernist historian suggests that there was a strong correlation between architectural thought and these new attempts to make sense of the new consumer society. Systems theory remained popular among some architects in the 1970s and 1980s, given new life by scholars like Christopher Alexander and his colleagues at Berkeley, who linked design methodology to taxonomic studies of building types (Alexander, Ishikawa and Silverstein 1977).
8 See Martin, R., The Organisational Complex, 2003.
9 See Lewis, P., The impact of ecological thought on architectural theory, October 2019. In an interview with Charles Jencks, June 2014, Jencks describes the Smithson's opposition to his attempts to criticise the Modern Movement in the 1970s.
10 Forty identifies two key influences on architectural thought following 1968. He argues that nature was reintroduced into the discourse (following its rejection by the Modern Movement) through the philosophy of the Frankfurt School on the one hand and the green movement epitomized by Rachel Carson on the other. The green movement was not only concerned about pollution, but it gave shape to an anxiety about technology (Forty 2000). Forty identifies *The Dialectics of the Enlightenment* (1947) by Adorno and Horkheimer as significant in that it is concerned primarily with man's exploitation of nature rather than man's exploitation of each other (Horkheimer 1997). 'Seen in these terms, the critique of capitalism shifted from the social relations of production to the relations between human beings and nature' (Forty 2000, 239).
11 "It was decided therefore to try to formulate some way of thinking which would consider the problem of urbanism as an entity, as a unique form of human association at a particular time and in a particular place. This might be termed the ecological concept of urbanism, a concept of obvious value when we are dealing with the problems of 'habitat' said the group…It was this ecological concept which also led us to reject the existing commission system which we considered as another analytical method which is not proving fruitful," wrote the Smithsons (Architecture 2006).
12 *Climate Register: Four Works by Alison and Peter Smithson* (Climate Register: Four Works 1994).
13 Letter from E.A. Gutkind to MARS group, in: CIAM, gta/ETH, (42-JT-13-347), s.d. in Avermaete (2003, 255).
14 The importance of the synoptic view for urban thinking in this period is explored by A Vidler in The scenes of the Streets and Other Essays, 2011, Vidler, A., The Monicelli Press, New York.
15 Jacobs, J., 1961. *The Death and LIfe of the Great Amercian City*. London: Jonathan Cape.
16 McHale (1922–1978) was an artist, graphic designer to sociologist, futurist and critic. He designed several exhibitions for the ICA during the Independent Group's lifespan and pioneered some of the ideas about the significant of the image and about the plurality in forms of modern representation that was taken up by the Post-Modernists. In the early 1960s, he had joined Fuller at the Southern Illinois University and becomes what is known as a 'techno-utopian.' While working with Fuller, he became increasingly interested in the world of science and the possibility of speculating on the future. In 1970, he published *The Ecological Context* in which he argues that humanity has reached a point where its potential to disrupt the global eco-system is significant, and yet, at the same time, the knowledge and technology that exits allows humankind to develop strategies that can deal with a complex global system (J. McHale 1970, 97). McHale was fascinated by science and the natural world, but pessimistic about the possibility of social progress and political emancipation. He recognised the tendency to view technology as a substitute for social progress and change; he recorded a shift in US society from a commitment to political and economic action to 'a belief in the inexorable law of scientific progress' (McHale, 1970).
17 Open Letter, Utopie, Aspen 1970 in the Banham collection, Getty Archives, LA. Accessed January 2017.

References

Alexander, C., S. Ishikawa, and M. Silverstein. 1977. *The Pattern Language*. Oxford: Oxford University Press.
Anker, P. 2005. "The Bauhaus of Nature". *Modernism/Modernity* 12, 229–251.
Arendt, H. 1998. *The Human Condition*. Chicago, IL: University of Chicago Press.
Avermaete, T. 2003. "Team 10: between Modernity and the Everyday." *Sociology, Production and the City*, 237–282.
Bookchin, M. 2005. *The Ecology of Freedom*. Chico, CA: AK Press.
Bramwell, Anna. 1989. *Ecology in the Twentieth Century: A History*. New Haven, CT: Yale University Press.
Forty, A. 2000. *Words and Buildings*. London: Thames and Hudson.
Giedion, Sigfried. 1948. *Mechanisation Takes Command: A Contribution to an Anonymous History*. 1975 Edition. New York and London: W.W. Norton and Co.
Gugger, Harry, and Macaes Costa. 2014. "Ecology." *San Rocco* (10), 32–40.

Gutkind, A.E. 1943. *Creative Demobilisation*. London: K PAUL, Trench, Trubner and Co.
Gutkind, E.A. 1953. *The Expanded Environment*. London: Freedom Press.
Haeckel. E 1866. *Generelle Morphologie der Organismen* Vols I and II, Berlin: Georg Reimer.
———. 2000. *Kunstformen der Natur: Art Forms of Nature 1899*. London: Dover Pictorial Archive.
Horkheimer, Adorno. 1997. *Dialectics of Enlightenment (1944)*. London and New York: Verso.
Jacobs, J. 1961. *The Death and Life of Great American Cities*. London: Jonathan Cape.
Jamison, A. 2001. *The Making of Green Knowledge: Environmental Politics and Cultural Transformation*. Cambridge: Cambridge University Press.
Jencks, C. 1971. *Architecture 2000 and Beyond*. London: Academy Publications.
Kitnick, A. (Ed.). 2011. *The Expendable Reader*. New York: GSAPP Sourcebooks.
Lewis, P. 2019. "The Impact of Ecological thought on Architectural Theory Phd thesis." Robert Gordon University, October 2019.
Lovelock, J. 1988. *Ages of Gaia*. Oxford: Oxford University Press.
Lukács, G. 1980. *The Destruction of Reason*. Brecon: The Merlin Press.
MacNaugthen, P., and Urry, J. 1998. *Contested Natures*. London; Thousand Oaks, CA; New Delhi: Sage.
Martin, Reinhold. 2003. *The Organisational Complex*. Cambridge: MIT Press.
McHale, J. 1969. *The Future of the Future*. New York: George Braziller.
———. 1970. *The Ecological Context*. New York: G. Braziller.
Moholy-Nagy, S. 1971. *Experiment in Totality*. MIT Press
Ockman, Joan. 2012. *Architecture School: Three Centuries of Educating Architects in North America*. Cambridge, MA: MIT Press.
Proctor, Robert. 2006. " Architecture from the Cell-soul: René Binet and Ernst." *The Journal of Architecture* 11(4), pp. 407–424.
Rampley, M. 2017. *The Seductions of Darwin*. Pennsylvania: Penn State University Press.
Rappaport, N. 2005. *Team 10: Utopia of the Present*. Rotterdam: NAI and TU Delft.
Salter, P. 1994. *Climate Register: Four works by Alison and Peter Smithson*. London: AA.
Spencer, D. 2016. *Neoliberalism and Affect: Architecture and the Patterning of Experience*. London: Bloomsbury.
Tafuri, Manfredo, and Francesco Dal Co. 1976. *Modern Architecture 1*. Milan: Electa.
Vidler, A. 2008. *Whatever Happened to Ecology? Technology and Sustainability from Banham to Today Lecture Syracuse University*. 12 November. Accessed August 21, 2016. https://www.youtube.com/watch?v=1UA0N4huxlw.
Worster, D. 1992. *Nature's Economy: A History of Ecological Ideas*. Cambridge: Cambridge University Press.
Yale School of Architecture. 2006. "Team 10 (Exhbition catalogue)." New Haven, CT: Yale.

Chapter 24

Opinions – or, from dialogue to conversation

Teresa Stoppani

Architectural discourse has often appropriated the dialogical construct to introduce and promote new ideas that would otherwise be uneasily accepted or polemically rejected. The dialectical dialogue is thus scripted – i.e. designed – from the onset, with a precise outcome in mind, as in a reverse whodunnit in which the reader/spectator always already knows who the culprit is. Part of the pleasure in the unfolding of the dialogue – often presented as a confrontation – is the witnessing of the dexterity (and triumph) of the argumentative mastermind that opposes the erring or architecturally mistaken one. In this narrative performance, the architect-writer is scriptwriter, editor, director, main actor, set designer, etc., and the proposed synthesis is already clear from the beginning. The pleasure lies in the argumentation, in the text, in the script and in the construction of the dialogue as "architectural project" – by definition unfinished and to be completed (and altered) only by inhabitation, use, weathering. So, perhaps, a dialogue in architecture is never resolutive, but it is used to open up and to inhabit contradiction. Only then can the audience/witness-turned-(potential)-inhabitant enter the conversation.

More recent forms of dialogue refuse a predefined oppositional scheme and take the form of the conversation, the interview, the debate, to produce a collaborative construction of ideas and positions. Here, authorship and originality dissipate – if the process of dissipation is associated to the etymology of *dissipare*, as the act of throwing widely apart, scattering. Authorship and originality are thus distributed. If we instead embrace the more recent meaning of the term, of dissipation as a disappearance, we could infer that the dissipation of authorship and originality is never fully achieved, never complete. Things and ideas that dis-appear can, and indeed do, appear again. They re-surface – transformed perhaps, perhaps improved.

Embedded authorship, in the sense of momentarily disappeared or concealed, is more complex, and perhaps more satisfying than a shared one: because its origins are present but no longer traceable, and something new becomes possible, perhaps unexpectedly.

Oscillating between a distributed and a disguised authorship, the construction of a non-dialectical dialogue in architecture is itself a project: it negotiates and produces a project that does not aim to fulfil a predefined solution or to achieve a satisfactory synthesis. Its project opens up the possibility of the new as an "other" original that both embraces and negates the given one (the predefined solution) and preempts its own possibility to produce a synthesis. Like the contemporary architectural project, the conversation *in* architecture "makes space," opening up and enacting relations with architecture's pasts and presents. It becomes the locus of the project.

In the more structured dialogical modality of the interview, it is usually the interviewer that puts forward topics and argument, plotting fixed points and parameters that are there to be adhered to, or transgressed. It is instead the "main character" – the interviewee – that, thanks to the asymmetry of the structured exchange, is offered the space to elaborate, indulge perhaps in details and in the anecdotal and even undo the thesis. This is skiing *en piste*. If the city better or otherwise reveals itself to the transversal transgressions of the skateboarder, as Ian Borden has shown us, and the risk of the project – urban, metropolitan, territorial – requires the dexterity of Rem Koolhaas's surfer on the waves, able to turn external forces to his advantage, the dialogue as interview triggers elaboration and virtuosity, but only as long as one plays within the tracks of the pre-disposed *piste*.

Further complications occur when voices multiply, and the dialogue becomes a *con*-versation (but not a convergence) of different interlocutors. No longer a dialectical exchange aimed at achieving a resolution or more often simply aimed at illustrating a resolution; no more the asymmetrical and "guided" argumentation of the interview; the conversation defines itself in its making.

In architecture, the dialogue as conversation is in itself a project, independently of its topic, as a process that belongs to, and belongs with, the design process: conversation as con-vergence towards a centre that does not exist, or that, starting as a given, is taken apart and dis-located as the exchanges evolve, accumulate, dis-agree and trans-mutate. There is no intent to find or propose resolutions here; there is instead the momentary con-vergence and intersection of otherwise perhaps impossible encounters. Undone, the dialogue, now plural, is no longer a dialectical project. Open to, and opening up, possibilities, it can move on only as "project." Here, there is a possible way of "making theory" in architecture – or, better, a theory *from* architecture, rather than *of* architecture.

The form of the dialogue as a moment of dissipation – as both distribution and momentary disappearance – of opposing positions, enables the setting in motion of a more complex and ambiguous role-playing. Far from synthesis, the dialogue suspends to enable a new space. If synthesis there is here, it can only be the occasional and provisional one produced by the project and its representations. This suspension, far from failure or irresolution, is a way to open up to the possibility of change and innovation, or, as Sanford Kwinter puts it, the "novelty."

In *Architectures of Time* (2001), Kwinter offers a critical guide to the modern history of time, observing how 'the demise of the concept of absolute time' and of the classical notion of space as a fixed background against which things occur have led to field theory.[1] In the book, he discusses the shift occurred in the 20th century, and the difficulties of the modern mind with "time's relentless fluidity [and] irreducible materiality, that the modern mind finds so impossible – or repellent – to think".[2] For Kwinter:

> Time always expresses itself by producing, or more precisely, by drawing matter into a process of *becoming-ever-different*, and to the product of this becoming-ever-different – to this inbuilt wildness we have given the name novelty.[3] …novelty is simply a modality, a vehicle, by or through which something new appears in the world. It is that ever fresh endowment that affirms a radical incommensurability between what happens at any given instant and what follows. What has made it a problem for thought … is the way it is seen to introduce a corrupting element or impure principle into the pristine and already full world of "Creation". The offending element here is no other than the principle of change…. All change is change over time; no novelty appears without becoming, and no becoming without novelty.[4]

Novelty as "corrupting element" and "principle of change" that triggers innovation and transformation is presented through a dialogue by Giovanni Battista Piranesi in his *Opinions on Architecture* (Parere sull'Architettura),[5] published in 1765 and part of his composite rebuttal to philoellene critic Pierre Jean Mariette's negative review of Piranesi's works.

The *Parere* (singular in the Italian title, to emphasise the argument expressed by the dialogue, but translated into English with the plural *Opinions*) is set to continue Piranesi's defence of the superiority of Roman architectural "invention" over the architecture of ancient Greece, but it does much more. Structured as a dialogue between two fictional characters, Didascalo and Protopiro, who animatedly argue on the origin and primacy – Greek vs. Roman – of architecture, and illustrated with a series of cryptic architectural designs, *Opinions* discusses issues of originality, creativity, language and freedom in architecture. Through the words of the dialogue and the etchings of ornament-overloaded architectural proposals, Piranesi discusses the role of ornament in architecture and the problem of imitation as a creative act. Didascalo (Piranesi's alter ego, but only apparently) propounds that all ornament in architecture should be recognised as independent of function and structure, and as a separate apparatus that satisfies the human desire for variety. In his argumentation, variety is linked to invention and innovation, and change is identified as an intrinsic quality of architecture, not restricted to the wearing and decay of the edifice, but as an operation that brings time

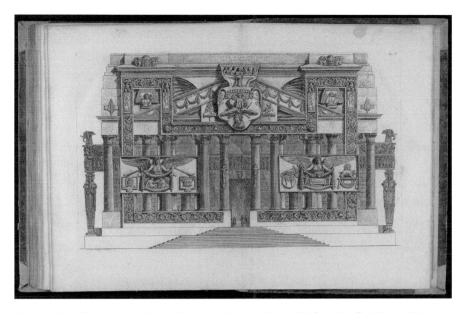

Figure 24.1 Giovanni Battista Piranesi, Parere, Plate IX (untitled), 410 × 645 mm. From *Osservazioni di Gio. Battista Piranesi sopra la lettre de M. Mariette.... E Parere su l'Architettura,...*, Paris: Firmin Didot, 1835–1839. (1st ed. Rome: Piranesi, 1765)

Courtesy of Ghent University Library, BHSL.RES.ACC.024064/07 [image – rug01:001634208]

into the very act of design, that is, in the project. Architecture, argues Piranesi through Didascalo, must be designed to change; otherwise, it can only repeat itself.[6] Intrinsic to architecture are change and its possibility of variation. Without change, architecture would become "a low trade, in which one would do nothing but copy," and architects would be "something less than masons."[7] In its very essence, architecture *is* only if it changes.

The voice of Didascalo in the dialogue is usually recognised as representative of Piranesi's position. But Piranesi's mind is in fact in both characters, and his dialogue is already a conversation of (at least) three: we have Didascalo and Protopiro, but we also have Piranesi as he develops his argument, dodging obstacles and juggling the contradictions of the two. The dialogical construction allows Piranesi to move between positions, transgress, leap – like the skateboarder, like the surfer, like the skier – to weave his project. Difficult to read, often circuitous and ambiguous, *Opinions* makes sense only if it is contextualised: read not only as Piranesi's response to his critics, but also as a development of Piranesi's earlier works – graphic, architectural and written. Built on their grounds, *Opinions* becomes a retroactive prologue to the interventions that both precede and follow it. And because it is a dialogue *on* architecture and a conversation *in* architecture, it "works" only *with* its images: not illustrations that complement the words, but veritable projects that further develop the argument discussed in the text.

Teresa Stoppani

In 1761, Piranesi had published *Della Magnificenza ed Architettura de' Romani*, a book that, Rudolf Wittkower explains:

> contains his view on art in a polemical form directed against two works: an essay by an anonymous English writer published in 1755, and *Les Ruines des plus beaux Monuments de la Grèce* published in 1758 by the Frenchman Le Roy. The latter was much the more important adversary, for he was the first to bring home to the West the Greek architecture of Athens, an event of far-reaching effect. In the text accompanying his engravings Le Roy explains that architecture is a Greek creation, from which all Roman buildings derive. As the Romans are only copyists, their architecture is decadent compared with that of the Greeks.[8]

In 1764, Pierre Jean Mariette published a letter against Piranesi in the *Gazette Littéraire de l'Europe*. "Piranesi, in a fury, prepared an answer at once. It appeared in 1765 and consisted of a title-page, 23 pages of text and 9 plates. The actual title-page already contains a programme and an attack,"[9] Wittkower observes.

Piranesi's *Observations on the Letter of Monsieur Mariette* are immediately followed by *Opinions on Architecture* (Parere sull'architettura), in which the 'fury' of the immediate response is diffused into the articulation of the voices of the dialogue. In *Opinions*, Protopiro is the rigorist, critical of Piranesi's designs because 'they are overloaded with ornament.' Protopiro "condemns Piranesi as illogical, for in *Della Magnificenza*, he was against ornament. And he concludes that, with these inventions, Piranesi *'si è dato a quella pazza libertà di lavorare a capriccio....'*"[10] But Piranesi's contradictions are only the preparation for his double attack in the dialogue: first, he dismisses the purity of the Greek architecture of the origins in favour of Roman hybridisation; then he also takes licence from Roman authority with the "capricious inventions" of his own designs. Didascalo, 'Piranesi's man,' according to Wittkower:

> defends his designs with unexpected arguments. He denies that severity, reason and adherence to rules are to be pursued for their own sakes. Not only Greek architecture, but also the rules of Vitruvius and the classicism of Palladio are rejected.[11]

This step is crucial, as Didascalo here opens the space for architecture to be no longer Greek or Roman, or even Etruscan or Egyptian, but to be all of them at once and ultimately none: to be Piranesi. This betrayal is necessary to architecture. As Didascalo argues in the dialogue, "If one carries the principles of Vitruvius to their logical conclusion the result will be a primitive hut."[12] "Without variation art is reduced to the mason's craft,"[13] and there is no architecture without hybridisation, transformations, betrayals and freedom to design.

Wittkower very clearly marks this shift, observing that

> the decisive break between his ideas in *Della Magnificenza* of 1761 and those expressed in the *Parere* of 1765 cannot be overlooked. In the earlier

book Vitruvius enjoys unchallenged authority, in the later the ancient author is rigorously criticized. Though Piranesi tries to find a way out by sophistry, he now recommends as indispensable those ornaments which he condemned before.[14]

But does Piranesi really recommend ornamentation as "indispensable"? Wittkower continues:

> The anti-Vitruvian, anticlassical theory expressed in the *Parere* is now not only in keeping with the character of much of the architecture which Piranesi had previously engraved, but coincides with his own pictorial interpretation of the[se] monuments [he had previously engraved]. His new views on architecture no longer permit him to illustrate them with engravings of ancient buildings, but he uses designs of his own invention which are now in complete accordance with his theory. … He shows how the whole heritage of antiquity can be used to develop new variations and to promote creative forces.[15]

The dialogue is accompanied by plates of architectures of Piranesian invention. Crucially, four of them bear inscriptions that further the position Didascalo defines in words, and push beyond it. Plate V bears a quotation from Terence's *Eunuch*: "It is reasonable to know yourself, and not to search into what the ancients have made if the moderns can make it." In plate VII, Piranesi inscribes on the façade of the building a verse from Ovid's *Metamorphoses* (XV): *Rerumque novatrix Ex aliis alias reddit natura figuras* (Nature renews herself constantly to create the new).[16] In plate VIII is a sentence from Le Roy: *Pour ne pas fair de cet art sublime un vil métier où l'on ne ferait que copier sans choix*. Last, in plate IX, borrowing from Sallust, Piranesi himself utters on stone: *Novitatem meam contemnunt, ego illorum ignaviam* (They despise my novelty, I their timidity).[17]

We have come full circle. The dialogue stages the two voices of Protopiro – tradition – and Didascalo – innovation – to let the third and multifaceted voice of Piranesi emerge through the illustrations and the short texts emblazoned on the buildings (or illusions thereof) that they represent. But the voice of Piranesi is also in the structuring of the exchanges of his two characters. Far from opposition, which is only apparent, and remains crucially unresolved and ambiguous, the merit of this dialogue *cum figuris* is to set the ground (a very treacherous one) for change in architecture, for Piranesi himself, and well beyond him. This is only a restart, a new beginning – as there had been many before, Piranesi intimates – for the true dialogue as conversation (architectural conversation) to develop, through many voices, across different times, and in many projects.

According to the inscriptions in the plates of the *Opinions* – which offer yet another dialogue, on stone on paper – nature remains a model for architecture only because it performs a constant renewal, and literal copying of ancient models is discouraged, in favour of a free combinatory work of contaminations. An architecture that does not imitate nature or architecture is called to reinvent itself. How? In *Opinions*

Teresa Stoppani

Piranesi offers the congestion of his images, and in the most famous plate, the ninth, he challenges: "They despise my novelty, I their timidity." As Wittkower observes, "Archeological material now becomes a weapon in the hands of a revolutionary modernist."[18] But the task at hand must go on, and will go on, well beyond archaeological materials and well beyond Piranesi. Materials will in the longer run be stripped, discarded and transformed by newly available technologies, and the experimentation will involve many architects.

In words and graphic provocation, Piranesi's dialogue establishes the autonomy of architecture. The excessive use of ornamentation proclaims a non-referentiality that dismisses a source, an external referent and a sole origin. As operation of manipulation of itself and on itself, architecture becomes autonomous. The congestion that clutters, structures, de-structures and re-structures his designs is ultimately self-effacing: by saturating architecture and its image, Piranesi erases all established orders, making room for a new language to come.[19] Referentiality is undone by excess, and his "too much" produces a critical mass that devours the existing orders and prepares the ground for the excess of its erasure and disappearance. The systematic congestion and manipulation of architectural orders, in fact, open the possibility of other orders, and trigger an unstoppable process that will eventually produce a naked architecture.[20]

For Wittkower, Piranesi is able to claim the right of invention because of "his intensity of purpose and his singularly sanguine fervour."[21] He argues that Piranesi "unconsciously hit upon a method which is deeply rooted in the Italian mentality,"[22] a systematic transgression and free play with given rules that he sees as continuity with "a tradition [16th century Manner] which has been taken by more than one independent artist since Michelangelo's days."[23]

The 'fury' of Piranesi's 'Italian mentality' is clear as he concludes his dialogue, by directly addressing Mariette:

> Now, what do you make of all this chatter, Signor Mariette? …. Demonstrate that without straying from beautiful and noble simplicity or without adopting a ridiculous and barbaric manner, and yet not wanting to reduce architecture to a low trade, in which one would do nothing but copy, there is nevertheless all possible scope for variation and for multiplying inventions. …. As for the difference of opinion between yourself and Piranesi, the matter is by no means closed. Listen to what he is preparing for you to review, in addition to the drawings mentioned in the debate: a treatise, of greater length than *Della magnificenza ed architettura de' romani*, …[24]

As we know, the announced treatise *On the Introduction and Progress of the Fine Arts in Europe in Ancient Times* will never come into being beyond its preface, which Piranesi appends to *Observations on the Letter of Monsieur Mariette* and *Opinions on Architecture*. But the dialogue staged by Piranesi continues as a remote conversation beyond Didascalo-Protopiro and Piranesi-Mariette, bringing in – in the order Wittkover refers to them in his 1938 essay on *Opinions*: Goguet, Caylus, Thomas Dempster, A.F. Gori, G.B. Passeri, M. Guarnacci, William Chambers, Abbé Laugier, Cordemoy, padre Lodoli,

Francesco Milizia, Andrea Memmo, J.F. Blondel, D'Hancarville, Winckelmann, Robert Adam, Bottari and also Ovid, Terence, Sallust. And then, later, we can add Wittkover himself, John Wilton-Ely and Manfredo Tafuri; and it still puzzles us.

Yet, the crucial space opened by the *Opinions* and its images is best occupied by the projects and buildings of those architects of the French Enlightenment that Emil Kaufmann has called "revolutionary."[25] Twenty years after Piranesi's dialogue, Claude-Nicolas Ledoux and Étienne-Louis Boullée will continue the stripping of ornaments that Piranesi had only timidly hinted at in Santa Maria del Priorato in Rome,[26] when he removed (omitted) mouldings from the back of the main altar he had designed for the renovation of the church, one of his few built works. According to Kaufmann, the works of Ledoux and Boullée marked only the beginning of an architectural revolution. And this stripping of architecture will not be skin deep: with the rich ornamentation will go also the possibility to rely on a fixed set of rules, on a universal language of orders and order, and architecture will need to learn to "speak" in other ways.[27] In 1933, with his *Von Ledoux bis Le Corbusier*,[28] Kaufmann had already indicated the direction of travel, suggesting a continuity from Ledoux's revolution to Le Corbusier's new architecture.

Yet, Piranesi's dialogue, with a complexity that reaches beyond dialectical opposition, and with the "monstrousness of his [architectural] contaminations,"[29] opened up for architecture a space of questioning and contradiction, from which many and other possible directions could be taken – still.

Notes

1. "In physics, the demise of absolute time is shown to give way to a theory of the 'field,' effectively superseding the classical notion of space as a substratum against which things occur, and consequently giving rise to a physics of the 'event'." Sanford Kwinter, *Architectures of Time. Towards a Theory of the Event in Modernist Culture*, Cambridge, MA: MIT Press, 2001, ix.
2. Kwinter, 4.
3. Kwinter, 5.
4. Kwinter, 5.
5. Giovanni Battista Piranesi, *Observations on the Letter of Monsieur Mariette: With Opinions on Architecture, and a Preface to a New Treatise on the Introduction and Progress of the Fine Arts in Europe in Ancient Times* (John Wilton-Ely, ed.), Los Angeles, CA: Getty Publications, 2002. [Osservazioni di Gio. Batista Piranesi sopra la Lettre de M. Mariette aux Auteurs de la Gazette de l'Europe: inserita nel supplemento dell'istessa gazzetta stampata Dimanche 4, Novembre MDCCLXIV & Parere su l'architettura, con una prefazione ad un nuovo Trattato della introduzione e del progresso delle belle arti in Europa ne' tempi antichi].
6. 'Let us imagine the impossible: let us imagine the world – sickened though it is by everything that does not change day to day – very gracefully to accept your monotony; what would architecture become? A LOW TRADE, IN WHICH ONE WOULD DO NOTHING BUT COPY, as a certain gentleman has said. So that not only would you and your colleagues become extremely ordinary architects, as I said before, but further you would be something less than masons. By constant repetition, they learn to work by rote; and they have the advantage over you because they have the mechanical skill. You would ultimately cease to be architects at all because clients would be foolish to use an architect to get a work that could be done far more cheaply by a mason.' And so Didascalo advocates: 'I ask only this: by all means treasure the rationality that you proclaim, but at the same time respect the freedom of architectural creation that sustains it.' Giovanni Battista Piranesi, *Observations on the Letter of Monsieur Mariette: with Opinions on Architecture, and a Preface to a New Treatise on the Introduction and Progress of the Fine Arts in Europe in Ancient Times* (John Wilton-Ely, ed.), Los Angeles, CA: Getty Research Institute, 2002, 110–111.
7. Piranesi, *Opinions on Architecture*, in *Observations....* 2002, 110–111.
8. Rudolf Wittkower, 'Piranesi's "Parere su L'Architettura"', *Journal of the Warburg Institute*, Vol. 2, No. 2 (October 1938), pp. 147–158. Quote from page 147.

9 Wittkower, 'Piranesi's "Parere su L'Architettura"', 150–151.
10 Wittkower, 152.
11 Wittkower, 152.
12 Wittkower, 152.
13 Wittkower, 152.
14 Wittkower, 152.
15 Wittkower, 154.
16 Ovid (Publius Ovidius Naso), *Metamorphoses*, 15.253.253.
17 In *Bellum Jugurthinum*, Sallust writes, 'Contemnunt novitatem meam, ego illorum ignaviam, mihi fortuna, illis probra obiectantur' [85,14]. 'They despise my recent nobility, I their ineptitude. I am reproached for my fortune, they for their shameful actions.' J.C. Rolfe translates this passage with 'They scorn my lack of pedigree [as a 'new man'], I their [of the arrogant nobles] worthlessness; I am reproached with my lot in life, they with their scandals.' Sallust, *The War with Catiline. The War with Jugurtha*, transl. by John Carew Rolfe, revised by John T. Ramsey, Loeb Classical Library, Cambridge, MA: Harvard University Press, 2013. Available online at DOI: 10.4159/DLCL.sallust-war_jugurtha.2013. This contextualised translation perhaps better explains Piranesi's appropriation of Sallust's words. While here he is illustrating the dialogue in which he argues his position, the truly innovative power of his works resides in his architectures, imagined or built.
18 Wittkower, 155.
19 I have discussed the process of erasure in the graphic works of Piranesi in Teresa Stoppani 'Material and Critical: Piranesi's Erasures', in Ivana Wingham (ed.), *Mobility of the Line. Art, Architecture, Design*, Basel: Birkhäuser, 2013, 234–246.
20 For Manfredo Tafuri, with the 'discovery of the *principle of contradiction*' in the San Basilio altar and with the unresolved confrontations of *Opinions* Piranesi demonstrates 'that the silence of architecture, the reduction to zero of its symbolic and communicative attributes, is the inevitable consequence of the "constraint" ["*costrizione*," as imperative] to variation...' Manfredo Tafuri, *The Sphere and the Labyrinth*, Cambridge, MA: The MIT Press, 1987, 49. My note.
21 Wittkower, 156.
22 Wittkower, 156.
23 Wittkower, 156.
24 Piranesi, *Opinions on Architecture*, in *Observations on the Letter of Monsieur Mariette ....* (John Wilton-Ely, ed.), 2002, 113–114.
25 Emil Kaufmann, *Three Revolutionary Architects: Boullée, Ledoux, Lequeu*, Philadelphia, PA: American Philosophical Society, 1953.
26 The Church of St. Mary of the Priory *(Chiesa di Santa Maria del Priorato)* on the Aventine in Rome was renovated in 1764–1766 according to Piranesi's designs. Manfredo Tafuri discusses the project, and the altar's detail as an important clue of Piranesi's modernity in Manfredo Tafuri, '"L'architetto scellerato": G.B. Piranesi, l'eterotopia e il viaggio', in *La sfera e il labirinto. Avanguardie e architettura da Piranesi agli anni '70*, Turin: Einaudi, 1980, 33–74; English translation, '"The Wicked Architect": G.B. Piranesi, Heterotopia, and the Voyage', in *The Sphere and the Labyrinth*, Cambridge, MA: The MIT Press, 1987, 25.
27 The French term *architecture parlante*, first used in an anonymous review of C.-N. Ledoux's work, was adopted by Emil Kaufmann in his work on Ledoux in *Three Revolutionary Architects*.
28 Emil Kaufmann, *Von Ledoux bis Le Corbusier: Ursprung und Entwicklung der Autonomen Architektur*, Vienna: Rolf Passer, 1933.
29 Tafuri, *The Sphere and the Labyrinth*, 47.

Chapter 25

Epilogue[1]

Penny Lewis and Vicky Richardson

Can we talk about collectivity after Covid?

As we go to press, a debate has broken out between the UK and the European Commission over the export and supply of Covid vaccines. The row exposes how difficult it is to talk about an 'international community' despite the fantastic collaboration that has taken place to produce the vaccines. It's a timely reminder of the difference between calling something a 'community' and it being one. Today, community, which by definition is "a body of people or things viewed collectively" or "a body of people having common or equal rights or rank, as distinguished from the privileged classes; the commons; the commonalty,"[2] has become shorthand for shared or publicly held assets rather than describing an ongoing relationship of social solidarity among equals. Many aspects of the Covid experience have highlighted the necessity and possibility of genuine social solidarity and, at the same time, have exposed the serious divisions in society and the obstacles to forming common bonds with our neighbours or beyond. In the UK, the question of how we live together and how we act together has moved to the forefront of public discussion as pundits and academics speculate on urban life post-Covid. Rory Sutherland said, those of us suffering from an urbanist obsession need to recognise that "the more that life is conducted digitally, the less location matters, and the less need there is for agglomeration of people."[3]

In the international arena, the World Economic Forum (WEF) promised a Great Reset in which green infrastructure would be a central concern.[4] And, in October, the Secretary-General of the UN identified cities and communities as being on the frontline

Figure 25.1 Jackson Heights Shop, Chen Yang 2021

of the Covid-19 response.[5] "The recognition of communities' value must be maintained beyond the virus outbreak. In the transition to a new sustainable urban normality, local communities must play an expanded role supporting government stimulus packages."[6]

Yet, at a local level, our community experience under Covid has created as many tensions as opportunities for social solidarity. Definitions of a key worker have shifted, at least in peoples' understanding of the term, as it became clear that society relies just as heavily on supermarket and delivery workers as it does on doctors and nurses. Madonna's proclamation that "Covid is a great equaliser"[7] is long forgotten; the reality is lockdown has heightened the social inequality. "As one dark wit remarked, 'Lockdown? No, middle-class people hid, while working-class people brought them things.'"[8] In the UK, the 'culture wars' have gained momentum; we appear to be more divided over lockdown itself, Brexit, race, gender and the environment; the 2020 summer protests in the UK (and USA) highlighted these divisions.[9] Expressions of collective dissent have taken place against a backdrop of the suspension of individual rights and freedom on an unprecedented scale, setting government against the people.

In this book, there are a wide range of views on collectivity, community and the commons. Historically, the idea of the collective has been used in many ways as explored in the introduction. Within this book, it is used to describe non-market economies, state welfare initiatives and civic values generated by self-governing local and radical organisations. Sometimes, we talk about collectivity in relation to the state and, at others, we mean the people. The experience of the second half of the 20th century tells us that these two ideas can often be polar opposites. The difficulty for architects and planners is that they stand in the middle, trying to meet the needs of users in a way that satisfies the very different needs of their public clients. In today's discourse, there is a tendency to see the three decades following the Second World War as a golden age of public commissioning;[10] but we should also recognise that post-war culture was one in which the technical experts could do as they pleased because war had politically demobilised urban inhabitants. The demand for housing and healthcare existed, but it was addressed by the professional class (and the officials of the Labour movement). Jacobs and other critics of post-war planning represented the beginning of an expression of the popular will and a reaction to technocratic and unsatisfactory aspects of public life, particularly, as they affected the city.

Orr argues that Aldo Rossi's (and by association Jacobs') opposition to the planners in the 1960s contributed to the success of neo-liberal ideas in the following decades. For Orr, 'anti-planning' is associated with "an ideologically suspect notion of urban society and collectivity". For others, state planning itself was seen as a barrier to the participation of urban inhabitants; Goodman describes how city leaders brought in the scientists and the professional planners in order to protect or insulate politicians from the demands of the urban population. Professionalising local planning took local decision-making from the people, and the result was passivity and a sense of inertia in public life[11]. Richard Sennett made similar observations in the *Fall of Public Man*. He wrote:

> public life has become a matter of formal obligation. Most citizens approach their dealings with the state in the spirit of resigned acquiescence … Manners and ritual interchanges with strangers are looked on as at best formal and dry, at worst phony,[12]

Today, in the UK, you don't need to be a sociologist or an anarchist (like Sennett or Goodman) to be sensitive to the fact that there is a spirit of resigned acquiescence when it comes to local politics.[13] During lockdown, many metropolitan authorities took advantage of the crisis to bring in measures without public consultation; the evacuation of the physical public realm due to Covid has emboldened authorities. The London Mayor's Streetspace strategy was launched without consultation in May 2020, and local roads were closed to cars, congestion charge periods extended and pavements widened in the interests of walking and cycling. The policy was declared illegal at a public hearing in January 2021 following popular demonstrations, but the approach has exacerbated the sense that policy is made by people who are privileged or "out of touch,"[14] *The Economist* described the battle over roads as "old London pitted against the new"[15] – new being the politicians and gentrifyers and the old being the long-standing locals. Although today's road closure may seem very different to Robert Moses' New York Expressway plans, they have much in common. Jane Jacobs objection to Moses' plans was not limited to the question of demolition: she disliked his paternalism. "The problems with paternalists is that they want to make impossibly profound changes and they chose impossibly superficial means for doing so"[16] wrote Jacobs.

Reinier de Graaf is critical of Jacobs, but he shares her discomfort about paternalistic experts and politicians. De Graaf believes that popular buzzwords among urbanists like 'community,' 'liveability' and 'happiness' are used by city leaders to gloss over a widening social inequality. While many of us may share his scepticism about politicians' and developers doublespeak, when it comes to terms such as community; it is important to recognise the dangers of an 'anti-community ideology.' Sociologist Frank Furedi writes about the rise of "a dogmatic anti-community ideology," which is borne out of a distorted cosmopolitanism, in which communities are often been condemned as old-fashioned, conventional and exclusionary.[17] David Harvey reminds us of the benefits of dense urban life as a place where people thrive as social animals. The city is

> the site where people of all sorts and classes mingle, however reluctantly and agonistically, to produce a common if perpetually changing and transitory life. The commonality of that life has long been a matter of commentary by urbanists of all stripes, and the compelling subject of a wide range of evocative writings and representations …that attempt to pin down the character of that life … and its deeper meanings[18]
>
> (Harvey 2012)

Even when economic life is at its rawest and most brutal, there are aspects of urban life that give us some sense of togetherness. First, we operate within a social division of labour; this is true for all aspects of life and production (and it is explicit within the construction industry). Second, the evolving division of labour tends to give rise to a concentration of human activity, and these centres need to be regulated according to 'civic values.' Values are usually worked out by people living side by side. Sometimes civic values are associated with the values of the powerful (such as the legal protection over private property), but often they express our shared concerns over questions such as freedom of speech or respect for privacy. Dealing with the differences in our collective interests and endeavours and our conflicting needs and concerns were the challenges facing New York when Jacobs wrote *Death and Life*.

Joan Ockman's AHRA conference keynote made an important link between Jacobs's work in the USA and the debates about human association between the younger members of CIAM/Team 10/The Independent Group. "An even closer affinity exists between Jacobs' idea of collectivity and that of the architectural protagonists of Team 10, who published the first edition of their *Team 10 Primer* one year after *Death and Life*,"[19] noted Ockman. She makes a connection between Jacobs' famous "sidewalk ballet" and the "doorstep philosophy" put forward by Peter and Alison Smithson, for whom "the doorstep was the place of primary encounter 'between man and men.'"[20] Concerns for residents' aspirations sat alongside the desire to organise and give shape to the new built environment. Somehow in that process of post-war redevelopment the modernist failed to win sustained popular support for their design proposals.[21] The enforced 'togetherness' that operated in the housing projects is sharply criticised by Jacobs in *Death and Life*. The failure of the modernist project is often understood as an aesthetic problem, but in reality it was a political one. People often see their immediate environment as a place where they can express their limited autonomy:

the modernist project was a reminder of the fact that so much of life is dictated by forces beyond our control.

1. Is there a new geography?

Jodi Dean's analysis of contemporary social relations – in particular, the idea of 'new feudalism' has emerged as part of a vibrant debate about post-Covid urban life and politics. The neo-feudal interpretation draws parallels between the unprecedented wealth of today's Big Tech entrepreneurs and feudal lords; and between police brutality and the arbitrary exercise of authority in medieval society. In this extended metaphor, today's middle-class professionals and experts are compared to the feudal clerics whose faith shored up the legitimacy of the lords. Today's supercities (New York, London, Shanghai, etc.) with their rich urban cores and poverty-stricken lawless hinterlands are likened to the feudal landscape (*The Coming of New Feudalism; A warning to the global Middle class* Kotkin 2020 Encounter New York).

Kotkin describes a significant trend in urban development: the departure from the idea of the city as an emblem of upward mobility. This shift has taken place because of urban policy and economic drivers and is particularly evident in the west where successful cities have become sites for serious consumption as much as production and exchange. Cities and towns seem to divide clearly into winners and losers. The focus of attention is the emergence of supercities with their active construction sites and gleaming towers, and urban cores in which the super-rich live alongside the super-poor while key workers and the middle class have moved on to the hinterlands or suburbs.

It is ironic that urban policy makers have talked about the liveable city for three decades, and their policies have given rise to safe retail environments which are unaffordable for most ordinary people. Kotkin also describes the losers, places like Detroit, which are de-industrialised and suffering from depopulation and crime. In both cases, he argues that the engines of upward mobility historically associated with the city have stalled. London's profile is typical of superstar cities: 37% of London's population are immigrants, who as a rule take on low paid work and have very little chance of upward mobility.

As Tahl Kaminer and his colleagues outline in Chapter 7, the process of gentrification has had a significant impact on the shape of urban development across Europe.

> The dynamics of the global city have seen its spatial and social forms increasingly shaped not by the political community, but by abstract, international pressures and forces driven by global imbalances...The reconfiguration of housing as a financial commodity necessarily effects the collective life of the city – it diminishes housing as a key social resource; it de-valorises housing's use value; it infuses increased precariousness into the lives of individuals, communities and cities. It reduces local governments' capacity to shape the city.[22]

Kotkin echoes this critique but is keen to stress that, although gentrification began life as a spontaneous process in 1960s London, it was consciously adopted by urban leaders in the 1980s; investment in cultural and leisure facilities rather than infrastructure and education was a strategy which was likely to transform the urban core into a centre for consumption rather than a place for families to live.

Dean paid attention to the power of the Big Tech oligarchs such as Mark Zuckerberg (Facebook) and Jeff Bezos (Amazon): the new oligarchy. In Chapter 6, Claudia Dutson analyses the way in which Big Tech companies have changed the urban form of the Bay Area and shifted the design of the workplace. Dutson argues that post-Covid the Big Tech campus arrangement may prove flexible for its owners. "Open-plan buildings can readily be adapted to lower density occupation and the campus affords tightly controlled access. Tech companies have both the physical and tech infrastructure – as well as the will – to create a proprietary bio-polis."[23] The new Big Tech workplace has several key features that are not so much aesthetic as they are strategic and relational – particularly in how they construct the identities of their employees. Apple, Facebook and Google have their own cultures with which employees are expected to align. The architecture follows these brand identities and even though each campus may be formally different, they share properties such as low-rise blocks and extremely large floor plates. Dutson describes how Facebook staff have been given a free space for creative activity with a screen-printing press – during their leisure time staff make and post political messages around the campus. Dutson and others have remarked that staff are encouraged to see political dissent as "just another mode of self-expression" while images of activists and Black Lives Matter marchers are "hollowed of the hard work of movement organising."[24]

Figure 25.2 Jackson Heights Subway, Chen Yang 2021

2. The real public and the digital realm under Covid

Outside Silicon Valley, the Covid lockdown will accelerate the trend towards downsizing of offices and the diversification of the use of central business districts. Corporate headquarters may come to be social spaces rather than predominantly spaces for desks and concrete expressions of corporate values. If Covid has provoked a rethink on the structure and character of the city, social distancing has made us think in a very tangible way about how closely we live together. Zoom-land has its positives: productivity may have increased temporarily and we are able to communicate with people all over the world without the inconvenience of international travel, but there is a fear that the digital will replace the public realm and that we will never be able to back-track to re-establish face to face dialogue and debate.

Pre-Covid, Ockman noted McLuhan's naivety about digital technology; "Despite all of McLuhan's enthusiasm for the possibilities of digital communication Jacobs had a better understanding of the process of urban democracy and the possibility of the citizens exercising control over the electronic revolution".[25] The relationship between digital and democratic life demands more discussion. Standing beside others in public debate is very different to engaging with them online because IRL you only engage with whole personality not simple one aspect of a being.[26]

One of the most significant things about the Covid pandemic is the evacuation of the public sphere as a physical space and the move to digital platforms of MS Teams and Zoom. In Real Life (IRL) is an expression that has taken on a new significance as our real lives have tended to be lived among a small group of family of friends in our homes. We may hope that we can return to the old ways of doing things to the old social conventions of shaking hands, joining a party, eating in a crowded room, etc., but we also know that there is likely to be a 'new normal.' There is a real danger that these temporary restrictions on our freedom and sociability become part of a new pattern of public life.

The policy of 'lockdown' began in China in January 2020 and was adopted as a means of halting the spread of Coronavirus in almost every country in the world. It has meant the closure of public life in physical space – the avoidance of collective experiences in shared spaces, whether in a shopping mall, museum, cinema or pub. The pandemic has focused attention on the public life that has been lost; we have realised the importance of pubs, cafes and restaurants as places where individuals feel themselves to be part of society.

The lockdown immediately accelerated the adoption of digital technology in the workplace. In the UK, during the pandemic approximately 50% of the workforce worked from home, creating divisions between those who continued in roles 'at the frontline,' and those who could carry on their work online. The understanding and appreciation of digital technology as a public space has swung between techno-utopianism and dystopianism. For the optimists, digital technology allowed the policy of lockdown to be workable; we could stay connected, and a large section of the economy could continue to function even as the people lived in isolation. For the pessimists, the 'new normal' was seen by many as a playing out of predictions of science fiction.

In his 1977 short story *Intensive Care Unit*, JG Ballard imagined a society where people live in isolation, but life carries on mediated by TV monitors. When the narrator decides to ignore the rules and meet his family in person for the first time, the happy peace of married life through technology breaks down. The vision is eerily close to the experience of social life we've all become familiar with under lockdown: Ballard writes:

> ... we were married, at a lavish ceremony in the most exclusive of the studio chapels. Over two hundred guests attended, joining a huge hook-up of television screens, and the service was conducted by a priest renowned for his mastery of the split-screen technique.[27]

The details of this sad tale are incredibly prescient, down to Ballard's use of the word 'zoom' to describe televisual social engagement. But, most significantly, the story is a tale about the breakdown of human relations, and the dystopian idea that the greatest danger we face is physical contact with other people.

For some, the Covid lockdown has been the chance to demonstrate the power of new digital activism. Myria Georgiou, a media professor at the LSE, celebrated the scale of 'digital mobilisation' at the start of the pandemic when thousands of people responded to the government's call for volunteers.[28] Architect Jeremy Till, Head of Central St Martins School of Art was among many who stressed that physical distancing did not have to mean social distancing. Through the use of technology, public life could even be extended and enhanced, argued Dr Gregory Asmolov, a lecturer in 'crisis communication' at King's College London:

> Technology has offered a variety of opportunities for engagement with the crisis and has continuously increased the scope for participation in terms of both the range of people who can participate and the diversity of the tasks they can fulfil.[29]

The use of zoom to facilitate lectures and discussion platforms has, say some, opened access and allowed a wider range of voices to be heard, while digital networks, such as WhatsApp support groups and social media, have been credited with enabling new forms of solidarity.

'Hyper-local,' digitally connected communities have come about as a result of the use of data and online platforms to rapidly convey information between people and allow new forms of collective action. The crisis, some argue, has not just accelerated existing trends towards the adoption of digital technology, but has qualitatively shifted the generative power of the internet to bring about social change. The idea that community and social networks can be recreated in the digital world is not restricted to dystopian fiction but has been put forward by techno-optimists and social theorists since the 1960s. Ockman discusses this in her essay: Jane Jacobs spoke of the New York City as a 'criss-cross network' in the late 1950s, while Melvin Webber wrote about 'community without propinquity' in 1963. The idea of society as a series of networks has reoccurred ever since and found purchase in architectural and urban theory in the 1990s with Manuel Castells' Rise of the Network Society. From here, it is an obvious step to argue that the public realm is little more than a series of encounters and activities that can equally be organised through digital information networks rather than in physical space. As Craig Calhoun points out, Webber's idea of 'community' is very weak, even allowing for a more fluid kind of community relations based on professional groups and non-place-specific relationships.[30] The idea of a dispersed digital community has gained some ground in higher education, where lectures and design tutorials have tended to take place online. Away from the privileged realm of academia, the experience of most people during lockdown is to yearn for the days of social interaction and free movement in the 'real' world. The impact of collective political will in real public space has not been entirely absent during the pandemic – in response to the killing of George Floyd, the instinct of many people was to express their horror and outrage by protesting collectively in cities around the US and UK.

Where there has been an appreciation of solidarity, it has tended to be framed by a tendency to medicalise social connections. Seth Holmes argues that solidarity is important for mental health and well-being.[31] *Connected Places Catapult* notes that "the current crisis has reinforced the vital role that public places play in bringing people together and promoting wellbeing."[32] This idea of collectivity as a health strategy for vulnerable individuals is very far from the free citizen celebrated by Jacobs. By and large, the lockdown restrictions on public space and free movement have not been met with resistance from the public. Advocates for public space, who in the past, have been vocal about the privatisation and regulation of public space have fallen silent. The Mayor of London, who, in 2019, launched a 'public charter' to safeguard rights in privately managed and owned public space, fully accepted lockdown and in fact pushed the government for more stringent restrictions.

The idea that digital networks are a good substitute for face-to-face encounters can only gain purchase because our public life was already undervalued pre-Covid. Social media has become an extension of the public square, but, increasingly, the digital realm has been becoming a privatised, regulated space. In January 2021, the censorship of President Donald Trump by Twitter opened the door for tech giants such as YouTube and Facebook to exercise unprecedented control over what is said in 'our' digital public realm. As people have been forced into using technology to work, socialise and increasingly as a platform for debate, there is a widespread recognition that this is not substitute for being with others and for the sense of engagement that comes from face to face dialogue and freedom to speak freely. However, on both sides of the physical/digital debate, there is a reduced and limited view of what constitutes collectivity. While the use of social media may have increased for causes such as environmentalism and the expression of cultural identity, it tends to be the outlet of choice for the "professional managerial class."[33] Working-class sentiments tend to be dismissed as racist or populist. In December 2020, when Millwall Football Club fans booed their own players for 'taking the knee,' it was widely assumed that the fans were racist, not that the booing was a spontaneous reaction against political posturing. Opportunities for the informal exchange of views between strangers and the opportunity to interact with those outside our usual social circle have made it harder for individuals to form an opinion or actively shape the debate.

The shift to homeworking (WFH) seems certain to bring about long-term change in the boundaries between private and public. Earlier variants of WFH, 'teleworking' and 'telecommuting,' were first discussed in the 1970s as part of a positive move towards flexibility brought about through new technology. From the 1990s, homeworking began to be put into practice, along with hot-desking and other arrangements designed to reduce corporate overheads and improve productivity. The increasing use of mobile devices over the past decade allowed people to bring their work home, and the division between working hours and leisure time has also been blurred by companies seeking to provide workplaces that mimic the home, with the provision of showers, kitchens and relaxation spaces. The Covid crisis will be remembered as a time when working from home (WFH) was tested to its limit. While the professional classes welcomed the change as an opportunity to redress a work/life balance, others highlighted the inadequacy of private space for work.

One of the lasting visual memories of the pandemic will be politicians and public figures being interviewed in their homes with their personal possessions and private space on full display. The idea of home as a private sphere of intimacy and individual autonomy has been under scrutiny for some time.[34] While public discourse has tended to focus on the lack of shared experience in urban spaces, much less concern has been expressed about the erosion of the private realm. So, what contribution does private space play in the formation of collective will and a sense of public agency? The modern-day concept of the home as a realm of personal freedom and choice was intrinsically connected to the development of democracy and a sense of collective in the public realm, particularly, during the 19th century. In order to participate in democracy, it had to be assumed that individuals would have the freedom to develop their own ideas, religious practices and lifestyle choices. The private sphere, and by extension our inner thoughts and subjective being, was by necessity free from state regulation and the laws that govern behaviour in public. We can see that, as the public are less trusted as individuals, and our speech and ideas are increasingly monitored in both public and private, the important distinction between the character of public and personal freedom has been lost.[35]

Conclusion

One very important lesson from the pandemic, particularly, in the UK, is that the contemporary state and its planning mechanisms are inadequate. Writing in *The Telegraph*, academic Lee Jones wrote: "When Britain finally escapes this nightmare of rolling lockdowns, we must completely rethink how we organise the state."[36] In the introduction to this book, we talked about how you can approach architecture in different ways; as a disciplinary activity producing buildings, and as a subject of investigation that provides a mechanism for us to understand the man-made world and see how it shapes our world and social life. One other way to look at architecture is as a political tool; activist architects have been popping up with plans for new ways of doing things throughout the pandemic. While this kind of design work can be useful, it would be wrong to imagine that architecture can become a substitute for politics. Architects cannot design collectivity or community. Our ability to develop social solidarity is a social and political question, not a technical or aesthetic one. Too often, over the course of the 20th century, architects as professionals have consciously or unconsciously taken on the role of the expert for the state without fully understanding their role. Post-war planning and redevelopment gave rise to some excellent buildings, but the sense in which they were genuinely 'public' was very limited. We should not be wary of over romanticising the architecture of the welfare state.

As Jones says: "We need a democratic state that is prepared to exercise authority, mobilise resources, and be accountable for its decisions – not a failed array of quangos, management consultancies and outsourcing firms."[37] This 'new state' accountable to its population would provide the best possible conditions in which architects and other designers can practice[38]. As Parker said:

> Democracy is not worked out at the polling-booths; it is the bringing forth of a genuine collective will, one to which every single being must contribute the whole of his complex life, as one which every single being must express the whole of at one point. Thus, the essence of democracy is creating.[39]

Notes

1. The images included in this essay and the introduction were taken by Chen Yang, a Wuhan and Dundee graduate, who travelled to the USA during the Covid crisis to study architecture at Columbia University.
2. OED Definition of community https://www.oed.com/view/Entry/37337?redirectedFrom=community#eid I. A body of people or things viewed collectively.
3. Rory Sutherland, *The Spectator*, 30 January 2021.
4. WEF in June 2020.
5. Unites Nations World Cities Day 31 October 2020 https://www.un.org/en/observances/cities-day "Community activities can no longer be taken for granted or under-resourced. Policy makers and urban managers need to engage communities systematically and strategically in urban planning, implementation and monitoring to co-create the cities of the future."
6. UN statement.
7. Madonna https://www.youtube.com/watch?v=5UYU4Slh34I. Madonna made a video in her bath in the early stages of the pandemic saying; 'The good and the bad thing about the virus is that it's a great equaliser.'
8. We could all do with a breath of fresh air; From the meaning of 'local' to the benefits of opening a window, there's a lot we can learn from the coronavirus crisis, Libby Purves, Monday, 18 January 2021, *The Times*. "Most of the infection surges look more like a poverty map than evidence of recklessness. … Even if a government felt deliberately callous and brutal about its poorest it would need to draw that conclusion now, simply because with a virus rampant, laissez-faire inequality ruins everybody's life."
9. The images from Minneapolis (May 2020), Portland Oregon, Kansas City and Seattle in the summer and more recently from Capitol in January 2021.
10. See Chapter 3 interview with Reinier de Graaf.
11. Paul Goodman *After the Planners* Pelican Book, London, 1972.
12. Richard Sennett, *The Fall of Public Man* Page 3 1976 Cambridge University Press.
13. Goodman.
14. https://www.opendemocracy.net/en/opendemocracyuk/these-figures-show-how-out-of-touch-uk-politicians-are-from-everyone-else/
15. *The Economist* October 2020.
16. Jane Jacobs, *The Death and Life of the Great American City*, 1992 page 271.
17. The anti-community sentiment ignores the fact that the root of democratic participation begins with the relations we form with neighbours and colleagues. "It is only as citizens interacting with one

another, within a clearly geographically bounded entity, that democratic decision-making can work. The demos have always existed in a bounded space," notes Furedi.
18. Harvey, D Rebel City 1990.
19. See Chapter 2 Joan Ockman *From Greenwich Village to the Global Village*.
20. See Chapter 2.
21. See Andrew O'Hagan *Our Father* 1999 Faber and Faber which reflects on slum clearance and tower block construction in Glasgow and how the main protagonist – Mr Housing was driven by his catholic faith and political idealism.
22. See Kaminer et al Chapter 7.
23. See Dutson Chapter 6.
24. See Dutson Chapter 6.
25. Chapter 2 Lewis et al. *Architecture and Collective Life 2021*, Routledge, London.
26. Craig Calhoun, In Communications Technology and the Transformation of the Urban Public Sphere. 1998 Community without Propinquity Revisited:
27. JG Ballard, *Myths of the Near Future*, 1982.
28. https://blogs.lse.ac.uk/medialse/2020/03/30/solidarity-at-the-time-of-covid-19-another-digital-revolution/
29. https://www.kcl.ac.uk/digital-innovation-and-social-resilience-how-can-covid-19-help-us-prepare-for-the-next-crisis
30. Craig Calhoun, In Communications Technology and the Transformation of the Urban Public Sphere. 1998 Community without Propinquity Revisited: Community and propinquity revisited Webber, he says, 'did not clarify differences in the patterns of relationships-e.g., density or multiplexity-that might vary with propinquity (and relative isolation), making the community of a remote coalmining town a different thing from the professional bonds and personal friendships of, say, the more dispersed "community" of social theorists.'
31. https://blogs.bmj.com/bmj/2020/04/30/seth-holmes-societies-re-open-pandemic-need-social-solidarity-survive/
32. https://cp.catapult.org.uk/news/innovation-brief-post-pandemic-public-space/
33. See Catherine Liu, *Virtue Hoarders: The Case against the Professional Managerial Class*.
34. The feminist critique of the family as a system of exploitation and oppression brought negative connotations, which have grown into a chorus of concern as incidences of domestic abuse have been described as a 'shadow pandemic' by the UN.
35. Arendt, Hannah The Human Condition (1958).
36. Lee Jones *The Telegraph* 26 Jan 2021 https://www.telegraph.co.uk/global-health/science-and-disease/rolls-royce-skoda-pandemic-has-exposed-britains-failed-regulatory/
37. Lee Jones *The Telegraph* 26 Jan 2021 https://www.telegraph.co.uk/global-health/science-and-disease/rolls-royce-skoda-pandemic-has-exposed-britains-failed-regulatory/
38. Mary Parker Follett The New State 1918. http://sunsite.utk.edu/FINS/Mary_Parker_Follett/Fins-MPF-01.html
39. Mary Parker Follett The New State 1918 p 20: We belong to our community just in so far as we are helping to make that community; then loyalty follows, then love follows. Loyalty means the consciousness of oneness, the full realization that we succeed or fail, live or die, are saved or damned together… Rows of houses, rows of streets, do not make a neighborhood. The place bond must give way to a consciousness of real union. http://sunsite.utk.edu/FINS/Mary_Parker_Follett/Fins-MPF-01.html

The Wally Close

Robert Wightman

The Wally Close was a collection of maquettes of the shared closes or stairs of a selection of Glasgow tenements produced by Robert Wightman.
Drawings and photo courtesy of Robert Wightman.

Robert Wightman

The Wally Close

Robert Wightman

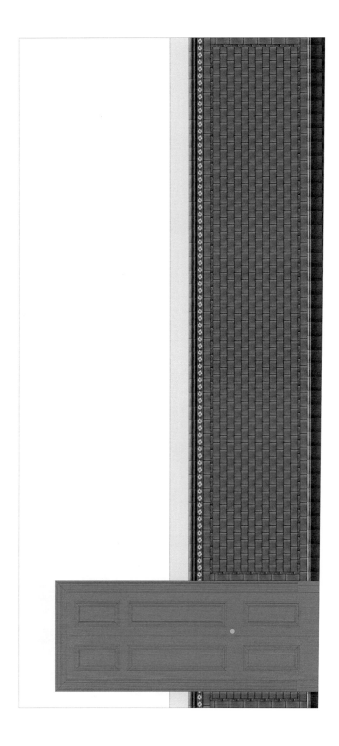

Tenement
The collective close

John Joseph Burns

Glasgow and the 'tenement' are synonymous. The tenement typology and the collective life which has emerged from its practical and pragmatic development as a typology have come to define Glasgow's social character and history. The consistency of the tenement as the main housing typology in Glasgow for a period of 400 years is remarkable considering the changing economic and social changes, upheavals and reforms throughout the city's history. Urban and industrial growth led to the creation of both overcrowded slums and new affluent middle-class areas. These seemed to reinforce the idea of collective living and the creation of relative social cohesion in respective tenement districts.

In Scotland, the term 'tenement' refers to a Victorian or Edwardian stone structure, three to five-storeys tall, with a common access stair, or 'close,' with two or three flats, or 'houses,' off each stair landing. They were built as speculative rental accommodation initially in the 18th century to house immigrant migrant workers and, as the city developed, even became a preferred housing type by an emerging middle class. The communal aspects of the shared semi-private space of the close and the sharing of facilities such as toilets, or 'cludgies,' and wash houses, or the 'steamie,' in the back court underpinned the collective life that emerged.

The early growth of Glasgow in the early 18th century, from trade with the new world primarily in tobacco, led to a wave of rural Scottish and Irish workers coming to the city. This growth led to the development of a standard typology from the Scottish Burgh system. Flats are accessed from a turnpike stair with multiple residences on each floor. This would've been an alien way of life for the rural migrants; but the dense living started to form small communities within the building linked by the common stair. As the city developed a substantial cotton industry in the late 18th century, the pressure on tenement design increased. 'Backland' tenements were now built to the rear of the street tenement in the Georgian period to accommodate the working class. The basic living arrangements are the same as the medieval burgh tenement but with a higher density using the shared facilities. Each backcourt of these tenements became their own community with various tenements sharing the provision of a few toilets.

Glasgow emerged in the mid-19th century as the 'Second City' of the British Empire, and this new wealth from trade, industry and commerce created a new affluent middle class. By the 1850s, the tenement reflected the aspirations and status of this new middle class. Queen's Park Terrace by Alexander 'Greek' Thomson is a fine example of this classical tenement with mannerist plays on details inspired by Renaissance Roman and Florentine Palazzos. The stone façade of the tenement became a display of wealth and status evolving the typology from a working-class form of housing to that of the city elite. W.M. Whyte further explored this in his design for Queen's Drive in 1884 choosing a free French Renaissance style, albeit with typical Glaswegian detailing, which was the height of fashion at the time. These tenements were built in the new suburbs of Glasgow's South Side; it is curious to note that although both these examples demonstrate a clear show of architectural grandeur, the way of life behind the façade is no different from the earlier examples. A common stair with shared communal faculties was present even in the high-end tenements, demonstrating that a communal life not only existed but was also expected in Glaswegian society at this time.

By the start of the 20th century, the tenement typology had been standardised and improved in terms of sanitary provision and room sizes through a series of Burgh Police Acts in the late 19th century. Number 19 Afton Street is an example of the standard tenement of this time, and although the toilets have been moved inside the flats the way of life of a shared close and backcourt remain. It is no surprise that after the failed centrally planned 'Comprehensive Development' of Post-WWII planning of 'Slab & Tower' that the desire to return to the tenement emerged. Ken McRae's Craigen Court for Maryhill Housing Association in 1989 returns to the idea of 'close' living and re-establishes the tenement in Glasgow; the continued construction of tenemental housing in Glasgow today is testament to the legacy of this tenement revival.

The development, endurance and revival of the tenement and its 'close' demonstrate that a collective life developed and evolved naturally and symbiotically. Glasgow is a city of tenements and as such is a city of collective communities.

The collective close

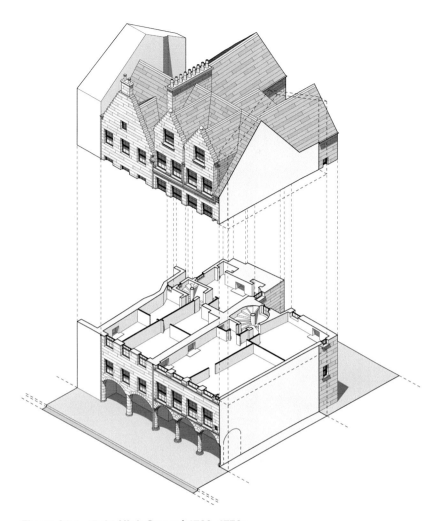

Figure A2.1 17–21 High Street | 1722–1750s
Scottish vernacular tenement with ground floor 'piazza' outside shops, turnpike stair and crow step dormers. Typical of early to mid-18th century following Burgh Council acts to produce a tenement typology in a 'uniform manner.'

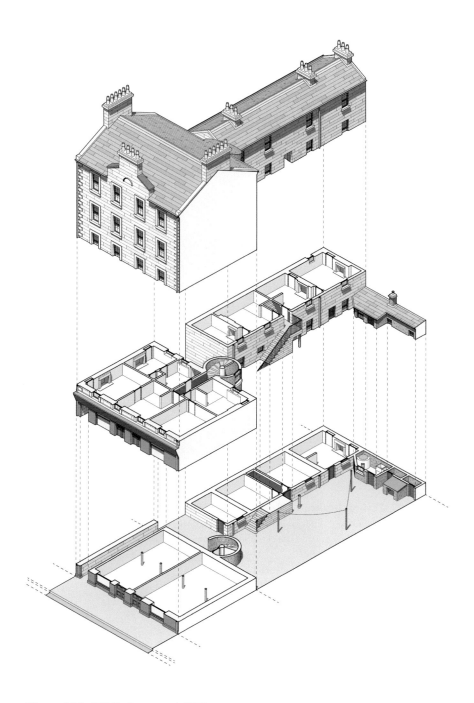

Figure A2.2 395 Gallowgate | 1771

Georgian working-class tenement with four-storey 'foreland' tenement on the street and 'backland' tenement behind the backcourt. Architectural features include a plain ashlar façade with nepus gable, ground floor shops and the emergence of a standard 'Room & Kitchen' arrangement for typical tenement flats.

The collective close

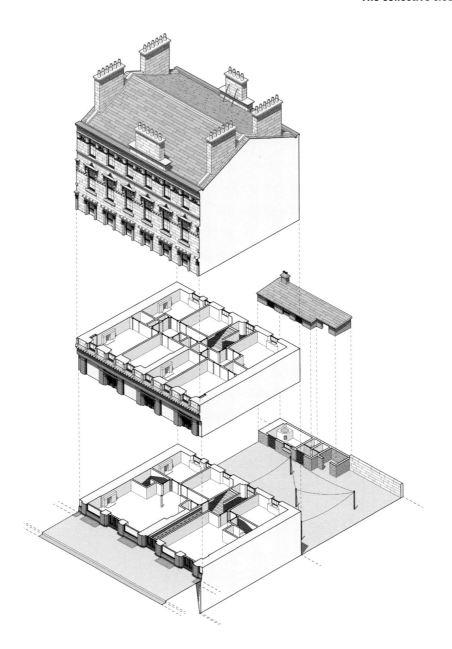

Figure A2.3 Queen's Park Terrace | Alexander 'Greek' Thomson | 1858
This decorative tenement is in the 'Classical' style with typical Thomson features including linking key stone band to second-floor windows and dwarf columns flanking third-floor windows. Internal layout comprises a mix of three and four-room flats off each stair landing; Thomson expertly hides this behind an equally spaced window arrangement on the façade.

John Joseph Burns

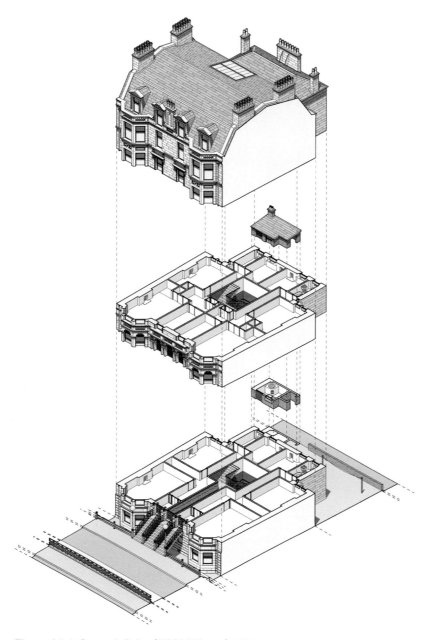

Figure A2.4 Queen's Drive | W.M. Whyte | 1884
Built on the expanding suburbs in Glasgow, this tenement provided an escape from the dense inner city with an outlook onto Queen's Park. The façade takes inspiration from the French Renaissance style but typical tenement features of the time such as bay windows make this unmistakably Glaswegian.

The collective close

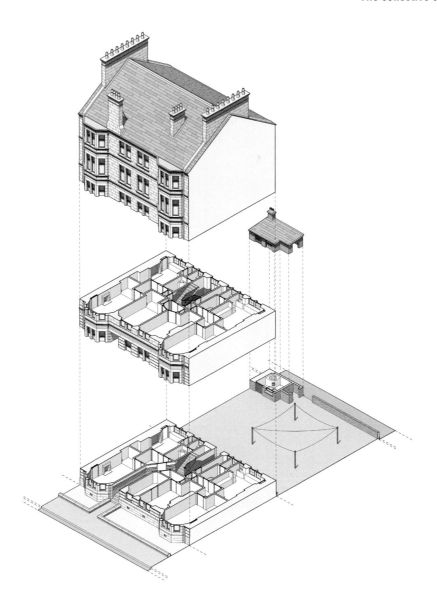

Figure A2.5 Afton Street | A.R. Crawford | 1901

A standard tenement from the 1900s demonstrating elements and layout common to most surviving tenements in Glasgow. A strong emphasis on verticality in the portrait windows and mullioned bay windows combined with linking horizontal string coursing is the main feature of tenement façade design of this period.

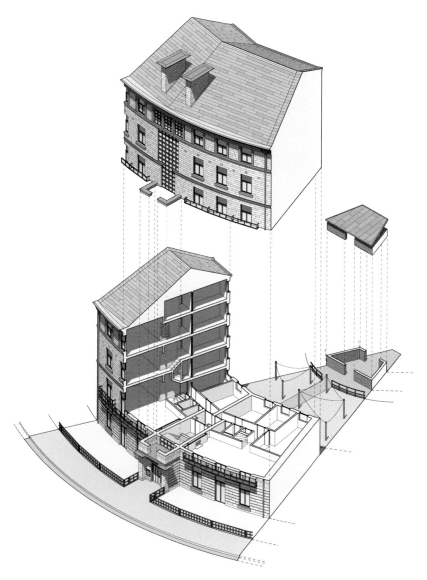

Figure A2.6 Craigen Court | Ken McRae with McGurn/Logan/Duncan & Opfer | 1989
This post-modern tenement takes its elevational design from the 'Classical' tenement period of the mid-19th century. Winner of the '21st Century Tenement Competition' this design imitates a standard tenement but the split section enables a diverse range of flat types and accommodation behind the façade, something not present in historical tenements.

Index

Note: *Italic* page numbers refer to figures and page number followed by "n" refer to end notes.

accessibility 3, 60, 65, 209, 266
Adam, Robert 291
adaptive reuse 163
A Discourse on Social Ecology (Gutkind) 277
Adorno, Theodor 105
affluence, paradox of 94–95
African American population 45
After the Planners (Goodman) 8
Afton Street 310, *315*
Age of Ecology: ecology movement 275; post-war British architects 274
Ahmed, Sara 254
AHRA conference 4, 9, 11, 31–41, *43*, 83, 296
Aichinger, Hermann 177
Airbnb 47
Akcan, Esra 264
alternative assets 84, 85
Amazon 45, 46, 50, 298
America and Cosmic Man (Lewis) 22
American: corporate capitalism 228; feminism 17; way of life *43*
American Appropriate Technology (AT) 238, 240–242
American Institute of Architects (AIA) 264
Amsterdam 83, 86–87
Analogue Research Lab (ARL) 77
Anderson, Perry 44, 46
Andy Yan 85
anti-communism 50
anti-gentrification campaigns 83
Anti-Oedipus (Guattari) 132
anti-perfectionism 208
Apartment House Syndicate 61
apocalypticism 49, 53
'apparatus of observation' 256

Apple 71–75
Apple Park 75
Arab Spring 80n15
The Archaeology of Knowledge (Foucault) 133
architectural authorship 116
Architectural Forum 15
architectural imagery 98
architectural parallax theory 102, 104
architectural theory 207, 276, 281n3, 282n7, 282n8, 282n10
"Architecture for Museums" 115, 117, 119
The Architecture of the City (Rossi) 10, 115, 117, 120–121
Architectures of Time (Kwinter) 286
Architecture without Architects (Rudofsky) 23
Arendt, Hannah 3, 5
Aristotelian ethics 260
Aristotle and the Virtues (Curzer) 262
artificial landscapes 164
Arts and Crafts-style 26
Asia: A Handbook 240
Aslund, Anders 52
Aspen Design Conference in 1970 280
Athenian style local democracy 8
audio transcriptions services 47
Aureli, Pier Vittorio 118, 121n4
Austen, Jane 32
authorship 7, 10, 116–117, 118, 201, 284, 285
autonomous project 115
autonomy-minded design 212, 213

Bacon, Ed 15
Ballygunge streets 220
Banham, Reyner 274, 280

317

Index

Barad, Karen 256, 257
Barrett-Kriegel, Blandine 129
Barthes, Roland 16
Basilico, Gabriele 146
Battle of the Styles 6
Baugruppen model 55
Bauhaus 35, 37
Bavarian Prince Otto 184, 191n5
Bebel-Hof layout plan *171*, 173
Bedford, Joseph 7, 10, 123–144
Beguin, Francois 129
Bekaert, Geert 159
Bender, Tom 238, 241–243, 246
Bengal Renaissance 218, 219
Benjamin, Walter 147, 148, 150, 154
Berlin 83, 86–87
Berlin Wall 36
Bernath, Doreen 10, 145–156
Bezos, Jeff 298
BiG (Bo i Gemenskap) 195; collective housing 197, 199; Fardknappen, different house 197–199; housing typology 195; legacy 201–202; model and concept 196–197; witness seminar 199–201
Big Tech developments 7, 11, 297, 298
The Birth of the Clinic (Foucault) 129
Blackhorse Lane 93
Black Lives Matter 39, 78
Blomberg, Ingela 195, 201
Blondel, J.F. 291
2004 Bloomberg-Pataki Hudson Yards synthesis 108
Blue House Yard (BHY) 97–98
Bonnis, Leonidas 186
Bontridder, Albert 159
Bookchin, Murray 241, 280; *Post-Scarcity Anarchism* 241
Boullee, Etienne-Louis 291
boundary conditions 209–210
boundary-making cuts 255
Bourdieu, Pierre 99
Bourgeois, Victor 11, 159; architectural tools 163; "Charleroi, region for urbanism" 163; cult of manual labour 164–165; 'detournement' strategy 164; earth-architecture 165; interdisciplinary work 168
Brand, Stewart 74, 240; holistic approach 241; How Buildings Learn 74
Brecht, Bertolt 147, 148, 154, 155n4
Brigate Rosse 132
Brinker, Menachem 155
British public land 47
British Townscape movement 16
Brown, Michael 45
"Buddhist Economics" 240
Bureau of Labor Statistics 50
The Burning Would (McLuhan) 26, *27*

Cacciari, Massimo 128, 130, 133
Calcutta, India: architectural modernity 218–220; cosmo-ecological collective life 220–223; environmentalism 223–225; tropical construction 218; urban margins 218
Callenbach, Ernest 242, 246; *Ecotopia: The Notebooks and Reports of William Weston* 241, 242
campus 71–79, 80n22, 298
capitalism 4, 28, 42–53, 43, 282n10
Caribbean campus 77
Carl, Peter 209
Carmona, Matthew 100n4
catastrophism 51
Catina, Aleks 5, 11
censorship 40
Centre d'etudes, de recherches et de formation institutionnelles (CERFI) 129
Centre Georges Pompidou, Paris (Rogers and Piano) 107
Cerny, Philip 48
Chambers, William 290
Charles, Prince 35, 36
cheap labour 46
Chelsea Hotel 61
Chipperfield, David *103*
Christophers, Brett 47
Churchill, W. 4
CIAM meeting at Doorn 1954 276
city, freedom of 12
The City in History (Mumford) 18
'City Planning and Urban Realities' 18
civic values 7
Claudius-Petit, Eugene 230
climatic reserves 160
Clossick, Jane 11, 207, 209, *213–216*
Colburn, Ben 11, 207–208
Collaborative Housing in Sweden 201
collective concept 7
collective housing model 57, 197, 199
collective life 7, 88, 188–189
collective ownership 57
collectivity idea 16
Colquhoun, A. 4, 6
Commentary 18
Commissariat Generale du Plan 230
Commons 7, 47, 51, 251, 294
communal housing project 265
communicative capitalism 43–44
communicative space 11, 211
communism 43, 44, 52–53
community 9, 13, 33, 202, 229, 293
Community and Environment (Gutkind) 277
Community Land Trust (CLT) 58, 59
Community Land Trust Brussels (CLTB) 63
complementarity 257
conservativism 93
construction process 166

Index

consumerist explanation 84
cooperative model 61
Coop Himmelblau 151
'cosmic' civilisation 22
cosmo-ecological collective life 220–223
The Cosmological Eye (Miller) 8
Courant Plan 230
Covid-19 shutdown 5
Covid vaccines 293
Craigen Court 316
Creative Demobilisation (Gutkind) 277, 278
"crusade for health" 160
cult of manual labour 164–165
cultural icons 7
da Cunha, Dilip 223
Curzer, Howard J. 262
cybernetics, post-war science of 21

Dalston Lane 92, 94
Dant, Adam 93
D'Arcy-Reed, Louis 7, 11, 102–110
dark enlightenment 49
David-*versus*-Goliath confrontation 24
Dean, Jodi 10, 42–54, 297
The Death and Life of the Great American City (Jacobs) 13, 14, 18, 21, 24, 279, 296
Debord, Guy 23
De-extinction (Huyghe) 149, 150
Defensible Space (Newman) 18
Deleuze, Gilles 129, 133
democracy *vs.* fascism 50
1968 Democratic National Convention in Chicago 26
demographic phenomena 230
Dempster, Thomas 290
Department of Thermal Springs in 1918 191n7
"depression and anxiety" 49
depth structure 11, 207, 209–211
design public buildings: autonomy and depth structure 207–208; depth structure 209–211; self-directedness and clarity 208–209
'detournement' strategy 164
Deviller, Christian 136
Dewey, John 20
D'Hancarville 291
dialectical dialogue 284
Discipline and Punish (Foucault) 133, 135
discursive community 98
distinctiveness: architectural tradition 99; concept of 98; definition of 92
doorstep philosophy 16, 23, 296
Dosse, Francoise 132
Dugin, Alexander 49
Dutson, Claudia 7, 11, 71–81, 298
dynamism 15

earth architecture 163
earthquake and reconstruction 185–186
East London Trader's Guild (ELTG) 93
'ecological concept of urbanism' 276
economic and political ideology 115
economic feudalism 52
economic liberalism 6
economic sustainability 232
Ecotopia: American Appropriate Technology 238; utopian society 240
Ecotopia: The Notebooks and Reports of William Weston (Callenbach) 241
edifice complex 72
'education of attention' 254
Edwardian stone structure 309
Eggers, Dave 72
Ehn, Karl 173
electronic environment 21
Emmaus: collective life 232–233; Emmaus ragpickers 232; post-war welfare state 229–232; social housing company 230
empty apartment buildings 265
energy-efficient alternative transit methods 243
environmentalism 223–225, 274, 276
Ericssonsgatan, John 199
erotic dimension 16
ethics in architecture 262–264
European feudalism 49
Europe, welfare state regimes 229
Evans, Robin 136
evolutive housing 64
"Existence, Space and Architecture" (Norberg-Schulz) 252
The Expanded Environment (Gutkind) 277

Facebook 46, 51, 71–75, 78, 79
Faim & Soif magazine 230
Fairchild Semiconductor 73
Fall of Public Man (Sennett) 295
The Family of Man (Steichen) 23
Fardknappen, different house 197–199
Federal Anti-Monopoly Service 52
1949 Federal Housing Act 18
The Feminine Mystique (Friedan) 17
feminist objectivity 255
1951 Festival of Britain 6
feudalism–military service 46, 49
2008 financial crisis 84
Finnegans Wake (Joyce) 21, 26
firmness, commodity and delight (Vitruvius) 3
First World War 8, 11, 230
Fisher, Mark 42
Five Year Plan 230
Flaubert, Gustave: *Madame Bovary* 154
Floor Area Ratio (FAR) 74
Flyover project 155
Fordism model 264

Index

Fortier, Bruno 129
Foster, Norman 72
Foucault, Michel 10, 123, 124; *The Archaeology of Knowledge* 133; *The Birth of the Clinic* 129; *Discipline and Punish* 133, 135; heterotopia concept 127; *The History of Madness* 129, 133; *History of Sexuality* 133; "L'Architecture dans le boudoir" 133; "L'ordre du discourse" 126, 132; "Of Other Spaces" 136; *The Order of Things* 123, 124, 127; *Theories and Histories of Architecture* 124
Fourier, Phalanstere 232
Francis Road 97
French post-war welfare state 229–230
Freud, Sigmund 104
Friedan, Betty 17
Friedman, Avi 64
Fröken Julie (Strindberg) 148
Fuchsenfeldhof layout plan *176*, 177
Fuller, R. Buckminster 28, 241, 276, 279; *Operating Manual for Spaceship Earth* 241
functionalism 105

Gaglio, Meredith 11
The Game of Thrones 42
Gans, Herbert 18, 29n24
Garden City 58
"G. B. Piranesi: Architecture as Negative Utopia" 125, 128
Geddes, Patrick 22, 32
Gehl, Jan 36
Gehry, Frank 72, 76
Gemeinschaft-Gesellschaft 33
gentrification: anti-gentrification campaigns 83; and collective life 88; hyper-gentrification 82; intervention-based redevelopment 102; sophistication and reference 93; super-gentrification 82
Georgian working class tenement 312
German Siedlung 277
Gibson, James 254, 275
Giedion, Sigfried 21, 29n37, 276
Glasgow University 210
Glissant, Edouard 253, 254
global village 22, 24–27
global wealth 45
Godin, Familistere de Jean-Baptiste 232
Goodman, Robert 8
Google 46, 47, 72–75, 79, 80n26
Googleplex 71
Gori, A.F. 290
Gosseye, Janina 11
de Graaf, Reiner 5, 6, 9, 10, 31–41, 295
Greater London Authority (GLA) 90, 94
Greek Civil War 188
greenery 174–176

Greenwich village 24
Griffiths, S. 91
Gruen, Victor 15
Guarnacci, M. 290
Guattari, Felix 129, 132
Guendelsberger, Emily 49
Guillerme, Jacques 136
The Gutenberg Galaxy: The Making of Typographic Man (McLuhan) 21
Gutkind, Erwin Anton 277; *Community and Environment* 277; *Creative Demobilisation* 277, 278; *A Discourse on Social Ecology* 277; *The Expanded Environment* 277; *Man and his Environment* 277; *Our World from the Air* 277; *Revolution of Environment* 277

Haeckel, Ernst 274, 281n2
Hall, Edward T. 22
Hall, Kelvin 207, 208; autonomy-minded design 212, 213; depth structure 210; public building 211–212
Haney, David H. 167
Haraway, Donna 255
Harvard's Graduate School of Design 15
Harvey, David 296
Haus-Rucker-Co 151
Hayden, Dolores 199
Hayek, Friedrich 115
healthcare systems 260
health tourism 190
Heatherwick, Thomas 72, 109
hedge city 85
Hegemann, Werner 172
Helsinki Department of Youth 265
heterotopia concept 123, 124
high street 98–99, 311
Hindu East Bengalis 218
Hinduism 219
Hinterland (Neel) 48
hinterlandization 48
Hippocrates 183
The History of Madness (Foucault) 129, 133
History of Sexuality (Foucault) 133
Home Club 60, 61
home ownership 59
homeworking (WFH) 302
Houdini act 35
housekeeping 61
Housing Act 59
housing financialisation 84–85
'housing for all' agenda 228
housing market mechanisms 57
housing tenure: alternative models 60–63; land property problem 57–60; private ownership 60–63; two proposals 63–65
Howard, Ebenezer 58
How Buildings Learn (Brand) 74

320

Index

Hubert, Philip G. 60
Hubusch, Heinrich 6
Hughes, David 149
human association 9, 274, 276, 282n11, 296
The Human Condition (Arendt) 4
Hunger Games 42
Husserl, Edmund 254
Huyghe, Pierre 149, 151; *De-extinction* 149, 150
hydrotherapy in Antiquity 183
hygiene-oriented social claim 160
hyper-gentrification: consumerist explanation 84; financialisation 83; housing financialisation 84–85; productivist rent-gap theory 84; real-estate value 84, 85; urbanisation of suburbia 85–86

Il Dispositivo Foucault 126, 128–130, 133
Illich, Ivan 241; *Tools for Conviviality* 241
immaterial labour 51
independence 208
Indian architectural modernity 218–220
Indian humanism: architectural modernity 218–220; cosmo-ecological collective life 220–223; environmentalism 223–225; as urbanism, literature, culture 223–225
industrial 'detournement' 163
industrialisation 55, 160
industrial tools 167–168
inequality 6, 9, 10, 39, 44–46, 50–52, 54, 107, 280, 294, 296, 303n7
infant mortality 260
infrastructure 161
Ingels, Bjarke 72
insecurity 49
Institut d'Etudes et de Recherches Architecturales (IERAU) 135
'intermediate technology' concept 240
International Relations scholars 48
interruptions: interrupted image 146–149; interrupted meal 149–151; interrupted way 151–155
intersubjective 151
intimacy and situatedness 257
intra-action notion 256
intravention: notion of 251, 252; situated architecture mode 251
intraventions-in-flux 255, 258
In What Style Should We build? (Hubusch and Pugin) 6
Isi Metzstein 5
Italian Communist Party (PCI) 131, 132
Italian urbanism 117
I-Thou relationship 279

Jacobs, Jane 6, 8–20, *14*, 28n1, 31, 32, 115, 264, 295; *The Death and Life of the Great American City* 13, 14, 279; "The Missing Link in City Redevelopment" 15, *15*
Jameson, Fredric 42
Jan Kattein Architects (JKA) 96
Jencks, Charles 19
Jentsch, Ernst 104
Johnson, Boris 90
Johnson, Lee 238, 245
Johnson, Peter 123, 243
Johnson, Steve 238, 243
Jones, Paul 99
Joyce, James 21

Kahn, Louis 12
Kalighat streets 220
Kaminer, Tahl 11, 297
Kandinsky, Wassily 35
Karl Seitz-Hof layout plan *175*, 175–176, 177
Karnekull, Kerstin 195, 202
Kaufmann, Emil 291
Kaufmann, Franz-Xaver 229
Keeley, Richard Carroll 29n32
Kennedy, Robert F. 26
Kent, Fred 36
Kittler, Friedrich 150
Koolhaas, Rem 72, 121, 285
Kotkin, Joel 52
Kristin, after Miss Julie in 2011 148
Kuma, Kengo *105*
Kwinter, Sanford 286

'laboratory' method 19
La Cerisaie 232
land: management of 58; organisation of 59; ownership model 59; privatisation 47; property problem 57–60
land-deprived peasants 58
Landi, Davide 11, *263*, 267
landscape of zones 209
language 124–135; architectural language 124; negative utopias 124
The Language of Post-Modern Architecture (Jencks) 19
Lanier, Jaron: *You Are Not a Gadget* 46
"L'Architecture dans le boudoir" (Foucault) 133
large-scale suburbanisation 85
Las Meninas (Velázquez) 133
Latour, Bruno 150, 151
Laugier, Abbe 290
Learning from Las Vegas (Venturi and Scott Brown) 189
Lebas, Louis-Hippolyte 135
LeBon, Gutave 7
Le Corbusier 6, 33, 34; *Vers une architecture* 118
Ledoux, Claude-Nicolas 291
Lefebvre, Henri 14

Index

Lefort, Claude 132
left-wing terrorism 132
Lévi-Strauss, Claude 102–104
Lewis, Penny 11, 31
Lewis, Wyndham 22, 26; *America and Cosmic Man* 22
Ley, David 84
Leyton High Road 96–97
'link-place' model 92
liveability 10, 33, 296
'Living in Community' 196
'living together' model 170, 199
localism 51
local 'rent-a-car' systems 243
lockdown 5, 10, 12, 294, 295, 299, 301
Lodoli, padre 290
London 55, 57, 63, 64, 82, 83, 85–87, 90, 91, 93–99, 295, 297, 300, 301
"L'ordre du discourse" (Foucault) 126, 132
Loutraki in Greece: collective life 188–189; doctors and buildings 184–185; earthquake and reconstruction 185–186; hydrotherapy and leisure 182; municipal hydrotherapy centre 186; thermalism 182; urban development 187
Lower Manhattan Expressway 24
Lundahl, Gunilla 195

machine-learning processes 47
Madame Bovary (Flaubert) 154
making theory 285
Man and his Environment (Gutkind) 277
de Man, Henri 160
Manning, Erin 256
'Man Plus' idea 280
Mariette, Pierre Jean 286, 288
Markelius, Sven 199
Marx 46, 47, 57, 58
Mathur, Anuradha 223
May, Ernst 172
Mazzadra, Sandro 132
McHale, John 274, 279, 280
McLuhan, Marshall 10, *20*, 21, 28n36; *The Burning Would* 26, *27*; *The Gutenberg Galaxy: The Making of Typographic Man* 21; half science-fiction 23; local and global villages 26; *The Medium Is the Massage* 23; *Understanding Media: The Extensions of Man* 21, 22; *War and Peace in the Global Village* 26
McRae, Ken 310
Measures of Success (Verso) 31
Mechanization Takes Command (Giedion) 21
The Medium Is the Massage (McLuhan) 23
Meiksins Wood, Ellen 44, 45, 48
Melnikov, Konstantin 35
Memmo, Andrea 291

Menlo Park Building 20 (MPK20) *73*, 75
metropolis 17, 18, 58
metropolitan 170, 240, 285
Meyer, Hannes 126
Meyrowitz, Joshua 28, 30n54
'mic-drop' moments 77
middle-class Indian homes 219
migratory movements 230
Milizia, Francesco 291
Miller, Henry 8–9
"The Missing Link in City Redevelopment" (Jacobs) 15, *15*
Mitchell, Katie 148, 149
modernisation 228
modernism 6
modernist 'method' 117–118
Modernist urbanism 281n4
Modern Movement 4, 115, 118, 120, 281n4
modern urban life 9, 275
Moffett Airfield 77
de Moll, Lane 238, 242, 243
monopoly capitalism 4
Morachiello, Paolo 136
moral imagination 263, 267
Moses, Robert 15, 24, 295
Mozingo, Louise 79
multi-family housing 87
multi-functioning arts complexes 102–103
Mumford, Lewis 15, 17, 18, 22, 32; *The City in History* 18; *Technics and Civilization* 22
Mungo, Raymond 242
municipal housing company 199
municipalism 51
Museum of Modern Art 23
Myrdal, Alva 199
mythological publication 242

Natapoff, Alexandra 45; *Punishment without Crime* 45
National Council of Architectural Registration Boards 264
National Organization of Women in 1966 17
Neel, Phil A. 48; *Hinterland* 48
negative utopias 124, 125, 127
neofeudal ideology 49
neofeudalism 10, 42–44; cities and hinterlands 47–48; communism 52–53; hierarchy and expropriation 45–47; insecurity and apocalypticism 49; neofeudal hypothesis 49–51; new peasants and lords 45–47; sovereignty, parcelisation of 44–45
neo-liberalism 6, 10, 295
neo-reactionaries 49
Neufert, Ernst 37
Neutra, Richard 15
New Economic Foundation (NEF) 92–93

Index

New Labour government 107
Newman, Oscar 18, 19, 29n26
New Objectivity movement 147, 150
The New State (Follett) 8
New York Expressway plans 295
New York Times 8, 25, 182
nonplace realm 21
Norberg-Schulz, Christian 252, 253
"Normative and Non-normative Theories" 262
Norrby, Ann 195
No Sense of Place: The Impact of Electronic Media on Social Behavior (Meyrowitz) 28
Nurses and Midwives code of conduct (NMC) 264

Observations on the Letter of Monsieur Mariette (Piranesi) 288
The Observer 240
Ockman, Joan 5, 6, 9, 10, 296
one-kitchen housing projects 199
Open Architecture (Akcan) 264
"open architecture" 262
open city 264–265
Operating Manual for Spaceship Earth (Fuller) 241
Opinions on Architecture 286, 288
"Order in Diversity: Community without Propinquity" 20
The Order of Things (Foucault) 123, 127
OREC (office for national recovery) 160
organisation 230, 232
Organisation for the Rehabilitation of Earthquake Victims (AOSK) 185, 186
orientations notion 254
Orr, William 5, 10
Orwell, G. 40
Our World from the Air (Gutkind) 277
oxymoron 167–168

Packard, Hewlett 73
Palestinian land 45
Palo Alto campus 77
Pantheon in Rome in 2010 146–147
Parker Follett, Mary 7, 8; Athenian style local democracy 8
participation 36, 38, 39, 43, 46, 77, 295
Passeri, G.B. 290
pattern recognition algorithms 47
pedestrian paths 173–174
Perrot, Jean-Claude 136
Peterson, Jordan 49
phenomenological tools 106–107
phonographs mechanisms 150
physical fallacy 18
Pichai, Sundar 79

"piecemeal and fragmented process" 47
Pierre, Abbe 229, 230
Piketty, Thomas 6
Piranesi, Giovanni Battista 286; *Della Magnificenza ed Architettura de'Romani* 288; *Observations on the Letter of Monsieur Mariette* 288
Pirard, Marie 11
placemaking 5, 9, 10, 33–36
The Plague Year 12
planning: economic impact 6, 91; modern planning 6, 9, 281; planning policies 6, 7, 11, 91, 170; planning theory 9; post-war planning 295, 303
Platform Capitalism (Srnicek) 46
platformisation 46
Playboy magazine 22
politicisation 50
politics 5, 43; definition of 39; political authority 5, 44; political-economic-choices 120
populist agenda 90
Porrotto, Alessandro 11
post-capitalist dystopias 42
post-covid 79
post-Covid urban life 297
post-modernism 3, 276; post-modern architecture 9
Post-Scarcity Anarchism (Bookchin) 241
post-war reconstruction 6, 11
post-work imaginary 51
primitive accumulation 58
Princeton Conference 1955 277
Princeton University 135
The principles of newspeak (Orwell) 40
private ownership 60–63
productivist rent-gap theory 84
property owning democracy 58
proprietary polis 71
Pruitt-Igoe complex in St. Louis 18–19
pseudo-scientific methodology 94
psychodynamic effects 107–109
psychological freedom 38
public land development 57
public life 276, 279, 295, 299–301
public realm 5–7, 92, 94, 97, 99, 301, 302
Pugin, Augustus 6
Punishment without Crime (Natapoff) 45
Puttemans, Pierre 159

Queen's Park Terrace 313, 314
Queer Phenomenology 254

RAIN: Journal of Appropriate Technology 238, *239*
Raquel Rolnik 85
Raz, Joseph 207

Index

real-estate value 84, 85
Red Vienna 170
Regional Advantage 79
relational identity 253
religious welfare organisations 11, 229
Rella, Franco 128, 130
Renger-Patzsch, Albert 147
Resurgence magazine 240
retribalization 21
Revolution of Environment (Gutkind) 277
'right to buy' legislation 58, 59
'Ring of Ten' 277
risk 49, 51, 73, 85, 102, 117, 264, 268
Rodler, Alfred 173
Roman architectural invention 286
romanticism 280
Roosevelt, Franklin D. 8
Rossi, Aldo 5, 10, 115–117, 120, 121n3, 124, 295; *The Architecture of the City* 117
Rotry, Richard 99
rough-and-ready design 209
Rowe, Colin 6
Royal Institute of British Architects (RIBA). 264
Roy, Raja Ram Mohan 219
Rudofsky, Bernard 6, 23; *Architecture without Architects* 23
Rudolf in Helsinki 260, 262; ethical dilemmas 267–269; living 266–267; thinking and making 265–266
Rudolf senior home project 265
Ryhmärakentaminen model 55

St John, Caruso *108*
Sangregorio, Inga-Lisa 195, 197, 201
Santa Clara Valley 71
Saxenian, Annalee 79
Scepticism 296
Schalk, Meike 11
Schatz, Diane 238, 242
Schmid, Heinrich 177
Schumacher, E.F. 238, 240
Schuttau-Hof layout plan 173, *174*
Scott Brown, Denise 189
Scottish Screen Archive 210
Scruton, Roger 32
Searle, Adrian 149
seasonal housing project 265
Second World War 21, 22, 58, 61, 188, 228, 295
self-directedness and clarity 208–209
'Semiology and Urbanism' (Barthes) 16
Sennett, Richard 264, 295
Senn, Rainer 232–234
Serres, Michel 150, 151
Sert, Josep Lluis 15
Shelden, Michael 40

Shockley, William 73
sidewalk ballet 16, 296
The Silent Language (Hall) 22
Silicon Graphics (SGI) 71
Silicon Valley 7, 11, 43, 49, 71, 72, 73
Simon, Boris 232
single-use development 264
Sitte, Camillo 172
situated choreographies 256–257
situatedness 255–256
'slow burn' approach 98
Small Sites Initiative 55
Smith, Neil 84, 88n1
Smithson, Alison 9, 16, 29n8, 274, 276
Smithson, Peter 9, 16, 274, 276
social ecology 277
social freedom 11
social housing 87, 228
social program 159
social reproduction theory 48
social surplus 42, 49
social sustainability agenda 91, 97
socio-economic challenges 57
SoHo 24
Sousakion, aroneion 191n11
sovereignty, parcelisation of 44–45
Soviet communism 228
Spadina expressway extension, protest *24*
Spanish Civil War 40
spatial practice 98, 256, 285
spatial relationships 207
The Sphere and the Labyrinth (Tafuri) 128
Srnicek, Nick 46
Stadtluft macht frei 17
Stewart, David 133
Stirling, James 124, 125
Stockholm 83, 86–87
Stonorov, Oscar 12, 29n25
Stoppani, Teresa 12, 146
strategic psychoanalytic methods 106–107
Strauven, Iwan 159
street life 86; streetspace strategy 295; suburban street 86
Strindberg, August 148; *Fröken Julie* 148
Strong, Frederick 182
Stutterheim, Alfred 173
suburban model 39
Sun Microsystems 71, 76
super-gentrification 82; discussions of 83
surveillance capitalism 46
sustainability 52
Sutherland, Rory 293
Swann, Robert 58
Swedish Association of Architects 196
Swedish Centre for Architecture and Design 195
Swedish feminist movement 196

Index

Tafuri, Manfredo 117, 120, 123–135, 136; *The Sphere and the Labyrinth* 128
Tattara, Martino 10
Team 10 6, 7, 16
Team X memorandum 279
Technics and Civilization (Mumford) 22
Teyssot, George 123, 127–128, 130, 135
'TGIF' (Thank God It's Friday) meeting 77
Thalamy, Anne 129
Thatcher, Margaret 36, 60; Thatcherism 6
Theories and Histories of Architecture (Foucault) 124
thermalism 182–184, 190
thermal medicine 183
Thiel, Peter 49
Tokyo Bay Project 264
Tools for Conviviality (Illich) 241
"Toward a Critique of Architectural Ideology" 120
Toyota Production System 77
traditional cultural values 218, 219
transnational solidarity 264
Tremmel, Ludwig 173
Trident and Polaris Inter Continental Ballistic Missile 77
Triste Tropique (Lévi-Strauss) 103
Tronti, Mario 132
tropical construction 218
Trump, Donald 35, 36
Twitter 79

Uber 47
Understanding Media: The Extensions of Man (McLuhan) 21, 22
unemployment 160
United States 7–10, 15, 20, 22, 25–27, 39, 40, 42, 44–45, 48, 50, 52, 53, 58, 60, 79, 160, 180, 238, 241, 245, 246, 274, 276, 279, 282n16, 294, 296, 301
Universal Basic Income 51
University of California at Berkeley 20
University of Milton Keynes 34
University of Pennsylvania 277
University of Toronto Faculty Club 25
urban freedom 12; concept of 14, 17
urban housing problem 55
urbanisation of suburbia 85–86
urbanism 16, 32, 165; radical theory of 21; urban landscape 11; urban layouts 177–180; urban life 14; urban morphology 172; urban management 8"The Urban Place and the Nonplace Urban Realm" 20
urban planning 172
urban renewal projects 19
urban theory 7, 31; radical theory of urbanism 21
The Urban Villagers (Gans) 18

US carceral system 45
US urban policy 8
utopian society 240

V&A design museum *105*
Vafas, Georgios 185
van der Rohe, Mies 34
van Eyck, Aldo 6, 16, 23
Velázquez, Diego 133
Venturi, Robert 6, 9, 126, 188, 190
verisimilitude construction 154
Vers une architecture (Le Corbusier) 118
Vesely, Dalibor 11, 210
Via Campesina 52
Viden, Sonja 195, 201
Vidler, A. 104, 106, 276
Vienna's Höfe: architectural idea 170; collective courtyards *179*; collective dimension 172; housing project 173; large courtyards 173–174; 'living together' model 170; pedestrian paths 173–174; speculative activities 172
Vietnam War 24
Vitruvius 3
Von Ledoux bis Le Corbusier (Kaufmann) 291

Wagner, Otto 172
Walking School 151–152, *152*
War and Peace in the Global Village (McLuhan) 26
'warehouse' buildings 85
Washington Square Park 24
wastelands 48
Webber, Melvin 20, 21, 26n35
Weiner, Nobert 276
welfare mix 229
welfare state 228
Werkbund, Deutche 280
western post-war architecture 117
white-collar employees 84
White Man's Burden 8
Whole Earth Catalog 240, 241
Wiszniewski, Dorian 11
William, H. 109
WilMa 19, at Magdalenenstrase 19 63
Winckelmann 291
witness seminar 199–201, 203n1
Wittkower, Rudolf 288–290
World Economic Forum (WEF) 293
Wright, Patrick 94
Wychwood Park 26
Wynants, Rene 160

Xenophon 191n10

You Are Not a Gadget (Lanier) 46

Index

Zaera-Polo, Alejandro 107
Zeitgeist modern 21
zero-institution culture 103–105; phenomenological tools 106–107; psychodynamic effects 107–109; strategic psychoanalytic methods 106–107; zero-institutionalist interventions 105–106
Žižek, Slavoj 42, 102–106, 121
zoom-land 299
Zuboff, Shoshana 46
Zuckerberg, Mark 77, 298